A Research Agenda for Food Systems

Elgar Research Agendas outline the future of research in a given area. Leading scholars are given the space to explore their subject in provocative ways, and map out the potential directions of travel. They are relevant but also visionary.

Forward-looking and innovative, Elgar Research Agendas are an essential resource for PhD students, scholars and anybody who wants to be at the forefront of research.

Titles in the series include:

A Research Agenda for Political Marketing
Edited by Bruce I. Newman and Todd P. Newman

A Research Agenda for Public–Private Partnerships and the Governance of Infrastructure
Edited by Graeme A. Hodge and Carsten Greve

A Research Agenda for Governance
John Pierre, B. Guy Peters, Jacob Torfing and Eva Sørensen

A Research Agenda for Sport Management
Edited by David Shilbury

A Research Agenda for COVID-19 and Society
Edited by Steve Matthewman

A Research Agenda for Civil Society
Edited by Kees Biekart and Alan Fowler

A Research Agenda for Tax Law
Edited by Leopoldo Parada

A Research Agenda for Food Systems
Edited by Colin L. Sage

A Research Agenda for Food Systems

Edited by

COLIN L. SAGE
Independent Research Scholar

Elgar Research Agendas

 Edward Elgar
PUBLISHING

Cheltenham, UK • Northampton, MA, USA

© Colin L. Sage 2022

With the exception of any material published open access under a Creative Commons licence (see www.elgaronline.com), all rights are reserved and no part of this publication may be reproduced, stored in a retrieval system or transmitted in any form or by any means, electronic, mechanical or photocopying, recording, or otherwise without the prior permission of the publisher.

Chapter 2 is available for free as Open Access from the individual product page at www.elgaronline.com under a Creative Commons AttributionNonCommercial-NoDerivatives 4.0 Unported (https://creativecommons.org/licenses/by-nc-nd/4.0/) license.

Published by
Edward Elgar Publishing Limited
The Lypiatts
15 Lansdown Road
Cheltenham
Glos GL50 2JA
UK

Edward Elgar Publishing, Inc.
William Pratt House
9 Dewey Court
Northampton
Massachusetts 01060
USA

Paperback edition 2023

A catalogue record for this book
is available from the British Library

Library of Congress Control Number: 2022943157

This book is available electronically in the **Elgar**online
Geography, Planning and Tourism subject collection
http://dx.doi.org/10.4337/9781800880269

ISBN 978 1 80088 025 2 (cased)
ISBN 978 1 80088 026 9 (eBook)
ISBN 978 1 0353 2035 6 (paperback)

Printed and bound by CPI Group (UK) Ltd, Croydon, CR0 4YY

Contents

Figures

Figures

Contributors

Mondira Bhattacharya is a postdoctoral researcher, University of Reading, working on the Robot Highways project. She has a PhD in Economic Geography from Jawaharlal Nehru University, New Delhi, and her research interests are in agrarian studies with a focus on India and other low- and medium-income countries.

Steffen Böhm is Professor in Organisation & Sustainability at the University of Exeter Business School. His research focuses on the political economy and ecology of the sustainability transition. His books include: *Ecocultures: Blueprints for Sustainable Communities* (Routledge, 2015) and *Upsetting the Offset: The Political Economy of Carbon Markets. Climate Activism* (with Annika Skoglund, Cambridge University Press) is forthcoming. More details at www.steffenboehm.net.

Martin Caraher is Emeritus Professor of Food and Health Policy, Centre for Food Policy, City, University of London. He was a founder member of the London Food Board and was the public health representative on the London 2012 Olympic Food Advisory Board. He has been 'Thinker in Residence' at Deakin University, Melbourne and an Australian Healthway's fellow (2016, 2008). His publications range from food access in local communities, food taxes, school food, cooking, fast food to food banks and food poverty.

Jennifer Clapp is a Canada Research Chair in Global Food Security and Sustainability and Professor in the School of Environment, Resources and Sustainability at the University of Waterloo, Canada. She is Vice Chair of the Steering Committee of the High-Level Panel of Experts on Food Security and Nutrition of the UN Committee on World Food Security and a member of the International Panel of Experts on Sustainable Food Systems. Among her recent books are *Food*, 3rd edition (Polity, 2020), *Speculative Harvests: Financialization, Food, and Agriculture* (co-author, Fernwood Press, 2018), and *Hunger in the Balance: The New Politics of International Food Aid* (Cornell University Press, 2012).

Laura Colombo is a Lecturer in Management at the University of Exeter Business School. Her research interests revolve around social enterprises and their role in transforming relationships among people and with nature. She is particularly interested in the scaling strategies of social enterprises, with a focus on alternative food networks, social agriculture and social cooperatives.

Auvikki de Boon is a PhD student in the Change in Agriculture group, University of Reading. Her research interests include governance of agricultural innovation, collaborative environmental governance, policy analysis, stakeholder participation, and climate change adaptation.

Carlos de Castro is Senior Lecturer in the Sociology Department, Autonomous University of Madrid. His research focuses on the political and institutional configuration of work and workers in the context of global production networks in several sectors. He has published a number of papers on the role of workers in global agricultural production.

Ram Kiran Dhulipala is Theme Leader, Digital Agriculture & Youth at ICRISAT, Hyderabad. Here he drives action research on the use of latest digital technologies in agriculture and has been instrumental in strategising and executing a private sector and partnership-based approach.

Kata Fodor is an architect and doctoral researcher focusing on the spatial preconditions/implications of sustainable urban food systems. She is a co-founder of the multidisciplinary design studio Atelier Kite, and a member of the Nodus Sustainable Design Research Group at Aalto University. Kata's ongoing PhD research, Kitchen Think-over, complements her design practice in developing collaborative urban food spaces across European cities.

Michael K. Goodman is Professor of Environment and Development at the University of Reading. His research interests centre around the cultural politics of food and topics have included fair trade and alternative food networks, celebrity politics in the context of food, climate change and global development. He is particularly interested in conceptualising how these issues are framed in the media in the process of building more sustainable societies.

Jess Halliday is a consultant and researcher specialising in urban and city region food system governance. She is an associate of the RUAF Global Partnership on Sustainable Urban Agriculture and Food Systems, working with the RUAF Secretariat and Partners on topics including resilience, gender and inclusion, and food environments. Jess received her PhD in food policy from the Centre for Food Policy, City University London in 2015.

Lewis Holloway is Professor of Human Geography at the University of Hull, UK. His research focuses on food, farming and the countryside. Recent projects have examined the relationships between humans, animals and technologies in agriculture including increasing use of genetics in breeding 'farmed' animals, and the deployment of robotic and information technologies in dairy farming. He is a co-author of *Geographies of Food: An Introduction* (2021, Bloomsbury).

Sophie Jackson is Project Manager and Research Assistant for Circular Food, University of Exeter. She has a particular interest in regenerative agriculture and sustainable agri-food.

Matt Lobley is Professor of Rural Resource Management and Co-Director of the Centre for Rural Policy Research at the University of Exeter. He was Editor of *The International Journal of Agricultural Management* (2015–20) and is Co-Editor of *The Agricultural Notebook*. Matt works extensively with farming families, the policy community, private sector business and NGOs.

Stefano Pascucci is Professor in Sustainability and Circular Economy, University of Exeter Business School, UK and visiting professor in Sustainable Business at the University of Auckland Business School, NZ. He is a social scientist interested in sustainability connected to organisation theories, innovation management, entrepreneurship, and value chain analysis.

Catherine Price is a sociologist who is Research Assistant in the Change in Agriculture group, University of Reading. Her research interests include the social and ethical impacts of agricultural technologies, and relationships between humans and the more-than-human world.

Alicia Reigada is a Senior Lecturer in the Anthropology Department, University of Seville (Spain) and member of the GEISA Research Group. Her studies focus on global agri-food chains, social organisation of labour, migrations, and gender relationships. She has participated in several international networks involving comparative analysis of Mediterranean and Latin American intensive agriculture. She has been a visiting scholar at CUNY, UC Davis (USA), UNAM (Mexico) and UFRRJ (Brazil).

David Christian Rose is Professor of Sustainable Agricultural Systems at Cranfield University and leads the Change in Agriculture group. His academic interests centre around the social impacts of agriculture 4.0, including extension, behaviour change, and ethics of new technologies, as well as policy co-design and farmer mental health..

Colin L. Sage is an independent research scholar who has worked on the interconnections of food systems, agriculture, and environment throughout his career. Previously at University College Cork and Wye College, University of London, he has held visiting research positions at the Universities of Tasmania and Bergamo and is currently Affiliated Professor with the Faculty of Nutrition and Food Sciences at the University of Porto and Visiting Professor in a teaching capacity at the University of Gastronomic Sciences and the American University of Rome. As founding Chair of the Cork Food Policy Council in 2013 Colin has long been actively engaged in exploring civic initiatives for social change as well as promoting transdisciplinary collaboration. He is the author of *Environment and Food* (Routledge, 2012); and co-editor of five books including: *Metaphor, Sustainability, Transformation* (Routledge, 2022); *Food System Transformations* (Routledge, 2021); *Transdisciplinary Perspectives on Transitions to Sustainability* (Routledge, 2017); and *Food Transgressions: Making Sense of Contemporary Food Politics* (Routledge, 2016). He is based in Portugal.

Rebecca Sandover is a Lecturer in Human Geography at the University of Exeter who undertakes engaged research using a knowledge co-production approach. In recent years she has been investigating action toward the formation of sustainable food networks in the South-West, UK.

Juliette Schillings is a PhD student in the Change in Agriculture group, University of Reading. Her research interests include animal welfare, animal behaviour and the ethics of Precision Livestock Farming technologies.

Alexandra E. Sexton is a Leverhulme Early Career Research Fellow, University of Sheffield. Her research examines the geographies, politics, and histories of food innovation, with a focus on high-tech meat and dairy alternatives. Her current project explores the implications of alternative proteins for rural landscapes and livelihoods in the UK and considers what role these technologies might play in a just protein transition for UK agriculture.

Foreword: The urgency of food systems research

Tim Lang[1]

From the moment it emerged in the literature, let alone in political discussion, the term 'food system' had intriguing connotations. For me, and for many engaged in the debates about the social implications of the food system over the last half century, the term 'food system' captured – and still captures – the scale of the entity good people were probably against, were certainly analysing to help tame or redirect, and were often painting as the leviathan against which alternative food systems were waging their heroic struggle.

The term's value surely lay in its implied values: an 'us' versus 'it' or 'them'; the baronial food class versus the mass; the giant corporation versus the decent, small food business; the influencers versus the led; the polluters versus the natural. And so on.

My memory may be playing tricks but, as the term crept into fairly widespread use in social discourse, nay normality, I for one used it for what I thought was its core 1970s political resonance. If 'the system' was what the 'counter culture' was against, as Theodor Roszak memorably called it (Roszak, 1970), then the food system was what the many strands of food movements were also against or trying to subvert or simply trying to understand (Lang, 1997). The term became useful because it conveyed the enormity of how modern food dynamics played out, and how understanding this would improve efforts to ameliorate its damage (Clutterbuck and Lang, 1982). That tension in food systems thinking was captured in Tansey and Worsley's mid-1990s book describing the food system, its dynamics and winners / losers (Tansey and Worsley, 1995).

Today hundreds if not thousands of publications use the term. It was not always so. But reading back into the literature which cite or focus on the food system, the connotations were in fact less shared than my colleagues and I felt at the time. Take Steinhart and Steinhart's 1974 paper on energy use in the US food system (Steinhart and Steinhart, 1974). This used the term to move beyond the previous convention that food came from agriculture. It clearly didn't. The farm is but one phase in what can be a long process between primary production and end consumption. That's why the language of 'systems' was borrowed into food systems from mechanical engineering and cybernetics, and post-Darwinian systems biology (Bertalanffy, 1949; Bertalanffy, 1968). Today we all benefit from the gorgeous systems maps with masses of spaghetti lines which amply illustrate complexity. Simply do a web search for 'images of food systems' to see what I mean! More importantly, policy-makers now have little excuse for ignoring the insights that follow from research which explains and reassembles the parts into the whole together (Gladek et al., 2016).

To understand how different food parts operate, one needs to understand where they fit in the bigger picture. It used to centre on the farm, but in urbanised and industrialised societies, this was no longer the case. The supermarket is a powerhouse. More value is added off the land. Energy is expended. The pull of urban consumers and the industrialisation of food processes are now key features of the US food system. In food, we see the speed and scale of the transition ever further from simpler, less developed societies' relationship with food to today's normality of mass food waste. Poor societies and households treat food with more respect.

No wonder the term began to be used in distinct bodies of knowledge, beyond the social perspective that my colleagues and I then thought it had. One strand of knowledge was certainly concerned with the 'macro' – the shape of the food economy and the dynamics of food supply chains. This was mostly a matter of tracking value and power. In fact, corporate and industrial interests were also mining systems analysis, not just the critics. An illustration is Crowder's 1976 paper analysing the research needs of the US food industry from a systemic perspective (Crowder, 1976). At the same time, in the 1970s, the term food system was being used by those focussed on 'micro' processes – whether this or that ingredient could be analysed for its effects in food processing. Hutton and Campbell's 1977 paper is an illustration, identifying the properties of soy and whether its emulsifying capacity could be useful in food processing (Hutton and Campbel 1977). It was. And today it is commonly and excessively used in processing too often with negative environmental impacts, as we now know.

My point is that food systems, far from bringing rigour and a material solidity to our radical studies, can actually also represent serious differences of perspective. Like the terms 'sustainability' or 'resilience' in modern discourse, we must be wary of – or at least clear about – food system's conceptual plasticity.

And that is why this book is so useful. If it had one single author, some of that plasticity might be lost by the term and book having one voice, one tone, one set of meanings. The authors here, however, bring a rich diversity of interests. Collectively, they embrace the term's plasticity rather than assume it. And that is valuable.

But now that the term is ubiquitous and respectable, we must also ask if it has lost that useful edge which I now realise I naively ascribed to it in the past. I think the answer is a definite 'no'. In my own writing, most recently trying to apply a critical policy analysis to the UK's food system (Lang, 2020), the characteristics I still find useful are there. Conceiving of a food system requires us to set boundaries. In the UK's case, it might be a set of islands that have left the European Union, but its flow of food transcends those boundaries. The 'British' food system is not British. A food systems analysis requires one to locate the UK within mostly EU and to a lesser extent global food flows, and to distinguish between food itself and the power and control.

A second feature is that the dynamics of any food system can be assumed to be complex. Even apparently simple supply chains or value-added chains require us to be clear about the scale and interactions between different parts or system actors. The North American food system is not the same as sub-Saharan Africa's.

A third valuable feature is the requirement to address change. Even 50 years ago, the environmental impacts and energy use of the food system were troubling (Meadows et al., 1972; Hirsch, 1976). And they still are (Randers, 2012; Jackson and Webster, 2016). Indeed, even more so. The food system is a huge user and emitter of carbon, and of water, and of biodiversity. And despite the seriousness of the data, policy-makers and consumers seem unable to jump off the treadmill. In 2021, the UN hosted the first Food Systems Summit (UNFSS) (UN 2020). Many of us might have hoped that this would be a moment when systemic or paradigmatic change could emerge. It didn't, and some denounced the UNFSS as corrupted by big business from the start . Indeed, the event was given only one day, hardly a sign of serious intent to grapple with a complex system, one might conclude.

And yet…. The notion of food systems still urges us to give attention to what 30 years ago I called food democracy, the pitching of the public interest; the movements which protect the public interest against the exploiters. The critics were right to amplify the question of power. Change, in whose name, for what, lies at the heart of any analysis of the food system. The chapters in this book are testament to that. Food systems need to be humanised and democratised.

Therein lies the value that the social sciences bring to food systems analysis, illustrated in this volume.

This leads to the fifth feature: the need to clarify who the actors are in the food system. Where does power lie? With whom? How is it held and maintained? In the name of what? Whether our research looks at flows of money, nutrients or labour, whether at the state or companies, at the use, abuse and framing of technology, at humans or plants or animals, the notion of a food system requires us to identify who does what in that system, and thus to be able to explain whether all interests are served equally. In modern parlance, where lies normality, and who or what are the disruptors? Crudely, who wins, who loses? And are democratic procedures and goals having any effect?

Finally, for me, the value of retaining the concept of the food system as a key element in our analysis is that it requires a multi-disciplinary perspective. No singular discipline can claim intellectual ownership or unique policy wisdom: rather, food systems analysis demands the widest range of disciplinary insights. Indeed, one might argue that the fragmentation of science and its pursuit of disciplinary independence has actively contributed to the mess that we have made of the food system.

The track record of the last three centuries is so mixed. On the one hand, humanity proved wrong the gloomy and racist 1798 analysis of Malthus that population growth would outpace food supply (Malthus, 1798). We know we could feed nine or ten billion healthily by 2050 without further destroying the environment . On the other hand, some of the forces that enabled this 'victory' so far – science, technology, intensification, displacement of labour, social movements demanding better food and conditions for all – has been turned into what Galbraith memorably called 'the culture of contentment' (Galbraith, 1992). With the rich world over- and mal-consuming, and also steadfastly maintaining millions in food poverty, few seem prepared to reduce consumption, and to eat less but better to allow the under-consumers to get a bigger slice of the food system. Public ill-health, social inequalities and eco-systems stress thus all continue within the food system, despite us knowing that a radical restructuring is required. On that point, there is vast evidence. The world could be fed well without destroying the infrastructure on which the food system depends. But to do so requires political imagination not just systemic thinking.

If academia jettisoned the kind of thinking and research outlined in this col-lection, the chances of holding policy-makers to account would be diminished, and the imagination that fuels social movements which press from 'below' would be shrouded. In short, the research agenda and the democratic agenda for food systems analysis have never been so acutely needed, nor more on a knife edge.

Note

1.   Professor Emeritus of Food Policy, Centre for Food Policy, City, University of London; author, *Feeding Britain: Our Food Problems and What to Do About Them* (Pelican, 2020); co-author, *Sustainable Diets* (Routledge, 2017); *Food Wars* (Routledge, 2015); *Ecological Public Health* (Routledge, 2012); *Food Policy* (Oxford University Press, 2009); and many more...

References

Bertalanffy, L. v. (1949). *Das biologische Weltbild*. Bern, A. Francke.

Bertalanffy, L. v. (1968). *General System Theory: Foundations, Development, Applications*. New York, Braziller.

Canfield, M., M. D. Anderson and P. McMichael (2021). UN Food Systems Summit 2021: Dismantling Democracy and Resetting Corporate Control of Food Systems. *Frontiers in Sustainable Food Systems* 5, 103: https://www.frontiersin.org/articles/10.3389/fsufs.2021.661552/full

Clapp, J., I. Noyes and Z. Grant (2021). The Food Systems Summit's Failure to Address Corporate Power. *Development* 64: 192–198.

Clutterbuck, C. and T. Lang (1982). *More Than We Can Chew: The Crazy World of Food and Farming*. London, Pluto Press.

Crowder, R. T. (1976). Research Needs and Priorities in the Food System: An Industry Viewpoint. *American Journal of Agricultural Economics* 58: 991–999.

Galbraith, J. K. (1992). *The Culture of Contentment*. New York, Houghton Mifflin and Company.

Gladek, E., M. Fraser, G. Roemers, O. Sabag Munoz, P. Hirsch and E. Kennedy (2016). The Global Food System: An Analysis – report to WWF. Amsterdam, WWF Netherlands and Metabolic: 188.

Hirsch, F. (1976). *Social Limits to Growth*. Cambridge, MA, Harvard University Press.

Hutton, C. W. and A. M. Campbel (1977). Functional Properties of a Soy Concentrate and a Soy Isolate in Simple Systems and in a Food System: Emulsion Properties, Thickening Function and Fat Absorption. *Journal of Food Science* 42, 2: 457–460.

Jackson, T. and R. Webster (2016). Limits Revisited: The Limits to Growth Debate Revisited. London, All Party Parliamentary Group on Limits to Growth.

Lang, T. (1997). Going public: food campaigns during the 1980s and 1990s. In Smith, D. (ed.) *Nutrition Scientists and Nutrition Policy in the 20th Century*. London, Routledge: 238–260.

Lang, T. (2020). *Feeding Britain: Our Food Problems and How to Fix Them*. London, Pelican.

Malthus, T. R. (1798). *An Essay on the Principle of Population, as it Affects the Future Improvement of Society with Remarks on the Speculations of Mr. Godwin, M. Condorcet and Other Writers.* London, Printed for J. Johnson.

Meadows, D. H., D. L. Meadows, J. Randers and W. W. Behrens (1972). *The Limits to Growth: A Report for the Club of Rome's Project on the Predicament of Mankind.* New York, Universe Books.

Randers, J. (2012). *2052: A Report to the Club of Rome Commemorating the 40th Anniversary of The Limits to Growth.* White River Junction VT, Chelsea Green Publishing.

Roszak, T. (1970). *The Making of a Counter Culture: Reflections on the Technocratic Society and its Youthful Opposition.* London, Faber and Faber.

Steinhart, J. S. and C. E. Steinhart (1974). Energy Use in the U.S. Food System. Science 184, 4134: 307–316.

Tansey, G. and T. Worsley (1995). *The Food System: A Guide.* London, Earthscan.

UN (2020). UN Food System Summit 2021: https:// www .un .org/ en/ food -systems -summit. New York, United Nations.

Willett, W., J. Rockström, B. Loken, M. Springmann, T. Lang et al. (2019). Food in the Anthropocene: The EAT-Lancet Commission on Healthy Diets from Sustainable Food Systems. *The Lancet* 393, 10170: 447–492.

Acknowledgements

First, I would like to thank all of the contributors to this volume for their patience and commitment as we went through various drafts in order to achieve chapters of the highest quality that readers will discover here. Together, I believe they provide complementary and critical insights in taking forward a research agenda for food systems. I would especially like to thank Tim Lang for his willingness to contribute a Foreword which places this exercise in historical context and, characteristically, provides an impassioned call for more research in this field. I am sure I speak for all of us involved in this volume when I suggest that present arrangements regarding the production, supply and dietary practices around food are far from satisfactory and that change is both necessary and urgent. We hope this volume will communicate our concern and call for more engaged research in the field.

Second, I would like to take this opportunity to express my appreciation to friends and colleagues with whom I have collaborated in various writing projects over the last three years or so, and which have been a source of uplifting distraction during the pandemic. My thanks, then, to Francesca Forno and Gloria Giambartolomei; to Maria Grazia Quieti and Maria Fonte; to Cordula Kropp and Irene Antoni-Komar; and to my good friends in Cork, Ed Byrne and Ger Mullally, together with Ian Hughes. I feel privileged to have worked with you all on our various writing projects. I would also like to give a special mention to Tara Kenny who, besides being a co-author keeps me supplied with a constant stream of 'must read' journal articles and packets of Barry's Tea. Thanks also to Mike Goodman for his friendship and support.

Third, I would like to acknowledge the opportunities that have been given to me to teach and test ideas and material found herein: principally at the University of Gastronomic Sciences, Pollenzo, where masters students there have been an important sounding board over many years and where staff in the Segreteria Didattica are always so welcoming. I would also like to thank Maria Grazia Quieti at the American University Rome for her collegiality and hospitality. Finally, thanks to Sara Rodrigues and Pedro Graça in the Faculty of Nutrition and Food Sciences at the University of Porto for the warmth of their welcome to a new arrival in their country.

As always, this book is dedicated to my two brilliant and beautiful daughters, Liadán and Aisling.

Colin L. Sage
Viana Do Castelo

PART I

Introduction

1   Introduction: *A Research Agenda for Food Systems*

Colin L. Sage

(We) have a global food system. It's based on large multinational companies, private
profits, … on the extreme irresponsibility of powerful countries with regard to the
environment… on a radical denial of the economic rights of poor people… (We)
have a global food system, but we need a different system. We cannot turn the global
food system over to the private sector. We already did that about 100 years ago, to the
private sector with the U.S. military behind it. That different system must be based
on the principle of universal human dignity, the principle of national sovereignty and
economic rights. (Selected text from transcript of speech made by Jeffrey Sachs at the
U.N. Food Systems Pre-Summit, July 27, 2021[1])

Today's food systems are no longer fit for purpose. (GLOPAN, 2020: 16)

Introduction

Food systems have changed radically over the past 70 years and they are
unfolding at an ever-greater pace. While the economic beneficiaries of current
arrangements are keen to defend the status quo in order to continue 'feeding
the world', a growing chorus of voices share the observations of Jeffrey Sachs
– a distinguished mainstream economist – that we need a different system.
This book examines some of the key issues that confront the contemporary
food system, explores some of the developments that are emerging as possible
design 'solutions' to system failings, and points to themes that should inform
a research agenda as we move through uncertain times.

Commonly we speak of 'the food system' in the singular that, while offering
a misleading sense of uniformity on the ways we eat, does accurately convey
the reality that food supply chains now criss-cross the world and interconnect many diverse regions, and do appear to be part of an integrated whole.
In reality it may be helpful to imagine the 'global food system' as a 'system
of systems' operating at different spatial scales with variations between and
within countries and with strong multi-level interconnectedness (Baker et al.,
2021). Individual nation states and their sub-national regions will likely have

their own particular composition of primary food production (agriculture, horticulture, pastoralism, wild capture) differentially oriented to provisioning domestic and international markets, with imported products ranging from the critical supply of basic carbohydrate needs to highly processed, internationally branded foods. Consequently, to speak of 'a food system' is to acknowledge the co-existence of multiple food systems, nested within different spatial scales, comprising many different actors from agricultural input providers through farmers to manufacturers and, ultimately, to eaters ('consumers') where food becomes the final resting place (almost!) for choices made. So, food systems enrol every one of us on this planet, and it is not just CEOs of transnational agribusiness corporations that have an interest as stakeholders in how the system performs.

Box 1.1   Food Systems: Two Definitions

Food systems comprise all the processes involved in keeping us fed: growing, harvesting, packing, processing, transforming, transporting, marketing, consuming and disposing of food. They include the inputs needed and outputs generated at each step. A food system operates within and is influenced by social, political, economic and natural environments. (GLOPAN, 2020: 14)

[A] food system gathers all the elements (environment, people, inputs, processes, infrastructures, institutions, etc.) and activities that relate to the production, processing, distribution, preparation and consumption of food, and the output of these activities, including socio-economic and environmental outcomes. (HLPE, 2017: 23)

While the term 'food systems' can be traced back into the late twentieth century, but often where it was treated synonymously with agricultural supply chains, it is only over the last decade or so where a more holistic analysis has brought food systems under greater critical scrutiny. The trigger arguably lies with the 2008–12 financial crisis where a concatenation of political, economic and social upheaval took place that further entrenched neoliberal managerialism. Rising food prices over the course of that first decade of the new millennium ultimately led to widespread civil disturbance in many countries but probably no more so than in North Africa where the rising cost of bread initiated the Arab Spring that saw the overthrow of several long-standing political regimes (Lagi et al., 2011). Food has always been a political weapon – from the Great Famines of Ireland, Bengal, Nigeria and elsewhere – to the selective deployment of relief and aid by powerful states (Sen, 1981; Crowley et al., 2012). The hungry have long known this, but now it would appear that well-fed citizens in rich countries are also becoming more conscious of the shortcomings of food systems: their inefficiencies, injustices, unsustainable foundations, and the burden of dietary ill-health for which they are responsible. In this respect more citizens, businesses and public bodies are observing that we need to create a food system that is fit for purpose. So, if the current UN Special Rapporteur on the Right to Food is correct that "The world's food systems have been failing people for a long time" (Fakhri, 2021), then this may be the moment to contribute to a process of re-imagining what a more equitable, sustainable, and healthier food system might look like.[2]

This collection, then, is a timely contribution to a growing debate about the kinds of food we eat; how, where and by whom these foods are produced; and the consequences of a productivist paradigm focussed on output volume over feeding people well. While this book will ideally attract the attention of food system scholars including graduate students exploring possible research topics that will deepen our understanding of food system failings and possible solutions, the subject matter is of greater public interest. While the act of eating connects us all to the wider, non-human world – and, indeed, can be regarded as a primary ecological practice – for most of us (at least, I assume, the readers of this book) the system which has underpinned our food security has also left us feeling dissatisfied and disempowered in decision making about our consumption choices. The food system has become a global behemoth that appears to pander to, but thoroughly controls, our dietary options. While this might appear a rather ungenerous or begrudging view given the 'success' of a system that today produces more food than at any time in history, the debit column of the balance sheet has been growing steadily longer as our awareness of the world has extended beyond filling our bellies. Section three below takes stock of the major shortcomings, which might be encapsulated here as constituting threats to both planetary health and human wellbeing.

Nevertheless, criticisms – and defence – of a system take many forms and reflect the ways in which we see the world, 'frame' its problems and consequently identify appropriate 'solutions' (Lakoff 2010). This framing process is extremely important in the ways we approach the food system and the priorities that we attach to possible 'pathways of transition' that might lead us toward a currently popular but rather rhetorical promised land: that of a 'sustainable food system'. As we shall see, it is important to pay attention to language and the ways in which powerful actors appropriate discourse in order to justify and defend their activities (maintain 'business as usual'). Distinguishing between the different narratives of where the food system is 'failing' and their respective 'priorities for action' is the focus of section four. From there this Introduction then explores the issue of sustainability largely through a focus on sustainable agriculture and sustainable diets.

Before proceeding further, it might be as well to establish the parameters of the volume and the perspective shared by its contributors. First, as residents of rich countries, with most of us based in Europe, we are mindful of being beneficiaries of a food system that provides a high degree of dietary choice as well as food security and that such privileges are not shared equitably within our own societies and certainly not globally. Consequently, we all share a concern for a substantial improvement – if not a radical transformation – of the existing food order. Second, all contributors are social scientists albeit with different disciplinary backgrounds stretching from health policy to urban design by way of geography, anthropology, sociology, and political science. While attentive to the large and growing body of health and nutrition evidence that highlight major food system failures, the volume does not examine dietary composition – what foods are eaten by whom – that might typically be found in accounts produced by scholars in the field of public health nutrition. Rather, a social science informed food systems analysis – as in other areas requiring problem-centred attention capable of developing a more holistic appreciation of the interconnections surrounding the field of study – the perspective is deliberately broader and where disciplinary boundaries are regarded as porous and capable of accommodating insights from adjacent fields. Thus, the general approach adopted throughout is one that critically evaluates existing practices and arrangements drawing upon a wide range of evidence and, where appropriate, offers a normative judgement on possible ways forward.

A further caveat on what this volume does not do. The reader will find no typology of food systems representing generalized configurations of production and provisioning arrangements in different societies. Such typologies generate categories ('rural', 'transitioning', 'mixed', 'industrialized') reflecting different levels of urbanization, reliance upon domestic food staples versus manufactured products, household expenditure on food and so on. This is work that has been done elsewhere (HLPE 2017; Marshall et al., 2021). It has been suggested that "a typology can help to identify countries with similar food systems that may be more likely to share common drivers of dietary, economic, and environmental change and be responsive to similar policy actions or technological or institutional innovations" (Marshall et al., 2021: 2). Clearly this is an exercise that would harness a range of quantitative universal variables capable of distinguishing between countries in the creation of a national 'type' yet one which can often conceal heterogeneity within countries. While such work has its place in planning exercises this volume does not provide a descriptive content of food systems or ascribe categorical labels, but rather offers insights into a number of different lines of research in the rapidly emerging field of food system studies.

Consequently, the book is organized as follows. After this extended Introduction, Part II ('Issues') comprises five chapters each dealing with separate challenges facing the food system: growing corporate concentration; the climate crisis and how we might respond; the role of migrant labour in agricultural enclave production; food poverty as a structural feature of food systems; and changing configurations of animals in protein supply chains. Part III, which is rather sceptically labelled 'Solutions?' (for it will soon become apparent that there cannot possibly be one way forward), also comprises five chapters. Topics here include: options for a high-tech 'Fourth Agricultural Revolution'; the development of the alternative proteins (AP) sector; the role of municipal authorities in food system governance; the policy and practice for more circular and regenerative food systems; and, finally, a stock-taking of the design implications for the rapidly evolving food environment. Each of these chapters is briefly discussed at the beginning of each Part rather than in aggregate later in this Introduction where an extended synopsis would likely prove rather indigestible.

Representing the Food System

It would be helpful at this early stage to identify some of the key elements of food systems and perhaps to attempt a schematic representation that might convey a visual sense of how these various elements are configured and inter-connect. Figure 1.1 has been substantially revised from the diagram included in the High-Level Panel of Experts on Food Security and Nutrition Report on Food Systems and Nutrition (HLPE, 2017). Their original drew upon earlier versions and has since subsequently been revised and published elsewhere (Leach et al., 2020; Fanzo et al., 2021). This reveals the efforts of researchers to grapple with and try to accurately represent the complex, dynamic and adaptive nature of food systems. For if there is one abiding truth on which all would agree, food systems maintain multiple interconnections, not only inter-nally amongst the different elements (as represented in the Figure), but also externally with a range of other systems including health care, energy, finance and transport (not shown here). Food systems, then, are complex entities and consequently subject to very different interpretations and schematic rep-resentations. In this version of what is consequently a highly iterative ongoing process, a central focus is given to the 'Food Environment', a concept that is of growing public policy attention and is creatively explored in Chapter 11.

Before explaining in some detail what is meant by the food environment, attention is drawn first to the five 'drivers' at the top of the Figure. While in the interests of visual clarity arrows are used parsimoniously, it should be emphasized that drivers are mutually and dynamically interconnected as well as with the 'food supply', 'food environment', and 'consumer practices' boxes. The first of the drivers, then, 'Science and technology innovation' has been an overwhelmingly influential driver of change in the way food systems have developed. Agricultural mechanization, plant and animal breeding and use of agrichemicals have transformed primary food production in most parts of the world and vested economic interests in this sector maintain a relentless pursuit of innovation, with some of the latest developments in digital farming outlined in Chapter 7. Food manufacturing, too, has witnessed extraordinary innovation giving rise to tens of thousands of processed and packaged products which meet stringent safety protocols, many of which have become internationally recognized brands – although they may not necessarily deliver optimal nutrition to their consumers. An opportunity to better understand the pace and sophistication of technological innovation in one area of food manufacturing – the field of alternative proteins – is provided in Chapter 8.

A second driver, labelled 'environmental', underpins the food system in the most fundamental way. The availability and sequestering of natural resources such as soil and freshwater together with a host of ecosystem services (the hydrological cycle, climate stability, insect pollination, genetic diversity, wild fish stocks) have enabled food production to grow. However, the demands of the food system have had enormous repercussions on the integrity and functioning of these systems, through depleting stocks and by exceeding their capacity to absorb waste streams. One of the most egregious examples here is the level of greenhouse gas emissions from agriculture that is contributing to destabilizing the global climate system and threatening food production in many parts of the world (discussed in detail in Chapter 3). Choices made about what we eat ('consumer practices') and how we produce ('supply') provide critical feedback loops to the environmental driver.

A third, labelled 'governance' might be regarded as encompassing all forms and levels of regulation, standards setting (including consumer protection), and promotion of economic growth linked to food (e.g. international trade). It ranges from the multilateral agencies of the United Nations (e.g. FAO, Codex Alimentarius) and the World Trade Organization, to supranational entities (the EU and its Directorates-General such as DG Sante and DG Agri), and trade blocs ('Mercosur', 'NAFTA') to national and local government and also food businesses. Globalization, which many of these institutions have promoted, has been a critical factor during the past forty years in reshaping diets

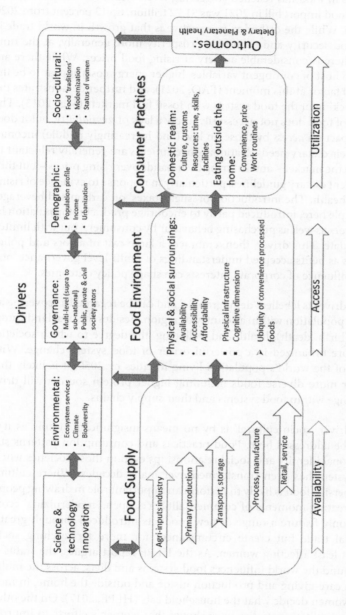

Source: Substantially revised from HLPE (2017) Nutrition and Food Systems. Report 12. FAO.

Figure 1.1 A conceptual framework for food systems

around the world and in driving the nutrition transition (discussed below). World trade in food has reached staggering levels with FAO estimating that the world's food import bill in 2021 was $1.72 trillion, up 12 percent from 2020 (FAO 2021). While the orthodox perspective is that growth in world trade is good for food security and economic prosperity more generally, at the time of writing there is considerable anxiety at rising food prices. While there are likely to be a host of contingent variables, higher energy costs appear to be the most critical factor at this moment (FAO, 2021), and further demonstrates the tight interlocking of the food system with fossil fuel markets (Sage 2013). The higher cost of food does not necessarily imply a lack of *availability*, but it does severely impact on *access* by those on low (and increasingly middle) incomes to secure their dietary needs. National governments are generally reluctant to intervene in the market – and so wring their hands over rising prices – but they can implement dietary guidelines, particularly in response to evidence of rising levels of ill-health. The introduction of 'sugar-taxes' on carbonated beverages is one example here, introduced partly to encourage product reformulation by manufacturers as well as purchasing behaviour by consumers, but with limited benefits to date. This driver, then, embraces a large cast of actors and policy instruments as befits accepted understandings of multi-level governance, and where the influence of corporate interests can shape policy outcomes.

The fourth driver is labelled 'demographic' and can be regarded as covering all aspects of a population within a country or region. Besides the usual indicators of growth (birth, death), health and wellbeing, the degree to which societies become more urbanized is a powerful driver of food system change. With two-thirds of the world's population living in cities by 2050, it is likely that demand for more diverse foods including higher protein sources will drive further change within food systems and their supply chains.

The final driver 'socio-cultural' is by no means insignificant simply as it is the last to be addressed here. Food practices and consumption patterns still reflect personal identity and social relationships even in those societies where the food system has been transformed over many decades. Where cultural traditions persist, food is likely to perform an important role in drawing people together, creating moments of commensality. Yet open, 'modernizing' economies not only feature a range of new products introduced through greater international trade but create circumstances for more far-reaching social change, not least affecting women. As the HLPE report argues, the status of women around the world influences food systems and diets: across the multiple roles of care-giving and production inside and outside the home, in most countries women decide what the household eats (HLPE, 2017). On the other hand, some qualitative studies have shown that women's efforts to improve family diets are resisted by male partners and children within the household who are reluctant to change their food preferences (McBey et al., 2019).

The food environment might be regarded as the 'interface' between food systems and diets and, at one level, provides a lens through which to examine physical and social surroundings that enable people to fulfil their dietary choices, with food being available, accessible, and affordable (Turner et al., 2018). In practical terms and at a neighbourhood level this might involve mapping the number and distribution of different food outlets, whether supermarkets, convenience stores, open air or municipal markets, take-away and other food service establishments. A great deal of research has established the limited availability of fresh and healthier food options in low-income neighbourhoods, many of which seem disproportionately served by fast food outlets (Pitt et al., 2017). However, beyond the physical infrastructure of the food environment lies a deeper cognitive world – revealed through the science of semiotics – where messages communicated through promotion, advertising, and incentivisation exert such a powerful influence over actual eating practices (Riley and Cavanaugh, 2017). It is this hidden dimension of food environments that play such a key role in unhealthy eating practices leading to weight gain (Neve and Isaacs, 2021). Paying closer attention to the complex dynamics unfolding in the food environment is consequently critical to understanding the process of nutrition transition (Popkin et al., 2012). This is especially characterized by rising levels of consumption of highly processed foods – foods high in salt, sugar, fats – that underpins the growing burden of diet-related disease in low and middle-income countries (Popkin and Reardon, 2018; Basu, 2015). In this regard it is important to remember that food environments are largely commercially driven spaces promoting and marketing products designed to optimize revenue streams rather than benefit public health. In doing so they translate patterns of demand into production signals that further entrench the availability of unhealthy and unsustainable foods (EU Food Policy Coalition, 2021).

In Figure 1.1 the food environment is sandwiched between boxes representing food supply and that of consumer practices. The first encompasses each of the steps involved in the production and supply of food products available to the food environment. The inclusion of the agricultural inputs sector is essential, given its power and influence over what is grown and how. The food processing stage should also be highlighted as its capacity to supply an extraordinary volume and array of durable, hyper-palatable, and convenient ultra-processed products has had far-reaching effects on many of its most loyal customers (see below). However, the overall sequence of stages – from farming, to processing and manufacturing of final foods and their delivery into retail and food service sectors – is straightforward and not under scrutiny here.[3] The food supply 'chain', with all of its logistical and technological sophistication consequently makes food available within the food environment. Consumer practices ultimately determine how food is utilized through the exercise of domestic and individual choice and then metabolically by our bodies as ingested nutrients give rise to dietary outcomes (health and vitality, accretion of body mass, susceptibility to disease etc.). However, this physiological observation should not disguise the fact that ultimately individual decisions about what to eat are shaped by advertising, social norms and the daily pressures (time, money, commitments and responsibilities) of life.

Consequently, a schematic mapping of the food system draws together: planetary-scale geo-physical processes; decision-making by powerful corporate actors; the work of over two billion farmers, agricultural labourers, food manufacturing operatives and retail staff; the everyday choices and actions undertaken by almost eight billion individual eaters; and, ultimately, the metabolism and microbiology of the human body as it converts food into life. In this respect it is vital to enquire into the nutritional value of food – its macro- and micro-nutrient composition, bioavailability of antioxidants, fibre and so on – and whether supply chains are providing the basis of a healthy, diversified, and balanced diet. Are supply chains, for instance, delivering into a given food environment sufficient quantities and quality of fruits and vegetables, minimally processed and fortified foods that are physically and economically accessible to citizens? Or is that food environment dominated by ready-to-eat products that contain higher amounts of saturated fat, sugar and sodium and which are heavily promoted – including online and television advertising to children and products that emphasize 'fun' – that result in unfavourable dietary health outcomes? (Chacon et al., 2015; Elliott, 2015; Tyrell et al., 2017) In this regard such questions help us to better understand the distribution of power and the real motivational drivers that lie behind the operation of the contemporary food system.

Food Systems Failings

Much has been made of the technological achievements of the contemporary food system to feed a world of almost eight billion people. As Barrett and colleagues point out, agri-food systems were engineered primarily to "boost productivity in delivering dietary energy supply" and they have "succeeded fabulously in that goal" (Barrett et al., 2020: 974). While world population doubled between 1961 and 2003, global food production increased by 2.5

times, increasing the average per capita availability of food (Caron et al., 2018). For others this 'intensification paradigm' has been "tremendously successful in increasing agricultural productivity and keeping food prices low" (Fanzo et al., 2020: 3). Yet while there has been generally continuing improvement in the per capita availability indicator over recent decades, regional crises have demonstrated inequalities in access to food due to limitations in people's purchasing power particularly, but not only, at times of food price volatility. In this respect a policy focus on boosting production to increase food supply has not significantly improved global food security with the numbers of hungry and malnourished people on the rise since 2015 (FAO et al., 2019). This suggests that it is becoming increasingly urgent to revise our understanding of what constitutes food system 'success' which has been so closely tied to food security, a concept which is examined in more detail below. For, as we will see, if there is one pillar that has anchored food security discourse over the second half of the twentieth century, it is the central role of interconnected technological developments, involving seeds, chemicals, and machinery, to achieve greater volumes of food output. This productivist paradigm is now coming under increasingly critical scrutiny, given the multiple problems that have arisen as part of this singular focus. Some of the key problems are briefly identified and discussed here as we take stock of food system failings.

Inadequate diets: More than one-quarter of the world's population experienced hunger or did not have regular access to nutrient-rich and sufficient food in 2019. An estimated three billion people lack access to affordable, healthy diets (GLOPAN, 2020). Currently, one in nine people – 820 million worldwide – are hungry or undernourished, with numbers rising since 2015, especially in Africa, West Asia and Latin America (FAO et al., 2019). Some 2.37 billion people – nearly one in three – faced food insecurity at the moderate or severe level in 2020. These numbers climbed steadily since 2014 and experienced a sharp increase in 2020 as the COVID-19 pandemic took hold (FAO, 2021; Béné et al., 2021). Globally in 2020 undernutrition was responsible for: nearly 150 million children aged under 5 estimated to be stunted (too short for age); 45 million estimated to be wasted (too thin for height); and around 45 percent of deaths among children aged under 5 years of age (WHO, 2021).

Diet-related disease: The links between diet and disease are becoming ever clearer and understood as a triple burden of undernutrition, deficiencies of vitamins and minerals, and diet-related noncommunicable diseases (NCDs). The paradox of the contemporary food system is that given the numbers that are chronically food insecure, almost two billion are overweight or obese with the fastest rate of growth in middle- and low-income countries. The co-existence of undernutrition, overnutrition (obesity) and climate change has been labelled 'The Global Syndemic', being a synergy of epidemics that interact and share common underlying societal drivers giving rise to complex outcomes (Swinburn et al., 2019). Changes in food systems that have led to the availability, indeed ubiquity, of highly processed foodstuffs that are affordable and convenient have resulted in unhealthy dietary patterns (Moodie et al., 2013). Sub-optimal diets are now responsible for 20 percent of premature (disease-mediated) mortality and at least 11 million people die every year from specifically diet-related illnesses (GLOPAN, 2020). Yet there is considerable inequality in health profiles, including within rich countries, reflecting differential access to healthy diets. For example, in the United States over 16 percent of youth aged between 10 and 17 years of age were obese, with Indigenous, Black, and Hispanic youth recording rates that were more than twice the level of White and Asian youth. This places them at much higher risk of type 2 diabetes and high blood pressure (Robert Wood Foundation, 2021).

Climate breakdown: the food system's contribution to global heating has come under increased scrutiny in recent years and it has been attributed with responsibility for between 21 and 37 percent of global greenhouse gas emissions (Xu et al., 2021; IPCC, 2021). Based on current trends, food system emissions alone would prevent the achievement of the 1.5°C target established under the 2015 Paris Agreement, irrespective of fossil fuel emissions reduction in other sectors (Clark et al., 2020). The largest source of uncertainty in the remaining carbon budget relates to the short-lived greenhouse gases methane and nitrous oxide, both strongly linked to agricultural production. The wider interconnections between climate and the food system, including the benefits from methane reduction efforts, are discussed in more detail in Chapter 3.

Loss of biospheric integrity: The production of food is the main cause of biodiversity loss through the conversion of land from primary ecosystems to agriculture. The area of land occupied by crop and livestock production has increased by around 5.5 times since 1600 and now occupies about 50 percent of the world's habitable land (Benton et al., 2021; Ritchie and Roser, 2020). The destruction of habitats such as forests removes sources of food and shelter on which wildlife depends. Since 1970, the collective weight of wild mammals has declined by 82 percent and now account for just 4 percent of global mammalian biomass, while a small number of domesticated livestock species (principally cattle and pigs) account for 60 percent of all mammals by mass, with humans representing 36 percent (Ritchie and Roser, 2020). A similar picture emerges from the realm of birds with 70 percent of global bird biomass now comprising domestic poultry, partly reflecting the catastrophic decline in farmland birds as well as a vertiginous increase in the numbers of broiler chickens. The loss of habitat, removal of sources of food and, of course, the widespread use of agri-chemicals have also been responsible for one of the greatest concerns among ecologists today: the disappearance of insects (Goulson, 2021).

Moreover, the expansion of high external input agriculture has resulted in the depletion and contamination of freshwater resources with two-thirds of global withdrawals from rivers, aquifers and groundwater extracted for irrigation. The production of water-intensive commodity crops for globalized supply chains can severely exacerbate the risks of local water scarcity (Qu et al., 2018). Meanwhile, the management of soil fertility under conventional agriculture has been largely reduced to ensuring the availability of three macro-nutrients – nitrogen, phosphorous and potassium – which are provided through copious applications of synthetic fertilizers. With nitrogen uptake by crops worldwide estimated at 43 percent, this means that over half of the fertilizer applied is lost to the environment and contributes atmospheric emissions of N_2O and leaching of nitrate into waterways that causes eutrophication (Sage, 2022). Food production creates around 32 percent of global terrestrial acidification and around 78 percent of eutrophication. These emissions threaten the biological composition and resilience of natural ecosystems (Poore and Nemecek, 2018). Overall, then, the food system constitutes a major driver of environmental degradation and requires a profound change if it is not to put at risk planetary boundaries that constitute a safe operating space for humanity (Springmann et al., 2018a).

Wider ecological and health consequences: The intensification of agricultural production has given rise to a wide range of problems, given the path-dependent pursuit of industrial technologies particularly around the use of chemicals. The rise of glyphosate, commercially developed by Monsanto under the label 'Roundup' to become by 2015 the most widely used herbicide around the world, is an illustrative example. Clapp (2021) traces the way in which glyphosate was taken up as a less toxic alternative to other herbicides. Yet one of the first problems to emerge, given its repeated field applications, was the development of glyphosate resistance in weeds. Subsequently, the toxicological effects on human health became more widely recognized, first through direct exposure in application (resulting in cases of non-Hodgkin's lymphoma and other cancers), and then through wider concerns arising from the ingestion of residues on food and through drinking water. Yet the entrenchment of glyphosate in agriculture, Clapp argues, was through overlapping configurations of technology, market, and regulatory forces – including the genetic engineering of herbicide tolerance in such crops as soy, cotton, maize, and rapeseed/canola. The rapid spread of genetically modified (GM) crops has been one of the most controversial issues within the food system over the past two decades and it remains a highly contested matter involving regulatory agencies, agrichemical corporations, farmers' representatives and civil society organizations.[4] Given glyphosate's seemingly irreplaceable role in conventional agriculture it is worth highlighting Arcuri and Hendlin's observation that it has the dubious distinction – alongside tobacco – of having multibillion dollar legal settlements made against it for health harms and deaths of hundreds of thousands of product users, while still being legally available on the market (Arcuri and Hendlin, 2020).

A second issue which we briefly note here is the role of pharmaceuticals in industrial livestock production; specifically, the prophylactic use of antibiotics to accelerate weight gain and control infection in food-producing animals. While the use of growth-promoting drugs has been banned in Europe, recombinant somatotropin, rBST (previously called bovine growth hormone), which is a genetically engineered hormone injected into dairy cows to increase milk production, is still widely used in the USA. Moreover, while there are complex pathways connecting human and animal health, the widespread veterinary use of broad-spectrum antibiotics commonly used to treat a range of infections in humans is of growing concern. Antimicrobial resistant infections were *directly responsible* for an estimated 1.27 million deaths worldwide and *associated with* 4.95 million deaths in 2019 (Antimicrobial Resistance Collaborators, 2022). This is simply a further illustration of the need to develop a more holistic One Health approach to life on earth that works to prevent zoonotic spill-overs of infection via food (as COVID-19) and to avoid inappropriately narrow 'techno-fix' responses such as mass application of veterinary prophylactics (Sinclair, 2019).

Labour in the food system: The first phase of the COVID-19 pandemic brought into sharp relief the issue of labour in the food system. A shortage of seasonal agricultural workers as a consequence of quarantine measures or illness affected many countries especially in the horticultural sector (Stephens et al., 2020) as well as meat processing and packing plants.[5] This sudden interest in labour in food was welcome but may yet be short-lived as supply chains return to normal. The conditions which characterize many intensive agricultural operations around the world persist. These include: exploitation – long hours, for low pay, often on piece rates; precarity – a lack of certainty about work and pay often on a day-to-day basis; unsafe and hazardous working conditions including exposure to toxic chemicals without adequate protection; and forced labour and human trafficking in global supply chains, including the use of child labour. One illustration of the latter is the 'caporalato' (gang-master) system that controls migrant agricultural labour in Italy and has long been linked with mafia networks in the South (Oxfam 2018). Chapter 4 provides a more detailed examination of agricultural labour in the food system.

However, it should also be noted that long hours for low pay is not confined within the farmgate: many factory operatives within food manufacturing and shop-floor staff in food retail experience poor working conditions. A continuous downward pressure on costs – including wages – has been an over-riding characteristic of the food system.

Food waste: There is general agreement that food waste is a problem that 'ought' to be addressed, given that around one-third of all food produced – around 1.3 billion tonnes per year – fails to reach a human stomach. It is an issue that has been extensively documented at the highest levels for well over a decade (FAO, 2011; HLPE, 2014; EU-FUSIONS, 2016) and so it is not discussed in detail here. Though often treated as an issue of morality – to throw away food when people are going hungry – it is vital to recognize that the production of surplus food in excess of demand is, in fact, a structural feature of the prevailing food system. As Messner and colleagues observe, "large-scale increases in supply, combined with the ongoing rise of food mass retailing and related dietary transitions, have contributed to food waste creation and overconsumption along the entire food supply chain" (Messner et al., 2020: 806). There are, of course, multiple issues arising from food waste creation and its management, not least the loss of embodied resources (energy, water) and the aggregated carbon footprint arising from these inputs and waste decomposition. Together these make food waste the third largest source of greenhouse gas emissions after China and the USA (EU-FUSIONS, 2016).

Corporate power and inequality: long-standing structural inequities related to class, gender, ethnicity, and the legacies of colonialism reflect the ways vested interests continue to disproportionately exercise power and influence across the food system. Injustices take many forms, for example small farmers lose access to land and other resources necessary for their livelihood as a consequence of state-sanctioned appropriations (land-grabbing) in favour of export commodity production. At the other end of the food system, nutritional security may be compromised through the unregulated availability of junk foods with little provision for healthier options. The concentration and market power of a small number of corporate entities that exercise enormous control over the food system and exert considerable influence over national and international policy is becoming a concern amongst many observers (Lauber et al., 2021; Clapp, 2018; Stuckler & Nestle, 2012). How do such structures reinforce or alleviate the widespread inequity and injustice in access to food experienced as a lived reality by billions of people? This is addressed in Chapter 5, which argues that the food system itself, *sui generis*, can be a cause of food poverty and food insecurity experienced both by those upstream (farmers, labourers) as well as those downstream (consumer-citizens). Arguably, the recent expansion of food banking across most wealthy countries reveals the sharp contradictions of a system oriented to structural over-production disposing of its unwanted surpluses through charitable food 'partners' to those in 'need'. While the dominant narrative is one of 'win–win' benefits – saving food from going to waste by giving it to those who cannot afford to buy it – corporate influence in this sector is powerful and serves to block a more critical analysis of the underlying drivers of food poverty and hunger in rich societies (Kenny and Sage, 2019; Riches, 2018).

In concluding this section, it is acknowledged that the above can only be regarded as a superficial treatment of some key failings of the food system, although subsequent chapters explore some of the issues in greater depth. It is also important to recognize how these different problem categories interconnect in complex ways and why they need to be approached in a manner that facilitates transdisciplinary enquiry. For example, it is not perhaps widely appreciated that rates of suicide amongst farmers are way above any other occupational category: 3.5 times that of the general population in the United States; with hundreds of thousands of lives lost in India since the mid-1990s. While a complex social pathology underpins such personal and domestic tragedies, indebtedness is invariably the single most common feature – revealing the capacity and determination of financial interests to extract value from land without itself being directly responsible for production – and where ready access to means, especially toxic agrichemicals, account for the majority of deaths. For agricultural labourers, meanwhile, exposure to extreme temperatures are exacerbated by climate breakdown, and this category accounted for almost half of the 295 billion potential work hours lost due to heat in 2020. Besides toiling in rising temperatures, it is these already vulnerable workers who will also experience the economic consequences as wages disappear in the face of crop failure and drive them, in desperation, into international migration as trafficked labour (Romanello et al., 2021).

While we cannot always anticipate the outcomes of dynamic systems as different elements within them synergize or collide, it does demand that food systems scholars develop a broader, transdisciplinary and longer-term perspective in their analyses. Events over recent years have clearly demonstrated that food systems at all scales around the world must become more resilient to the kinds of 'black swan' events represented by COVID-19 or cyber-attacks. Instead, the pursuit of 'just-in-time' practices within supply chains leaves the food system vulnerable to breakdown (see Jack, 2021 for an analysis of UK supermarkets).[6] Let us now turn to better appreciating the different ways in which food system failures are framed and potential solutions for improvement are proposed.

Food System Narratives

As noted above, many diverse sources of commentary and analysis have highlighted the 'failings' of contemporary food systems and urged the need for change. In an in-depth review of this literature, Béné and colleagues (2019) sought to identify the different narratives within these documents and the ways they framed the failures of food systems and where the priorities for action (the 'solutions') might be found. Their analysis led them to propose four distinctive narrative themes with each identifying a different structural problem and for which resolution would require divergent trajectories of intervention.

Their first, which they label 'food security', reminds us of the persistent pre-occupation with producing sufficient food to feed the global population. This is, of course, a valid anxiety given, that barely half a century ago, before the production achievements of the Green Revolution were visible, large areas of the Global South survived precariously with barely sufficient availability of cereals. Today, however, although the evidence demonstrates that we produce enough food to feed everyone well, as noted above billions of people remain malnourished. The popular food security narrative, however, speaks of the need to 'close the yield gap', that is, to produce a greater quantity of calories to feed the growing population. Most frequently it is expressed plaintively as 'How will we feed a population of ten billion by 2050?' (UNEP, 2020).

The concept of food security has existed for many decades, although interpretations of how it is understood have evolved. A long-standing definition that emerged from the 1996 World Food Summit proposed that food security is said to be achieved when "all people, at all times, have physical, social and economic access to sufficient, safe, and nutritious food to meet their dietary needs and food preferences for an active and healthy life". This definition has long rested on four pillars: availability, accessibility, utilization and stability where availability is regarded as necessary, but not sufficient for access; access as necessary but not sufficient for effective utilization; and stability as a cross-cutting factor that is necessary for the others to hold (Clapp et al., 2022). Arguably this hierarchy has served to privilege availability with an implicit bias toward a global solution: producing more food to feed a growing world population – a neo-Malthusian framing frequently forming part of this narrative. In this way, food security is treated as a scientific problem requiring purely technical solutions and where proponents of this narrative focus on the low yields of indigenous farming systems and argue that modern technologies could do much to achieve food security across the poorest countries. Consequently, it is of little surprise that this narrative has been so enthusiastically promoted by those largely in favour of 'business-as-usual' solutions where genetic engineering of seeds (and animal bodies) together with chemicals (proprietary herbicides) alongside new technologies (AI, drones, robotics) are presented as potential saviours.[7]

Such a framing of the problem narrowly circumscribes the kinds of solutions that are consequently proposed. A focus on projected population numbers encourages a sense of urgency, an imperative, for which agricultural technology appears to provide a ready-made solution. This globalized perspective fails to recognize, of course, that food security should largely be embedded in local ecosystems managed by local people (Sage, 2019). This helps to better understand the need to add two further dimensions to the existing four pillars of food security: agency and sustainability (Clapp et al., 2022). Agency can be regarded as the ability to express, exercise, and execute personal views and decisions in the interests of oneself and wider community wellbeing. However, it extends beyond the idea that people have a voice in matters of food security but, rather, become effective stakeholders within food systems, a change that will unsettle existing inequalities in the distribution of power.

The second additional dimension, sustainability, emphasizes "the connections between ecosystems, livelihoods, society, and political economy to maintain food systems and support food security into the distant future" (Clapp et al., 2022: 5). We explore issues surrounding sustainability in a little more detail below. However, here it is clear that both concepts help to establish a much broader systems perspective that take us from a linear 'problem → solution' approach and toward a place where socially and ecologically appropriate, multi-dimensional measures might be formulated by local people that offer different visions and options for bridging this 'yield gap'. Such measures might include changes in crops and farming methods, dietary practices including efforts to reduce food loss and waste, as well as social initiatives (work and labour practices, new institutional arrangements, networked collaborations etc).

Béné et al.'s second narrative focusses upon the inability of the food system to deliver a healthy diet and might be captured by the label 'nutrition security'. Here, as they observe, the problem has shifted from quantity to quality: the reviewed literature acknowledges that sufficient food is being produced today yet so many still remain malnourished with serious implications for human health. Here, issues become more nuanced as we move from the supply of sufficient calories to an appreciation of micro-nutrient deficiencies and even the availability of foods that contribute to dietary ill-health and obesity. This more strongly nutrition-centred disciplinary approach segues into their third narrative category which might be labelled 'social justice'. This builds upon the second but rather highlights the gross social inequities that underpin differentials in accessing healthy diets. Furthermore, this distributional injustice is intrinsic to a food system increasingly concentrated in fewer corporate hands that reinforces existing structures creating greater vulnerability.

As one might expect, although the second and third narratives share a concern for human wellbeing, their 'priorities for action' take quite different pathways: targeted nutrition interventions to improve diets in the former as opposed to a range of social, economic and political measures challenging injustice. However, if the latter might be encapsulated by aspirations for greater food sovereignty – where communities exercise control over what foods are produced and distributed within their territory in the interests of local livelihoods and dietary health – then we might imagine the possibilities for bridging the second and third narratives through the promotion of greater agricultural biodiversity. It has been noted that while 10,000 plant species have been used for food since the origin of agriculture, only 30 crops now provide 90 percent of the world's calorie intake with four – rice, wheat, maize and potatoes – supplying 50 percent of energy needs (Hunter and Fanzo, 2013). The nutritional and ecological importance of underutilized indigenous crops has been widely recognized (Fanzo et al., 2013) yet remains marginalized by a dominant food system centred upon the intensive production of a narrow range of commercially bred seeds. The greater deployment of plant genetic diversity by communities offers a pathway toward improving nutritional security while also addressing structural inequities in accessing food, and thereby reveals possible synergies between different narratives if the lens is widened.

The fourth, and final narrative that Béné and colleagues identify is that surrounding the impact of the food system on the environment and natural resources. Some of the most egregious impacts were outlined above, including land use change and biodiversity loss; freshwater depletion, and greenhouse gas emissions. Although the entire food system shares responsibility – from primary production through distribution and retail to consumption – the evidence is clear that the greatest impacts occur at the agricultural stage and this has driven calls for more sustainable farming methods in producing our food. However, much as the term 'food security' has required careful consideration with the deployment of additional dimensions to make it 'fit' for our contemporary circumstances, so the term 'sustainable' needs review and recalibration. This is especially so given the way in which it has become a prefix *de nos jours*, appropriated by powerful interests and promiscuously deployed often with little concern for precision or honesty. In order to render more transparent the practice of 'greenwashing', making environmental claims for a product or process that are not borne out in practice, we turn to examine the meaning of 'sustainable' in relation to the food system.[8]

'Sustainable' Food Systems

Approaching the topic of *sustainable* food one is reminded of a character from Lewis Carroll's Through the Looking Glass:

> "When I use a word," Humpty Dumpty said, in rather a scornful tone, "it means just what I choose it to mean—neither more nor less." "The question is," said Alice, "whether you can make words mean so many different things." "The question is," said Humpty Dumpty, "which is to be master—that's all." (Knowles, 2009: 203)

As is generally well known, the term 'sustainable development' first gained currency in the wake of the 1987 report of the World Commission for Environment and Development (the 'Brundtland Commission'). It famously captured the necessity of longer-term thinking through a definition that drew attention to ensuring that meeting the needs of the present generation would not compromise the ability of future generations to meet their own needs. Moreover, it sought to give equal weighting to the pursuit of economic, social and environmental objectives often represented as overlapping circles across which trade-offs would be determined. Given the hazards of attempting to universalize human needs across cultures and over time the notion of 'needs' left unanswered questions about how these might be defined in the context of development, population growth, changes in patterns of consumption and environmental capacities. For many, the sheer vagueness of the term as well as being an oxymoron – how can economic development and environmental conservation actually be reconciled? – meant outright hostility in certain quarters where it was regarded as providing 'green cover' for development planning and environmental managerialism. Others, however, saw in the term not strict definitional clarity but the promise of a shared discourse, the basis of a 'thinkable opposition' to the capitalist status quo, and the space to (re-) imagine environmental justice, ecological rationality, and human wellbeing (Springett and Redclift, 2015).

'Sustainable' is now a ubiquitous feature of the food system vocabulary and while it might 'promise' a shared discourse, it remains subject to many different interpretations and is vulnerable to being used as something of a Trojan Horse to greenwash 'business-as-usual' practices, as is briefly outlined with regard to Irish agricultural policy in Chapter 3. Nevertheless, with the adoption by the

United Nations in 2015 of the 17 Sustainable Development Goals (SDGs), the world has begun to appreciate the embeddedness of food to human wellbeing and planetary health. As evidence, of the 17 SDGs there are 160 specific targets with around 70 of these connected to food. There is widespread and high-level agreement that the current food system is not sustainable nor just (Group of Chief Scientific Advisors, 2020) yet there is little agreement beyond generalised statements of what a sustainable food system would look like.[9]

A major part of the problem here lies with the multiplicity of components that need to be incorporated and evaluated if a food system is to be assessed on a performance scale of sustainability. Such components might include a host of environmental impacts (greenhouse gas emissions, water pollution, biodiversity loss etc.); resource use (land, water); effects on human wellbeing (dietary health); animal welfare; and remuneration and working conditions along supply chains. Measurement of these many different variables then involves a system of trade-offs between them to ultimately deliver some 'index of performance' that might then be communicated to the consumer of a product or service (Broom, 2021).

However, given the complexity of this process, it is probably more helpful to look in greater detail at two key areas where the term has been applied more concretely: as sustainable agriculture and as sustainable diets. Selecting these points at either end of the food system does neglect the commercial activities of companies working along the food chain in processing, manufacturing, food service and retail. However, there is a wide variety of positions here: from defensiveness including active lobbying against proposed labelling and regulations to improve environmental performance, to enthusiastic engagement with a sustainability agenda. Such diverse attitudes from different boardrooms reflect on the particular sector and product mix in which businesses are engaged. For example, the global giant food service company Sodexo, with nearly half-million employees worldwide, has recently renewed its partnership with WWF to improve its "sustainable food offer and purchasing practices" (Sodexo, 2020). Besides 'doing good' it must see in this strategy an opportunity, inter alia, to differentiate itself from competitors; enhance its brand; build customer loyalty; make efficiency savings and reduce costs; raise staff motivation; and, ultimately, improve profit margins (Mason and Lang, 2017). Elsewhere start-up companies have proclaimed their sustainability credentials through engagement with, for example, alternative proteins as meat substitutes. Overall, however, there is too much motivational and interpretive diversity across the entire food system to do justice to an analysis of the term and so we focus on, first, sustainable agriculture, and then sustainable diets.

Sustainable Agriculture

First, it should be noted that this term is itself a gateway to a rich and diverse landscape of different technical, environmental and, above all, ethical visions of food, farming, and the place of nature in securing human sustenance from the land.[10] Second order labels provide some sense of this agricultural diversity: agroecology, biodynamic, conservation farming, organic, low external input, permaculture, regenerative, sustainable intensification and so on, each with their own array of standards. One of many issues that differentiate sustainable agriculture approaches is with regard to the use of land and the optimal way of conserving biodiversity. For some, 'land sparing' represents the best option whereby agricultural land is farmed intensively to maximize food output, but other land is set aside – spared – for habitat restoration and species protection. Others suggest 'land sharing' might work better, where agriculture retains landscape features such as hedgerows, ponds and woodland and reduced chemical inputs lead to lower overall yields. Despite such differences, all proponents of sustainable agriculture agree, however, that the dominant paradigm of industrial, productivist agriculture levies too high a cost in externalities (consequences not reflected in market prices) when set against food output. Indeed, many of the multi-dimensional system failings discussed earlier are largely located within the realm of agriculture and while its own supporters claim to be improving their social and environmental performance while 'feeding the world' (e.g. by developing 'climate-smart' farming solutions), the case for change is becoming increasingly apparent.

One approach that appears to have gained considerable momentum in international policy circles is that of agroecology with the UN's Food and Agriculture Organisation finally acknowledging its potential contribution to resolving many of our contemporary challenges. Drawing upon the FAO's Agroecology Knowledge Hub (FAO, 2022) – which derived from extensive stakeholder consultation and expert input – some of the essential principles of agroecology are briefly outlined here as a way of illustrating the alternative paradigm of sustainable agriculture.[11]

Diversity: Possibly the single most important *practical* feature of agroecology is diversity: of plant and animal species and varieties, including intercropping (companion planting) and crop rotations (succession planting) which provides spatial and temporal diversity. Diversified systems might include crop-livestock or crop-fish (aquaculture) combinations. Increasing agrobiodiversity contributes nutritional and environmental benefits by enhancing the provisioning of ecosystem services, including pollination and soil health. Maintaining plant genetic resources in situ – that is in farmers' fields – is recognized as vital to future adaptation to a hotter world. Polycultures – the simultaneous cultivation of different crops – has been a distinctive feature of small-scale farming throughout much of the world yet despite its overall yield advantages (measured by numbers of people nourished, not by yield volume of a single cereal) it has been increasingly displaced by high-input monocultures.

Knowledge: Agroecology depends on context-specific knowledge and where practices are tailored to fit local circumstances. Co-creation and sharing of knowledge will be vital in building adaptive, synergistic and resilient food systems in the face of climate disruption. This does not exclude learning from Western scientific expertise where this is appropriate, but it rejects the imposition of top-down models of technology transfer in favour of farmer field schools and farmer-to-farmer extension practices.

Efficiency: Avoiding the unnecessary use of external inputs is an essential feature of any sustainable agriculture. Rather, the objective is to optimize the use of natural resources, to enhance biological processes and recycle nutrients. The application of integrated pest management to replace chemical pesticides, and the planting of legumes for biological nitrogen fixation instead of synthetic fertilizers are examples here. Closing nutrient cycles and eliminating waste also reduces dependency on external inputs, increasing autonomy and reducing vulnerability to unpredictable market shocks and other risks. This enhances the resilience of farming communities and improves their capacity to ensure food security.

Circular and solidarity economy: As the Knowledge Hub states, 'Agroecology seeks to reconnect producers and consumers through a circular and solidarity economy that prioritizes local markets and supports local economic development...' (FAO, 2022). This feature marks the sharpest contrast with industrialized agriculture and its drive to maximize output for distant markets ('food from nowhere'). By reterritorializing the food system, agroecology restores the essential connection between food, people, and place. It also demonstrates that agroecology – and one might arguably extend this to other forms of sustainable agriculture – is a great deal more than a set of farming practices designed to produce food; rather it embodies social, economic, and political objectives.

As one can see from this all-too-brief summary of some of its key features, agroecology offers an integrated approach that applies ecological and social principles to the redesign and management of food and farming systems. The notion of *redesign* is very important: it is not an ad hoc 'tweaking' of unsustainable practices but rather promises transformative change (Pretty, 2020; Pretty and Bharucha, 2018). It embodies a more deliberative process whereby changes in farming practices – to maximize biodiversity, build healthy agroecosystems while producing nutritious food – are accompanied by a rebalancing of power relations that strengthen local livelihoods and enable greater participation by all food system stakeholders, perhaps best expressed by the term 'food sovereignty'. Agroecology possesses a universal logic for the redesign of food systems: it is not simply a model for smallholder farmers. Yet as IPES-Food (2016) outlines, there are a number of deeply entrenched 'lock-ins' that maintain the hegemony of productivist agriculture: path dependency based on financial investments and returns; globalization and export orientation (underpinned by claims of comparative advantage); the continuing expectation of 'cheap' food (where true costs are shunted to 'externalities'); and a great deal of short-term and compartmentalized thinking (especially in agricultural research) amongst other factors. Such obstacles make clear that food system change cannot be left to farmers alone by improving agricultural practices but must proceed together with governments, municipal authorities, civil society organizations and, ultimately, food consumers themselves. This latter group is critical for those in rich countries, especially, need to embark upon a process of dietary change if there is to be any hope of achieving a sustainable food system.

Sustainable Diets

In pursuit of a more sustainable food system, the chapter has suggested a necessity for less resource-intensive diets as a way of mitigating climate change, to achieve a lower environmental footprint that will reduce pressure on use of land and freshwater resources, and reduce pollution of aquatic and terrestrial ecosystems (Willett et al., 2019; Springmann et al., 2018a; Tilman and Clark, 2014). As already noted, this means there are a number of very different ecological components, each with their own metrics that must be taken into account and traded off in order to create some aggregate measure of environmental performance. Invariably this process involves prioritization as some components are regarded as more important than others. In a systematic literature review of empirical research studies on sustainable diets it was found that greenhouse gas emissions followed by land use then levels of meat consumption were identified as primary measures while other important components were disproportionately underrepresented (Jones et al., 2016).

Yet the ongoing process of nutrition transition continues to enrol greater numbers of people into more westernized diets featuring higher intakes of meat, sugar, fats and salt which not only exert a high environmental load but have increased the global burden of disease (GLOPAN, 2020). Consequently, the notion of a sustainable diet has become inextricably entangled with individual wellbeing such that human and planetary health are increasingly regarded as inseparable. This has led Tim Lang to ask whether this presents a new benchmark for what constitutes a 'good' or desirable diet; labels which carry moral and cultural weight as well as practical implications (Lang, 2021). That the term has come to embody a high degree of complexity given the range and importance of policy issues it represents, as well as extraordinary malleability in the meanings it conveys, it is as well to reprise a long-standing and robust definition here:

> Sustainable diets are those with low environmental impacts which contribute to food and nutrition security and to healthy life for present and future generations. Sustainable diets are protective and respectful of biodiversity and ecosystems, culturally acceptable, accessible, economically fair and affordable; nutritionally adequate, safe and healthy; while optimizing natural and human resources. (Burlingame & Dernini, 2012: 8)[12]

What, however, should this mean in practice? Mason and Lang (2017) have set out at length and in some depth why sustainable diets matter and they argue strongly for maintaining complexity in the way it should be approached: it cannot be reduced, they make clear, to a matter of 'carbon + calories' but must accommodate, equally, a range of dimensions. These they elaborate under six broad headings: health, social values, economy, food quality, governance, and environment, each with their own set of constituent issues and measures that simply cannot be 'traded-off' one against another and where experience tells us that the economic calculation invariably prevails. It means approaching sustainable diets holistically and in a transdisciplinary manner capable of understanding the interactions between the many different variables that ultimately influence the choices and actions of food consumers. As the preceding discussion in this chapter has suggested, unidimensional narratives of food system failure and singular solutions ('productivism will feed the world') will not resolve the complex challenges facing us, nor bridge the large and widening gaps between scientific evidence, public policy, and everyday behaviours.

Nevertheless, a focus on the realm of consumption is essential, particularly in rich and upper middle-income countries, to tackle the planetary and human health burden of contemporary dietary practices. This implies that deep-rooted shifts in values, norms, consumer culture and underlying worldviews will be an inescapable part of the necessary transition (UNEP, 2019). Yet there is considerable personal investment in maintaining eating habits that deliver the tastes and satisfaction to which individuals have become accustomed and many will be hostile to change, despite the fact that consumption patterns have been transformed over the past 50 years. Constructing the notion of a 'sustainable diet' is consequently a deeply challenging goal that will need to carefully navigate recommendations of what 'should' or 'should not' be eaten. There can be no *a priori* 'demon' or 'saviour' foods though the scientific evidence points clearly to more ecologically, nutritionally, and culturally appropriate forms of consumption. One way may be to restore a greater sense of the social, cultural, nutritional, medicinal and territorial dimensions of our customary food practices and to communicate the ways these have been transformed – or entirely lost – as a consequence of the modern, industrial food system.

Sustainable diets are most closely associated with greater levels of plant-based consumption, which has been shown to reduce food-related environmental impacts and improve health outcomes (Springmann et al., 2018b). In the context of this evidence, the EAT-Lancet Commission – a consortium of 39 distinguished scientists from 16 countries – published a report in 2019 that elaborated a planetary health diet and made a call for dietary change (Willett et al., 2019). The EAT-Lancet diet can be labelled 'flexitarian', where plant-based foods predominate – with recommended increases in whole grains, fruit and vegetables, nuts and seeds, and legumes – supplemented by small amounts of meat (one serving of red meat per week), fish, and dairy (one serving or glass per day). Modelling the adoption of the EAT-Lancet diet recommendations was associated with large net reductions in greenhouse gas emissions (42 percent or 1.8 Gt CO_2-eq), freshwater use (10 percent) and nitrogen and phosphorus applications. Besides delivering a reduction in environmental resource use in line with global environmental targets (e.g. the 2015 Paris Accord on Climate Change), the EAT-Lancet diet also achieved greater health benefits (a 34 percent reduction in premature mortality, saving around 11 million lives/year) than all national food-based dietary guidelines compared in a recent study (Springmann et al., 2020).

Predictably, the EAT-Lancet report quickly acquired a certain notoriety, as sectors threatened by its recommendations (the meat and livestock industry) pushed back. However, more considered responses have since emerged, highlighting the importance of regionalizing any reference diet (including promoting existing territorial patterns such as the Mediterranean Diet); re-evaluating prohibitions on meat, dairy and fish consumption amongst pastoralist and coastal communities where these are key staples; and to ensure that healthy dietary recommendations are also affordable to those on low incomes (Vaidyanathan, 2021). But it is clear that the EAT-Lancet study has opened up space for making planetary and human health an inseparable part of ongoing discussion and policy formulation on sustainable diets and around the food system more generally.

Conclusions

This chapter has presented a broad overview of the dominant system that drives the production, distribution, and consumption of food across much of the world today. It has not sought to provide descriptive detail but rather to offer a critical analysis of some of its key features, dynamics, and outcomes. It identified the main constituent components and mapped the ways in which they inter-relate. While conventionally much attention is focussed upon the stages of the food supply chain, with all of its logistical sophistication, it was suggested that the food environment – comprising both the physical infrastructure (food outlets) as well as the more 'virtual' cognitive world – is key to appreciating how such a commercially successful system can result in sub-optimal, arguably disastrous, outcomes. Major problem areas were only briefly reviewed but together provide sufficient evidence to demonstrate that the current food system is simply not fit for purpose if judged by the criteria of feeding people well. Yet while there may be widespread agreement for change, it was clear that how problems are framed determines what solutions might be identified and pursued. While many readers might agree that the case for radical and urgent structural reform of the food system is overdue, others would make the case for more incremental improvements, perhaps using the language of sustainability to prove their green credentials.

The chapters that follow provide more detailed examination of significant issues confronting the food system and, indeed, confront us all as participants to some degree – whether we are willing to accept them or not! The rise and concentration of corporate power within key stages of the supply chain – from seeds to food retailers – should concern us. So, too, the conditions faced by those who pick and pack the fresh produce found on our supermarket shelves, or the animals whose bodies have been so thoroughly reconfigured and commodified. But writing this is not to generate guilt: it is rather a contribution to clearing away the smokescreen of disguise, deception and denial that has concealed much of the workings of the food system from the public gaze. Above all, it makes clear the importance of developing a research agenda for food systems that highlights key areas requiring interrogation and which can bring insight to wider public attention. There is much work to be done in this regard and social scientists, in particular, have an important role in using their skills by undertaking research that not only documents cases of food system failure but in a way that can engage with and support local stakeholders (farmers, workers, food citizens) in devising strategies for their resolution. It is in this spirit that this volume has been prepared.

Notes

1. Jeffrey Sachs, Speech to UN Food Systems Pre-Summit. Transcript and video here: https://www.jeffsachs.org/recorded-lectures/5jf86pp5lxch35e6z3nct6xnmb8zy5. Also video of this speech available here: https://sandersinstitute.org/blog-jeffrey -sachs-speech-at-the-un-food-systems-pre-summit/?cat=economy-economic -justice and here: https://www.youtube.com/watch?v=WZ1xc491mnU.

2. This is not to overlook the work that has been ongoing both prior and subsequent to the financial crisis of 2008-12. In particular the landmark publication of the first International Assessment of Agricultural Knowledge, Science and Technology for Development (IAASTD) report in 2009 should be acknowledged not least for establishing the maxim, "Business as usual is not an option". Herren et al. (2020) provide an excellent evaluation of efforts to transform food systems since that publication.

3. More detail on the various stages of the food supply chain can be found in Sage (2012), and Tansey and Worsley (1995).

4. There is not space here to unpick the complex interconnected configurations of technology, market, and regulatory aspects that explain how glyphosate has become so central to productivist agriculture. Besides Clapp's article (2021) interested readers are directed to the special issue of the *European Journal of Risk Regulation* (11, 3; 2020) which contains a Symposium on the Science and Politics of Glyphosate edited by Arcuri and Hendlin.

5. The animal slaughter and carcass processing industry has been characterized by unsafe working conditions and low pay for more than a century since the work of Upton Sinclair. These plants – especially in the United States but in Europe too – became notorious for the rapid spread of COVID-19 amongst workers as a consequence of close contact in the working environment. A highly critical piece is provided by Chang et al. (2021). On Covid, agricultural labour and the food system more generally see the special issue of *Agricultural Systems*, volume 183: https://www.sciencedirect.com/journal/agricultural-systems/special-issue/ 10D1KTPPCQ5.

6. Cyber-attacks can seriously undermine the functioning of the food system given the complex logistics of supply chains that connect product bar-code scanning at the supermarket checkout to ordering stock via wholesalers (the case of Spar, UK 5 December 2021). On the vulnerability of the UK food system to COVID-19 see Rivington et al. (2021).

7. At the time of writing, BBC Global News is showing on its platform a second series of programmes under the title, 'Follow the Food' which is sponsored by Corteva Agriscience, the rebranded company arising from the merger of Dow and DuPont. The programmes are presented by James Wong, a British botanist with a boyish enthusiasm for all things tech. As the BBC describes it, "Follow the Food is a TV and digital series showcasing the latest in technological innovation and modern agriculture. Sponsored by Corteva Agriscience, it takes audiences on a journey from field to fork; exploring the ways in which the world's rapidly growing population can be fed, without exhausting the Earth's resources." It is instructive to note how reference to population growth prefaces every item in each episode. https:// www.bbc.com/future/bespoke/follow-the-food/ (accessed 7 August 2022).

8. Making claims for the sustainability of a product is only part, of course, of the myths that are spun as a way of deceiving customers, policymakers and less

than vigilant regulators. A good example is the Spanish pork industry which has boomed in recent years on the back of a narrative that claims it is based on small, artisanal firms, creating large numbers of quality jobs in rural areas, and helping to reverse population decline; that it is a model of sustainable production and economic success. The reality is that the sector is heavily industrialized, extremely polluting, and guilty of violating basic human rights (Win, 2021).

9.   "A sustainable food system delivers food security and nutrition for all in such a way that the economic, social and environmental bases to generate food security and nutrition for future generations are not compromised" (Group of Chief Scientific Advisors, 2020: 14). And "food system practices that contribute to long-term regeneration of natural, social, and economic systems, ensuring the food needs of the present generations are met without compromising food needs of future generations" (HLPE, 2020: 10).

10. A sense of this diversity of perspectives – which extend back to the work of Sir Albert Howard in colonial India – and which far exceed any notion of narrow technical disputes over how to farm, can be garnered from the reader compiled by Pretty (2005).

11. An immensely rich yet concise introduction to agroecology highlighting a wealth of web-based resources is provided by Anderson and Anderson (2020).

12. A collection of articles exploring many different aspects of sustainable diets appear as a special issue of the *International Journal of the Sociology of Agriculture and Food* edited by Sage, Quieti and Fonte (2021).

References

Anderson, C., Anderson, M. 2020. Resources to inspire a transformative agroecology: A curated guide. In Herren, H. et al. (eds) *Transformation of our Food Systems: The making of a paradigm shift.* Berlin: Zukunftsstiftung Landwirtschaft, pp. 167–180. https://www.globalagriculture.org/fileadmin/files/weltagrarbericht/IAASTD-Buch/PDFBuch/BuchWebTransformationFoodSystems.pdf.

Antimicrobial Resistance Collaborators 2022. Global burden of bacterial antimicrobial resistance in 2019: a systematic analysis. *The Lancet* https://doi.org/10.1016/S0140-6736(21)02724-0.

Arcuri, A., Hendlin, Y. 2020. Introduction to the Symposium on the Science and Politics of Glyphosate. *European Journal of Risk Regulation*, 11, 3: 411–421.

Baker, P., Lacy-Nichols, J., Williams, O., Labonté, R. 2021. The political economy of healthy and sustainable food systems: an introduction to a special issue. *International Journal of Health Policy Management*, 10, 12: 734–744.

Barrett, C., Benton, T., Cooper, K. et al. 2020. Bundling innovations to transform agri-food systems. *Nature Sustainability*, 3: 974–976.

Basu, S. 2015. The transitional dynamics of caloric ecosystems: changes in the food supply around the world, *Critical Public Health*, 25, 3: 248-264, https://doi.org/10.1080/09581596.2014.931568.

Béné, C., Bakker, D., Chavarro, M. et al. 2021. Global assessment of the impacts of COVID-19 on food security. *Global Food Security*, 31, 100575.

Béné, C., Oosterveer, P., Lamotte, L. et al. 2019. When food systems meet sustainability: current narratives and implications for actions. *World Development*, 113: 116–130.

Benton, T., Bieg, C., Harwatt, H., Pudasaini, R., Wellesley, L. 2021. Food system impacts on biodiversity loss: three levers for food system transformation in support of nature. Research Paper, Chatham House, London.

Broom, D. 2021. A method for assessing sustainability, with beef production as an example. *Biological Reviews*, 96: 1836–1853.

Burlingame, B., Dernini, S. 2012. Sustainable diets and biodiversity: directions and solutions for policy, research and action. Proceedings of the International Scientific Symposium 'Biodiversity and Sustainable Diets United against Hunger', 3–5 November 2010, FAO Headquarters, Rome. Rome: FAO and Bioversity International.

Caron, P., Ferrero y de Loma-Osorio, G., Nabarro, D. et al. 2018. Food systems for sustainable development: proposals for a profound four-part transformation. *Agronomy for Sustainable Development*, 38: 41. https://doi.org/10.1007/s13593-018-0519-1.

Chacon, V., Letona, P., Villamor, E., Barnoya, J. 2015. Snack food advertising in stores around public schools in Guatemala. *Critical Public Health*, 25, 3: 291–298. https://doi.org/10.1080/09581596.2014.953035.

Chang, A., Sainato, M., Lakhani, N., Kamal, R., Uteuova, A. 2021. The pandemic exposed the human cost of the meatpacking industry's power: 'it's enormously frightening'. *The Guardian*, 16 November. https://www.theguardian.com/environment/2021/nov/16/meatpacking-industry-covid-outbreaks-workers.

Clapp, J., Moseley, W., Burlingame, B., Termine, P. 2022. The case for a six-dimensional food security framework. *Food Policy*, 106, 102164.

Clapp, J. 2021. Explaining growing glyphosate use: the political economy of herbicide-dependent agriculture. *Global Environmental Change*, 67, 102239.

Clapp, J. 2018. Mega-mergers on the menu: corporate concentration and the politics of sustainability in the global food system. *Global Environmental Politics*, 18, 2: 12–33.

Clark, M., Domingo, N., Colgan, K. et al. 2020. Global food system emissions could preclude achieving the 1.5° and 2°C climate change targets. *Science*, 370: 705–708.

Crowley, J., Smyth, W., Murphy, M. (eds) 2012. *Atlas of the Great Irish Famine*. Cork: Cork University Press.

Elliott, C. 2015. 'Big food' and 'gamified' products: promotion, packaging, and the promise of fun. *Critical Public Health*, 25, 3: 348–360. https://doi.org/10.1080/09581596.2014.953034.

EU Food Policy Coalition 2021. Food environments and EU food policy: discovering the role of food environments for sustainable food systems. https://foodpolicycoalition.eu/.

EU-FUSIONS. 2016. About food waste. https://www.eu-fusions.org/index.php/about-food-waste.

Fakhri, M. 2021. 'The world's food systems have been failing people for a long time'. *The Guardian*, 23 September. https://www.theguardian.com/global/commentisfree/2021/sep/23/un-summit-food-systems-families-michael-fakhri.

FAO. 2022. Agroecology Knowledge Hub. https://www.fao.org/agroecology/overview/overview10elements/en/ (accessed 23 January 2022).

FAO. 2021. *Food outlook – biannual report on global food markets*. Food Outlook, November 2021. Rome. https://doi.org/10.4060/cb7491en.

FAO. 2011. Global food losses and food waste – extent, causes and prevention. Rome: FAO.

FAO, IFAD, UNICEF, WFP, WHO. 2019. The state of food security and nutrition in the world 2019. Rome: FAO.

Fanzo, J., Haddad, L., Schneider, K. et al. 2021. Viewpoint: rigorous monitoring is necessary to guide food system transformation in the countdown to the 2030 global goals. *Food Policy*, 104: 102163.

Fanzo, J., Covic, N., Dobermann, A., Henson, S. et al. 2020. A research vision for food systems in the 2020s: Defying the status quo. *Global Food Security*, 26: 100397.

Fanzo, J., Hunter, D., Borelli, T., Mattei, F. (eds) 2013. *Diversifying Food and Diets: Using agricultural biodiversity to improve nutrition and health.* Abingdon, UK: Routledge Earthscan.

Global Panel on Agriculture and Food Systems for Nutrition (GLOPAN). 2020. *Future Food Systems: For people, our planet, and prosperity.* London, UK.: GLOPAN.

Goulson, D. 2021. *Silent Earth: Averting the insect apocalypse.* London: Jonathan Cape.

Group of Chief Scientific Advisors, 2020. Towards a sustainable food system: moving from food as a commodity to food as more of a common good. Scientific Opinion No.8, DG Research & Innovation, Brussels.

Herren, H. et al. (eds) 2020. *Transformation of our Food Systems: The making of a paradigm shift.* Berlin: Zukunftsstiftung Landwirtschaft. https://www.globalagriculture.org/fileadmin/files/weltagrarbericht/IAASTD-Buch/PDFBuch/BuchWebTransformationFoodSystems.pdf.

HLPE, 2020. Food security and nutrition: building a global narrative towards 2030. A report by the High Level Panel of Experts on Food Security and Nutrition of the Committee on World Food Security, Rome.

HLPE, 2017. Nutrition and food systems. A report by the High-Level Panel of Experts on Food Security and Nutrition of the Committee on World Food Security, Rome.

HLPE 2014. Food losses and waste in the context of sustainable food systems. A report by the High-Level Panel of Experts on Food Security and Nutrition of the Committee on World Food Security, Rome.

Hunter, D., Fanzo, J. 2013. Introduction: agricultural biodiversity, diverse diets and improving nutrition. In Fanzo, J., Hunter, D., Borelli, T., Mattei, F. (eds) *Diversifying Food and Diets: Using agricultural biodiversity to improve nutrition and health.* Abingdon, UK: Earthscan, pp. 1–13.

IPES-Food 2016. From uniformity to diversity: A paradigm shift from industrial agriculture to diversified agroecological systems. International Panel of Experts on Sustainable Food systems. https://www.ipes-food.org.

Intergovernmental Panel on Climate Change (IPCC) 2021. Climate change 2021: the physical science basis. Contribution of Working Group I to the Sixth Assessment Report of the Intergovernmental Panel on Climate Change. https://www.ipcc.ch/report/ar6/wg1/.

Jack, L. 2021. The secrets of supermarketing: a model balanced on a knife-edge. FRC Food Policy Discussion Paper, Centre for Food Policy, City University London. https://foodresearch.org.uk/publications/the-supermarket-system-balanced-on-a-knife-edge/.

Jones, A., Hoey, L., Blesh, J., Miller, L., Green, A., Shapiro, L. 2016. A systematic review of the measurement of sustainable diets. *Advances in Nutrition*, 7: 641–664. https://doi.org/10.3945/an.115.011015.

Kenny, T., Sage, C. 2019. Food surplus as charitable provision: Obstacles to re-introducing food as a commons. In Vivero-Pol, J.L., Ferrando, T., de Schutter, O., Mattei, U. (eds) *Routledge Handbook of Food as a Commons.* Abingdon, UK: Routledge, pp. 281–295.

Knowles, E. 2009. *Oxford Dictionary of Quotations.* Oxford: Oxford University Press.

Lagi, M., Bertrand, K., Bar-Yam, Y. 2011. The food crises and political instability in North Africa and the Middle East. New England Complex Systems Institute, Cambridge, MA. necsi.edu.

Lakoff, G., 2010. Why it matters how we frame the environment. *Environmental Communication: A Journal of Nature and Culture*, 4, 1: 70–81.

Lang, T., 2021. The sustainable diet question: reasserting societal dynamics into the debate about a good diet. *International Journal of Sociology of Agriculture & Food*, 27: 12–34.

Lauber, K., Rutter, H., Gilmore A., 2021. Big food and the World Health Organization: a qualitative study of industry attempts to influence global-level non-communicable disease policy. *BMJ Global Health*, 6: e005216. https://doi.org/10.1136/bmjgh-2021 -005216.

Leach, M., Nisbett, N., Cabral, L., Harris, J., Hossain, N., Thompson, J. 2020. Food politics and development. *World Development*, 134, 105024.

Marshall, Q., Fanzo, J., Barrett, C., Jones, A. et al. 2021. Building a global food systems typology: a new tool for reducing complexity in food systems analysis. *Frontiers in Sustainable Food Systems*, 5, 746512.

Mason, P., Lang, T., 2017. *Sustainable Diets: How Ecological Nutrition can Transform Consumption and the Food System*. Abingdon: Routledge Earthscan.

McBey, D., Watts, D., Johnstone, A., 2019. Nudging, formulating new products, and the lifecourse: a qualitative assessment of the viability of three methods for reducing Scottish meat consumption for health, ethical, and environmental reasons. *Appetite*, 142. https://doi.org/10.1016/j.appet.2019.104349.

Messner, R., Richards, C., Johnson, H. 2020. The "Prevention Paradox": food waste prevention and the quandary of systemic surplus production. *Agriculture and Human Values*, 37: 805–817.

Moodie, R., Stuckler, D., Monteiro, C. et al. 2013. Profits and pandemics: prevention of harmful effects of tobacco, alcohol, and ultra-processed food and drink industries. *Lancet*, 381: 670–679.

Neve, K., Isaacs, A. 2021. How does the food environment influence people engaged in weight management? A systematic review and thematic synthesis of the qualitative literature. *Obesity Reviews*. https://doi.org/10.1111/obr.13398.

Oxfam 2018. *Human Suffering in Italy's Agricultural Value Chain*. Oxford: Oxfam.

Pitt, E., Gallegos, D., Comans, T., Cameron, C., Thornton, L. 2017. Exploring the influence of local food environments on food behaviours: a systematic review of qualitative literature. *Public Health Nutrition*, 20, 13: 2393–2405.

Poore, J., Nemecek, T. 2018. Reducing food's environmental impacts through producers and consumers. *Science*, 360, 6392: 987–992.

Popkin, B., Reardon, T. 2018. Obesity and the food system transformation in Latin America. *Obesity Reviews*, 19, 1028–1064.

Popkin, B., Adair, L., Ng, S., 2012. Global nutrition transition and the pandemic of obesity in developing countries. *Nutrition Reviews*, 70, 1: 3–21. https://doi.org/10.1111/j.1753-4887.2011.00456.x.

Pretty, J., 2020. The agroecology of redesign. *Sustainable Organic Agric Systems*, 70, 2: 25–30. https://doi.org/10.3220/LBF1605102089000.

Pretty, J. (ed.) 2005. *The Earthscan Reader in Sustainable Agriculture*. London: Earthscan.

Pretty, J., Bharucha, Z. 2018. *Sustainable Intensification of Agriculture: Greening the world's food economy*. Abingdon, UK: Routledge.

Qu, S., Liang, S., Konar, M., Zhu, Z., Chiu, A., Jia, X., Xu, M. 2018. Virtual water scarcity risk to the global trade system. *Environmental Science & Technology*, 52: 673–683.

Riches, G. 2018. *Food Bank Nations: Poverty, corporate charity and the right to food*. Abingdon, UK: Routledge.

Riley, K., Cavanaugh, J. 2017. Tasty talk, expressive food: an introduction to the semiotics of food-and-language. *Semiotic Review*, 5. https://semioticreview.com/ojs/index.php/sr/article/view/1.

Ritchie, H., Roser, M. 2020. Environmental impacts of food production. Published online at OurWorldInData.org. https://ourworldindata.org/environmental-impacts-of-food.

Rivington, M., King, R., Duckett, D. 2021. Food and nutrition security during and after the COVID-19 pandemic: project report and recommendations. The James Hutton Institute, UK. https://www.hutton.ac.uk/research/projects/uk-food-and-nutrition-security-during-and-after-covid-19-pandemic.

Robert Wood Foundation. 2021. From crisis to opportunity: reforming our nation's policies to help all children grow up healthy. https://www.rwjf.org/ (accessed 7 January 2022).

Romanello, M., McGushin, A., Di Napoli, C. et al. 2021. The 2021 report of the Lancet countdown on health and climate change: code red for a healthy future. *The Lancet*. https://doi.org/10.1016/S0140-6736(21)01787-6.

Sage, C. 2022. Nitrogen, planetary boundaries, and the metabolic rift: using metaphor for dietary transitions toward a safe operating space. In Hughes, I., Byrne, E., Mullally, G., Sage, C. (eds) *Metaphor, Sustainability, Transformation: Transdisciplinary perspectives*. Abingdon, UK: Routledge, pp. 46-64.

Sage, C., Quieti, M-G., Fonte, M. 2021. Sustainable food systems <--> sustainable diets. *The International Journal of Sociology of Agriculture and Food*, 27, 1: 1-11. https://doi.org/10.48416/ijsaf.v27i1.449.

Sage, C. 2019. Food security. In Richardson, D., Castree, N. et al. (eds) *The International Encyclopaedia of Geography: People, the earth, environment, and technology*. New York: John Wiley & Sons.

Sage, C. 2013. The inter-connected challenges for food security from a food regimes perspective: energy, climate and malconsumption. *Journal of Rural Studies*, 29, 1: 71-80.

Sage, C. 2012. *Environment and Food*. Abingdon, UK: Routledge.

Sen, A. 1981. *Poverty and Famines: An essay on entitlement and deprivation*. Oxford: Clarendon Press.

Sinclair, J., 2019. Importance of a One Health approach in advancing global health security and the Sustainable Development Goals. *Rev Sci Tech*, 38, 1: 145-154. https://doi.org/10.20506/rst.38.1.2949.

Sodexo 2020. Sodexo and WWF renew their global partnership after ten years of successful collaboration. https://www.sodexo.com/media/sodexo-and-wwf-renew-partnership.html (accessed 20 January 2022).

Springett, D., Redclift, M. 2015. Sustainable development: history and evolution of the concept. In Redclift, M., Springett, D. (eds) *Routledge International Handbook of Sustainable Development*. Abingdon, UK: Routledge.

Springmann, M., Spajic, L., Clark, M., Poore, J. et al. 2020. The healthiness and sustainability of national and global food based dietary guidelines: modelling study. *BMJ*, 370: m2322. https://doi.org/10.1136 bmj.m2322.

Springmann, M., Clark, M., Mason-D'Croz, D. et al. 2018a. Options for keeping the food system within environmental limits. *Nature*, 562, 7728, 519. https://doi.org/10.1038/s41586-018-0594-0.

Springman, M., Wiebe, K., Mason-D'Croz, D. et al. 2018b. Health and nutritional aspects of sustainable diet strategies and their association with environmental impacts: a global modelling analysis with country-level detail. *Lancet Planet Health*, 2: e451–e461.

Stephens, E., Martin, G., van Wijk, M., Timsina, J., Snow, V. 2020 Editorial: impacts of COVID-19 on agricultural and food systems worldwide and on progress to the sustainable development goals. *Agricultural Systems*, 183 https://doi.org/10.1016/j.agsy.2020.102873.

Stuckler D., Nestle M., 2012. Big food, food systems, and global health. *PLoS Medicine*, 9, 6: e1001242.

Swinburn, B., Kraak, V., Allender, A. et al. 2019 The global syndemic of obesity, undernutrition, and climate change: the Lancet Commission report. *The Lancet*, 393: 791–846. http://dx.doi.org/10.1016/S0140-6736(18)32822-8.

Tansey, G., Worsley, T. 1995. *The Food System: A guide*. London: Earthscan.

Tilman, D., Clark, M. 2014. Global diets link environmental sustainability and human health. *Nature*, 515: 518–522.

Turner, C., Aggarwal, A., Walls, H. et al. 2018. Concepts and critical perspectives for food environment research: a global framework with implications for action in low- and middle-income countries. *Global Food Security*, 18: 93–101.

Tyrell, R., Greenhalgh, F., Hodgson, S. 2017. Food environments of young people: linking individual behaviour to environmental context. *Journal of Public Health*, 39, 1: 95–104.

UNEP. 2020. How to feed 10 billion people. https://www.unep.org/news-and-stories/story/how-feed-10-billion-people. (accessed 14 January 2022).

UNEP 2019. Emissions Gap Report. 2019. United Nations Environment Programme, Nairobi.

UN World Population Prospects. 2019. The 2019 revision of world population prospects. https://population.un.org/wpp/.

Vaidyanathan, G. 2021. Healthy diets for people and the planet. *Nature*, 600, Dec 2: 22–25.

WHO. 2021. Malnutrition. https:// www .who .int/ news -room/ fact -sheets/ detail/ malnutrition (accessed 14 January 2022).

Willett, W., Rockström, J., Loken, B., Springmann, M., Lang, T., Vermeulen, S. et al. 2019. Food in the Anthropocene: the EAT-Lancet Commission on healthy diets from sustainable food systems. *The Lancet*, 393, 10170: 447–492.

Win, Thin Lei 2021. How clean are Europe's food supply chains? The myths fueling the massive growth of Spain's pork industry. Open Society Foundations https:// www .op ensocietyf oundations .org/ publications/ how -clean -are -europe -s -food -supply -chains.

World Food Summit. 1996. Rome Declaration on World Food Security and Plan of Action. World Food Summit, 13–17 November 1996, Rome, Italy. Rome: FAO. https://www.fao.org/3/w3613e/w3613e00.htm.

Xu, X., Sharma, P., Shu, S. et al. 2021. Global greenhouse gas emissions from animal-based foods are twice those of plant-based foods. *Nature Food*, 2, 724–732. https://doi.org/10.1038/s43016-021-00358-x.

PART II

Issues

Introduction to Part II

The five chapters that make up this second Part of the volume present a series of quite different 'issues' but in the course of their analysis ultimately raise profound questions about the *governance* of food systems. Understanding the distribution and exercise of power is clearly central to any serious examination of the food system. Invariably this means identifying the principal actors and the ways in which they influence and shape policy decisions that can affect the whole system. While we might naively assume that international agencies and national governments establish the regulatory framework and ensure compliance to the rules in the interests of the 'public good', close attention to the exercise of private power reveals the enormously influential role played by corporate actors. A glimpse of this power can be gained by consideration of the level of economic concentration in particular sectors of the food system. This topic is addressed in Chapter 2 by Jennifer Clapp who, besides outlining the state of corporate concentration across the entire food system – from agri-input manufacturers to supermarkets – explains how this consolidation has emerged. The interweaving of financial and technological developments, together with a more relaxed regulatory environment (the retreat of the state from the public realm as neoliberalism took hold), have created circumstances where large corporations have been able to bend food system narratives and regulations to their advantage. As Clapp demonstrates, corporate mergers creating ever larger entities now exercise enormous influence within their sector: the top four companies now control around 70 percent of the global pesticides market and around 60 percent of the global seed market. Their influence, of course, extends beyond market capture and into the corridors of government through lobbying of politicians and by making use of the 'revolving door' through which senior company personnel take up posts in state agencies in order to soften – or remove – regulatory controls.

Chapter 2 provides a justification, as if any were needed, for the indispensability of a political economy approach to the food system. The value of this perspective is that it brings into sharp relief the asymmetrical distribution and exercise of power. It also highlights the weakness – the lack – of effective global governance of food beyond toxicological rules designed to prevent dietary sickness. This absence of a coherent framework through which to monitor and regulate food system activities is no more clearly demonstrated than by their impact on the planetary system, which is the subject of Chapter 3. Here, Sage argues that agency and responsibility must be redistributed across the various stages of the food system and so while powerful corporate players are clearly the most influential drivers of change, decisions made in the realm of consumption, of eating, are also important and require close attention. Focussing upon the urgent issue of climate breakdown and the demonstrated dietary measures that could help mitigate the pace of deterioration, the chapter addresses the challenge of ensuring nutritional security for all within planetary limits and guided by aspirations for a greater sense of mutual obligation. Sage considers whether there are grounds for recovering the notion of 'contraction and convergence' and other such metaphorical devices in seeking greater collective agency and responsibility in order to help ensure we remain within the Paris Agreement targets. Can such ideas as conviviality and commensality help capture a spirit of mutual support that would enable us to adopt dietary practices such that we are eating within 1.5°C?

Bringing human agency into the frame is vital for food systems research which, for too long, has been dominated by technocratic agendas preoccupied with yields and output. As noted earlier, the COVID-19 pandemic revealed for many the issue of labour in the food system, a topic which has been more extensively discussed and for longer in North America (e.g. the Bracero programme was signed into agreement between the governments of USA and Mexico in 1942) than it has in Europe. However, this is changing as cases of exploitation emerge from different intensively farmed agricultural regions across Europe (Schneider et al., 2020). The drive to increase output, supported by subsidies from the EU's Common Agricultural Policy, while continuing to reduce costs – principally wages – in order to remain competitive in international markets, has led to agricultural labourers becoming the most vulnerable to exploitation within the fresh-food supply chain. For example, the system known as 'caporalato' (gang-master) in Italy has long been linked with mafia networks in the South, yet to regard it as just another illustration of criminal power in a weak state would be to fail to recognise the role of supermarket contracts that squeeze producer margins and impact on the conditions experienced by farm workers (Jones and Awokoya, 2019).

Chapter 4 addresses the labour market structures that support intensive production systems in agricultural enclaves. Tracing the development of global value chains in fresh food that includes the introduction of private standards by retailers reveals the complex subordination strategies facing small and medium sized producers. Alicia Reigada and Carlos de Castro, the authors of Chapter 4, highlight the transformations in labour practices that have taken place not just in Spain but in the intensive horticultural operations of Mexico, Brazil and Argentina that are now fully part of global value chains. Their chapter draws particular attention to strategies that ensure the availability of a cheap, unprotected, and segmented labour force involving the construction of gender, class and ethnic capabilities 'suited' to the performance of different tasks. Their analysis alerts us to appreciating that while exploitative labour practices are characterised by some common regularities, careful field research reveals the importance of local particularities in the ways in which production enclaves recruit and manage labour to maintain their foothold in global fresh food supply chains.

Chapter 5 presents the proposition that the food system itself, *sui generis*, can be regarded as the cause of food poverty and food insecurity. In other words, it is not market imperfections or distortions that lead to such outcomes, rather it is a structural feature of its operation. Martin Caraher finds evidence to support this argument both upstream (amongst producers) as well as downstream (the consumer-citizen). His focus on the different dynamics affecting the coffee and cocoa commodity chains reveal the incessant downward pressure on farm-gate prices and rising costs – including those resulting from the imposition of quality standards by highly concentrated corporate intermediaries – that leave farmers' share at 3–6 percent of the retail price of a chocolate bar. Such structural impoverishment, Caraher argues, has even brought forth responses by companies, under the banner of corporate social responsibility, anxious about the long-term consequences of the asymmetrical distribution of benefits across the supply chain. Meanwhile, the provision of 'cheap' and convenient ultra-processed foods to growing numbers of consumer-citizens is linked to rising levels of obesity and an increase in diet-related, non-communicable diseases. At a time of rising food prices and increasing employment precarity, food poverty should increasingly be regarded as a public health emergency, yet governments appear to prefer to leave interventions to the charitable sector and their corporate partners to supply surplus food as emergency provisions to 'people in need'. Such an approach, as Caraher makes clear, does not ensure the right to food.

The final chapter of Part II addresses the increasingly vexed issue of animals within the food system. We do not need to be reminded at this stage of just how significant is the role played by animal-sourced protein in the diets of rich and middle-income countries with global meat and dairy consumption continuing to rise, given industry efforts to drive down costs and increase its affordability to an ever-widening market. While this has meant the deepening of exploitative labour practices and externalising many of the environmental consequences associated with intensive livestock rearing, as discussed in Chapters 1 and 3, there is probably insufficient appreciation of how the subjectivity of animals themselves is changed in such systems. Without rehearsing arguments about the cruelty or otherwise of confined animal feeding operations, Chapter 6 takes us directly to the issue of how animals have been both physiologically and subjectively reconfigured. Through a consideration of breeding practices, the deployment of technologies such as robotic milking systems, and an exploration of the wider meaning and agency of animals, Lewis Holloway makes a powerful argument for food system analyses to be attentive to the ethically problematic practice of farming animals.

While these five chapters of Part II cannot possibly cover the full range of challenges that call into question the prevailing architecture of the contemporary food system, they do provide important insights into some key issues, all of which require further investigative work at different scales and in diverse locations. Yet, as Chapter 1 made clear, building a research agenda for food systems requires the development of a more holistic, transdisciplinary approach capable of interconnecting many of these issues rather than attempting to find a singular solution. Given the particularities of place, research efforts must ensure the widest possible inclusion of all stakeholders, especially food citizens. Such engagement will ultimately lie at the heart of building effective food system governance arrangements and create possibilities for food system transformation (van Bers et al., 2019).

References

Jones, T., Awokoya, A. 2019. Are your tinned tomatoes picked by slave labour? *The Guardian*: https://www.theguardian.com/world/2019/jun/20/tomatoes-italy-mafia-migrant-labour-modern-slavery (accessed 8 Aug 2022).

Schneider, J., Götte, M. et al. 2020. Are agri-food workers only exploited in Southern Europe? Case studies on migrant labour in Germany, the Netherlands, and Sweden. Open Society Foundations. https://www.opensocietyfoundations.org/publications/are-agri-food-workers-only-exploited-in-southern-europe.

van Bers, C., Delaney, A., Eakin, H. et al. 2019. Advancing the research agenda on food systems governance and transformation. *Current Opinion in Environmental Sustainability*, 39: 94–102.

2 The rise of big food and agriculture: corporate influence in the food system

Jennifer Clapp

Introduction

Corporate concentration has become a dominant feature of the modern industrial food system. In nearly all stages of global food supply chains, from farm inputs, through production, trade, processing and food retail, a common pattern is that just a handful of firms tend to dominate the market. Scholars from across a range of disciplines in the food studies literature have noted this trend, raising important questions about the impact of corporate influence on food system outcomes. For example, sociologists draw our attention to the ways in which neoliberal economic policies have institutionalized market relationships that privilege agribusiness as part of a "corporate food regime" (McMichael, 2013). Political scientists have focused on the multiple ways in which corporations can exercise power in the food system to shape policy and governance (Clapp and Fuchs, 2009). Economists are concerned about whether concentration undermines efficiency of markets in the sector (Maisashvili et al., 2016; Hovhannisyan et al., 2019). Lawyers focus on the application and limits of antitrust law in the food sector (Lianos et al., 2016). Nutritionists have raised concerns about corporate engagement in setting nutritional standards and the health claims they make about processed foods (Nestle, 2013; Scrinis, 2016). And political economists examine debates over a range of potential consequences – economic, political, and environmental – of consolidation in the sector (Howard, 2016; Bonny, 2017; Clapp, 2018).

Drawing on these various literatures, this chapter attempts to provide an inter-disciplinary assessment of corporate consolidation in the sector. It outlines the state of corporate concentration in the global food system and examines some of the key drivers of this trend as well as its wider implications. It makes the case that a combination of financial incentives, technological change, and changes in the broader regulatory environment have been important factors in the trend toward increased concentration in the sector in recent decades. It also outlines how concentration has lent enormous power to the firms at the top to shape the parameters of markets as well as the broader policy and regulatory context. It shows that access to and exercise of power in these realms by the largest agri-food firms has shaped food systems in ways that tend to serve corporate interests and has important implications for broader food system goals such as equity, participation, sustainability, and choice.

The State of Corporate Consolidation in the Agri-food System

Growing corporate concentration in the agri-food system has followed patterns of corporate consolidation in the broader economy in recent decades. In this period, for example, some of the biggest corporate mergers have been in the agri-food sector as witnessed by giant deals such as the combinations of Kraft and Heinz, Dow and Dupont, and Anheuser Busch In-Bev and SAB Miller, each of which formed firms worth over US$100 billion (Heinrich Böll Foundation et al., 2017). Alongside these massive deals, a series of other mergers and acquisitions have also occurred in recent decades such that today agri-food supply chains are quite concentrated.

In the agricultural inputs sector, recent mergers resulted in a reduction in the number of dominant players in the sector from six to just four giant firms (IPES-Food, 2017; Bonny, 2017). In 2015, Dow and Dupont announced a "merger of equals" bringing together significant market share for agrochemicals and seeds into a new entity "Corteva". Shortly after the Dow and Dupont deal was announced, Syngenta, a major Swiss agrochemical producer, was purchased by ChemChina, which was subsequently purchased by Sinochem, to form China's largest chemical company. In the wake of these two deals, Bayer purchased Monsanto, bringing together the latter's strength in biotech seeds with the former's strength in agrochemicals. Meanwhile, BASF, a chemical company specializing in agrochemicals that was one of the original six dominant companies in the sector, acquired seed technology assets that Bayer was forced to sell to enable its purchase of Monsanto to be approved. With the global commercial seed market worth around US$39 billion annually, and the global pesticide industry worth around US$57 billion, a consolidation in the market among the top firms has cemented their position as dominant players. In 2018, as the Bayer acquisition of Monsanto was being finalized, approximately 60 percent of the global seed market was held by the top four firms (IHS

Markit, 2019), while around 70 percent of the global agrochemical market was controlled by those same four firms (Statista, 2020).

Consolidation has also occurred in other parts of the agricultural input sector. For example, while the global fertilizer market – worth over US$150 billion – is not as concentrated as that for seeds and chemicals, the sector is quite concentrated within countries. In 2016, for example, the first and fourth largest global fertilizer companies – Canadian firms Agrium and Potash Corp – merged to create a new fertilizer giant called Nutrien, which is now the largest fertilizer company in the world. This single firm accounts for over 60 percent of North America's potash production, 25 percent of its phosphate production, and 22 percent of its ammonia production (Wiggerthale, 2021). Before this most recent merger, the top four firms – Agrium, Yara, Mosaic and Potash Corp – accounted for around one quarter of the global market (ETC Group, 2015).

The farm equipment sector is also characterized by high levels of concentration. Just four firms – Deere & Co, CNH Industries, AGCO, and Kubota – account for around 40 percent of the US$115 billion market (Mooney, 2018). Many of the mergers and acquisitions in the farm equipment sector in recent years have been the purchase of data software firms by traditional equipment makers in their bid to develop "digital farming" platforms that tap into big data via satellites direct to tractor cabs to improve farm decision-making and enable more precise applications of fertilizers and pesticides on the farm. Deere & Co, for example has acquired several technology and software firms in recent years as it seeks to be a leader in digital agriculture (Cornish, 2017).

The commodity trading sector has long been highly concentrated, with the dominance of the ABCD firms (Archer Daniels Midland, Bunge, Cargill, and Louis Dreyfus Commodities) in the grain trade. Because Cargill and Dreyfus are privately owned firms, it is difficult to obtain reliable statistics on the market share of these firms, although some estimates have indicated that together these four firms control around 70 percent or more of the global grain trade (Murphy et al., 2012). This level of concentration may be weakening, however, as several Asian commodity trading firms, including the Singapore-based Wilmar and the Chinese state trading firm COFCO, are increasingly challenging the power of the ABCD firms, particularly in Asia and in Latin American commodity trading (Clapp, 2015). Concentration is also high in the trade of other food commodities. For example, three firms – Cargill, ADM and Barry Callebaut – control 60 percent of the world's cocoa grinding business (Terazono, 2014). Just five firms control 75 percent of the world's banana trade, and seven firms control 85 percent of the world's tea trade (Fairtrade International, 2013).

The food processing sector, often referred to as Big Food, is not as concentrated as the raw commodities trade, but the largest companies are globally recognized with known brands, giving them influence in the sector, particularly with respect to setting trends. The top 10 food and beverage companies, for example, account for around 40 percent of the sales of the top 100 firms in the sector. Those same 10 firms are each bringing in over US$35 billion per year in revenues (IPES-Food, 2017). Certain subsectors are especially concentrated, as in the case of the meat sector, particularly at the national level. In the US, for example, just four firms – Tyson, Cargill, Swift and Co., and National Beef Packing Co – control 85 percent of the market for beef processing (USDA, 2020). Consolidation in the processed foods sector has continued at a fairly steady pace in the past decade. As noted above, in 2015 Kraft and Heinz combined to create a firm worth over US$100 billion (Fontanella-Khan et al., 2015a), while the 2016 merger between Anheuser Busch InBev and SAB Miller resulted in a firm worth over US$275 billion with a nearly one third share of the global beer market (Fontanella Khan et al., 2015b). These are just some of the largest of the recent mergers. Firms in the sector are constantly buying smaller rivals and engaging in deals to buy or sell different units or specific products.

The global grocery retail market, worth around US$7.5 trillion, is also concentrated. Globally, the top four retail firms are Walmart, Schwartz Group, Kroger, and Aldi, while Costco, Carrefour, and Tesco are also major players. At the international level, the top 10 grocery retailers accounted for nearly 30 percent of the global food retail market in 2014 (IPES-Food, 2017). Concentration in the grocery retail sector is higher at the domestic level. In the USA, for example, the top four grocery retailers account for around 40 percent of the market (IPES-Food, 2017). In Canada, the five largest grocery chains command over 80 percent of the food retail market (CBAN, 2020). And in Australia, just two firms – Coles Group and the Woolworths Group – each control around 30 percent of the Aus$90 billion food retail market (Statista, 2021). Mergers and acquisitions are common in the food retail sector. In 2017, Amazon, the world's largest online retail corporation, acquired Wholefoods in a deal that foreshadowed major changes in the retail market toward online sales (Nicolaou et al., 2017). Other deals have been proposed, but have fallen through – such as a proposed merger between Asda and Sainsburys in the UK, and the attempt by Canada's convenience store chain Couche-Tard to purchase France's Carrefour – due to concerns about excessive market concentration (Eley and Massoudi, 2019; Abboud, 2021).

As this brief review shows, the growing dominance of the key firms is in some cases a result of horizontal consolidation – where firms that normally compete with one another at the same stage of supply chains join up forces to command a greater share of that market. But it is also in some cases a result of vertical integration – where firms at different stages of supply chains merge to control adjacent or related markets. Both types of consolidation matter for food systems. In the case of the former, greater concentration of market shares in fewer players can lead to uncompetitive outcomes that can affect prices and consumer choice. In the case of the latter, firms can lock in consumers and farmers by tying different products together in ways that increase market shares for both.

Forces Encouraging Consolidation in this Food System

What explains the trend toward corporate concentration in the food system, especially heightened consolidation among some of the biggest agri-food sector players in the past decade? Historically, consolidation and concentration in the agri-food sector has been the product of several different forces, some relating to the broader economic context, and some specific to the sector and subsector in which consolidation has been a feature. One can group these forces into three main categories: financial incentives; technological change; and the increasingly relaxed regulatory environment. All three of these types of forces have been at play in the process of food system concentration, especially in recent decades, although in some subsectors, some of these forces have been more prominent than others, depending on the context and specifics of the industry.

Financial Incentives

Financial factors are typically one of the forces leading to greater consolidation in the global economy more generally, and they certainly matter in the agri-food sector. Firms facing a decline in sales or a drop in profitability may be targets of acquisitions by other firms with more resources that are seeking to increase their market share or expand their product offerings by acquiring rivals. Several firms facing economic hardship may seek to merge their activities to reduce costs, which can be achieved through the elimination of duplicating activities.

As the global economy has become more "financialized" in recent decades – that is, the rise in importance of financial actors, institutions and motives in the economy more broadly – these financial incentives have played an important role in encouraging corporate consolidation, including in the agri-food sector

(Burch and Lawrence, 2013; Clapp and Isakson, 2018). Financialization has resulted in a higher prioritization of shareholder value in corporate decision making, such that firms seek to maximize returns to investors over other goals and functions of the firm. The reason for this prioritization is clear – unless they do so, financial investors will move on to other companies in which to invest, which could result in a negative spiral for the firm. Thus, there are strong incentives for firms to ensure high profitability and the engagement in mergers and acquisitions is one strategy to bolster returns.

Financial incentives appear to have played a strong role in the consolidation in the agricultural input company mergers that took place after 2015. After 2013, for example, agricultural input firms – including the Big Six seed and chemical firms as well as the fertilizer firms – began to experience weak performance compared to other firms on the S&P 500 stock market index. This was a change from the high profits they earned during the global food crisis in the 2008 to 2012 period that was driven by higher and more volatile commodity prices, which drove up demand for agricultural inputs as farmers globally sought to increase production in the face of higher prices. The seed and chemical firms, for example, benefited from increased demand in Latin America for their products in the immediate wake of the food crisis. But after 2013, agricultural commodity prices fell, weakening economic growth in the Latin American agricultural economies, dampening profitability for the input companies as farmers scaled back their demand for inputs (Clapp, 2018).

In this context, shareholders in the Big Six firms put pressure on management of these firms to increase returns. In the case of the Dow and DuPont merger, the first of the three big mergers to take place after 2015, "activist" investors – that is, large investors who hold a significant stake in the firm and can influence management decisions as a result – pushed for restructuring of both Dow and DuPont. In this case, separate large hedge fund investors in each firm made clear their desire for restructuring to improve the firms' financial performance. Nelson Peltz and his Trian hedge fund pushed on the DuPont side, while Daniel Loeb's Third Point hedge fund pushed on the Dow side. The merger of Dow and DuPont occurred shortly after (Crooks, 2015).

Financial factors and the drive for shareholder value also loomed large in the merger of Kraft and Heinz in 2015. To understand this merger, it is important to go back to 2013, when billionaire investor Warren Buffett's Berkshire Hathaway teamed up with private equity firm 3G Capital – backed by Jorge Paulo Lemann, a billionaire investor from Brazil – to purchase Heinz, the US-based processed food firm. Heinz had already been pushed by Nelson Peltz to slash costs after he joined the board in 2006, to make up for flagging sales as consumers increasingly sought healthier food options. The deal made Heinz a private company and resulted in a huge payout to shareholders. 3G Capital, focused on cutting costs to improve profits, then orchestrated the subsequent merger of Kraft and Heinz into a new publicly traded firm that consistently ranks in the top ten food and beverage companies in the world. As Warren Buffett noted upon the closing of the deal "This is my kind of transaction, uniting two world-class organizations and delivering shareholder value" (quoted in Fontanella Khan and Massoudi, 2015a). In 2017, Kraft Heinz attempted to purchase Unilever for US$143 billion in what would have been the second largest takeover in history, but the acquisition ultimately fell through after Unilever's chief executive pushed back (Massoudi and Fontanella-Khan, 2017).

Agri-food sector financialization has also influenced patterns of corporate ownership, which also appears to be contributing to consolidation and concentration in the sector. The agri-food sector has seen a rise in "common ownership" – where large institutional shareholders, such as asset management firms, hold significant shares across a range of firms within the same sector. This type of ownership pattern has become prominent across a number of industries in recent years, with the top asset management companies BlackRock, Vanguard, and State Street, for example, collectively owning some 15 to 30 percent of most American companies (Schmalz, 2018). At least one study of this type of ownership pattern has found that merger and acquisition events are more likely to occur in commonly owned firms (Brooks et al., 2018). Most of the large corporations that dominate agri-food supply chains have a significant proportion of their shares owned by the five largest asset management companies. The recent mergers in the seed and agrochemical sector, for example, occurred in a context where over 30 percent of DuPont shares, over 20 percent of Monsanto and Dow shares, and over 15 percent of Bayer shares were owned by the same five large asset management firms (Clapp, 2019). Common ownership patterns are also prominent in the processed foods sector.

A further financial dimension of the recent mergers is simply low interest rates that have been prevalent since the 2008 financial crisis. Most governments sought to stimulate their economies in the wake of the financial crash by lowering interest rates in a bid to encourage borrowing as a means to kick-start their economies. Over a decade of rates near zero has encouraged many firms to engage in corporate tie-ups because it has been incredibly cheap for them to borrow the funds to do so. Investment banks have also been active in encouraging the financing of such deals which further increases their own profitability (Turner, 2016). A number of mergers in the agri-food sector have been financed by debt in this way, including Bayer's purchase of Monsanto, which saw its debt increase by a factor of four as a result of the deal.

Technological Change and Complementarities

Consolidation in the agri-food sector has also been encouraged in some cases by technological change and complementarities between different types of firms or firms in the same sector but which specialize in different activities. These types of mergers can be considered either "vertical" or "horizontal" depending on the specifics of the case, but both types of mergers bring together different functionalities in ways that can reinforce market dominance of the resulting firms in new ways.

The recent mergers in the agricultural seed and chemical sector, for example, were in part the latest iteration of consolidation based on technological change and tighter product complementarity. Consolidation in the seed sector dates back a century to the development of hybrid seed technologies. While hybrids brought higher yields, they needed to be repurchased on a regular basis because those higher yields would not be maintained over time if farmers saved and reused seeds from previous harvests. This technological change encouraged the rise of a private sector seed industry (Fernandez-Cornejo, 2004; Howard, 2016). Since that time, consolidation has continued apace in the sector, due to the rise of new agricultural biotechnologies and the ways in which those new technologies articulated seeds more closely with chemical herbicides. When these new biotechnologies first emerged in the 1980s and 1990s, this technological change sparked a wave of consolidation in the sector that brought agrochemical firms and seed firms together to form new agricultural input companies (Fuglie et al., 2012).

The most recent round of consolidation in the agricultural seed and chemical sector has resulted in a tightening of technological complementarity among the dominant firms. Prior to the most recent mergers, some of the Big Six firms were focused more on agrochemicals while others were more focused on seeds. For example, DuPont had significant investment in the seed business since its acquisition of seed company Pioneer in 1999, while Dow focused mainly on agrochemicals. Similarly, Monsanto, although it started out as a major chemical firm that first commercialized the glyphosate-based herbicide Roundup in the 1970s, by the 2000s had become a major producer of genetically modified seeds. Bayer, meanwhile, although it had developed some expertise in seeds since the 1990s, was focused more on agrochemicals prior to its purchase of Monsanto. The recent mergers have thus resulted in a more even distribution of seed and chemical sales across the now four dominant firms (Clapp, 2018).

These mergers were also, in part, an attempt by some of the large firms to acquire rivals that had been acquiring other, smaller firms that had expertise in digital technologies – the latest technological change that is reshaping the agri-food system (Rotz et al., 2019). Monsanto, for example, had previously purchased Climate Corp, a digital agriculture firm, that Bayer was interested in acquiring to build up its own expertise in digital farming (Clapp and Ruder, 2020). Within the new Bayer, the digital service is now called "Climate Fieldview" and is the leading farm software program.

Other nodes in food systems have also teamed up with software firms, including farm equipment firm Deere & Co., which recently acquired several digital farming software firms (Cornish, 2017). The rationale behind these acquisitions is that farm equipment firms are increasingly outfitting tractors with satellite-connected equipment to enable big data to feed into on farm decision-making. In this case, big data can inform settings on variable spray equipment to refine the quantity of herbicides and pesticides that are used on any particular field. Deere's equipment now links directly with Bayer's Climate Fieldview software.

In the processed foods sector, technological change is also reshaping firms and their markets. The development of newer plant-based meat and dairy products, for example, has drawn attention to some of the biggest market players. Danone, one of the world's leading dairy firms, acquired White Wave Foods, makers of Silk plant-based milks, in 2016. More recently, large meat firms, like Tyson and Cargill have invested in plant-based alternative meat and cell-based synthetic meat start-up firms, which, if successful, could expand their already commanding market share in the protein sector (Terazono, 2020; see also Chapter 8, this volume). Finally, Amazon's acquisition of Wholefoods brought together two firms with different expertise – online retail and food – as the former was interested in developing an online grocery shopping business (Kestenbaum, 2018).

A Changing Regulatory Environment

While not necessarily intentional on the part of states, regulatory change has also had an impact on corporate concentration in the agri-food sector. Government regulations regarding intellectual property rights and competition policy, for example, have shaped markets in ways that, at least in recent decades, have encouraged corporate consolidation in the sector.

The adoption of plant-breeders rights in the 1960s and 1970s in the US as well as international plant breeders' rights via the Union for the Protection of New Varieties of Plants (UPOV) in the 1970s encouraged consolidation in the industry as firms sought to invest more in research and development (R&D) because they would be guaranteed profits on new varieties for a period of 20–25 years (Howard, 2016; Fernandez-Cornejo and Just, 2007). These new regulations sparked the purchase of smaller, independent seed companies by larger firms throughout the 1970s and 1980s (Fernandez-Cornejo, 2004). When states began to pass legislation allowing for intellectual property rights and in some cases patents on genetically engineered micro-organisms as well as plant varieties derived from biotechnology in the 1980s and 1990s, firms were further incentivized to ramp up R&D in the sector, sparking a further wave of consolidation not just between seed companies, but also between seed and agrochemical firms, as noted above. The consolidation in this instance enabled these firms to pay for increasingly expensive R&D into agricultural biotechnology, something that they were incentivized to do by the fact that patent protection would enable them to recoup the higher costs to bring those products to market. It was this wave of mergers that reduced a large field of agricultural seed and chemical companies that operated in the 1970s and 1980s to just six dominant firms by 2009 (Fuglie et al., 2011).

The tendencies toward concentration encouraged by technological change and the shifts in the financial context could, in theory, be kept in check by robust competition law and policy that would disallow mergers that were likely to encourage anti-competitive behaviour. But at the same time that technological and financial changes were encouraging anti-competitive practices and consolidation among firms, the political interpretation and application of competition law shifted in important ways that effectively loosened the controls on the very kinds of market concentration we are witnessing today (Wu, 2018; Khan, 2017). This shift began to take place, first in the USA, and then globally, over the course of the 1970s to 1990s, coinciding with the rise of neoliberal economic policies that sought to reduce government intervention and oversight of the market.

The result of this shift in the interpretation of competition law was that proposed mergers and growing market control were reviewed not with an eye to whether they stifled competition by reshaping market structures. Rather, they were reviewed on the much narrower basis of whether they led to increased consumer prices or led to market inefficiencies (Ergen and Kohl, 2019). Interpreted through this more outcome-focused lens that zeroed-in on specific price and efficiency metrics, mergers that previously would likely have been prevented because they would have allowed dominant firms to amass significant market share (for example through horizontal mergers that result in fewer players controlling the bulk of the market), or to dominate in multiple areas along supply chains in ways that stifled competition and locked in customers (as would be the case with vertical mergers), were deemed to be permissible if they led to lower consumer prices or an increase in market efficiencies (Kwoka, 2017). This more economistic and effects-based approach to evaluating mergers is reflected in the various overhauls of the US merger guidelines since the 1980s, rules which were mirrored in other countries. In the following decades, not surprisingly, there were fewer challenges to mergers, especially vertical tie-ups (Khan, 2017).

Recent mergers in the agri-food sector have, as a result, faced relatively little push-back from regulatory authorities. For example, the Kraft and Heinz merger, which created one of the largest firms in North America, was easily approved in the US and Canada. The statement on the merger from the Canada Competition Bureau noted that its assessment found that the two firms had enough different products that they were not undercutting competition, and thus were unlikely to lead to price increases (Government of Canada, 2015). Similarly, the combination of Agrium and Potash Corp, two Canadian-based fertilizer giants, also went uncontested by competition authorities. Again, regulators deemed that their operations were sufficiently different – with Potash Corp dominant on potash mining, and Agrium focusing on other fertilizer ingredients as well as retail operations – that the combination was unlikely to lead to higher prices. In both cases, the firms that were created are large, powerful and dominate in key markets. Regulators did require some asset sales in the mergers between Dow and DuPont and Bayer and Monsanto, although these were different in different countries, depending on the local market specifics. All three mega-mergers in the seeds and chemicals sector were eventually allowed to proceed even though they resulted in increased market share for the remaining four dominant firms.

Why Corporate Consolidation in Food Systems Matters

Just because an agri-food firm is large does not necessarily mean that it will pursue strategies that have a negative impact on food systems. However, when specific markets are dominated by just a handful of firms, there are concerns that those firms have access to different kinds of power that could be used to advance their own interests at the expense of society more broadly. The food system has often been likened to an hourglass, with many producers on one end, and many consumers on the other end, and few corporations in the chokepoint in the middle. When the chokepoint becomes more constrained, the firms that dominate that space are able to gain more power to control how food items pass through the middle: how commodities are grown, at what price they are bought and sold, how they are processed, and, ultimately, how they are retailed. Large powerful firms in the sector have the capacity to shape both the parameters of markets and the broader policy context in which they operate.

Shaping Market Parameters

Most governments have competition policies that seek to ensure fair market competition, which has implications for equity and innovation. Regulators typically weigh the cost of market concentration against any efficiencies that may arise from economies of scale and scope, as well as innovation. If proposed mergers or other forms of concentration in markets result in corporate dominance that will stifle competition and raise prices, then the effects are most likely to be assessed as negative. But if they result in more efficient markets resulting from economies of scale, even if there are fewer suppliers in the market, then they might be viewed more positively by regulators.

Different metrics are used to calculate concentration and its likely impact on markets, primarily the concentration ratio of the top four firms (CR4) and the Herfindal Hirschman Index (HHI) (Howard, 2016). The CR4 measures the market share of the top four firms within a given market. A CR4 rating under 40 percent is widely considered to be competitive; markets with a CR4 rating in the 40–60 percent range are considered to be moderately concentrated; while markets with a CR4 over 60 percent are regarded as highly concentrated. The HHI measures market concentration by adding the square of the market share of each firm participating in the market for a particular product. As it is more difficult to measure HHI because the market share of all firms must be known in a given market, which is especially difficult to ascertain in a global context, most analysts concerned with the market dominance of transnational firms in the food sector focus on the CR4 even though it is less precise than the HHI.

The recent mergers in the agricultural seeds and chemical sector are a good illustration of how consolidation can affect market concentration as measured by the CR4. Before these mergers, the global CR4 in 2009 was 54 percent for seeds and 53 percent for agrochemicals, figures that were already markedly higher than the 1994 figures of 21 percent and 29 percent, respectively (Fuglie et al., 2011). In other words, both sectors were already near the threshold of what most economists consider as a highly concentrated market prior to the most recent mergers. This latest round of mergers has now led to CR4 ratios of around 70 percent for the global pesticides market and around 60 percent for the global seed market (Statista, 2020; IHS Markit, 2019).

Dominant firms in concentrated markets have more capacity to shape those markets in ways that may be good for their own bottom line, but which may impose costs on others. As noted above, a key concern is whether concentration can lead to higher prices. In some markets, such as seeds, most pricing data is not publicly available, making assessment especially difficult. Some studies, however, have found that concentration is associated with higher prices for genetically modified seeds, especially where the market is particularly concentrated (Shi et al., 2010; Torshizi and Clapp, 2021). If farmers are in fact paying high prices for inputs due to concentration, these costs can affect equity because they are either reflected in lower returns for farmers, or potentially passed on to consumers in the form of higher food prices.

Concentrated firms can also shape the prices paid to suppliers, which can exacerbate inequities in the food system. When certain food trading, processing and retail firms dominate markets, they can set the terms of purchase from farmers, which can mean lower prices paid to farmers for their goods because there are few other options available to them. This kind of power is prevalent in markets for tropical commodities where large transnational buyers have bargaining leverage over multiple small-scale producers in developing countries (de Schutter, 2010). It is also evident in the meat sector in countries where the industry is highly concentrated, as is the case in the US. Most chickens raised in the US, for example, are grown under contract farming arrangements, where farmers must follow strict procedures as stipulated by the large meat packing firms. These farmers are not easily able to shop around for different buyers, because the market is dominated by just a few firms in most regions (Kelloway and Miller, 2019). Similar dynamics of buyer leverage occur in other parts of the meatpacking as well as the dairy sectors in the US.

Labour conditions are also affected in subsectors of the food system where just a few large firms dominate. Buyer power often pressures farmers and producers to cut costs where they can, which can lead to the use of child labour and other forms of modern slavery like work conditions, including on plantations and also for seasonal and migrant workers (LeBaron, 2020). Large food corporations also directly shape working conditions for other food system workers in their bid to cut costs. For example, the COVID-19 pandemic shone a bright light on working conditions and poor pay faced by meat packers and workers in food production plants (Klassen and Murphy, 2020).

Corporate power additionally shapes the food system in terms of the products made available to both farmers and consumers. On the farmer side, corporate concentration in the agricultural input sector has narrowed innovation pathways such that agricultural biotechnology and associated herbicides have become the dominant technologies for key crops such as maize and soy. As a result, the glyphosate-based herbicides have become widely applied globally, and while the risks of this chemical in terms of weed resistance and possible health effects are becoming more apparent, the input companies have not invested in alternative weed control technologies because doing so was less profitable than relying on glyphosate (Clapp, 2021).

The problem of concentration also affects consumer choice because it is the large firms that determine what ends up on grocery store shelves. While it may appear that there are endless varieties of products available for purchase, many of these products are similar due to the fact that different brands are often owned by the same food processing conglomerates, and it is primarily the packaging that is different (Kelloway and Miller, 2019). Firms often market foods based on nutritional or health claims (Scrinis, 2016), also appearing to give choice. But while there may be many differentiated types of breakfast cereal on grocery store shelves, for example, just three firms – Kellogg, General Mills and Post Holdings – command 79 percent of the breakfast cereal market in the USA (Hyslop, 2017). Similarly, the large food retailers typically own multiple grocery chains within concentrated domestic markets, giving the false appearance of choice to consumers.

Shaping Policy and Governance

The dominance of large, concentrated firms across multiple subsectors of the food system tends to lend those actors power to shape policy and governance that matters for their own business survival, and which also has broader implications for equity and representation within food systems (Clapp and Fuchs, 2009; McKeon, 2015). There are multiple ways in which powerful firms in the food system can influence policy, including both direct and indirect means.

When fewer firms dominate in a market, they are more able to coordinate their lobbying activities, and face less competition with other firms to gain access to government policymakers (Khan and Vaheesan, 2017). Lobbying by large corporate players is widespread across the entire agri-food sector; both direct lobbying by consultants hired directly by the firms themselves, as well as lobbying through industry associations in which the firms are members (Clapp, 2020). The sums firms spend to shape policy this way can be huge. For example, in 2019, the year US regulators reviewed whether to register glyphosate-based herbicides, Bayer AG – which specializes in seeds designed to work with glyphosate after its purchase of Monsanto – spent US$9 million lobbying the US government (US Senate, 2021). According to disclosure forms submitted by the firm, the leading topics on which it lobbied policymakers included pesticide registration, GM labelling, and biotech innovation. The other firms that dominate the input sector – Corteva, BASF, ChemChina – also each spent between US$1.3 million and US$1.6 million lobbying that year (ibid.).

Actors promoting the specific interests of agri-food firms often end up working as government regulators through what is termed the "revolving door" between business and government. There are numerous cases where governments have appointed former corporate employees and lobbyists into regulatory positions, who then often cycle back into business. An example of this is Barbara Gallini, a former lobbyist for the UK Food and Drink Federation – that represents firms such as Coca-Cola, Kellogg, and Unilever – who was appointed in 2016 as Head of Communications and External Relations at the European Food Safety Authority (Clapp, 2020). Large agri-food firms also give liberally to election campaigns to support candidates who will be sympathetic to their interests (Center for Responsive Politics, 2021). It is hard to know for sure the extent to which such lobby campaigns, the revolving door, and political sponsorship result in the outcomes firms are aiming for, but one can say that the practice privileges the voice of industry while doing little to open up space for more open and democratic participation in the design of food systems.

Corporate actors can also influence food system governance through their involvement in multi-stakeholder supply chain standards-setting initiatives. While governments have long set standards for food safety, corporate actors are increasingly establishing voluntary private standards – sometimes also involving other stakeholders such as NGOs – that govern other aspects of food supply chains, including environmental and labour standards. For example, the Roundtable on Sustainable Palm Oil (RSPO) is an initiative dominated by large corporate players involved in palm oil trade, including the ABCD grain trading firms (Grabs and Carodenuto, 2021). Other commodity focused certification initiatives include the Roundtable on Responsible Soy (RTRS), Bonsucro (sugar) and the Global Roundtable for Sustainable Beef (e.g. Buckley et al., 2019; Fortin and Richardson, 2013).

Food retail companies also often require standards to be met for certain products, such as seafood. Walmart and Tesco, for example, have requirements in place for the seafood they sell to be certified by some sort of sustainability standards, such as those of the Marine Stewardship Council (MSC). While such standards initiatives seek to assure consumers that the products they purchase are sustainable, some analysts have pointed out that the traders and retailers that require such certifications often download the cost of compliance onto small-scale producers (Fuchs and Kalfagianni, 2010) while others have noted how these initiatives suffer from structural flaws that make them weak in practice (LeBaron, 2020). Critics, for example, argue that palm oil governance schemes have done little to reduce deforestation, biodiversity loss, and carbon emissions in the largest palm oil producing regions (Dauvergne, 2018).

A less direct way that corporate giants shape food systems policy and governance is via their "discursive power": that is, their attempts to shape discourses and narratives about their products and their corporate image more broadly. Discursive strategies are often pursued through public relations campaigns carried out through everyday advertising, strategic placement of opinion articles in newspapers and magazines, and the use of websites and social media to get their message out. Corteva, for example, recently sponsored a series of documentaries, entitled "Follow the Food", on the future of agriculture that puts the kinds of high-tech products in which the firm specializes in a positive light (BBC, 2021). Large corporations also influence public discourse by sponsoring scientific studies that relate to food products or production inputs in a bid to direct the kinds of the research questions that get asked, often in ways that are more flattering to the firms' products (Nestle, 2013). This kind of corporate engagement in academic research projects raises concerns about conflicts of interest, which are not always divulged in resulting publications (Fabbri et al., 2018; Rowe et al., 2009).

Finally, dominant agri-food firms can influence policy and governance simply because they are large and dominant – meaning that governments often hold back on imposing regulations for fear that those firms might take flight and relocate to other jurisdictions and take their investment and jobs with them – either within countries or between countries. This capacity to threaten flight gives large firms a kind of "structural power" to influence the regulatory context (Fuchs, 2007; Clapp and Fuchs, 2009). A recent example of the attempt to wield this kind of influence, which is often difficult to document, occurred when the CEOs of Bayer and Monsanto met privately with Donald Trump just before he took office to promise the creation of 3000 new jobs in the US if their proposed merger would be approved (Sink and Parker, 2017). Although this was not a direct threat to leave if the merger was not approved, it was clear that there was a "carrot" of new jobs being dangled in front of the incoming administration as a reward for approving the merger.

Conclusion

This chapter has provided a sketch of the trend toward corporate concentration in the dominant industrial food system, which has affected all stages of global supply chains from agricultural inputs through commodity trade, food processing, and food retail, albeit to varying degrees. This trend toward more concentrated markets has become more pronounced in recent decades, to the extent that in some subsectors, such as seeds and agrochemicals, just a handful of firms dominate the market. Several interacting forces have contributed to growing consolidation in the sector. Financial factors have been prominent and have become more pronounced in recent decades with the rise of the financialization of the global economy, which has had an especially profound influence on the food system. Technological change has also played a role in firms joining up in the sector, especially with the rise of agricultural biotechnology and digital transformation of the global economy. And the broader regulatory context has also been important, especially its role in establishing intellectual property rights for innovators of agricultural biotechnology as well as changes in the interpretation and application of antitrust laws that have become increasingly focused on narrow price and efficiency metrics over broader questions of market structure and corporate influence.

The firms that tower over the agri-food system have been key players in a reconfiguration of the global industrial food system toward globalized agri-food supply chains that articulate with one another in ways that reinforce the power of those firms. As they have become more concentrated, firms that dominate in the sector have increasingly been able to exercise different kinds of power to shape the parameters of markets as well as the broader regulatory context. This means that they have the capacity to influence not only prices in the sector – both the prices at which they sell their products as well as the prices at which they buy from food producers – but also working conditions and compensation for food system workers as well as consumer choice. They also have the capacity to influence regulatory decisions via lobbying, the revolving door, industry standards-setting, and the shaping of public discourse about the products which they sell. All of these ways in which corporate actors shape food systems matter because they affect broader goals society has set for food systems, including equity, sustainability, health, and democratic participation and governance.

The future agenda for research on corporate concentration in the food system is enormous. This chapter could only provide an outline of the many ways in which corporations become more concentrated and the mechanisms by which they can influence food system outcomes. Detailed work is needed at each of the points along supply chains where these forces are playing out. As the trend toward concentration continues, it is important to continue to track ongoing consolidation both within and between subsectors within the food system as well as the ways in which food system consolidation interfaces with financialization, technological change, and the broader regulatory context. Finally, there is a need for detailed studies – both disciplinary and interdisciplinary – linking these processes to outcomes in the food system, using a variety of methods that can give both a qualitative and quantitative picture of the broader implications of these processes which can inform policymaking going forward.

References

Abboud, L., 2021. Couche-Tard Faces Clash with French Government over Carrefour Bid. *Financial Times.* January 13. Online at: https://www.ft.com/content/05319282-cddc-4022-b31b-e5ad09b0ad0c.

Bonny, S., 2017. Corporate Concentration and Technological Change in the Global Seed Industry. *Sustainability* 9(9): 1632.

British Broadcasting Corporation (BBC), 2021. "Follow the Food" documentary series. Online at: https://www.bbc.com/future/bespoke/follow-the-food/.

Brooks, C., Chen, Z., Zeng, Y., 2018. Institutional Cross-Ownership and Corporate Strategy: The Case of Mergers and Acquisitions. *Journal of Corporate Finance* 48(February 2018): 187–216. https://doi.org/10.1016/j.jcorpfin.2017.11.003.

Buckley, K., Newton, P., Gibbs, H., McConnel, I., Ehrmann, J., 2019. Pursuing Sustainability through Multi-Stakeholder Collaboration: A Description of the Governance, Actions, and Perceived Impacts of the Roundtables for Sustainable Beef. *World Development* 121: 203–17.

Burch, David, and Geoffrey Lawrence. 2013. Financialization in Agri-Food Supply Chains: Private Equity and the Transformation of the Retail Sector. *Agriculture and Human Values* 30(2): 247–58.

Canadian Biotechnology Action Network (CBAN), 2020. *GMOs in Your Grocery Store: Ranking Company Transparency.* https://cban.ca/wp-content/uploads/GMOs-in-your-grocery-store-report-2020.pdf.

Center for Responsive Politics, 2021. Politicians & Elections. Online at: https://www.opensecrets.org/elections/.

Clapp, J., 2021. Explaining Growing Glyphosate Use: The Political Economy of Herbicide-Dependent Agriculture. *Global Environmental Change* 67: 102239.

Clapp, J., 2020. *Food.* 2nd edition. Cambridge: Polity.

Clapp, J., 2019. The Rise of Financial Investment and Common Ownership in Global Agrifood Firms. *Review of International Political Economy* 26(4): 604–29.

Clapp, J., 2018. Mega-Mergers on the Menu: Corporate Concentration and the Politics of Sustainability in the Global Food System. *Global Environmental Politics* 18(2): 12–33.

Clapp, J., 2015. ABCD and Beyond: From Grain Merchants to Agricultural Value Chain Managers. *Canadian Food Studies* 2(2): 126–35.

Clapp, J., Ruder, S-L., 2020. Precision Technologies for Agriculture: Digital Farming, Gene-Edited Crops, and the Politics of Sustainability. *Global Environmental Politics* 20(3): 49–69.

Clapp, J., Isakson, R., 2018. *Speculative Harvests: Financialization, Food, and Agriculture.* Halifax: Fernwood.

Clapp, J., Fuchs, D. (eds), 2009. *Corporate Power in Global Agrifood Governance.* Cambridge, MA: MIT Press.

Cornish, C., 2017. John Deere Ploughs a New Furrow with Algorithmic Acquisition. *Financial Times.* September 11.

Crooks, E., 2015. Dow Chemical and DuPont Unveil $130bn Mega-Merger. *Financial Times.* December 11. Online at: https://www.ft.com/content/dfcde2d2-a006-11e5-8613-08e211ea5317.

Dauvergne, P., 2018. The Global Politics of the Business of "Sustainable" Palm Oil. *Global Environmental Politics* 18(2): 34–52.

de Schutter, O., 2010. Addressing Concentration in Food Supply Chains: The Role of Competition Law in Tackling the Abuse of Buyer Power. *Briefing note by the Special Rapporteur on the right to food* (December). Online at: http://www.srfood.org/en/briefing-note-addressing-concentration-in-food-supply-chains.

Eley, J., Massoudi, A., 2019. Sainsburys Faces Tough Battle to Keep Asda Deal on Track. *Financial Times.* January 13. Online at: https://www.ft.com/content/1115a9b0-0477-11e9-9d01-cd4d49afbbe3.

Ergen, T., Kohl, S., 2019. Varieties of Economization in Competition Policy: Institutional Change in German and American Antitrust, 1960–2000. *Review of International Political Economy* 26(2): 256–86.

ETC Group, 2015. *Breaking Bad: Big Ag Mega-Mergers in Play: Dow + DuPont in the Pocket? Next: Demonsanto?* Communiqué #115. Online at: https://www.etcgroup.org/content/breaking-bad-big-ag-mega-mergers-play.

Fabbri, A., Holland, T., Bero, L., 2018. Food Industry Sponsorship of Academic Research: Investigating Commercial Bias in the Research Agenda. *Public Health Nutrition* 12(18): 3422–30.

Fairtrade International, 2013. *Powering Up Smallholder Farmers to Make Food Fair: A Five Point Agenda.* Fairtrade International. May. Online at: https://files.fairtrade.net/publications/2013_PoweringUpSmallholderFarmers.pdf.

Fernandez-Cornejo, J., 2004. *The Seed Industry in U.S. Agriculture: An Exploration of Data and Information on Crop Seed Markets, Regulation, Industry Structure, and Research and Development.* Washington, D.C.: USDA. Online at: http://ageconsearch.umn.edu/handle/33671.

Fernandez-Cornejo, J., Just, R., 2007. Researchability of Modern Agricultural Input Markets and Growing Concentration. *American Journal of Agricultural Economics* 89(5): 1269–75.

Fontanella-Khan, J., Massoudi, A., Daneshkhu, S., 2015a. Heinz Swallows Kraft in Deal Engineered by Warren Buffett and 3G. *Financial Times.* March 25. Online at: https://www.ft.com/content/fe532334-d289-11e4-9c25-00144feab7de.

Fontanella-Khan, J., Massoudi, A., Daneshkhu, S., 2015b. Anheuser-Busch InBev Eyes Takeover of Rival SAB Miller. *Financial Times.* September 16. Online at: https://www.ft.com/content/52162e9c-5c3e-11e5-9846-de406ccb37f2.

Fortin, E., Richardson, B., 2013. Certification Schemes and the Governance of Land: Enforcing Standards or Enabling Scrutiny? *Globalizations* 10(1): 141–59.

Fuchs, D., 2007. *Business Power in Global Governance.* Boulder, CO: Lynne Rienner.

Fuchs, D., Kalfagianni, A., 2010. The Causes and Consequences of Private Food Governance. *Business and Politics* 12(3): 145–81.

Fuglie, K., Heisey, P., King, J. Schimmelpfennig, D., 2012. Rising Concentration in Agricultural Input Industries Influences New Farm Technologies. *Amber Waves.* December 3. Online at: https://www.ers.usda.gov/amber-waves/2012/december/rising-concentration-in-agricultural-input-industries-influences-new-technologies/.

Fuglie, K., Heisey, P., King, J. et al., 2011. *Research Investments and Market Structure in the Food Processing, Agricultural Input, and Biofuel Industries Worldwide*. United States Department of Agriculture, Economic Research Service. https://www.ers.usda.gov/webdocs/publications/44951/11777_err130_1_.pdf?v=4816.8.

Government of Canada, 2015. Competition Bureau Statement Regarding the Merger Between Heinz and Kraft. June 17. Online at: https://www.competitionbureau.gc.ca/eic/site/cb-bc.nsf/eng/03965.html.

Grabs, J., Carodenuto, S., 2021. Traders as Sustainability Governance Actors in Global Food Supply Chains: A Research Agenda. *Business Strategy and the Environment* 30(2): 1314–32.

Heinrich Böll Foundation, Rosa Luxemburg Foundation, Friends of the Earth Europe, 2017. *Agrifood Atlas*. Online at: https://www.boell.de/sites/default/files/agrifoodatlas2017_facts-and-figures-about-the-corporations-that-control-what-we-eat.pdf?dimension1=ds_agrifoodatlas.

Hovhannisyan, V., Cho, C., Bozic, M., 2019. The Relationship between Price and Retail Concentration: Evidence from the US Food Industry. *European Review of Agricultural Economics* 46(2): 319–45.

Howard, P., 2016. *Concentration and Power in the Food System*. London: Bloomsbury.

Hyslop, G., 2017. Cold Cereals USA: The Top 10 Brands in the First Half of 2017. *BakeryandSnacks*. Online at: https://www.bakeryandsnacks.com/Article/2017/08/03/Cold-cereals-USA-The-Top-10-brands-in-the-first-half-of-2017.

IHS Markit Agribusiness Consulting, 2019. *Analysis of Sales and Profitability Within the Seed Sector*. Independent Report by IHS Markit (Phillips McDougall) for the Co-Chairs of the Ad-hoc Open-ended Working Group to Enhance the Functioning of the Multilateral System of FAO's International Treaty on Plant Genetic Resources for Food and Agriculture. Online at: http://www.fao.org/3/ca6929en/ca6929en.pdf.

International Panel of Experts on Sustainable Food Systems (IPES-Food), 2017. *Too Big to Feed*. Online at: http://www.ipes-food.org/_img/upload/files/Concentration_FullReport.pdf.

Kelloway, C., Miller, S., 2019. Food and Power: Addressing Monopolization in America's Food System. Open Markets Institute. Online at: https://static1.squarespace.com/static/5e449c8c3ef68d752f3e70dc/t/5ea9fa6c2c1e9c460038ec5b/1588198002769/190322_MonopolyFoodReport-v7.pdf.

Kestenbaum, R., 2018. Amazon and Whole Foods After A Year: Supermarkets Will See Massive Changes. *Forbes*. December 18. Online at: https://www.forbes.com/sites/richardkestenbaum/2018/12/16/amazon-whole-foods-supermarkets-grocery-massive-change/?sh=5fce0a769cc9.

Khan, L., 2017. Amazon's Antitrust Paradox. *Yale Law Journal*, 126: 710–805.

Khan, L., Vaheesan, S., 2017. Market Power and Inequality: The Antitrust Counterrevolution and Its Discontents. *Harvard Law & Policy Review*, 11: 235–94.

Klassen, S., Murphy, S., 2020. Equity as Both a Means and an End: Lessons for Resilient Food Systems from COVID-19. *World Development* 136: 105104.

Kwoka, J., 2017. U.S. Antitrust and Competition Policy amid the New Merger Wave. *Washington Center for Equitable Growth*. Online at: https://equitablegrowth.org/research-paper/u-s-merger-policy-amid-the-new-merger-wave/.

LeBaron, G., 2020. *Combatting Modern Slavery: Why Labour Governance is Failing and What We Can Do About It*. Cambridge: Polity.

Lianos, I., Katalevsky, D., Ivanov, A., 2016. *The Global Seed Market, Competition Law and Intellectual Property Rights: Untying the Gordian Knot*. Centre for Law, Economics and Society, UCL. Online at: https://www.ucl.ac.uk/cles/research-papers.

Maisashvili, A., Bryant, H., Raulston, M. et al., 2016. Seed Prices, Proposed Mergers and Acquisitions Among Biotech Firms. *Choices*, 31(4). Online at: http:// www .choicesmagazine .org/ choices -magazine/ submitted -articles/ seed -prices -proposed -mergers-and-acquisitions-among-biotech-firms.

Massoudi, A., Fontanella-Khan, J., 2017. The $143bn Flop: How Warren Buffett and 3G Lost Unilever. *Financial Times*. February 21.

McKeon, N., 2015. *Food Security Governance: Empowering Communities, Regulating Corporations*. London: Routledge.

McMichael, P., 2013. *Food Regimes and Agrarian Questions*. Halifax: Fernwood Press.

Mooney, P., 2018. *Blocking the Chain: Industrial Food Chain Concentration, Big Data Platforms and Food Sovereignty Solutions*. Ottawa: ETC Group. Online at: http:// www .etcgroup .org/ sites/ www .etcgroup .org/ files/ files/ blockingthechain _english _web.pdf

Murphy, S., Burch, D., Clapp, J., 2012. Cereal Secrets. Oxfam. https://www.oxfam.org/en/research/cereal-secrets-worlds-largest-grain-traders-and-global-agriculture.

Nestle, M., 2013. *Food Politics: How the Food Industry Influences Nutrition and Health*. Berkeley, CA: University of California Press.

Nicolaou, A., Fontanella-Khan, J., Samson, A., Hook, L., 2017. Amazon Agrees to Buy Wholefoods for $13.7 bn. *Financial Times*. June 16. Online at: https://www.ft.com/content/bb5a7dae-5296-11e7-a1f2-db19572361bb.

Rotz, S., Duncan, E., Small, M., Botschner, J. et al., 2019. The Politics of Digital Agricultural Technologies: A Preliminary Review. *Sociologia Ruralis* 59(2): 203–29.

Rowe, S., Alexander, N., Clydesdale, F., Applebaum, R. et al., 2009. Funding Food Science and Nutrition Research: Financial Conflicts and Scientific Integrity. *The American Journal of Clinical Nutrition* 89(5): 1285–91.

Schmalz, M., 2018. Common-Ownership Concentration and Corporate Conduct. *Annual Review of Financial Economics*, 10(1): 413–48.

Scrinis, G., 2016. Reformulation, Fortification and Functionalization: Big Food Corporations' Nutritional Engineering and Marketing Strategies. *The Journal of Peasant Studies* 43(1): 17–37.

Shi, G., Chavas, J-P., Stiegert, K., 2010. An Analysis of the Pricing of Traits in the US Corn Seed Market. *American Journal of Agricultural Economics* 92(5): 1324–38.

Sink, J., Parker, M., 2017. Bayer-Monsanto Pledge Investment, Jobs After Trump Meeting. *Bloomberg Politics*. January 17. Online at: https:// www .bloomberg .com/ politics/ articles/ 2017 -01 -17/ bayer -to -invest -8 -billion -and -add -3 -000 -jobs -trump -aide -says.

Statista, 2021. Supermarkets and Grocery Retail in Australia – Statistics and Facts. https:// www .statista .com/ topics/ 6399/ supermarkets -and -grocery -retail -in -australia/.

Statista, 2020. Market Share of Five Largest Agricultural Chemical Companies Worldwide as of 2018. https:// www .statista .com/ statistics/ 950490/ market -share -largest-agrochemical-companies-worldwide/.

Terazono, E., 2020. Impossible Foods Steps up Challenge to Meat Producers, *Financial Times*, March 3. Online at: https://www.ft.com/content/452c5718-5d6c-11ea-8033 -fa40a0d65a98.

Terazono, E., 2014. Welcome to the World of Big Chocolate. *Financial Times*, December 18. Online at: https://www.ft.com/content/80e196cc-8538-11e4-ab4e-00144feabdc0.

Torshizi, M., Clapp, J., 2021. Price Effects of Common Ownership in the Seed Sector. *Antitrust Bulletin* 66(1): 39–67.

Turner, M., 2016. We Just Got a Rare Insight into How Wall Street Dealmakers Make Their Money. *Business Insider*. September 12. Online at: http://www.businessinsider .com/mergers-acquisitions-advice-on-wall-street-2016-9.

US Department of Agriculture (USDA), 2020. *Packers and Stockyards Programs Annual Report 2019*. Online at: https://www.ams.usda.gov/sites/default/files/media/ PSDAnnualReport2019.pdf.

US Senate, 2021. Lobbying Disclosure Act (LDA) Reports. Online at: https://lda.senate .gov/system/public/

Wiggerthale, M., 2021. Corporate Power in the Food System: Facts and Figures on Market Concentration in the Agri-food Sector. http:// marita -wiggerthale .de/ mediapool/16/163463/data/Corporate_power_food_system_Jan_2021_1_.pdf.

Wu, T., 2018. *The Curse of Bigness: Antitrust in the New Gilded Age*. New York: Columbia Global Reports.

3

The food system, planetary boundaries and eating for 1.5°C: the case for mutualism and commensality within a safe and just operating space for humankind

Colin L. Sage

Introduction

More cultivated food is produced today than at any time hitherto and has enabled world population to grow to nearly 8 billion people. Yet while at least two-fifths of humanity do not eat or absorb sufficient nutrients for a healthy life (IFPRI, 2016) the global ecological costs of feeding the rest of us are becoming ever more apparent. Across a range of key biophysical indicators, the consequences of food system activities – from agricultural input manufacturing through farming and food processing to retail, consumption and waste – have been raising concern for some time (Foley et al., 2011; Sage, 2012; Tilman & Clark, 2014; Springmann et al., 2018; Rockström et al., 2020) and life cycle assessment (LCA) studies are providing an abundance of quantitative evidence (Cucurachi et al., 2019; Notarnicola et al., 2017; McAuliffe et al., 2016). However, it is the food system's contribution to global warming and impacts of climate disruption that has recently come under the sharpest focus and one which will preoccupy us here.

As highlighted in Chapter 1, voices from a range of policy fields have created a sense that the food system is 'in crisis'. As we saw, there are several different ways in which this 'crisis' has been framed and, consequently, the kinds of solutions that have been presented. One of the key 'saviour' terms to emerge from this process has been that of sustainability. Although deployed as something of a Trojan horse by those who wish to maintain business as usual, the frequent occurrence of the word 'sustainable' as a prefix to food systems reveals the extent to which the environmental consequences of current practices have become more widely recognised. In this respect it is relatively straightforward to itemise multiple first-order impacts associated with food production, putting to one side for the moment that of climate disruption.

Land use change in favour of food growing and livestock rearing has led to deforestation, habitat destruction, biodiversity loss and likely greater biological insecurity given the suspected origins of COVID-19 (Rulli et al., 2021). The expansion of high external input agriculture has resulted in the depletion of freshwater, soil fertility, and mineral resources and has been the primary contributor to the disruption of global geochemical flows (Poore & Nemecek 2018). The global food system, then, can be regarded as the primary driver of biodiversity loss through the conversion of natural ecosystems to crop production or pasture (Benton et al., 2021; Dudley & Alexander, 2017; Alexander et al., 2015). Ecosystems perform multiple complex functions including the sequestration of atmospheric carbon, buffering the effects of adverse weather, and providing ecosystem services such as the purification of air and water and insect pollination of food crops. It is increasingly recognised that natural ecosystems provide other vital functions to human health and wellbeing, including psychological benefits. Yet with the widespread destruction of host ecosystems "biodiversity is declining faster than at any time in human history, and perhaps as fast as during any mass extinction" (Benton et al., 2021: 5). In this process the production of food is primarily responsible, having driven land conversion such that 50 percent of the world's habitable land is now under crop cultivation and animal grazing (Ritchie & Roser, 2013).

Another concern arises from analysis of stocks and flows of *virtual water*: the amount of freshwater required to produce a certain volume of food and which might therefore be regarded as virtually embedded in it (Chapagain & Hoekstra, 2008; Allan, 2011). The mapping of international hydrological resources has revealed the considerable risk posed by local water scarcity to downstream economies through globalised supply chains (Qu et al., 2018). Moreover, global heating and climate breakdown are exacerbating regional and local issues around water management presenting societies with unprecedented challenges of both drought and flooding. Yet aquatic resources are also being damaged by pollution arising from intensive food production, particularly run-off from animal agriculture and heavily fertilised fields (Mateo-Sagasta et al., 2017).

Drawing upon the framework of planetary boundaries (Rockström et al., 2009a, 2009b; Steffen et al., 2015a), serves to reveal nine key Earth system processes of which five are deeply affected by food production. These are changes to land-use, the climate system, freshwater availability, the biogeochemical cycles of nitrogen and phosphorus, and biosphere integrity (biodiversity loss). The other four – stratospheric ozone depletion, novel entities, aerosol loading and ocean acidification – may not be entirely disconnected from food but can be disregarded here. The value of the planetary boundaries model is that it helps to foster a more holistic and systemic approach to understanding the interconnected and cascading nature of the environmental consequences of all human activity – including food production – while proposing critical thresholds that represent limits to a 'safe operating space' for humankind. In this respect it invites us to consider a broader 'planetary turn' in our efforts to comprehend and act upon the conjoined conditions of human and global ecosystem health that are most closely entangled in the securing of food (Beacham, 2021).[1]

Consequently, the chapter proceeds, first, by unpacking the planetary boundaries model before examining in greater detail one sector – climate – which is widely regarded as having breached 'safe limits' and in which the food system is playing a critical role (Campbell et al., 2017). Indeed, the entire food system is regarded as contributing between 21 and 37 percent of total greenhouse gas (GHG) emissions that are responsible for atmospheric heating and associated climatic changes (IPCC, 2019: A3). Based on current trends food system emissions alone would prevent the achievement of the 1.5°C target established under the 2015 Paris Agreement – irrespective of fossil fuel emissions reduction (Clark et al., 2020).

A central feature of taking a food systems perspective is not to attribute responsibility for environmental harms solely to the realm of production without fully acknowledging all other actors at different stages of the system including that of human consumption. It is vital to challenge received 'wisdom' that consumers are simply acting in economic self-interest and responding somewhat passively to the incentives placed before them by producers and retailers. But food purchasers have *agency* and the choices that they make have *consequences*, with demand driving market signals upstream leading to agricultural expansion, specialisation, and intensification. For this reason, the chapter regards current dietary practices within rich and upper middle-income countries as shouldering particular responsibility for the ways in which environmental pressures have developed (Wiedmann et al., 2020; Loki, 2021). This has had the effect not only of pressing against and, ultimately, forcing the transgression of planetary boundaries, but of undermining the social and ecological foundations that support people in low-income countries, making them more vulnerable to environmental hazards. Utilising the notion of a safe and just operating space for humanity, the chapter makes the case for higher-income consumers to make radical shifts in dietary practices such that these achieve a lower environmental footprint that will help enable others of lower-income countries to achieve nutritional security. This sense of mutualism echoes the contraction and convergence model originally proposed by Aubrey Meyer over three decades ago (www.gci.org.uk) and more recently by discussion of what constitutes 'fair shares' (Rajamani et al., 2021). It also resonates strongly with the 'consumption corridors' model that represents a metaphorical space between a minimum level that ensures the satisfaction of all basic needs and maximum consumption standards that provides a check on levels or ways of consuming that prevent others from realising their needs. Consumption corridors "combine the pursuits of a good life and of justice within planetary boundaries" (Fuchs et al., 2021: 4). Building a sense of commensality – the act of eating *together* (Jönsson et al., 2021) – within the food system might just provide a metaphorical crystallisation of the need for nutritional security within a safe operating space bounded by a social minima and an ecological maxima and guided by the principle of intra- and inter-generational justice.

Planetary Boundaries

The framework of planetary boundaries originally set out by Rockström et al. (2009a, 2009b) and further developed by Steffen et al. (2015a) highlighted nine key Earth system processes previously mentioned. Each of these processes are directly affected by human activity and for each the cited authors have attempted to establish critical thresholds that represent limits to a safe operating space for human societies. The framework has emerged as a way of monitoring trends in Earth system processes with particular concern for deviation from the conditions that marked the past 12,000-year Holocene era which, Steffen et al. (2015a) suggest, is the only state of the planet that has appeared capable of supporting contemporary human societies. It presents a precautionary, systems integrity approach in proposing boundary limits at a distance from possible tipping points, thus establishing parameters for stable and resilient global ecosystems to support human wellbeing (Häyhä et al., 2016). However, while planetary boundaries emphasise the urgency of global environmental problems, the model has been subject to critique for using a language of universals that fail to speak to the differentiated interests, concerns and capabilities of people (Hajer et al., 2015). Others have argued that the framework deploys a narrow conception of planetary thresholds (Cornell, 2012) while different behaviours and practices can give rise to breaching some regional boundaries, which may not affect other regions. Criticisms have also been levelled at the accuracy of singular quantitative measure to mark boundary thresholds (Jaramillo & Destouni, 2015). Consequently, the planetary boundaries framework should be regarded as a work in progress that may involve translating global boundaries into specific national and regional contexts for effective policy making besides further development and refinement of what constitutes a 'safe operating space'.

Steffen et al. (2015a) have contributed to such work, especially by introducing a two-tier approach for several of the Earth system processes to account for regional heterogeneity; and by updating boundary limits in light of new findings. Their paper also makes clear that the segmented architecture of the framework should not disguise the complex interactions between processes. They argue that two of the boundaries – climate change and biosphere integrity – are highly integrated, emergent system phenomena that are connected to all of the other planetary processes that operate at the level of the whole Earth system, and provide the planetary-level overarching systems within which the other boundary processes operate. Furthermore, large changes in the climate or in biosphere integrity have likely, on their own, pushed the Earth system out of the Holocene state and into a new era widely recognised as the Anthropocene (Steffen et al., 2015b; Castree, 2017).

The planetary boundaries framework has also undergone an important and extended development with the emergence of the Doughnut model. This is an idea developed by the economist Kate Raworth (Raworth, 2012, 2017). The model takes the nine sectors of the planetary boundaries framework and assumes the safe operating space for each to constitute an 'environmental ceiling'. However, its novelty derives from its close alignment with the UN Sustainable Development Goals to establish twelve dimensions that constitute a social foundation comprising food, water, health, energy, and other basic human needs including gender equality, social equity, and peace and justice. It is between these social and planetary boundaries where an environmentally safe and socially just space exists within which humanity can flourish (O'Neill et al., 2018) (see Figure 3.1).

The doughnut model has attracted interest as a potential 'bottom-up' approach to the planetary boundaries framework that otherwise appears somewhat neglectful of scale and the differentiated responsibilities arising from past and present levels of resource use. The doughnut's visual simplicity and holistic approach provides for a certain 'cosmological vision' that encompasses shared assumptions, values and attitudes around social justice, and where a common 'world view' presents an effective means of translating international scientific discourse ('planetary boundaries') into the potential for social and political action (Sage, 2014). The Doughnut Economics Action Lab (DEAL) provides

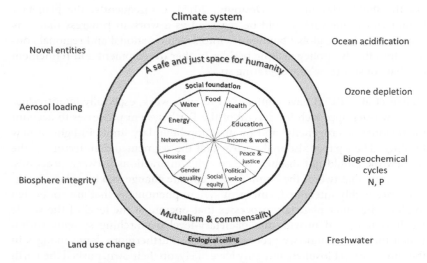

Source: This version adapted from various online Creative Commons versions.

Figure 3.1   The doughnut model: locating mutualism and commensality between the ecological ceiling and social foundation

an online community platform, sharing tools and stories designed to encourage a proto-movement of interested activists to apply the doughnut model and turn a radical idea into transformative action at local level (DEAL, 2021). The work of translating planetary boundaries insights into supporting the development of local and regional plans is clearly important and part of the growing network of globally connected civic initiatives motivated by a different vision for greater social justice, climate action, and sustainable food systems (Sage et al., 2021). Critically, it presents an argument for a 'safe operating space' that sits between a planetary ceiling and a social floor that establishes both a minimum threshold for all human beings and a constraint on consumption for the wealthiest. To what extent, then, might this safe operating space serve as an 'SOS' providing a metaphorical frame through which we might come to recognise the indispensable state of mutual co-existence under which the inhabitants of rich, middle and low-income countries live? Indeed, could this mark the beginning of a new planetary imaginary no longer rooted in the nation state but where there is a profound understanding of the inextricable interdependence of human beings and other forms of life on Earth (Pedersen, 2020)?

Given what we know about the environmental burden of affluence (Wiedmann et al., 2020) it is vital that efforts are made to reduce the ecological footprint of modern lifestyles caught up in a web of conspicuous consumption. And it is with regard to food production systems and the kinds of dietary consumption patterns they support in rich and upper-middle income countries where action needs to focus by making the case for mutual co-existence within planetary boundaries alongside guaranteed assurance of food and nutritional wellbeing. Although the planetary boundaries work has identified three sectors where thresholds have been transgressed – climate, biodiversity and biogeochemical flows – it is with respect to climate which presents the most urgent and, arguably, best opportunity for leveraging the kinds of collective behavioural changes which are needed to ensure that global heating stays below 1.5°C.

Climate

At the time of writing this chapter the IPCC had just published the Working Group 1 documentation for its Sixth Assessment Report (AR6; IPCC, 2021). The Report's headline findings are stark particularly given its moment of publication (August 2021). It highlights, for example, that each of the last four decades has been successively warmer than any decade that preceded it since 1850 and that this process will continue for at least the next three decades due to existing concentrations of atmospheric greenhouse gases (IPCC, 2021, SPM A.1.2). One of the consequences of atmospheric warming is the intensification of the water cycle, that is the movement of moisture between oceans, atmosphere, cryosphere and land. With a warmer atmosphere capable of holding greater amounts of moisture, more extreme precipitation events are becoming a more regular feature: the catastrophic flooding that resulted in loss of life in Germany, UK, India, Japan and China during July and August 2021 bears testament. Meanwhile drought, "an exceptional lack of water compared with normal conditions" (UNDRR 2021: xi), remains a dominant hazard of climate in major food-producing regions including the western United States, Southern Australia, Southern Europe, West Africa, Mexico and South America. Exceptionally hot and dry conditions have also given rise to fire events that have swept through forest areas and rural communities in 2021 in western North America, Siberia and Mediterranean countries.

All of these climate-induced hazards – flooding, drought, fire – present a challenge to primary food production and threaten the livelihoods of farmers with their episodic destructive effects. Yet such hazards will have quite different consequences for local food systems, the food security of their populations and the livelihoods of food producers depending upon the extent and nature of their interconnections with regional networks, national government supports and global commodity markets. In this respect it is vital to acknowledge the growing divergence between high and low latitudes (aka the Global 'North' and 'South'; or 'minority' and 'majority' worlds) in terms of exposure to climate and other risks and the availability of welfare supports – emergency provision, social safety nets, compensation for crop loss and so on – both to farmers and their wider populations. Recognising the vulnerability of local populations to environmental hazards is a first step in helping to identify ways in which this can be mitigated across individual, household, community, and regional scales. For wealthier and comparatively more secure food purchasers in the Global North, however, even preliminary analysis motivated by long-term self-interest would reveal the vulnerabilities of global supply chains that currently deliver tropical food commodities to their supermarket shelves.

Within the tropics there is particular concern for the effects of sustained higher temperatures, with resulting heat stress on crops, animals, and farmers; changing precipitation patterns, disrupting established cycles of rain-fed farming, and associated livelihood activities; rising sea levels that will not only cause inundation of coastal farmland but trigger saline intrusions of freshwater aquifers used for drinking and irrigation; as well as the emergence of new pests and disease. For example, changes in temperature and in the amount, timing, and intensity of rainfall can result in reduced yields and lower overall levels of food production. This leaves households with inadequate amounts to sustain their consumption needs until the next harvest and/or sell into local and regional markets. This decline invariably exacerbates price fluctuations which are likely to be transmitted into national urban food markets. Here access to food will be determined by the ability to pay higher prices and, depending on how these price rises occur alongside changes in income, can make existing food secure populations vulnerable to food insecurity in the future. In urban areas, food availability is seldom the major constraint, but rather it is lack of access to food for the urban poor, especially children.

It may be possible to make agricultural systems more resilient to climate change effects by changing farming practices, for example, from staggering planting dates to practicing water conservation methods such as using mulches or rainwater harvesting techniques. The introduction of more heat- or drought-tolerant varieties of existing crops, or replacing those with new crop species, may also be an option but may have profound implications for household labour and other resources. Amongst resource-poor, low-income households, agriculture has a significant bearing on poverty reduction and therefore in reducing hunger and malnutrition, every effort must be made to make farming systems in vulnerable regions more resilient to the effects of climate change. Might this involve prioritising food sovereignty and ensuring greater provisioning of staple crops for domestic markets over engagement in global supply chains? What might be the implications of such policy decisions for food importing countries of both North and South?

Climate change can deepen the fault lines of existing inequalities that operate along multiple social axes, principally of gender, age, marital status, ethnicity, and ascribed status within the prevailing society (e.g., caste). This has implications for entitlement relations and access to food, as outlined above, and consequently for nutritional security. Even within the household under normal conditions, it has been well documented that the allocation of food frequently favours males over females. Tightening stocks may disproportionately affect women and girls who eat what remains in the pot after the men have fed. Yet the work performed by women and girls may increase as a consequence of climate warming and drying. The gender roles of water and fuel collection may make journeys longer and leave women little time to pursue income-generating activities.

Furthermore, in developing countries as a whole, women constitute approximately 43 percent of the agricultural labour force yet are typically disadvantaged in terms of access to inputs (water, fertilisers, and seeds) and credit and lack titles to land. This affects farm productivity and leaves female-headed households more vulnerable to food insecurity. Women farmers are generally more likely to produce a greater variety of foods for household consumption than men who are more connected with extension services encouraging commodity production. Small-scale production of fruits and vegetables by women has a greater chance of maintaining nutritional security.

Improving access to food will not automatically result from increased agri-commodity production especially under the prevailing model of highly mechanised, large-scale, high-input farming that dominates throughout the developed world and is being promoted as the solution for the South by agri-food corporations and philanthropic organisations such as the Bill and Melinda Gates Foundation. While this industrial model currently produces enough food to feed the world, almost one billion are hungry and food insecure and demonstrate that such technologies do not enhance the human right to adequate food (De Schutter, 2011).

Overall, then, we begin to see the multiple and cascading consequences that climate change will have in poorer countries, and although these will vary between regions, the impacts on people's lives will be enormous if not catastrophic. In light of the publication of the IPCC WG1 AR6 report, which has brought into much sharper relief the role of shorter-lived greenhouse gases in atmospheric heating and which are more closely tied to agriculture, it becomes vitally important to ask whether, in the interests of the most vulnerable, immediate efforts must be made in the food system to move away from the production of certain foods and farming methods in order to stay within this planetary boundary.

The Food System inside the Global Greenhouse

Around two-thirds of the atmospheric warming that has occurred since 1750 is attributed to the release of CO_2 from the burning of fossil fuels (coal, oil, gas) that generates energy for industrial, commercial and domestic use and for the transportation of goods and people. Until recently there has been little popular appreciation about the contribution of the food system to climate beyond, perhaps, the sense that extended supply chains and the carbon emissions resulting therefrom ('food miles') had a role. This is now changing as media coverage of deforestation in the Amazon and South-East Asia has highlighted the extension of the agricultural frontier for soybeans, palm oil and cattle ranching. The intensity of arable and livestock operations across many high- and middle-income countries has also come under increased scrutiny and revealed that agriculture has become one of the most important anthropogenic activities contributing to climate disruption. As previously noted, the entire food system – from agricultural input manufacture to waste disposal – is responsible for between 21 and 37 percent of anthropogenic greenhouse gas emissions (IPCC, 2021) and agriculture (along with forestry and other land use) represent 23 percent (IPCC, 2019). Critically, agricultural activities emit large amounts of important non-CO_2 greenhouse gases – methane (CH_4, 44 percent of emissions arising from human activity) and nitrous oxide (N_2O, 81 percent) – while land use change (deforestation) accounts for 13 percent of CO_2. Beyond the farm gate in its processing, refining, manufacturing, distribution, and retail activities the food system and ancillary activities also emit significant amounts of CO_2.[2]

Methane (and nitrous oxide) levels are now higher than at any point in the past 800,000 years. According to AR6 methane has contributed about 0.5°C of warming (compared to 0.75°C for CO_2) when assessing 2010-2019 warming relative to 1850-1900 (IPCC, 2021). Methane is a powerful greenhouse gas and although it has an atmospheric lifetime of only a decade or so it is attributed with a 100-year global warming potential (GWP) 28-34 times that of CO_2 and over a 20-year period that ratio grows to 84–86 times (Costa et al., 2021; further discussion below). Although it has a number of different sources – with around one-third comprising fugitive emissions from hydrocarbon extraction, with smaller shares from the decomposition of organic material, and, in agriculture from rice paddies – its growing significance has been most closely tied to the expansion in numbers of ruminant livestock, especially dairy and beef cattle. Methane is a consequence of enteric fermentation, the microbial process by which ruminants digest plant matter and convert this into carcass tissue and/ or milk. This source accounts for almost one-third of anthropogenic methane and two-thirds of all agricultural methane (Lynch, 2019).

The overall number of animals reared worldwide for their meat, milk or hides has risen dramatically over the past 60 years, with an estimated 80 billion creatures slaughtered in 2018 (Ritchie & Roser, 2019). It has been estimated that global meat production has quadrupled since 1961 reaching 340 million tonnes in 2018. Despite continuing growth of output in North America, Europe and Oceania, the most dramatic increase has been witnessed in Asia where meat production has increased 15-fold since 1961 with China achieving the most spectacular growth (Ritchie & Roser, 2019). Given the high unit cost reduction achieved through the pursuit of economies of scale, the inevitable consequence has been ever-larger herd and flock sizes managed in high capacity, more technologically sophisticated enterprises (confined animal feeding operations or CAFOs), with a consequent fall in the price of meat to consumers. It is this which has led to the apparently insatiable demand for meat across large parts of the world and the 'meatification' of diets (Neo & Emel 2017; Weiss, 2013).

However, this has been accompanied at considerable cost to natural capital and ecological services. Livestock now account for 75 percent of all agricultural land, including pasture and rangeland, with over one-third of global arable land given over to the production of animal feeds, which account for around a quarter of global crop production by mass. As feed crops are dense in both calories and protein content, feed crops now account for 36 percent of global calorie production and 53 percent of global plant protein production (Cassidy et al., 2013). Moreover, it is calculated that livestock are now directly responsible for around 37 percent of anthropogenic methane, 65 percent of nitrous oxide and 9 percent of carbon dioxide. Taken together this suggests that livestock rearing – and the consumption of their products – is contributing significantly to the destabilisation of the climate system as well as placing pressures on other planetary boundaries including the global nitrogen cycle, freshwater stocks, biosphere integrity and land use change. How should such challenges be addressed?

First, it should be emphasised that this discussion puts to one side extensive pastoral systems which, though not generally regarded as commercially signifi-cant, are vital to support livelihoods in often marginal environments. Rather, it is the intensive livestock production system which has become largely discon-nected from its local resource base, has scaled up numbers of animals, output volumes of meat, milk, and eggs, and driven multiple ecological consequences that is the concern.

Second, dietary patterns that are high in the consumption of animal products are closely linked to escalating rates of chronic non-communicable diseases. Red and processed meat consumption has been associated with an increased risk for heart disease, stroke, type 2 diabetes, certain types of cancer, and mortality (Health Care Without Harm, 2017). Consequently, planetary and human health are becoming inextricably intertwined as the combined burden of existing dietary practices are exposed by mounting ecological and epidemi-ological evidence (Swinburn et al., 2019). It is in this context that the growing narrative around the contribution that plant-based diets could make to bio-spheric and human wellbeing is met by the powerful commercial interests of the meat industry. Inevitably, there has been a significant push-back by the industry anxious to retain business-as-usual practices.[3] Rose and colleagues have recently outlined some of the strategies used by the meat industry in the United States by which it has successfully shaped the federal Dietary Guidelines for Americans in order to exclude sustainability from considera-tion, amongst other practices (Rose et al., 2021). Such strategies illustrate the kinds of instrumental, discursive and structural power enjoyed by the 'Big Food' corporations in protecting their interests (Sievert et al., 2020). Yet it is not simply business that seeks to maintain the status quo, as governments too can be fearful of change.

In Ireland the Department of Agriculture has recently published its latest agri-food strategy, 'Food Vision 2030 – A World Leader in Sustainable Food Systems'.[4] Containing a level of hubris that even outshines its previous strategies – Food Harvest 2020, FoodWise 2025 (Kenny et al., 2018; Sage & Kenny, 2017) – all of the discursive power that can be enrolled is brought to bear through portentous deployment of key buzz words such as 'climate smart', 'environmentally sustainable', 'resilience' and even 'regenerative'. Such terms are an attempt to disguise the fact that agriculture was the sector with the largest greenhouse gas emissions in Ireland over the 1990–2017 period with 33 percent of the total in 2017 which helped ensure that it had the third highest per capita emissions in the EU28 at 13.3 tonnes CO_2-equivalent, which was 51 percent higher than the EU average (CSO, 2019). This is because Irish agriculture is now largely based around a national herd of over seven million cattle (and rising) and an export strategy focussed upon beef, infant formula, and cheese.

'Food Vision 2030' and its proponents in government, research and extension, the food industry and farming organisations, variously deploy many of the discourses identified by Lamb and colleagues (2020) in their analysis of climate delay tactics. Those discourses that resonate most strongly include the 'free rider' excuse ("if we don't produce beef then the Brazilians will"); 'whataboutism' (as in "our carbon footprint is tiny; what about China?"); 'all talk, little action' ("we are world leaders" and other forms of illusory rhetoric); and, above all, technological optimism. As one might expect, Food Vision 2030 makes a strong case for finding technological fixes to reduce methane emissions – its single biggest problem. This involves work on novel feed additives and supplements (e.g., seaweed), animal genetics, and exploiting emerging technologies (whatever these might be). In other words, a great deal of hope is pinned upon achieving new efficiencies (feed conversion to carcass weight and milk yield without co-production of methane) while rising livestock numbers promise to outstrip whatever marginal reductions are made in emissions per animal. The irony here, of course, is that a notion of commensality is drawn upon through a discourse of Irish agriculture as contributing to 'feeding the world' yet is entirely disregarded when it is clear that many of Ireland's export target markets (Asia, the Middle East, Africa) will experience the worst effects of climate breakdown. It illustrates how the selective and self-serving deployment of buzz-words such as sustainability are believed to convey the same concealing properties as Harry Potter's invisibility cloak: while that garment enabled him to move undetected along the corridors of Hogwarts, so rhetorical greenwash will magically disappear the environmental costs of excessive livestock numbers. Consequently, intransigent, export-focussed governments can present as big an obstacle to staying within planetary boundaries as Big Food corporations. How, then, will the food system operate within a 1.5°C threshold?

Eating for 1.5°C

In advance of the COP26 Summit in November 2021, much of the policy chatter revolved around efforts by countries to commit to new nationally determined contributions (NDCs) that will achieve net zero carbon by 2050 – and which must involve the effective elimination of fossil fuel use. Yet the AR6 makes clear the vital importance of immediate and significant efforts to reduce emissions of short-lived climate pollutants (SLCP, including methane and nitrous oxide) in order to slow the pace of climate disruption. Here a lifeline is offered in its statement that "Strong, rapid and sustained reductions in CH_4 (methane) emissions would also limit the warming effect" (IPCC, 2021: 36).

This rather hopeful tone has been recently echoed in a short paper (Costa et al., 2021) which examines the global warming potential (GWP) metric used by climate scientists. While this has conventionally focussed upon the capability of a greenhouse gas to warm the atmosphere over a 100-year time horizon (GWP_{100}), the paper argues for a different calculation – GWP^* – that better reflects the short-lived, non-cumulative behaviour of methane. In other words, unlike CO_2 which maintains a cumulative warming effect for thousands of years, methane's decade-long lifespan permits relatively quick gains in atmospheric concentration if emissions were lowered. As the paper argues: "The application of GWP^* to CH_4 emissions accounting suggests that avoiding further warming due to CH_4 emissions in agriculture is more attainable than previously understood. CH_4 reductions can have a rapid and highly substantial impact, which underscores the importance of making significant cuts in CH_4 emissions immediately" (Costa et al., 2021: 5).

While methane has other anthropogenic sources, it is a stark fact that if the livestock sector were to continue with business as usual, this sector alone would account for almost half of the emissions budget for 1.5°C by 2030, requiring other sectors to reduce emissions beyond a realistic or planned level. Consequently, it is becoming an unavoidable conclusion that substantially reducing if not avoiding meat and dairy products is the single biggest way to reduce our environmental impact on the planet (Poore & Nemecek 2018). Moreover, the human health co-benefits would be considerable, given the weight of clinical evidence pointing to the deleterious consequences of diets rich in red and processed meats. Yet warnings about unsustainable and unhealthy diets by experts in the fields of planetary science and public health (each embracing many different specialist disciplines) seems to have had an imperceptible influence over a global food system driven by powerful corporate interests and the relatively benign disinterest of governments. Amongst the first serious effort to outline a road map toward a healthier food future operating within planetary boundaries was the Eat-Lancet report (Willett et al., 2019). Yet that 'experts' would have the audacity to propose a 'Reference Diet' comprising a healthy, fair and just food intake for the entire global population within a safe operating space was met with considerable criticism (Garcia et al., 2019).

Tackling dietary practices in the wealthiest countries has to be a priority for it would immediately ease environmental burdens while improving human health (Tilman & Clark, 2014). Healthier diets – comprising more vegetables, fruit, and plant-based oils rather than animal products – require less crop-land, ease pressure on freshwater resources, provide more opportunities for co-existence with nature, create more potential for nutrient cycling without excessive disruption to the global nitrogen cycle and, above all, lower levels of greenhouse gas emissions. But while the necessary direction of travel is clear, the obstacles to moving forward are numerous.

One potential hazard in focussing upon methane is the demonising of meat and dairy, which would invariably prove a counter-productive strategy that will serve to rally more than the usual roster of denialists.[5] Within wealthier countries there are those who would be disproportionately affected by, say, the imposition of carbon taxes on meat and dairy. These would include live-stock farmers in upland environments with few, if any, alternative livelihood options, while low-income households with few resources (time, budget, skills) with which to make dietary changes would underline the socially regressive nature of such measures. In middle-income countries, too, there will be highly differentiated concerns particularly amongst populations which have only relatively recently experienced an improvement in income and diets and will be reluctant to sacrifice such gains. To speak of a 'just transition' is therefore to recognise that any food system transformation will require long and arduous discussions across societies with all stakeholders represented. This means building more participatory fora such as civic assemblies, citizen juries, public deliberation, digital tools and so on to enable effective and inclusive conversa-tions through which to identify potential transition pathways to emerge.

With respect to public policy more generally, small steps are being made to reform a food system that is currently structurally unsuited to operate within a safe operating space. At EU level the Farm to Fork Strategy is emerging but is hamstrung by the lobbying power of Big Food and the vested interests of farmers' organisations unwilling to relinquish the system of Common Agricultural Policy subsidies. Individual member states have their own agendas, too, as we have seen in the case of Ireland. The UK is in transition following Brexit but where the current Conservative government appears to be more interested in long-distance trade arrangements than building sustainable food sovereignty at home. Meanwhile the global food system carries on as before with unprecedented rates of deforestation in Amazonia opening new lands for soybeans that are harvested to feed poultry sold in UK supermarkets and fast-food restaurants (Watts et al., 2020).

The urgency of the warnings from climate science that implore strong and rapid action by governments does not then appear to be having the required response. It would appear that slow and incremental efforts in public policy simply will not be sufficient to stabilise the climate system. What about business interests operating through the market to bring about change? There are signs here of an emerging planetary awareness though mostly within the investment community which often takes a longer-term perspective. For example, the FAIRR Initiative is working "to leverage the power of institutional capital to effect change in the livestock and farmed fish sectors" which it pointedly observes has enjoyed a 'lack of scrutiny' which "has meant that these companies have been allowed to scale their operations, markets and production volumes without clear controls. This creates systemic risks: not just for companies, but also their global food customers, investors, consumers and society at large" (FAIRR, 2020). While these appear to be strong words coming from business insiders, we must remind ourselves that they presage a likely investment surge into alternative proteins as a market solution to the climate crisis rather than a call to reduce consumption so as to ensure we remain within planetary boundaries. The notion of a new global ethic around the principles of mutualism and commensality are unlikely, then, to be received enthusiastically by the investment community desiring to present consumers with yet more choice from which they can derive profit, rather than restraint.

Conclusions

This chapter has sought to outline the range and depth of environmental consequences generated by the global food system in its headlong pursuit of increased output. Yet we must remind ourselves that while two-fifths of humanity do not eat sufficient nutrients for a healthy life, around two billion are overweight primarily as a consequence of excessive food energy intake. With 2.8 million people dying each year from being overweight and obese, according to the WHO, this represents a human health crisis that sits alongside the crisis of planetary health. This is the predicament, arguably, to which the contemporary food system has brought us: a system that has enshrined the sovereign rights of consumers to eat what they like as the market delivers cheaper, more convenient novelties that titillate the palate but may do harm to our waistline, cardio-vascular organs and to the global ecological system.

Although there are many environmental problems that can be traced to the food system, the chapter has focussed upon the especially urgent matter of climate breakdown and the window of opportunity presented by methane reduction. It was suggested that efforts to reduce levels of meat consumption in rich and upper-middle income countries would offer a potential win–win outcome for climate and human health. Yet at this moment in time, one must ask the question: will the present governance arrangement comprising market-based solutions (e.g., the development of alternative proteins as a partial replacement for animal-derived proteins) and public policy nudges that do not infringe consumer choice be sufficient to ensure global nutritional security within a safe and just operating space where climate heating does not exceed 1.5C? We must doubt that it will. Indeed, the present regime of food governance, where much is left to the market and to the conscience of individual consumers, appears unfit to tackle the gravity of the predicament before us. Simply offering more choice options such as the provision of plant-based burgers alongside conventional fare will not lower environmental impacts. In this respect it becomes clear that the market and the state work best by maintaining an ideology of individualism through which value extraction from our lives is most easily managed.

Creating a sense of mutual co-existence between human beings – in our buildings, neighbourhoods, cities, and across the world – is a first step in finding collective solutions to our climate predicament. Thinking AND acting both locally AND globally – no room for either/or here – demonstrates the new planetary imaginary that is required. Clearly there is enormous scope for truly vital transdisciplinary research to be undertaken in pursuit of better understanding the links between food consumption practices and climate breakdown and effectively communicating such knowledge in order to achieve social change. This chapter has made the case for two terms that might help us bridge this cognitive dissonance between recognition and action. Mutualism demonstrates our acknowledgement that it is only through cooperation where we can harvest the synergies to be gained from working collectively to protect our precious biosphere. Commensality reminds us that ultimately the food system is supposed to feed people and we share whatever is available on that common platter at the centre of all humankind. Consequently, there are very strong grounds to suggest that further research could begin to develop and apply such concepts as mutualism, commensality and conviviality within local food systems as tools to help consciously and deliberatively reshape diets in the interests of achieving global nutritional security within planetary boundaries.

Notes

1. A new documentary film, *Breaking Boundaries: The Science of Our Planet* was released on Netflix in July 2021. Directed by Jon Clay and with narration by David Attenborough the film seeks to explain the planetary boundaries model

and the urgency of action to stabilise the rate of environmental change on Earth. It makes impressive use of CGI to portray the transgression of critical thresholds by hordes of zombie like humans but this seems to suggest a neo-Malthusian cause ('over-population') rather than the responsibility of a neoliberal economic system driven by the avarice of huge corporations. Nevertheless, a formidable effort in tackling a complex subject for a TV audience.

2.   Any apparent anomalies in the attribution of emission figures must recognise the range reflecting different research findings, varying levels of confidence (critical to IPCC procedures) and the existence of carbon sinks (forestry, soils) that provide some (small) compensation on emissions.

3.   Although as Sexton and Goodman explain in Chapter 8 of this volume, some of the biggest corporations are also hedging their bets and investing heavily in alternative protein initiatives.

4.   Available here: https://www.gov.ie/en/publication/c73a3-food-vision-2030-a-world-leader-in-sustainable-food-systems/.

5.   A constituency that appears to be growing albeit with very different core grievances – climate, COVID-19 and its vaccines, electoral fraud in the US, 5G etc.

References

Alexander, P., Rounsevell, M., Dislich, C., Dodson, J., Engstrom, K., Moran, D., 2015. Drivers for global agricultural land use change: the nexus of diet, population, yield and bioenergy. *Global Environmental Change* 35, 138-147.

Allan, T., 2011. *Virtual Water: Tackling the threat to our planet's most precious resource.* London: I.B. Tauris.

Beacham, J., 2021 Planetary food regimes: understanding the entanglement between human and planetary health in the Anthropocene. *Geographical Journal.* https://doi.org/10.1111/geoj.12407.

Benton, T., Bieg, C., Harwatt, H., Pudasaini, R. Wellesley, L., 2021. Food system impacts on biodiversity loss: three levers for food system transformation in support of nature. Energy, Environment and Resources Programme Research Paper. Chatham House, London.

Campbell, B., Beare, D., Bennett, E. et al., 2017. Agriculture production as a major driver of the Earth system exceeding planetary boundaries. *Ecology and Society* 22, 4: 8. https://doi.org/10.5751/ES-09595-220408.

Cassidy, E., West, P., Gerber, J., Foley, J., 2013. Redefining agricultural yields: from tonnes to people nourished per hectare. *Environmental Research Letters* 8. http://dx.doi.org/10.1088/1748-9326/8/3/034015.

Castree, N., 2017. Anthropocene and planetary boundaries. In *The International Encyclopedia of Geography: People, the Earth, Environment, and Technology* (Richardson, D., Castree, N., Goodchild, M., Kobayashi, A., Liu, W., Marston, R., eds.). New York: John Wiley & Sons.

Chapagain, A., Hoekstra, A., 2008. The global component of freshwater demand and supply: an assessment of virtual water flows between nations as a result of trade in agricultural and industrial products, *Water International*, 33, 1: 19-32.

Clark, M., Domingo, N., Colgan, K. et al., 2020. Global food system emissions could preclude achieving the 1.5° and 2°C climate change targets. *Science* 370: 705–708.

Cornell, S., 2012. On the system properties of the planetary boundaries. *Ecology and Society* 17, 1: r2. http://dx.doi.org/10.5751/ES-04731-1701r02.

Costa Jr. C., Wironen, M., Racette, K., Wollenberg, E., 2021. Global Warming Potential* (GWP*): understanding the implications for mitigating methane emissions in agriculture. CCAFS Info Note. Wageningen, the Netherlands: CGIAR Research Program on Climate Change, Agriculture and Food Security (CCAFS).

CSO 2019. Environmental indicators Ireland 2019. https:// www .cso .ie/ en/ rele asesandpublications/ep/p-eii/eii19/greenhousegasesandclimatechange/ Accessed 23 August 2021.

Cucurachi, S., Scherer, L., Guinée, J., Tukker, A., 2019. Life cycle assessment of food systems. *One Earth* 1, 3: 292-297. https://doi.org/10.1016/j.oneear.2019.10.014.

De Schutter, O., 2011. The right of everyone to enjoy the benefits of scientific progress and the right to food: from conflict to complementarity. *Human Rights Quarterly* 33:304–350.

Doughnut Economics Action Lab (DEAL), 2021. https:// doughnuteconomics .org/ Accessed 21 December 2021.

Dudley, N., Alexander, S., 2017. Agriculture and biodiversity: a review. *Biodiversity* 18, 2–3: 45–49.

FAIRR 2020. Coller FAIRR Protein Producer Index 2020. https://www.fairr.org/index/ Accessed 21 September 2021.

Foley, J.A., Ramankutty, N., Brauman, K.A. et al., 2011. Solutions for a cultivated planet. *Nature*, 478, 7369: 337–342. https://doi.org/10.1038/nature10452.

Fuchs, D., Sahakian, M., Gumbert, T. et al., 2021. *Consumption Corridors: Living a Good Life within Sustainable Limits*. Abingdon: Routledge.

Garcia, D., Galaz, V., Daume, S., 2019. EAT-Lancet vs yes2meat: the digital backlash to the planetary health diet. *The Lancet*, 25 November. https://doi.org/10.1016/S0140 -6736(19)32526-7.

Hajer, M., Nilsson, M., Raworth, K. et al., 2015. Beyond cockpit-ism: four insights to enhance the transformative potential of the Sustainable Development Goals. *Sustainability* 2015, 7: 1651-1660. https://doi.org/10.3390/su7021651.

Häyhä, T., Lucas, P., van Vuuren, D., Cornell, S., Hoff, H., 2016. From planetary boundaries to national fair shares of the global safe operating space: how can the scales be bridged? *Global Environmental Change* 40: 60–72.

Health Care Without Harm, 2017. Redefining protein: adjusting diets to protect public health and conserve resources. Reston, VA: HCWH.

Intergovernmental Panel on Climate Change (IPCC), 2021. Climate change 2021: the physical science basis. Contribution of Working Group I to the Sixth Assessment Report of the Intergovernmental Panel on Climate Change. https://www.ipcc.ch/ report/ar6/wg1/ Accessed 15 August 2021.

Intergovernmental Panel on Climate Change (IPCC), 2019. Summary for Policymakers (SPM). In: Climate Change and Land: an IPCC special report on climate change, desertification, land degradation, sustainable land management, food security, and greenhouse gas fluxes in terrestrial ecosystems. https://www.ipcc.ch/srccl/chapter/ summary-for-policymakers/ Accessed 3 September 2021.

International Food Policy Research Institute (IFPRI), 2016. Global nutrition report. Washington, DC: International Food Policy Research Institute.

Jaramillo, F., Destouni, G., 2015. Comment on "Planetary boundaries: guiding human development on a changing planet". *Science* 348, 6240): 1217.

Jönsson, H., Michaud, M., Neuman, N., 2021. What is commensality? A critical discussion of an expanding research field. *International Journal of Environmental Research and Public Health* 18, 6235. https://doi.org/doi.org/10.3390/ijerph18126235.

Kenny, T, Cronin, M., Sage, C., 2018. A retrospective public health analysis of the Republic of Ireland's Food Harvest 2020 strategy. *Critical Public Health* 28, 1: 94–105.

Lamb W., Mattioli, G., Levi, S., Roberts, JT. et al., 2020. Discourses of climate delay. *Global Sustainability* 3, e17: 1–5. https://doi.org/10.1017/sus.2020.13.

Loki, R., 2021. Humanity's #1 environmental problem is consumption: climate change is just one of the by-products. https://braveneweurope.com/reynard-loki-humanitys -1 -environmental -problem -is -consumption -climate -change -is -just -one -of -the -byproducts Accessed 21 December 2021.

Lynch, J., 2019. Agricultural methane and its role as a greenhouse gas. Food Climate Research Network, University of Oxford.

Mateo-Sagasta, J., Marjani Zadeh, S., Turral, H., 2017. Water pollution from agriculture: a global review. Rome: Food and Agriculture Organization. http:// www .fao .org/3/a-i7754e.pdf.

McAuliffe, G., Chapman, D., Sage, C., 2016. A thematic review of life cycle assessment (LCA) applied to pig production. *Environmental Impact Assessment Review* 56: 12–22.

Neo, H., Emel, J., 2017. *Geographies of Meat: Politics, economy and culture.* Abingdon: Routledge.

Notarnicola, B., Tassielli, G., Renzulli, P., Castellani, V., Sala, S., 2017. Environmental impacts of food consumption in Europe. *Journal of Cleaner Production* 140: 753–765.

O'Neill, D., Fanning, A., Lamb, W., Steinberger, J., 2018. A good life for all within planetary boundaries. *Nature Sustainability* 1: 88–95.

Pedersen, S., 2020. Planetarism: a paradigmatic alternative to internationalism. *Globalizations,* 18, 2: 141–154. https://doi.org/10.1080/14747731.2020.1741901.

Poore, J., Nemecek, T., 2018. Reducing food's environmental impacts through producers and consumers. *Science* 360, 6392: 987–992.

Qu, S., Liang, S., Konar, M. et al., 2018. Virtual water scarcity risk to the global trade system. *Environmental Science & Technology* 52, 673–683.

Rajamani, L., Jeffery, L., Höhne, N. et al., 2021. National 'fair shares' in reducing greenhouse gas emissions within the principled framework of international environmental law. *Climate Policy,* 21, 8: 983–1004. https://doi.org/10.1080/14693062.2021 .1970504.

Raworth, K., 2012. A safe and just space for humanity. Oxfam Discussion Paper, February. Oxford: Oxfam.

Raworth, K., 2017. *Doughnut Economics: Seven ways to think like a 21st-century economist.* London: Random House.

Ritchie, H., Roser, M. 2013. Land use. Retrieved from: https://ourworldindata.org/land -use Accessed 14 July 2021.

Ritchie, H., Roser, M., 2019. Meat and dairy production. Retrieved from: https:// ourworldindata.org/meat-production Accessed 19 August 2021.

Rockström, J., Edenhofer, O., Gaertner, J., DeClerck, F., 2020. Planet-proofing the global food system. *Nature Food* 1: 3–5. https://doi.org/10.1038/s43016-019-0010-4.

Rockström, J., Steffen, W., Noone, K. et al., 2009a. Planetary boundaries: exploring the safe operating space for humanity. *Ecology and Society* 14(2). http:// www .ecologyandsociety.org/vol14/iss2/art32/.

Rockström, J., Steffen, W., Noone, K. et al., 2009b. A safe operating space for humanity. *Nature* 461, 7263: 472–475.

Rose, D., Vance, C., Lopez, M.A., 2021. Livestock industry practices that impact sustainable diets in the United States. *International Journal of Sociology of Agriculture & Food*, 2021, 27, 1: 35–53.

Rulli, M.C., D'Odorico, P., Galli, N., Hayman, D., 2021. Land-use change and the livestock revolution increase the risk of zoonotic coronavirus transmission from rhinolophid bats. *Nature Food*, 2: 409–416.

Sage, C., 2012. *Environment and Food*. Abingdon: Routledge.

Sage, C., 2014. The transition movement and food sovereignty: from local resilience to global engagement in food system transformation. *Journal of Consumer Culture* 14, 2: 254–275.

Sage, C., Kenny, T., 2017. Connecting agri-export productivism, sustainability and domestic food security via the metabolic rift: the case of the Republic of Ireland. In Barling, D. (ed.) *Advances in Food Security and Sustainability*, vol.2. Oxford: Elsevier, pp. 41–67.

Sage, C., Antoni-Komar, I., Kropp, C., 2021. Grassroots initiatives in food system transformation: the role of food movements in the second 'Great Transformation'. In Kropp, C., Antoni-Komar, I., Sage, C. (eds.) *Food System Transformations: Social movements, local economies, collaborative networks*. Abingdon: Routledge, pp. 1–19. https:// www .taylorfrancis .com/ books/ edit/ 10 .4324/ 9781003131304/ food -system -transformations-irene-antoni-komar-cordula-kropp-colin-sage.

Sievert, K., Lawrence, M., Parker, C., Baker, P. et al., 2020. Understanding the political challenge of red and processed meat reduction for healthy and sustainable food systems: a narrative review of the literature. *International Journal of Health Policy Management*. https://doi.org/10.34172/ijhpm.2020.238.

Springmann, M., Clark, M., Mason-D'Croz, D. et al., 2018. Options for keeping the food system within environmental limits. *Nature* 562: 519–525. https:// doi.org/ 10 .1038/s41586-018-0594-0.

Steffen, W., Richardson, K., Rockström, J. et al., 2015a. Planetary boundaries: guiding human development on a changing planet. *Science* 347, 6223. http://www.sciencemag .org/content/347/6223/1259855.

Steffen, W., Broadgate, W., Deutsch, L., Gaffney, O., Ludwig, C., 2015b. The trajectory of the Anthropocene: the great acceleration. *The Anthropocene Review* 2, 1: 81–98.

Swinburn, B., Kraak, V., Allender, A. et al., 2019. The global syndemic of obesity, undernutrition, and climate change: The Lancet Commission report. *Lancet* 393: 791–846. http://dx.doi.org/10.1016/S0140-6736(18)32822-8.

Tilman, D., Clark, M., 2014. Global diets link environmental sustainability and human health. *Nature* 515, pp. 518–522.

United Nations Office for Disaster Risk Reduction (UNDRR), 2021. GAR special report on drought 2021. Geneva. https:// www .undrr .org/ publication/ gar -special -report -drought-2021 Accessed 13 August 2021.

Watts, J., Wasley, A., Heal, A., Ross, A., 2020. Revealed: UK supermarket and fast-food chicken linked to deforestation in Brazil. *The Guardian*, 25 November. https://www .theguardian .com/ environment/ 2020/ nov/ 25/ revealed -uk -supermarket -and -fast -food-chicken-linked-to-brazil-deforestation-soy-soya

Weiss, T., 2013. The meat of the global food crisis. *Journal of Peasant Studies* 40, 1: 65–85.

Wiedmann, T., Lenzen, M., Keyßer, L., Steinberger, J., 2020. Scientists' warning on affluence. *Nature Communications* 11, 3107, 2020. https:// doi.org/ 10.1038/ s41467 -020-16941-y.

Willett, W., Rockström, J., Loken, B., Springmann, M. et al., 2019. Food in the Anthropocene: the EAT-Lancet Commission on healthy diets from sustainable food systems. *The Lancet* 393, 10170, 447–492.

4 Agricultural labour in the global food system

Alicia Reigada and Carlos de Castro

Introduction

In the current context of increased global competitiveness in food products and the power of large-scale supply and distribution systems, rural areas that are closely tied to agricultural production have had to adapt to become part of global value chains. One key element of these adjustments has been the organisation and management of labour. One of the principal transformations undergone by the global agricultural production system over recent decades has rested upon the availability of a flexible, cheap, and socio-politically vulnerable workforce (Bonanno and Cavalcanti, 2014; Gertel and Sippel, 2014; Corrado et al., 2017a). The mobilisation and control of this workforce is an integral component of changes occurring within the agri-food system. Agriculture is the most emblematic sector of the food system and its trans-formation constitutes a paradigmatic example of the neoliberal globalisation process that has been gaining ground since the 1980s (Busch and Bain, 2004). McMichael (2013) has argued that this globalisation process is a transition towards a corporate food regime. Every food regime represents a specific configuration of relationships between state and market, involving a specific set of trade, technological, investment and employment policies, all aimed at guaranteeing the stable accumulation of capital in agriculture and ensuring the satisfaction of consumption demands in accordance with the different diets of each social class. According to McMichael, what we are currently witnessing is the consolidation of the corporate food regime initiated at the end of the 1970s.

This chapter addresses the labour market structures that support intensive production systems within the current phase of agri-food globalisation. After locating fresh food production within the framework of the corporate food regime and the configuration of global value chains, the analysis turns to the main processes involved in the construction of labour markets. These include: proletarianisation processes in the rural world; the diversification of labour categories and recruitment channels; the growing segmentation of the labour

89

force in accordance with class, sex and ethnicity; and the different means of ensuring a more flexible, temporary and precarious workforce. These diverse and complex processes are examined by drawing upon a range of published literature reporting empirical studies conducted in some of the main agri-export regions of the world.

The Development of Global Value Chains in Fresh Food

In order to better understand the changes that have occurred in the organisation of agricultural labour, we first briefly identify developments that enabled the emergence of global food supply chains. For since the 1990s, there has been a huge worldwide increase in the number of export-oriented intensive agricultural production enclaves that have been connected to global agri-food chains controlled by large-scale distributors. This has given rise to a new spatial organisation of agricultural production which poses major challenges in terms of coordination and control.

Within the corporate food regime, the growing power of food retailers, coupled with trade liberalisation policies, has played a key role in transforming agricultural production. The 'supermarket revolution' (Reardon et al., 2003; McMichael and Friedmann, 2007) has turned global agricultural production into an oligopolistic system controlled by a small number of supermarket chains based in Europe and the United States (Corrado et al., 2017b). A recent study by Deloitte (2020: 15) ranking the world's 250 leading retailers found that over 10 of the 20 top positions were occupied by those in the food distribution business. Groups such as Walmart, Schwarz (Lidl, Kaufland), Kroger, Aldi, Tesco, Ahold Delhaize (Albert Heijn), Edeka and Auchan have the capacity to purchase agricultural products from almost anywhere in the world, which intensifies their market power and increases competition between agricultural enclaves. However, control of the production chain is not based solely on control of product retail channels, but also on the ability to demand a deep-rooted redesign of production methods through the application of private standards, such as Global Good Agricultural Practices (Global GAP), British Retail Consortium (BRC) and International Featured Standards (IFS) (Konefal et al., 2005; Ramson et al., 2013).

In the literature on global value chains, this issue has long been a focus of attention in terms of governance. In the early 1990s Gereffi observed the emergence of a new type of multinational company, involving large-scale distribution of well-known brands, which were gradually concentrating power through the establishment and control of production chains in export countries without the need for ownership. Their power was based on the coordination and control of the production of numerous, geographically dispersed suppliers and the distribution of production to core countries. The agricultural industry was given as an example of these buyer-driven chains (Gereffi, 1994).

Nevertheless, the complexity of the relationships between leading global distributors and local companies, in both the agri-food and other chains, belied Gereffi's simple categorisation. Indeed, some years later, Gereffi argued that the key to the different forms of governance lay in the fact that positions in the chain are open to permanent dispute among actors. They therefore analysed the way in which local suppliers and producers compete with each other and with leading companies by developing upgrading strategies aimed at improving their position in global value chains (Gereffi et al., 2005).

In relation to global agri-food chains, previous studies have analysed both the strategies used by food retailers to maintain their hegemonic position (Burch and Lawrence, 2007), and the production and technology-based upgrading strategies employed by local businesses to try to improve their competitive and strategic position (Konefal et al., 2005; Bain, 2010). Private standards are the element linking the strategies employed by local producers and those used by food retailers.

Private standards (Global GAP for primary production and BRC and IFS for post-harvest production) represent a new form of governance that enables large-scale distributors to exercise strict control over producers' agricultural practices (Bain, 2010). However, standards are designed and supervised within the framework of an institutional structure (Loconto and Busch, 2010), which, while controlled by large-scale distributors (de Castro et al., 2021), nevertheless provides local producers with the opportunity to introduce upgrading and organisational innovation strategies aimed at improving their position in the chain.

It is within the framework of this trend connecting global agri-food production and distribution chains that some of the principal transformations in agriculture have taken place (Bonanno et al., 1994; McMichael, 1994; Burch and Lawrence, 2005; van der Ploeg, 2008). One of the most important is the shift towards corporate concentration. Connecting to a global agri-food chain involves a major investment in organisational, technological, and training infrastructure, and this has tended to exclude smaller farmers, thereby generating a process of greater corporate control of agriculture to the detriment of family-based production for local and regional markets. Corporate control is

evident in the increased average size of farms and the expansion of the cultivated area in those agricultural regions with ties to global value chains.

The inferior position in which small producers join these chains, in comparison
with their large and medium-sized counterparts, explains their greater fragility
and inability to hold their own against the power of the agents who control the
chain, as well as their subordination to the industrial and scientific-technical
knowledge that governs the functioning of the current agri-food model (van
der Ploeg, 2008). As Etxezarreta (1994) warned, knowledge, technology and
means of production are now mainly induced from outside agriculture, dilut-
ing the autonomy once enjoyed by traditional farmers. Their work depends
on the demands of technology and product regulation, in a process which is,
to Etxezarreta's mind, the 'agricultural' version of the subsumption of labour
to capital.

Moreover, the agri-food industry has implemented major biotechnological
and productive innovations, including new varieties and seeds which give
greater yields, increase the durability in transport from field to supermarket
shelves and are better able to withstand climatic adversity, moulds, and pests.
The artificially selected varieties guided by genetic engineering, following
standardised procedures, dependent on industrial inputs and large amounts
of irrigation water, displace the autochthonous seeds selected year after year
through traditional methods, historically linked to a particular place and to
local ecosystems, farming techniques, diets and cultures.

Other technological innovations include the appearance in some agricultural
enclaves of new structures for protecting crops, such as netting or greenhouses.
These structures have enabled producers to increase their yields, multiply their
harvests, improve their control over ripening times and reduce the risk of crop
loss due to adverse climate conditions. Drip irrigation is another of the innovations introduced in many different enclaves, and has helped producers to
optimise water consumption. The management and intensive use of water are
decisive factors for increasing crop yield and achieving the products' required
organoleptic qualities (colour, size, flavour).

Post-harvest technologies have also become extremely important in the
agri-food system. Local producers have used different types of packaging as
a means of making their products stand out in the value chain. As a consequence, in some enclaves, large industrial facilities have been built near the
farms for automating and standardising the entire food processing operation,
with the aim of improving product quality and adapting to consumer expectations. It is important to note that these packing houses are usually located close

to logistics distribution platforms (transport hubs) since it not only facilitates swift access to markets but also ensures uninterrupted movement of goods within a cool chain where products remain at refrigerated temperatures from the moment they enter the packing houses until they reach the supermarket shelves.

Labour Markets in Globalised Fields

The onset of agri-food globalisation has been accompanied by major transformations in work systems. Some of these changes are linked to the processes of proletarianisation which have occurred in rural areas throughout the world. This proletarianisation should be understood within a framework characterised by the advance of capitalist corporate agri-food, the increased influence of large-scale production companies and the diminishing importance of family agriculture within the sector. This scenario has forced many peasants to become salaried agricultural or industrial workers and has given farmers no choice but to integrate themselves into global agricultural chains if they want to survive.

Alongside the concentration of capital in relatively large production units, Pedreño (1999) identified the need for plentiful labour for intensive crop farming, and the expansion of the phase dedicated to the post-harvest processing of agricultural products as the two basic causes of the increasing percentage of salaried employees among the working agricultural population. The replacement of traditional and locally evolved crop cultivation by industrial farming based on the intensification of production, the difficulty of mechanising certain crops and tasks, and the privileged place occupied by packaging and processing plants for ensuring added value to products, all resulted in a significant increase in demand for labour. In many different agricultural enclaves these changes, which coincided with the decline and gradual abandonment of the family farm, necessitated the mobilisation of non-local reserve sources of labour. This new workforce was mainly made up of international migrants, who constituted an inexhaustible reserve of vulnerable, cheap and flexible labour for large agricultural companies.

Although they maintained some of the principles of Taylorism and Fordism, as evident in the assembly line set up of many of the packing houses, these companies mainly opted for the labour norms established under post-Fordism. It is worth remembering that the employment norm in global agricultural enclaves is based on the fragmentation and segmentation of labour and working conditions characterised by a high level of informal employment, temporary and seasonal contracts, variable and intense working days, low wages, the absence of collective bargaining and extreme flexibility (de Castro, 2014). We shall now examine these aspects in more detail.

Diversification of Labour Recruitment Strategies and Channels

Satisfying demand for high volumes of labour requires mobilising the workforce using different recruitment and hiring strategies. We should start by highlighting the persistence of traditional recruitment methods, in which migratory labour networks are the main channel for supplying the required workforce. Within frameworks often characterised by relationships based on paternalism and control, networks of relatives, neighbours and acquaintances come into play in both domestic and international migration. Although there is no formal intermediary, farm managers often play a key role in recruitment activities.

In the case of permanent employees (who are mostly men) and temporary workers who are kept on throughout most of the season, the existence of verbal agreements between producers and workers facilitates the repetition and continuity of the working relationship. In such cases, contracts are usually signed on arrival. Another part of the workforce is made up of (male and female) workers recruited solely for peak moments of the season. Some of these workers have legal contracts, while others do not. Under this system, producers often recruit from their immediate environment, with town squares and streets being the principal markets for this reserve workforce. Lack of continuity and planning, uncertainty regarding how many days a week they will be required to work, periods of forced unemployment and rotation around different farms all contribute to generating a situation characterised by insecurity and vulnerability, in terms of both employment and living status.

Alongside the traditional system, the labour intermediation model is of great importance in industrial agriculture and one of its main references is found in Californian agriculture. Revisiting the classic study by Thomas (1985), Quaranta (2007) compares two recruitment models used in lettuce farms there. The first is where a company hires undocumented workers through a decentralised, foreman-based system, in which hiring and supervision are carried out in accordance with a web of social obligations and reciprocal actions established by this network. The second is where the company is subject to trade union action and does not have recourse to the mass hiring of undocumented workers, but rather resorts to the power of the foreman, establishing a system of recruitment by seniority.

In Spain, labour intermediation is particularly common in Murcia where the system of *furgoneteros* (literally, van-drivers; referring here to those responsible for recruiting and transporting labourers) underwent a major expansion due to the arrival of migrant workers, the exponential increase in the mobilisation of the reserve workforce and the periodic return of large numbers of illegal immigrants (Pedreño and Riquelme, 2006). As the dismal working conditions imposed by this system became more widely known, the labour inspectorate took action to redress (or at least limit) the situation. Over recent years, particularly since the 2012 labour reform, the *furgonetero* system has gradually lost ground to temporary employment agencies and services companies, two systems in which irregular employment situations are not uncommon (Gadea et al., 2017). Similar arrangements to *furgoneteros* have been identified in many other regions of the world. Examples include *enganchadores* (or contractors) in Argentina (Bendini and Steimbreger, 2010) and Northwest Mexico (de Grammont and Lara, 2004; Lara, 2012), *capitanes* in Morelos, central Mexico (Sánchez, 2006), *caporale* in Italy (Avallone, 2017) and the informal intermediation systems observed in Greece (Papadopoulos and Fratsea, 2017).

In other agricultural enclaves, traditional recruitment systems coexist alongside a very different model, namely seasonal agricultural labourer programmes.[1] These programmes are based on a bilateral agreement which establishes a formal, institutionalised workforce recruitment process involving the governments of the countries of origin and destination, business organisations, trade unions and seasonal migrant workers. The size of the quotas is approved once the government of the country of destination establishes the number and characteristics of the required workforce and the country of origin indicates the availability of its nationals. The country of origin then undertakes to carry out a pre-selection process and to facilitate the administrative infrastructure required to enable employers to make the final selection. Contracts are limited to a specific period, crop and region. In general, producers are obliged to guarantee accommodation for hired labourers at their destination, and to organise transport. This system also includes the principle of commitment to return home, which obliges labourers to go back to their country of origin once the season is over.

For years, bilateral agreements between countries have played a key role in supporting global agricultural value chains. Of particular importance are the experiences identified in North America, with the Bracero programme between Mexico and the USA (1942–1964), the current H2-A programme between those same two countries and the Seasonal Agricultural Workers Programme (SAWP), which was established between Mexico and Canada in 1974 (Binford et al., 2004; Preibisch and Binford, 2007). In the European agri-food industry, the OMI (Office of International Migration) contracts created in France in 1946 are of particular interest, since they represent a model that articulates both a colonial outlook on production and the means of production employed by the agri-industry (Décosse, 2013). The equivalent of this programme in England is the Seasonal Agricultural Workers Scheme (SAWS) and in Spain it is the Contracting in Country-of-Origin system (*Contratación en origen*), which has been operating now for just over two decades. These programmes are excellent examples of the utilitarianism of policies which combine the interests of both the State and capital, reducing the migratory phenomenon to its economic usefulness (Morice, 2006; 2007). As several different empirical studies have pointed out, seasonal migration schemes establish dependent, non-free forms of work, derived from work permits limited to a single economic sector, a single geographical region or a specific pattern (Décosse, 2013).

The different systems described above are accompanied by a diversification of migratory circuits and an increased complexity of migratory patterns (Pedreño et al., 2014). During the 1990s, in what is now a seminal text, the Italian sociologist Enrico Pugliese (1991) demonstrated that the changes occurring in the structure of the labour market brought to light the different ways in which agricultural work was becoming increasingly fragmented as a result of the multiplication of recruitment channels. It should be remembered that the drop in the number of labourers hired directly by farmers due to the increase in subcontracting and the use of intermediaries, is one of the characteristic traits of the post-Fordist model. Moreover, the coexistence of multiple channels has a marked influence on labour segmentation and precarisation.

Labour Segmentation, a Key Element in the Model

The power concentrated in large-scale food distributors and retailers has exerted enormous pressure on the production sector of intensive agriculture enclaves throughout the world. Local producers have responded to this competitive pressure by developing not only production and organisation-related innovation strategies, but also (and mainly) strategies for controlling and ensuring the availability of a cheap, unprotected, and segmented labour force (Bonanno and Cavalcanti, 2014; Corrado et al., 2017a); strategies which have, in many cases, enabled them to maintain their profit margins.

Any examination of the segmentation dynamics that structure labour markets in the globalised agri-food system must necessarily take into account the trends followed by workforce substitution processes. Following the restructuring of production that paved the way for the corporate food regime, the segmentation of the workforce in accordance with class, ethnicity and sex became a key strategy for reducing costs in the only link in the chain still under the control of producers: workers.

The workforce substitution processes that have occurred throughout the social history of intensive crop farming are good indicators of the role played by certain social groups, such as immigrants and women, in the maintenance of agri-food production. Even though many different factors have contributed to the increase in, and internationalisation of, labour-related migratory flows, the demand generated by labour markets and the orientation of public policies are two decisive elements that help model the social composition of the working class employed in the sector. The trends which have been present for some time now in Californian agriculture, considered by many to be the global benchmark, reveal how political forces, economic organisation and class relations intervene in the construction of a strongly segmented labour market (Thomas, 1985; Wells, 1996). Many analyses coincide both in highlighting the link between the globalised agri-food system and the ethnicisation and feminisation of work (Lara, 1998; Barrientos et al., 2004; Figueroa, 2015), and in identifying the work carried out by migrant women in global value chains as one of the facets of the new political economy of gender (Anthias, 2014).

While from a global perspective it is important to detect regularities, it is also crucial to pay careful attention to local particularities. In other words, we should be alert to the differences which exist between enclaves in terms of selection criteria, migratory patterns and specific forms of segmentation. Such differences are clearly evident in the continued importance of internal migration in certain leading agri-export regions of Mexico and Argentina, which contrasts sharply with the key role played by international migration in the United States, France, Italy and Spain. For example, in the case of green bean farming in the State of Morelos (Sánchez and Saldaña, 2011) and of horticulture in Sinaloa (Lara, 2012), both in Mexico, indigenous labourers mainly come from the States of Guerrero, Oaxaca and Puebla. Similarly, the expansion of agriculture in the Río Negro Basin (Argentina) is mainly based on internal migration, with most labourers coming from the north-western part of the country, principally the Tucumán Province, whereas international migration from Chile has fallen (Bendini et al., 1999).

In the agricultural regions of the Spanish coast (Catalonia, Valencia, Murcia and Andalusia), on the other hand, domestic labourers from other parts of the country have been largely replaced by international labour migration (Torres, 2009; Pedreño et al., 2014; Reigada et al., 2017). Migrants from the Maghreb, who began working on Mediterranean farms during the second half of the 1980s, were followed a decade later by those from Mauritania and sub-Saharan

Africa (Senegal, Mali, Nigeria, Côte d'Ivoire). In France, for example, migration from the Maghreb (especially Morocco) remains important (Décosse, 2013), while in Italy, the local workforce has gradually been replaced by labourers from Morocco and sub-Saharan Africa, mainly Senegal. Within Spain's Mediterranean agriculture most migrants were young men who were hired on site on a temporary basis. Some were legal immigrants, some were not, and all were characterised by a high degree of mobility between farms, following the circuit of agricultural seasons around Spain. This migration had a pull effect and was followed by settlement strategies and processes of family reunification. In addition to the labour force from the Maghreb and sub-Saharan Africa, there are also many migrants from Latin America (mainly Ecuador and Colombia) and Eastern Europe (particularly Romania) working in the agricultural sector. Migration from Ecuador follows a different pattern from the others mentioned above, since coming to Spain to find work often forms part of a family migration plan, and Ecuadorian migrants tend not to move around the different agricultural regions, preferring instead to settle in one place.

The specificities linked to ethnic and national origin appear also to be connected to variability in terms of sex. Whereas many different types of agriculture are characterised by a clear feminisation of handling and packaging tasks, the same is not true of field labour. The feminisation of harvesting work, which has been evident in strawberry farming in Spain since the beginning of this millennium, following the displacement of male labourers from the Maghreb and sub-Saharan Africa (Moreno, 2009; Reigada, 2012; Hellio, 2017), clashes, for example, with the masculinisation observed in strawberry harvesting in Canada (Preibisch and Encalada, 2010). Furthermore, although grape harvesting in Northeast Brazil has become gradually more feminised, vegetable harvesting in Southeast Spain continues to be a predominantly male domain.

The labour segregation that structures globalised agriculture prompts questions about the cultural values and ideologies that legitimate and orient it. An entire set of capacities, qualities and abilities attributed to women and certain groups of immigrants are mobilised within these production systems, contributing to naturalising ethnic, sexual and class assumptions (Anthias, 2014; de Castro et al., 2020). Let us return to the example of green bean farming in Mexico. More than fifty years after the crop was first introduced in the region, cutting became a job carried out by immigrants rather than local cutters. This taxing activity, which is carried out in the full heat of the sun with no fixed number of working hours, is considered by the local population to be a job fit only 'for those from the other side'; moreover, the local mindset tends to define the Mixtecos as 'more savage' and 'better suited to hard labour' than the Nahuas (Sánchez, 2006). Similar conclusions have been reached by studies analysing the ideological frameworks underpinning the construing by political and economic institutions of foreign male agricultural labourers in Canada as a source of cheap, seasonal and racialised labour (Preibisch and Encalada, 2010).

Delicacy, patience, flexibility and capacity for hard work are just some of the values culturally construed as female in the dynamics of sexual segmentation. For example, whereas the strawberry farms of Morocco mainly demand young, unmarried women from rural areas (Moreno, 2014) and in Spain the profile of an ideal worker is a middle-aged woman with children in her care (Reigada, 2021; Hellio and Moreno, 2017), in Canada, other projected values take precedence, mainly linked in this case to male workers. It should not be forgotten that agriculture based on the masculinisation of work requires careful attention to be paid to gender relations. As Marie France Labrecque (2014) points out, the fact that only 3 percent of the workers recruited in Canada through the Seasonal Agricultural Worker Programme (SAWP) are women shows the extent to which public policies are based on a cultural representation of the differential roles of men and women in agriculture. Grape farming in the San Francisco Valley in Brazil reveals the association between the recent demand for high-quality products, the establishment of private standards and female work; a relationship which is accompanied by new forms of stress, pressure, and control mechanisms in the workspace (Cavalcanti, 2014). This same association has also been identified in other types of farming (Bain, 2010; Lee, 2010; Bonanno and Cavalcanti, 2012; Moraes and Cutillas, 2014).

It should be remembered that the discrimination which occurs as a result of the ethnic and sexual division of labour, according to which migrant workers and women are excluded from better paid jobs (management, supervision and control, marketing, technical tasks and agricultural engineering), gives rise to wage discrimination. Female migrant workers are assigned to harvesting and handling tasks not so much due to their supposed manual dexterity as to their willingness to work for low wages. Sexual ideologies use the values of sensitivity and delicacy to disguise what is actually hard, monotonous and repetitive work in both the packing house and the fields. The jobs are poorly paid and exhausting, and usually involve maintaining uncomfortable, unhealthy postures for long periods of time, often giving rise to injuries and sick leave.

Arguments based on certain skills and some people's greater capacity for work must be understood within the framework of those linked to greater availability and responsibility and the lower levels of social-labour conflict associated with employing a foreign, indigenous, or female workforce, which is less organised and unionised than its native, male counterpart. As de Grammont and Lara (2004) point out, the search for workers in poor, dispersed and distant regions is not only prompted by a scarcity of available local labour; rather, it stems mainly from the desire to find a cheap and vulnerable workforce with less organisational experience.

Their position in the social, political and occupational structure explains the obstacles that limit the capacity for mobilisation of this new class of day labourer. It is important to start by highlighting the role played in this by immigration laws and labour policies, which are based on an instrumental conception of immigration that categorises migrants as either seasonal or illegal workers. The division created by migratory policies between legal and illegal immigration serves to create a hierarchy of worker categories, and forces a connection between the labour market, political institutions and the legal system. This division also exacerbates the criminalisation and vulnerability of undocumented seasonal migrant workers, annulling their citizenship rights. The conditions under which they work (mobility, substitution and rotation, temporariness, vulnerability), the forms of fragmentation derived from labour intermediation, and labour segmentation business strategies all serve to impede migrant workers' ability to organise themselves (Pedreño et al., 2014). Alongside these obstacles, we should also bear in mind the fact that class unionism has a hard time adapting to the new social-labour scenario of globalised agriculture. Indeed, as Mills (2005) argues, in relation to labour-intensive industries (electronics, textile, food products), the question is not whether workers can organise themselves, but rather what conditions will enable them to mobilise despite all the obstacles in their path.

The Flexibility, Temporariness, and Precariousness of Agricultural Work

One of the changes currently occurring in the organisation of work in the agri-food industry is the spread of labour flexibility formulas (Lara, 1995). The increased flexibility of labour management has given rise to an intensification of worker exploitation and precariousness. As shown previously, business strategies based on outsourcing labour supply to informal and formal intermediaries have, alongside ethnic and sexual segmentation, contributed to establishing a framework of labour relations characterised by extreme precariousness. We will now summarise the principal aspects of the precariousness of agricultural work.

A key feature of intensive agricultural production enclaves is that most labour is hired on a temporary or seasonal basis by intermediaries, while many work with no contract at all but rather are sourced through informal community networks. The result is that agricultural workers usually sign various temporary contracts throughout the year, thanks to the staggered nature of crop harvests in neighbouring regions. Moreover, a significant, yet hard to quantify, proportion of these contracts are informal. As a result of the circumstances described above, only a small part of the workforce has a stable contract. These workers tend to be family members and trusted employees who occupy positions requiring a high level of technical qualification, or administrative and financial management posts.

This high proportion of temporary contracts is partly linked to the seasonal nature of agricultural activity. Although the technological modernisation of agricultural production has somewhat attenuated this seasonality, there are still huge differences between labour demands at different times of the year. In Latin America, a good example of this is the agricultural activity which takes place in one municipality in the State of Pernambuco (Brazil), which was responsible for 121,000 of the 222,681 jobs created from 2000 to 2009 and of which 118,000 were seasonal. Other similar examples can be found in Argentina (Bendini and Steimbreger, 2010) and Mexico (Lara, 2012). In Europe, the presence of seasonal workers moving from harvest to harvest across various regions is a common occurrence in France (Mésini, 2014; Crenn, 2017), Spain (Reigada, 2012; Hellio, 2017, Gadea et al., 2017), Italy (Perrotta, 2017; Avallone, 2017) and Greece (Papadopoulos and Fratsea, 2017). The seasonal nature of the work therefore prevents these labourers from finding full-time employment throughout the entire year. The economic shortcomings of temporary work are often partially compensated for by the concatenation of harvests, unemployment benefits (providing they exist) and employment in other sectors.

Day labourers may work for between 6 and 10 months a year, as reflected in the cases of Sinaloa and Morelos in Mexico, Murcia and Huelva in Spain, Neuquén and Pomán in Argentina and Pernambuco in Brazil (Cavalcanti, 2014; Cruz and Quaranta, 2014; Lara et al., 2014; Moraes et al., 2012; Reigada, 2012). Working days during active periods tend to be increasingly long, intense and variable (Lara, 2012; de Castro, 2014; Hedberg, 2014). This is because, first, workers need to make the most of periods of maximum activity to compensate wage-wise for the months in which they do not work; and, second, employers are eager to harvest their crops as quickly as possible in order to avoid deterioration and to market them in the shortest possible time frame, circumstances which are key factors in the intensification of work. Moreover, working days are made longer by the journeys labourers must often make to reach the farms on which they are employed. For example, in the Spanish region of Murcia, a survey carried out among day labourers in 2001 revealed that 62 percent were working between 9 and 10 hours a day, without counting daily travel (CES Informe, 2001). Among Thai workers harvesting berries for two months a year in Sweden, Hedberg (2014) reported working days of between 13 and 17 hours, including transport.

As regards salaries, official statistics do not usually reflect the complexity of the situation. Moreover, they are misleading in that they do not take into account the fact that most jobs exist within the shadow economy or through intermediaries. A study on European labour relations in the agricultural sector carried out in 2006 by the European Foundation for the Improvement of Living and Working Conditions concluded that farming is a sector in which the mean wage is below the EU mean.[2] Qualitative studies on the sector have reached similar conclusions in different countries (Segura et al., 2002; Rogaly, 2008; Muzlera, 2014).

It is also important to highlight the fact that the most frequent remuneration system in these enclaves is the piecework model (Rogaly, 2008; Lara, 2012). In Pomán (Argentina), remuneration depends on the value assigned to each box of harvested olives, which is negotiated with the employer or intermediary. Daily wages can reach up to 150 pesos (27 euros) (Cruz and Quaranta, 2014). In Pernambuco (Brazil), for example, labourers are paid between 0.10 and 0.50 centavos per corn plant (Cavalcanti, 2014). In Morelos and Sinaloa (Mexico), a value is also assigned to the amount of produce harvested, with labourers earning up to 134 pesos (approximately 8 euros) per day (Lara et al., 2014). This remuneration system serves to further intensify working days, as labourers strive to earn as much as possible. Piecework remuneration also renders wages more variable, since if working hours are reduced due to unfavourable climate conditions, for example, labourers' earning power is also diminished. Moreover, it is important to highlight the fact that, in these enclaves, intermediaries often hold on to part of the wages paid by companies, for services such as intermediation, transport, food or accommodation (Lara, 2012; Pedreño, 1998; Sánchez, 2006).

In a context increasingly characterised by informal employment, temporary contracts and the extreme flexibility of labour legislation, which hardly sets any limits at all on work management, the power wielded by employers and intermediaries has grown, severely constraining workers' capacity for collective bargaining (Selwyn, 2007). There are two reasons for this. First, workers are heavily dependent on their employers, since they represent the only pathway through which they can gain employment, season after season. And, second, the temporary nature of the contracts and the informal nature of labour relations make it difficult for collective bargaining mechanisms, such as trade union organisations, to develop. Consequently, conflicts tend to be managed on an individual basis, giving rise to situations in which workers' negotiating power is very weak. From the workers' perspective, the most frequent conflicts are mainly related to wages (piecework negotiation), length of contract, type of contract (formal or informal), suitable qualifications, work intensity, the unjustified prolongation of working days and the reduction of rest periods; whereas from the producers' perspective, they are usually linked to lack of occupational discipline and unjustified absenteeism.

Collective bargaining is poorly developed in these enclaves. Although, when establishing salary levels, the parties involved occasionally have recourse to the collective agreement signed in another sector or to some other regulation with more authority (Cruz and Quaranta, 2014), more commonly, conflicts are managed coercively using diverse control mechanisms (Selwyn, 2007). One of the most direct control mechanisms used is dismissal, either for lack of discipline or lack of productivity. Furthermore, intermediaries often monitor productivity, the duration of rest periods, bathroom breaks (Bendini and Steimbreger, 2010; Riella et al., 2011) and even labourers' behaviour and habits outside work, particularly in the case of those they deem to be conflictive or who attempt to unionise labour relations. In some regions, such as Sinaloa (Mexico), for example, there is also another figure in play, namely that of the 'social worker'. These are generally women who are hired to ensure workers comply with certain rules, such as not eating the products they harvest or package while working, not listening to music through earphones, not defecating outside and wearing long-sleeved shirts, and so on (Lara et al., 2014).

All this has resulted in a trend towards the individualisation of conflict negotiation. Workers are forced to negotiate their working conditions on an individual basis, mainly with the intermediary, something which weakens their negotiating position. This weakness is even greater if we take into consideration the fact that most of them are migrants and their legal situation renders them particularly vulnerable from a legal perspective. This is due to the fact that residence permits are commonly linked to work contracts, a circumstance that gives employers or intermediaries disproportionate negotiating power. This subordinate relationship is further exacerbated in the case of illegal migrant workers.

Conclusions

The key argument of this chapter is that the integration of agricultural producers into the fiercely competitive global fresh food production system, which is
now largely under the strict control of food retailer groups, was only possible
thanks to business strategies designed to render agricultural work more flexible and precarious. We have described the ways in which worker recruitment
strategies and the ethnic and sexual segmentation of labour have contributed
to establishing highly precarious working conditions. In terms of recruitment,
we have shown how both informal and formal intermediation tends to select
(differently in each region) mainly foreign workers in situations of political
weakness and strong institutional dependence. As regards segmentation, we
have shown how cultural values and sexual ideologies have been used to justify
task assignments whose real purpose is to cut labour costs.

The result is the general deterioration of working conditions that reflect the
political and institutional weakness of workers' negotiating position, and
which are embodied by unstable, insecure and vulnerable contract relations,
low and variable wages and increasingly long and intense working days. In
sum, the corporate food regime is structurally based upon the reproduction
and management of cheap, flexible and socio-politically vulnerable labour.
The COVID-19 pandemic has generated a paradoxical situation since, on the
one hand, agricultural workers were declared essential workers, but, at the
same time, their working conditions worsened not only due to their exposure
to the risk of infection but also due to an intensification of work. However, the
impact of the pandemic on agricultural workers goes beyond the workplace.
They have had greater difficulties in accessing public health services and the
programmes and resources offered by trade unions and non-governmental
organisations. They have lived with great anxiety being away from their loved
ones during the health crisis. In addition, the closing of borders between countries that source and receive workforce delayed the return of many seasonal
workers to their homes after the end of the agricultural season, generating
situations of tension and uncertainty. The pandemic, therefore, has contributed to accentuate in several ways the structural position of subordination of
agricultural workers.

Our final thought is that the structural crisis of agricultural work within the
global food system offers an important opportunity to undertake and intensify
research in three key areas. First, to examine the implications – as well as
the drivers – of the new migrant mobilities on farm recruitment strategies.
Second, to analyze the continuing development and influence of private and

international labour standards on working conditions. And third, to explore forms of collective action and informal organisation of agricultural workers in different parts of the world and the opportunities to be gained from sharing these through international collaborative networks.

Notes

1. For a compilation of empirical studies on the principal seasonal agricultural labourer programmes worldwide, see Sánchez and Lara (2015).
2. http://www.eurofound.europa.eu/eiro/2005/09/study/tn0509101s.htm.

References

Anthias, F., 2014. The Intersections of Class, Gender, Sexuality and 'Race': The Political Economy of Gendered Violence. *International Journal of Politics, Culture and Society*, 27: 153–171.

Avallone, G., 2017. The Land of Informal Intermediation: The Social Regulation of Migrant Agricultural Labour in the Piana del Sele, Italy. In Corrado, A., de Castro, C., Perrotta, D. (eds) *Migration and Agriculture: Mobility and Change in the Mediterranean Area*. London: Routledge, pp. 217–230.

Bain, C., 2010. Governing the Global Value Chain: GLOBALGAP and the Chilean Fresh Fruit Industry. *International Journal of Sociology of Agriculture and Food*, 17 (1): 1–23.

Barrientos, S., Kabeer, N. and Hossain, N., 2004. *The Gender Dimensions of the Globalization of Production*. Geneva: International Labour Organization.

Bendini, M., Radonich, M., Steimbreger, N., 1999. Historia de la vulnerabilidad social de los 'golondrinas' en la cuenca frutícola del río Negro. In Bendini, M., Radonich, M. (eds) *De golondrinas y otros migrantes*. Buenos Aires: La Colmena, pp. 5–23.

Bendini, M., Steimbreger, N., 2010. Trabajadores golondrinas y nuevas áreas frutícolas. Las mismas temporadas, otros territorios. In Lara, S. (ed.) *Migraciones de trabajo y movilidad territorial*. México: Miguel Ángel Porrúa, pp. 281–307.

Binford, L., Carrasco Rivas, G., Arana Hernández, S., 2004. *Rumbo a Canadá. La migración canadiense de trabajadores agrícolas tlaxcaltecas*, México, Ediciones Taller Abierto.

Bonanno, A., Busch, L., Friedland, W., Gouveia, L., Mingione, E., 1994. *From Columbus to ConAgra: The Globalisation of Food and Agriculture*. Lawrence: University Press of Kansas.

Bonanno, A., Cavalcanti, J.S., 2012. Globalization, Food Quality and Labor: The Case of Grape Production in North-Eastern Brazil. *International Journal of Sociology of Agriculture and Food* 19, 1: 37–55.

Bonanno, A., Cavalcanti, J.S., 2014. *Labour Relations in Globalized Food*. Bingley: Emerald Press.

Burch, D., Lawrence, G., 2005. Supermarket Own Brands, Supply Chains and the Transformation of the Agri-food System. *International Journal of Sociology of Agriculture and Food*, 13, 1: 1–18.

Burch, D., Lawrence, G. (eds) 2007. *Supermarkets and Agri-food Supply Chains. Transformations in the Production and Consumption of Foods*. Cheltenham, UK and Northampton, MA, USA: Edward Elgar Publishing.

Busch, L., Bain, C., 2004. New! Improved? The transformation of the Global Agrifood System. *Rural Sociology* 69, 3: 321–346.

Cavalcanti, J., 2014. De los extremos de la calidad y la permanente vulnerabilidad: los trabajadores del valle de Sao Francisco en el nordeste de Brasil. In Pedreño, A. (ed.) *De cadenas, migrantes y jornaleros. Los territorios rurales en las cadenas globales agroalimentarias*. Madrid: Talasa Ediciones, pp. 219–236.

CES Informe. 2001. *Condiciones de trabajo en el sector agroalimentario de la región de Murcia*. Murcia: Consejo Económico y Social de la Región de Murcia.

Corrado, A., de Castro, C., Perrotta, D. (eds) 2017a. *Migration and Agriculture: Mobility and Change in the Mediterranean Area*. London: Routledge.

Corrado, A., de Castro, C., Perrotta, D. (eds) 2017b. Cheap Food, Cheap Labour, High Profits. Agriculture and Mobility in the Mediterranean. In Corrado, A., de Castro, C., Perrotta, D. (eds) *Migration and Agriculture: Mobility and Change in the Mediterranean Area*. London: Routledge, pp. 1–24.

Crenn, C., 2017. Wine Heritage and the ethnicization of labour: Arab workers in the Bourdeaux vineyards. In Corrado, A., de Castro, C., Perrotta, D. (eds) *Migration and Agriculture: Mobility and Change in the Mediterranean Area*. London: Routledge, pp. 42–57.

Cruz, R., Quaranta, G., 2014. La conformación de un mercado de trabajo a través de un proceso de restructuración agrícola: la actividad olivícola en el departamento de Pomán, Argentina. In Pedreño, A. (ed.) *De cadenas, migrantes y jornaleros. Los territorios rurales en las cadenas globales agroalimentarias*. Madrid: Talasa Ediciones, pp. 78–93.

Décosse, F., 2013. Experimentando el utilitarismo migratorio: los jornaleros marroquíes bajo contrato OMI en Francia. In Aquino A., Varela A., Décosse F. (eds) *Desafiando Fronteras. Control de la movilidad y experiencias migratorias en el contexto capitalista*. Oaxaca: Frontera Press, Sur+ Ediciones, pp. 113–128.

Deloitte, 2020. Global Powers of Retailing. Business Report https:// www2 .deloitte .com/ content/ dam/ Deloitte/ at/ Documents/ consumer -business/ at -global -powers -retailing-2020.pdf (last visit: 28 March 2021).

de Castro, C., 2014. La desdemocratización de las relaciones laborales en los enclaves de producción agrícola. In Pedreño, A. (ed.) *De cadenas, migrantes y jornaleros. Los territorios rurales en las cadenas globales agroalimentarias*. Madrid: Talasa Ediciones, pp. 59–77.

de Castro, C., Reigada, A., Gadea, E., 2020. The devaluation of female labour in fruit and vegetable packaging plants in Spanish Mediterranean agriculture', *Organization*, 27, 2: 232–250. https://doi.org/10.1177/1350508419883387.

de Castro Pericacho, C., Gadea Montesinos, E., Sánchez García, M., 2021. Estandarizadores. La nueva burocracia privada que controla la calidad y la seguridad alimentaria en las cadenas globales agrícolas. *Revista Española de Sociología*, 30, 11, a16. https://doi.org/10.22325/fes/res.2021.16.

Etxezarreta, M., 1994. Trabajo y agricultura: los cambios del sistema de trabajo en una agricultura en transformación. *Agricultura y Sociedad*, 72: 121–166.

Figueroa, T., 2015. Gendered Sharecropping: Waged and Unwaged Mexican Immigrant Labor in the California Strawberry Fields. *Signs: Journal of Women in Culture and Society*, 40, 4: 917-938.

Gadea, E. Pedreño, A., de Castro, C., 2017. Producing and Mobilizing Vulnerable Workers. The Agribusiness of the Region of Murcia, Spain. In Corrado, A., de Castro, C., Perrotta, D. (eds) *Migration and Agriculture: Mobility and Change in the Mediterranean Area*. London: Routledge, pp. 79-94.

Gereffi, G. 1994. The Organization of Buyer-Driven Global Commodity Chains: How U.S. Retailers Shape Overseas Production Networks. In Gereffi, G., Korzeniewicz, M. (eds) *Commodity chains and global capitalism*. Westport, CT: Praeger, pp. 95-122.

Gereffi, G., Humphrey, J., Sturgeon, T., 2005. The Governance of Global Value Chains. *Review of International Political Economy*, 12(1), 78-104.

Gertel, J., Sippel, S.R. (eds), 2014. *Seasonal Workers in Mediterranean Agriculture. The Social Costs of Eating Fresh*. London: Routledge.

Grammont, H. de, Lara, S., 2004. *Encuesta a hogares de jornaleros agrícolas migrantes en regiones hortícolas de México*. Mexico: IIS–UNAM.

Hedberg, C., 2014. Restructuring Global Labour Markets: Recruitment Agencies and Work Relations in the Wild Berry Commodity Chain. In Bonanno, A., Cavalcanti, J. (eds) *Labor Relations in Globalized*. London: Emerald Group Publishing, pp. 33-56.

Hellio, E., 2017. They Know You'll Leave, Like a Dog Moving onto the Next Bin: Undocumented Male and Seasonal Contracted Female Workers in the Agricultural Labour Market of Huelva, Spain. In Corrado, A., de Castro, C., Perrotta, D. (eds) *Migration and Agriculture: Mobility and Change in the Mediterranean Area*. London: Routledge, pp. 198-216.

Hellio, M., Moreno, J., 2017. Produciendo fresas en el Mediterráneo occidental: deslocalización productiva, contrataciones en origen y feminización del trabajo en los sectores exportadores de Marruecos y España. *Revista Navegar. Revista de Estudos de E/Inmigraçao*, 5, 3.

Konefal, J., Mascarenhas, M., Hatanaka, M., 2005. Governance in the Global Agro-food System: Backlighting the Role of Transnational Supermarket Chains. *Agriculture and Human Values*, 22: 291-302.

Labrecque, M. F., 2014. Economía política feminista e interseccionalidad: retos para la etnografía. In Oehmichen, C. (ed.) *La etnografía y el trabajo de campo en las ciencias sociales*. México D.F.: UNAM/IIA, pp.195-214.

Lara, S., 1995. La feminización del trabajo asalariado en los cultivos de exportación no tradicionales en América Latina: efectos de una flexibilidad salvaje. In Lara, S. (ed.) *Jornaleras, temporeras y bóias-frias: el rostro femenino del mercado de trabajo rural en América Latina*. Caracas: Nueva Sociedad, pp. 13-34.

Lara, S., 1998. *Nuevas experiencias productivas y nuevas formas de organización flexible del trabajo en la agricultura mexicana*, México D.F.: Juan Pablos Editor.

Lara, S. 2012. Los territorios migratorios como espacios de articulación de migraciones nacionales e internacionales. Cuatro casos del contexto mexicano. *Política y Sociedad*, 49, 1: 89-102.

Lara, S., Sánchez, K., Saldaña, A., 2014. Asentamientos de trabajadores inmigrantes en torno a enclaves de agricultura intensiva en México: nuevas formas de apropiación de espacios de disputa. In Pedreño, A. (ed.) *De cadenas, migrantes y jornaleros. Los territorios rurales en las cadenas globales agroalimentarias*. Madrid: Talasa Ediciones, pp. 150-171.

Lee S., 2010. Unpacking the Packing Plant: Nicaraguan Migrant Women's Work in Costa Rica's Evolving Export Agriculture Sector. *Signs: Journal of Women in Culture and Society*, 35, 2: 317–342.

Loconto, A., Busch, L., 2010. Standards, Techno-Economic Networks, and Playing Fields: Performing the Global Market Economy. *Review of International Political Economy*, 17, 3: 507–536.

McMichael, P., 1994. Introduction: Agro-Food System Restructuring-Unity in Diversity. In McMichael, P., *The Global Restructuring of Agro-Food Systems*. Ithaca, NY: Cornell University Press.

McMichael, P., Friedmann, H., 2007. Situating the 'Retailing Revolution'. In Burch, D., Lawrence, G. (eds) *Supermarkets and Agri-food Supply Chains. Transformations in the Production and Consumption of Foods*. Cheltenham, UK and Northampton, MA, USA: Edward Elgar Publishing, pp. 291–319.

McMichael, P., 2013. *Food Regimes and Agrarian Questions*. Halifax and Winnipeg: Fernwood Publishing.

Mésini, B., 2014. The Transnational Recruitment of Temporary Latino Workers in European Agriculture. In Gertel, J., Sippel, S.R. (eds) *Seasonal workers in Mediterranean Agriculture. The Social Costs of Eating Fresh*. London: Routledge, pp. 71–82.

Mills, M., 2005. From Nimble Fingers to Raised Fists: Women and Labor Activism in Globalizing Thailand. *Signs: Journal of Women in Culture and Society*, 31, 1: 117–144.

Moraes, N., Gadea, E., Pedreño, A., de Castro, C., 2012. Enclaves globales agrícolas y migraciones de trabajo: convergencias globales y regulaciones transnacionales. *Política y sociedad*, 49, 1: 13–34.

Moraes, N., Cutillas, I., 2014. Nuevos dispositivos de regulación transnacional: un análisis sobre los estándares de calidad y responsabilidad social y su impacto en los enclaves globales agrícolas. In Pedreño, A. (ed.) *De cadenas, migrantes y jornaleros. Los territorios rurales en las cadenas globales agroalimentarias*. Madrid: Talasa Ediciones, pp. 120–135.

Moreno, J., 2009. Los contratos en origen de temporada: mujeres marroquíes en la agricultura onubense. *Revista De Estudios Internacionales Mediterráneos*, 7: 58–78.

Moreno, J., 2014. Labour and Gender Relations in Moroccan Strawberry Culture. In Gertel, J., Sippel, S. (eds) *Seasonal workers in Mediterranean Agriculture. The Social Costs of Eating Fresh*. London: Routledge, pp. 199–210.

Morice, A., 2006. Pas de séjour sans travail, ou les pièges du contrat saisonnier. *Migrations Société*, 18, 107: 211–231.

Morice, A., 2007. El difícil reconocimiento de los sin papeles en Francia. Entre tentación individualista y movilización colectiva. In Suarez-Navas, L., Macià, R., Moreno, A. (eds) *Las luchas de los sin papeles y la extensión de la ciudadanía*. Madrid: Traficantes de Sueños, pp. 39–71.

Muzlera, J., 2014. Capitalization Strategies and Labor in Agricultural Machinery Contractors in Argentina. In Bonanno, A., Cavalcanti, J. (eds) *Labor Relations in Globalized Food* (Research in Rural Sociology and Development, Volume 20), Bingley: Emerald Group Publishing, pp. 57–74.

Papadopoulos, A., Fratsea, L., 2017. Migrant Labour And Intensive Agriculture Production in Greece: The Case of Manolada Strawberry Industry. In Corrado, A., de Castro, C., Perrotta, D. (eds) *Migration and Agriculture: Mobility and Change in the Mediterranean Area*. London: Routledge, pp. 128–144.

Pedreño, A., 1998. *Del jornalero agrícola al obrero de las factorías vegetales*. Madrid: Ministerio de Agricultura, Pesca y Alimentación.

Pedreño, A. 1999. Taylor y Ford en los campos: trabajo, género y etnia en el cambio tecnológico y organizacional de la agricultura industrial murciana, *Sociología del Trabajo* (nueva época), 35: 25-56.

Pedreño, A., Riquelme, P., 2006. La condición inmigrante de los nuevos trabajadores rurales. *Revista española de estudios agrosociales y pesqueros*, 211: 189-238.

Pedreño, A, Gadea, E., de Castro, C., 2014. Labor, Gender, and Political Conflicts in the Global Agri-food System: The Case of the Agri-export Model in Murcia, Spain. In Bonanno, A., Cavalcanti, J. (eds) *Labor Relations in Globalized Food* (Research in Rural Sociology and Development, Volume 20). Bingley: Emerald Group Publishing, pp. 193-214.

Perrotta, D., 2017. Processing Tomatoes in the Era of Retailing Revolution: Mechanization and Migrant Labor in Northern and Southern Italy. In Corrado, A., de Castro, C., Perrotta, D. (eds) *Migration and Agriculture: Mobility and Change in the Mediterranean Area*. London: Routledge, pp. 58-76.

Ploeg van der J.D., 2008. *The New Peasantries. Struggles for Autonomy and Sustainability in an Era of Empire and Globalization*. London: Earthscan.

Preibisch, K., Binford, L., 2007. Interrogating Racialized Global Labour Supply: An Exploration of the Racial/National Replacement of Foreign Agricultural Workers in Canada. *Canadian Review of Sociology and Anthropology*, 44, 1: 5-36.

Preibisch, K., Encalada, E., 2010. The Other Side of el Otro Lado: Mexican Migrant Women and Labor Flexibility in Canadian Agriculture. *Signs: Journal of Women in Culture and Society*, 35, 2: 289-316.

Pugliese, E. 1991. Agriculture and the New Division of Labor. In Friedland, W. et al. (eds), *Towards a New Political Economy of Agriculture*. Boulder, Westview Press, pp. 137-150.

Quaranta, G., 2007. *Reestructuración y organización social del trabajo en producciones agrarias de la región pampeana argentina*. Tesis de doctorado. ISEC-UCO. Córdoba.

Ramson, E., Bain, C., Higgins, V., 2013. Private Agri-food Standards: Supply Chains and the Governance of Standard. *International Journal of Sociology of Agriculture and Food*, 20, 2: 147-154.

Reardon, T., Timmer, C.P., Barrett, C.B., Berdegue, J., 2003. The Rise of Supermarkets in Africa, Asia and Latin America. *American Journal of Agricultural Economics*, 85, 5: 1140-1146.

Reigada, A., 2012. Más allá del discurso sobre la 'inmigración ordenada': contratación en origen y feminización del trabajo en el cultivo de la fresa en Andalucía. *Política y Sociedad*, 49, 1: 103-122.

Reigada, A., Delgado, Pérez, D., Soler, M., 2017. La sostenibilidad social de la agricultura intensiva almeriense: una mirada desde la organización social del trabajo. AGER: Revista de Estudios sobre Despoblación y Desarrollo Rural, 23: 1-26.

Reigada, A., 2021. A Link in the Global Agri-food Chains: Hiring Policies, Labor, and Sexuality in the Strawberry Fields in Andalusia. *Current Anthropology*, under review.

Riella, A., Tulio, M., Lombardo, R., 2011. Los jornaleros de las cadenas de producción de alimentos en fresco: el caso del arándano en Uruguay. In Pedreño, A. (ed.) *De cadenas, migrantes y jornaleros. Los territorios rurales en las cadenas globales agroalimentarias*. Madrid: Talasa Ediciones, pp. 94-109.

Rogaly, B., 2008. Intensification of Workplace Regimes in British Horticulture. The Role of Migrant Workers. *Population, Space and Place*, 14: 497-510.

Sánchez, K., 2006. *Los capitanes de Tenextepango. Un estudio sobre intermediación cultural*. Mexico: UAEM, Miguel Ángel Porrúa.

Sánchez, K., Saldaña, A., 2011. Configuración de corrientes migratorias alrededor del mercado de trabajo de la Okra en Morelos. In Lara, S. (ed.) *Los 'encadenamientos migratorios' en espacios de agricultura intensiva*. México: Miguel Ángel Porrúa, pp. 151-211.

Sánchez, M. J., Lara, S. (eds) 2015. *Los programas de trabajadores agrícolas temporales ¿una solución a los retos de las migraciones en la globalización*. México: UNAM-Instituto de Investigaciones Sociales.

Segura, P., Pedreño, A., De Juana, S., 2002. Configurando la Región murciana para las frutas y hortalizas: Racionalización productiva, agricultura salarial y nueva estructura social del trabajo jornalero. *Revista Áreas*, 22: 71-93.

Selwyn, B., 2007. Labor Process and Workers' Bargaining Power in Export Grape Production, North-East Brazil. *Journal of Agrarian Change*, 7: 526-553.

Thomas, R.J., 1985. *Citizenship, Gender and Work. Social Organization of Industrial Agriculture*. Los Angeles: University of California Press.

Torres, F., 2009. La inserción residencial de los inmigrantes en la costa mediterránea española: 1998-2007, co-presencia residencial, segregación y contexto local. *Areas*, 28: 73-87.

Wells, M.J., 1996. *Strawberry Fields: Politics, Class, and Work in California Agriculture*. Ithaca: Cornell University Press.

5 Food systems and food poverty

Martin Caraher

Introduction

Food poverty has been defined as the inability to acquire or consume an adequate quality or sufficient quantity of food in socially acceptable ways, or uncertainty that one will be able to do so (Radimer, Olson & Campbell, 1990). Food poverty includes the element of the now more widely used term 'food insecurity', but it is broader in its scope and includes income, job security and what is known as the 'poverty premium' where those on low incomes pay a higher price for essential goods including food (Tait, 2015; Caraher & Furey, 2018). Food insecurity tends to be measured using a set of questions to indicate the problem of food access at a point in time (Beacom et al., 2021). The measures used are not predictive and do not address the uncertainty issues in the above definition of food poverty (Daly et al., 2018). Fisher (2017) says that use of the term food insecurity suggests that the problem can be ameliorated by the provision of food at times of economic or social stress, whereas in fact the issues of insecurity do not go away in the days that people have sufficient to eat. Food insecurity does not address the wider issue that food poverty encompasses, and it undoubtedly does not address the influence and impact of the food system on levels of poverty along the food chain. This results in a tendency to see behaviours and food choices as fallouts from the food system and the responsibility of the individual and lifestyle choices (Williams & Fullagar, 2019).

Sen and Drèze argue that the issue is not always that of the availability of food but of how access is defined or interpreted (Drèze & Sen, 1989; Sen & Drèze, 2012; Sen, 1992). The COVID-19 crisis has highlighted the fragility of people's access and rights to essential goods and services within existing food systems and this includes the role of governments in addressing, regulating and monitoring how food is delivered and made affordable. When the impact of supply chains is assessed, the tendency is to evaluate the accessibility of goods within a consumer frame of reference and not from the perspective of citizenship and rights or to consider the impact of the food system on how rights are conceived and defined (Caraher & Furey, 2018). An international report highlighted three aspects of the dominant food system which expose its vulnerabilities. These are:

- A food system based on industrial agriculture is driving habitat loss and creating the conditions for viruses to emerge and spread across national borders following trade routes.
- The emergence of a range of disruptions which test the resilience of food supply chains and reveal underlying vulnerabilities at both the grower/producer and consumer ends of the food system.
- And third, hundreds of millions of people are living permanently on the cusp of hunger, malnutrition, and extreme poverty, and are therefore highly vulnerable to the effects of a global recession and/or disruptions in the supply chain (IPES-Food, 2020).

Arguably, one might add a fourth which is the current lack of regulation and accountability of the global food system. This system ties together many countries and players from growers to financial speculators. National governments are not only accountable to their domestic populations but also exist within a global community involving policy commitments and moral responsibilities, such as reductions in greenhouse gas emissions or efforts to reduce global poverty. Many of these are set out in the 17 United Nations' Sustainable Development Goals (SDGs) which are designed to achieve three primary objectives by 2030:

- Protect the planet;
- End poverty, and
- Create prosperity and peace for all (IFPRI, 2016).

These objectives offer a way to set inter-connected goals that apply to both governments and the private sector (Biermann, Kanie & Kim, 2017). The food system has particular relevance to specific SDGs: #1 (no poverty); #2 (zero-hunger); #3 (good health and well-being); #4 (quality education); #5 (gender equality); #8 (decent work and economic growth); #10 (reduced inequalities); #11 (sustainable cities and communities); #13 (climate action); and #14 and #15 (life below water and on land respectively). Although regarded as vital in order to meet the 2030 objectives, progress to achieve these Goals has been slow: the poverty reduction targets were not being met even before the COVID-19 crises and inequalities have increased over the period of the pandemic (HLPE, 2021).

The stance taken in this chapter is that the food system itself, *sui generis*, can be a cause of food poverty (and food insecurity) in the same way that social class itself is an influence on health outcomes (Townsend, Whitehead & Davidson, 1992). The focus is on how the structures and organisation of the food system impact on those both upstream (growers, producers) as well as downstream (the consumer citizen). Impacts on producers include incessant downward pressure on farm-gate prices and the imposition of quality standards without recompense for the cost of these. Impacts on consumer citizens, meanwhile, include the promotion of 'cheap' but unhealthy processed foods which come at a cost: 'cheap' food is an illusion that contains hidden externalities (Caraher, 2019). The chapter examines these two ends of the food system starting with primary producers and ends by examining the consequences arising from the consumption of ultra-processed foods (UPF).

In exploring the issues for primary producers, the chapter draws upon the cases of coffee and cocoa. Both share characteristics such as:

- In terms of nutrition both are non-essentials, although for many societies are socially and culturally important.
- They are 'cash crops', which are arguably not abundantly consumed in the countries in which they are grown (the exception being coffee in Latin America), and both therefore can be considered luxury goods for countries of the global north.
- Compared to the overall value of the commodity chain, the economic footprint in the producing countries is relatively minor with added value occurring as the products are exported and processed.
- They are grown in areas which are at risk from climate change and, in some areas of production, political upheaval.
- Both are generally grown in small enterprises and rely on migrant and family labour.
- As global commodities both are subject to intense trading and financial speculation.
- Ironically they are transposed crops of the Columbian exchange. The botanical origin of coffee is located in Africa but its major area of production is South America. Cocoa, meanwhile, has its origin in Central America but now 80 percent of global production is in West Africa (Ghana and Côte d'Ivoire).

While these two commodity chains are used as examples to illustrate the ways in which the food system generates food poverty amongst producers, other food commodity chains might have served as well. In other words, similar processes are at work in grains, soy, or meat production and can occur within countries as well as in cross border food chains (Blas & Farchy, 2021).

In contrast, food poverty in rich and middle-income countries has become entangled with issues of dietary health and where one consequence of the industrial food system is that it has made cheap processed food ubiquitous. Despite rising global concerns about the incidence of diet related non-communicable diseases (DR-NCDs) and its strong association with increases in the consumption of UPF, there has been a failure to recognise in governance frameworks that the food system is a major contributor to the consumption of UPF and, ultimately, to poor dietary health.

The 2008-11 Great Recession had a major impact on global food poverty and contributed significantly to political unrest (the Arab Spring). Subsequent events have created further instability including the simmering US-China trade war; the UK's departure from the EU (Brexit); periodic outbreaks of zoonotic diseases (such as swine flu in Germany and China); regional climate and weather crises (drought, floods, storms); and, of course, COVID-19. All have highlighted flaws in the existing food system especially the vulnerability of many people in low and middle-income countries to rising food prices. Specifically, there was a 20 percent rise in global food prices between January 2020 and January 2021 which disproportionately affects households that spend a higher proportion of their income on food – while at the same time likely to be more vulnerable to reductions in such income (World Bank, 2021). In the USA an average of 6 percent of income is spent on food compared to 42 percent in Pakistan, and so rising prices means families being able to put less food on the table and malnourishment increasing. In rich countries, on the other hand, higher retail food prices combined with static or reduced incomes (from precarious employment or COVID layoffs) have resulted in families cutting down on the quality of their food purchases with a consequent likelihood of weight gain linked to consumption of cheaper ultra-processed foods.

One must be cautious about making singular attributions of cause and effect: the faults in the food system are not the result of COVID-19 – they have always been there. But the pandemic has exposed many of them simultaneously, often accentuating different features. Depending upon context, then, an increase in malnourishment can be exacerbated by income loss due to lockdown: from labour shortages and barriers to food distribution driving food price increases, to the sharp decline in export income as a consequence of demand collapse with consequences for currency depreciation. But there are other factors in play as well, including climate and political upheaval (FAO, 2020). In other words, there may be many contingent variables, but as this chapter will demonstrate through its focus on primary commodity producers and downstream consumers, the food system is structurally responsible for generating a great deal of food poverty.

Poverty in Commodity Chains: Coffee and Cocoa

As a consequence of latitude and altitude that provide the right growing conditions, around 80 percent of coffee is produced by 25 million small farmers. The economic footprint left in the country of production is around 10 percent with only 3–6 percent going to the grower. Meanwhile, greater beneficiaries are the coffee roasters, the international traders, export houses and retailers (Perez et al., 2017). The same inequitable principle also occurs in purely domestic markets for many commodities such as potato growers in the US and the UK. Generally speaking, those who invest most in the growing and production of food are those who are least likely to benefit, often being forced to sell at below farm gate production costs.

The coffee chain is controlled by two sets of actors: traders and roasters. Both of these sectors are highly concentrated and have developed through mergers and acquisitions. There are a limited number of trade houses that source coffee globally with the main players being Neumann Kaffee Gruppe, ED&F Man Volcafe and ECOM. To give an idea of the scale of concentration, the family owned Neumann group handles ten percent of the global green (before roasting) coffee trade. The largest roasting companies are Nestlé, JAB, Kraft, Sara Lee, Smucker's (P&G), Dalmayr, Starbucks, Tchibo, Aldi, Melitta, Lavazza, and Segafredo. Nestlé is the number one global roaster but is being challenged for supremacy by a German investment firm JAB Coffee, which spent US$350 billion acquiring coffee chains and restaurant chains that sell large amounts of coffee. These large roasting companies operate in many countries but often keep local brands and ownership identities separate; for example, JAB Coffee is not a high street brand as it leaves the local branding of the companies it acquires. A recent entrant Coca-Cola has acquired the Costa coffee chain of restaurants as it sees the future of coffee and caffeine containing drinks as important and this gives it a high street presence.

Added value occurs along the beverage supply chain. In areas where coffee is grown climate change is impacting on production, future supply and livelihoods. In July 2021 a major frost in the coffee growing areas of Brazil had a huge impact on the sector although it was not just coffee affected as Brazil is a large global producer of oranges, sugar, soy and corn and many of these crops sustained frost damage. Brazil is the world's largest producer of coffee with the 2020 crop accounting for 40 percent of global output (69 million bags of coffee). Production estimates for 2021 were 45–50 million bags as Brazil was in its '*off*' year in its biennial cycle. Estimates of the frost damage are a loss of around 10 percent of Brazil's production, equating to 4.5 to 5 million bags of coffee or 5 percent of world production. Add to this the difficulties with COVID-19 and the global freight shipping situation and we start to understand the serious supply problems but, more importantly, the issues facing growers as they wait for payment. For example, Vietnam, the world's second largest exporter of coffee, is struggling to transport beans to its ports as a consequence of tight COVID-19 lockdown measures. This has been described as a 'perfect storm in the global coffee market' which will lead to much higher prices (Ratcliffe, 2021). Retail prices will therefore continue to rise; however, the grower often gains little from these price increases. Political instability is also a factor in many countries and can flare up quite suddenly and can be further exacerbated by natural disasters and trade barriers. For example, during 2021 serious security and safety issues affected western and southern areas of Colombia, preventing farmers from getting their coffee beans into the market. Ongoing political protests against the government, as well as COVID-19 restrictions meant that fuel prices rose, transport between rural and urban areas was significantly disrupted, and small and medium coffee producers simply do not have the resources to hire secure means of transport to take their coffee to market. Meanwhile global prices for Colombian coffee are rising due to this shortage of supply.

The global standards body for coffee, the International Coffee Organization (ICO), has proven to be largely ineffective in maintaining commodity prices through the mechanism of the 2007 International Coffee Agreement (from which the US withdrew in 2018). In its place global traders and speculators have stepped in to fill the gap, with prices being established on trading floors in New York and London. Although prices are predictably driven by the pursuit of profit, there is a growing sense of unease amongst many coffee companies (traders and roasters) about future supply. Many have now stepped forward to invest in infrastructure projects, training for farmers and even helping set up local welfare schemes (Daviron & Ponte, 2005).

In the lead up to and in the wake of the 2008 Great Recession when food commodities became a focus for financial speculation, some of the big transnational coffee and cocoa companies were shocked by the lack of global accountability and the fact that the actions of some of the hedge funds threatened the viability of their supplies. In futures markets it is not the food commodity that is traded but the prospect of cash flows based upon further speculative investments in future harvests. World trade, much of which is untaxed and, as it occurs outside of national boundaries, is largely unregulated. There is financial speculation at a global level where the benefits do not accrue to communities, individuals or nation states or involve the movement of goods but focus upon currency trades. Currency speculators trade over $US5.4 trillion each day across national borders. How much of this is food related is not clear. The Tobin tax is a proposal for a simple sales taxes on currency trades across borders which would raise sufficient to meet urgent global health and environmental concerns including disease and poverty by funding UN agencies such as WHO and UNICEF. A side effect would be the strengthening of national economies and more money flows at this level by restricting international speculation thereby contributing to local wealth.

This speculative trading in food between 2008 to 2012 spurred many companies into taking action to protect their supply chains and to address food poverty among growers and producers. They were aware that increasing poverty and flight from the land compromised their future supplies and that they needed to protect the source of their primary product and this involved moving beyond mere business relationships to helping growers and producers in other ways. In the areas of coffee and cocoa, major firms are investing in training of farmers, small loan schemes and setting up pension schemes. This refocus also allowed companies an opportunity to rebrand civil activism demands within a consumer activism model, usually under a corporate social responsibility (CSR) banner (Belasco, 2007).

With cocoa, as with the coffee supply chain, there are concentrations with the 'Big Five' chocolate manufacturers (Mars, Hershey, Nestlé, Mondelēz [includes Cadbury] and Ferrero) and three main grinders/processors (Barry Callebaut, Cargill, and Olam). Cargill and Olam have no public face in the retail end of chocolate or confectionary sales. Within this 'Big Three' there are further concentrations and links with the Big Five chocolate manufactures. Olam sells cocoa to four of the five major manufactures, while Barry Callebaut supplies Unilever with 70 percent of its cocoa requirements and accounts for about 25 percent of all cocoa grinding; it also makes chocolate for Nestlé, Mondelēz and Hershey. Between them the grinders and chocolate manufacturers control the cocoa chain to the disadvantage of the 20 million growers, who receive between 3 and 6 percent of the final price of a chocolate bar. Amongst cocoa producers, roughly 4 million individuals and their families live on less than US$3 a day, perilously close to the World Bank's official poverty line of US$1.90/day.

With respect to quality there has been an emergence of many industry based voluntary sustainability standards (VSS) which serve to establish quality parameters for cocoa or coffee but have little to say about international or 'true' pricing. This is a form of policy making by industry. Much like the ICO for coffee, the International Cocoa Organization (ICCO) is an intergovernmental body with objectives to develop and strengthen international cooperation, providing a forum for discussion of cocoa related matters but does not establish pricing regimes. A second body, the International Office of Cocoa, Chocolate and Sugar Confectionery (IOCCC) is an industry association established to encourage scientific research in the cocoa, chocolate and confectionery industry. Both of these act for the dominant voices in the industry and are not lobbying or advocacy interests on behalf of growers. This is not to say that that companies are not helping development locally. With 80 percent of the world supply of cocoa coming from West Africa (Ghana and Côte d'Ivoire) the danger of a catastrophe – whether climate-related, political unrest or the effects of a pandemic – runs the risk of supply chains being compromised.

Recent moves in both the coffee and cocoa fields show a shift from third-party certification schemes led by international NGOs, such as Fairtrade and Rainforest Alliance, to in-house schemes run by the large companies. In the case of fair trade, the slightly higher price that a customer may pay for a product contributes to a premium that supports a community fund, rather than a direct payment to the grower. The value of this fair-trade premium is that it builds shared resources such as drinking water, health care and educational facilities that enhances the community, particularly the lives of women and children.

In contrast, in-house schemes which are strong in company branding, offer no such incentives. Examples here include Mondelēz International's 'Cocoa Life'; Barry Callebaut with its 'Cocoa Horizons' scheme and, increasingly, many Cadbury's products use its 'Cocoa Life' symbol. These in-house standards are set and monitored internally, potentially a case of the 'fox in the hen-house'. A glance at some of the larger high-street coffee chains show similar developments as in-house VSS standards take hold. There is an argument that companies have been forced to take this route in the absence of effective international standard setting protocols and governance. Across the food system – and extending well-beyond the case of coffee and cacao – it is evident that national governments have found it easier to hand quality control – de facto regulation – of the food system to private companies and confine governance to consumer protection matters such as labeling, health and hygiene, and nutritional recommendations.

In both the coffee and cocoa supply chains there is a move by companies, however, to source less from conventional production (using agri-chemicals) and more from the organic sector. This shift reflects companies' careful monitoring of consumer awareness of sustainability and health concerns. It is also in line with SDG #2: "to end hunger, achieve food security and improve nutrition and promote sustainable agriculture". Such moves come with costs and risks, however, and growers need to be supported through conversion and compensated for increased costs of production. The challenge of ensuring their interests in supply chains may also explain why many of the chocolate manufacturers are establishing their own private certification over third-party schemes. The conundrum is that those powerful players in the food chain set standards for markets in the global north, the additional costs of which it expects countries in the global south to absorb. Such standards can be demanding of local resources, such as using scarce potable water for washing and cleaning of export produce. As small producers find it ever harder to meet increasingly onerous contract demands, this exacerbates the 'squeeze' on incomes and ultimately increases flight from the land. Meanwhile larger producers with more favourable economies of scale are able to benefit while further illustrating concentration within the supply chain.

The makeup of the coffee and cocoa chains at the growing stage relies on small scale farming (coffee growing in Brazil is an exception) and family labour. The more that small-scale family farming is squeezed by price the more that education suffers as child labour becomes an ever more critical feature of hidden production. This gives rise to two forms of poverty: first, the lack of food safety networks supplied via school feeding systems; and, second, the long-term effects on future life chances through lost schooling (SDGs 1 to 5) (Leissle, 2018; Ryan, 2011; Purcell, 2018).

The plight of growers/producers in developing and emerging economies, are also being impacted by decisions to cut aid budgets. In the UK the government recently announced a cut from 0.7 to 0.5 percent of gross national income (Kobayashi, Heinrich & Bryant, 2021). As countries such as the UK and the US roll back on foreign aid budgets, their role is being replaced by private companies which, with a mix of corporate social responsibility (CSR) and welfare capitalism, are providing support to growers in Africa and Asia. Many transnational companies see this as investment in their future by supporting training for farmers and supporting capital investment projects. The mechanics of this process vary but as many have pointed out, such a process is not rights-based and, according to some, undermines the state's role as a provider and defender of citizens' rights (De Schutter, 2013; Silvasti & Kortetmäki, 2017).

Food Systems and DR-NCDs: The New Markers of Food Poverty

Changes in dietary intake are being driven by increasing urbanisation and the provision of 'cheap' ultra-processed foods (UPF) (Baker et al., 2020). Cheapness comes at a cost, which is an increase in diet-related, non-communicable diseases (DR-NCD) as well as damage to the environment. Increases in urbanisation make it easier to provide processed and convenience foods to populations who are often cash rich but time poor. There are arguments that processed foods build dependency via their convenience but also by contributing to a less food skills-based population (Stitt, 1996). UPF can be better understood through the use of a taxonomy called the NOVA classification which fits foods into four groups: (i) unprocessed or minimally processed foods; (ii) processed culinary ingredients; (iii) processed foods; and (iv) ultra-processed foods (Monteiro et al., 2019). UPF are favoured by the food industry as the addition of substances such as fat, salt and sugar contribute to increased preservation and prolonged shelf-life, palatability and ease of storage, transport and distribution. There are consumer advantages to processed foods including reduced labour in the kitchen, ease of preparation and potential waste reduction.

High levels of consumption of UPF are associated with rising levels of obesity (Luiten et al., 2016). A study of consumption in Europe found that availability in households ranged from 10.2 percent in Portugal and 13.4 percent in Italy to 46.2 percent in Germany and 50.4 percent in the UK (Monteiro et al., 2018). There is clear evidence of a link between increasing purchasing of UPF, urbanisation and rising incomes and that while sales have been highest in Australasia, North America, Europe and Latin America they are growing rapidly in Asia, the Middle East and Africa (Baker et al., 2020).

Using the NOVA classification for dietary analysis shows that those on low incomes suffer two forms of food poverty. First, that of poor-quality food, which has undergone many changes in the food chain; and, second, a nutritionally poor quality diet (Caraher, 2019) which ultimately contributes to a higher incidence of DR-NCD and obesity (Monteiro et al., 2019). Within countries there is a double burden of disease related to poor diet. In low-income countries (the global south) there is a rising level of DR-NCD (e.g. Type II diabetes) alongside diseases of under-nutrition. This places a significant additional burden on already underfunded health care services. In middle and high-income countries there is likewise a double burden with those on low-incomes suffering from hunger and DR-NCD, and while whole populations are gaining weight (rising average BMI), the trend is more acute in lower-income groups. There is also a corresponding relationship between the use of UPF and work contracts. So those on insecure, part time contracts who work in the 'gig-economy' are more likely to consume take-aways and UPF which fits with the nature of their work, which is often unplanned and where pay is by the 'piece' or the performance of tasks as opposed to a regular wage. Lacking resources, including time, determines the (poor) quality of diets and increases the likelihood of consuming energy dense or UPF.

As food prices increase, food is the most 'elastic item' in the household budget. This often means choosing poorer quality food items that may carry long-term health consequences, but for most people in straitened circumstances, the key issue is averting hunger – especially for their children – from day to day. An associated development of rising prices, increasing employment precarity and growing food poverty has been the growth in charitable food provisioning (e.g. food banks) whereby retail surpluses ('waste food') are redistributed through third-sector agencies. Unfortunately, much of this surplus comprises energy-dense, nutrient-poor UPF that wards off hunger and ticks the box of reducing food waste but provides no long-term health benefit (Kenny & Sage, 2021). Hence we witness a double burden and food poverty trap: cheap and time-saving unhealthy diets that result in people becoming overweight and experiencing ill-health. Temporary periods of hunger give rise to people eating unhealthy and energy-dense food when resources are available, and this is because such foods are cheap, energy-dense and filling (Peña & Bacallao, 2000).

To the above double burdens of disease related to the consumption of UPF can be added the third or triple burden of damage to the environment. The links between ultra-processed foods and the degree of sustainability inherent in the product are clear from the NOVA classification. The relationship between ultra-processed food and distance travelled along the food chain, while not a perfect match, is sufficiently strong to suggest the model can be used to assess and attribute accountability to food manufacturers for their contributions to damage to the environment – as well as ill-health (via DR-NCD). Generally, the more processing a food has undergone the greater the damage to the environment. There are some critics of the classification system claiming that it is too simplistic and arguing that the links with ultra-processed foods are tenuous (Gibney et al., 2017). The NOVA classification has also been used to present information to consumers which links healthy eating with sustainable sourcing. But it is clear that in terms of food poverty, those on low incomes suffer from low quality and much travelled foods. Paradoxically, we have seen a shift in the food system as part of this nutrition transition from a situation where 'the poor' ate locally grown food and 'the rich' consumed imported exotic and processed foods, to one where locally produced and grown food is now sold at a premium and consumed by the better-off while the poor eat a diet of semi and ultra-processed foods which has often travelled many miles.

Discussion and Conclusions: Implications for Future Research

It was apparent even before the COVID-19 crisis that the food system was not fit for purpose and is one which currently delivers 'cheap' UPF to the many while threatening livelihoods and the environment and benefitting those who control food supply chains. Cheapness comes at a cost to many, mainly those working in the fields and frontline supermarket workers and ultimately the customer. From 'farm to fork' and 'paddock to plate' inequalities occur at both ends of the food chain with the main financial benefits going to inter-mediaries in the system such as traders, manufacturers, and retailers. Yet the solutions to ongoing food insecurity and poverty are not regarded as requiring macro-structural changes in the supply system but in piece-meal efforts pro-viding aid through charities and public private partnerships (PPPs). Many of the current responses to the pandemic have not been based on state policy but on handing more control to the food sector often without safeguards or external monitoring or guarantees of long-term support (Berners-Lee et al., 2018; Biermann, Kanie & Kim, 2017). Modern food policy is now shaped as much by the influence of the food industry ('Big Food') as it is by state policy. Neoliberal trade environments with low-taxes and low-regulation of labour safeguards form the context for food policy and conditions in food chains (Navarro, 2020).

A survey by Visual Capitalist ranked companies by their positive or negative contribution to each of the 17 SDG goals. The findings were that global companies fell mostly in the middle ranking with approximately 38 percent aligned and 55 percent misaligned or neutral. Only 0.2 percent of companies were strongly aligned to meeting the UN SDGs (Neufeld, 2021). One of the strongly aligned goals was 'Responsible Production and Consumption'. This indicates that while there is commitment, often under a corporate social responsibility (CSR) banner, the obligation is tempered by the demands of shareholders and markets. In terms of food poverty prevention and alleviation the private sector are, of course, part of the solution but cannot be the only part as solutions favoured by the food industry will be located within business and consumer models of access and consumption (Prahalad & Hammond, 2002). Inevitably such approaches are targeted and not universalist in their application and do not address the right of people to food. Olivier De Schutter, the United Nations' Special Rapporteur on the Right to Food from 2008 to 2014, saw the right to food as being transformative and not a substitute for commercial or charity responses (De Schutter, 2014).

The COVID-19 crisis has made more apparent what can best be described as a 'whack a mole' policy approach (i.e. one that is concerned with tackling problems individually as they emerge) as opposed to one that is precautionary or strategic. This has resulted in short-term emergency responses to problems but little foresight or anticipation in tackling the underlying causes, the key to which is the structure of the food system and supply chains themselves that contribute strongly to food poverty. Food poverty now demands attention as a public health emergency; one that national governments appear to have absolved themselves from solving, leaving the charitable sector to bridge the growing chasm (Lorenz, 2012). However, the long-term solution lies not in the provision of emergency food aid to those who are food insecure and living in food poverty as charitable provisioning does not guarantee a *right* to food and, besides, is socially stigmatising. Sen reminds us that the problem is not one of a lack of food but of the right of *access* to food (Sen, 1981, 1992). The fallout from a food system which isolates many in our societies has seen a rise in the charity sector for food aid, often hand-in-hand with the food industry which contributes to the problem in the first instance and often results in the donated food being highly processed thus further widening inequalities (Caraher & Furey, 2017).

There are now a growing number of calls for an overhaul and more regulation of the food system including restrictions on speculation of agri-food commodities and preventing further corporate concentration across the food chain (Clapp & Scott, 2018; Clapp & Isakson, 2018; see also Clapp, Chapter 2 in this volume). The time is therefore ripe to look at food systems as contributors to food poverty and to readjust the social protection networks around food to alleviate and prevent this. Research effort might be directed to calculating the contribution of food chain supply of particular commodities to ill health and food poverty and ways these might be regulated, including the imposition of levies. The UPF categorisation scheme offers a way of identifying problematic 'hotspots' across the food system. It also has the advantage of linking health and eco-sustainability agendas as outlined by Mason and Lang under the heading of eco-nutrition or sustainable diets (Mason & Lang, 2017).

One of the issues to have emerged in recent years concerns the use of taxation as an instrument to regulate behaviour, whether of businesses or consumers. Despite debate over how taxes are to be levied and collected evidence from the deployment of soda taxes shows these can be resolved with political willingness (Pan American Health Organization, 2021). In relation to the Tobin currency transaction tax mentioned earlier, there has been some interest in its application to prevent the kinds of predatory trading and speculation that occurred in the lead up to and following the 2008-11 recession. Undoubtedly, these activities drove food prices and contributed to rising levels of world food poverty. Moreover, the growing trend for companies to introduce their own voluntary sustainability standards (VSS) demonstrates that there is concern in the food sector over the medium to long-term sustainability of supplies. There is currently a gap in research on how such developments fit with statutory initiatives and the food system.

The shift in policy focus from governance by the state to that by the private and charity sectors clearly needs more research especially in relation to the growth of welfare capitalism. There are positive features to such moves; many corporations have resources bigger than many nation states and can often move faster than state institutions. The downside is the unregulated nature of such developments with businesses investing where they can gain most profit and only in commodities in which they trade (coffee, cocoa, palm oil, etc.). Such an approach may also limit benefits to those growers who fall within the commercial interests of the sponsoring company, and still does not guarantee them an increase in income. For example, cocoa production is concentrated in 30 countries with 90 percent grown on plots of less than ten hectares often with limited capacity to expand within a land tenure system such as the 'cotter' system in West Africa (Leissle, 2018). Cases such as this are not confined to low-income and emerging economies, as dairy and beef farmers in the global north have experienced similar problems with falling farm incomes and ongoing downward pressure on prices controlled by processors and retailers.

It is not that welfare capitalism is without merit but that it needs to be located within broader frameworks of rights and to include voices of the dispossessed, marginalised and the wider community (Richards, Kjærnes & Vik, 2016). Governments defer to welfare capitalism based on the belief that commerce, not aid, is the way to lift people out of poverty (Moyo, 2010). Too often such initiatives prioritise the concerns of the funder not the right to food and citizenship and ways to ensure universal coverage in a population. Moreover, as the state retreats in favour of private and philanthropic interests there is the problem of limited investment in public infrastructures such as transport and education. This is the fall-out from a low regulation, low tax economy, where there is declining state income to spend on public infrastructure. Unsurprisingly, while agri-food businesses may contribute to some infrastructure projects under their CSR initiatives, they are likely only to invest in those that benefit them directly. Corporate welfare is clearly not universal in its coverage and is unlikely to subscribe to a universalist principle or citizenship of rights.

Finally, the COVID-19 crisis has made us aware of the people who really keep the system going and these are largely those who gain little from it. We are not hearing demands for more stockbrokers or bankers but rather for nurses, health care assistants, shop assistants, farm workers and delivery drivers. To date little has been done about improving their income or security of employment: for example, in the UK, retail workers earn, on average, £9.72/hour with little security of tenure and are dependent on work for income with few financial resources to fall back on. This introduces a double burden of poverty: not enough income to afford a healthy diet while being more exposed and at risk to COVID-19. As opposed to the current system of food prices being determined in stock exchanges in New York or London, we need to refocus research on global governance which can ensure farm gate prices are fair and sufficient to allow families along food chains – whether as producers or as citizen-consumers – to afford to live healthy and sustainable lives.

References

Baker, P., Machado, P., Santos, T., Sievert, K. et al., 2020. Ultra-processed foods and the nutrition transition: global, regional and national trends, food systems transformations and political economy drivers. *Obesity Reviews*, 21: e13126. https://doi.org/10.1111/obr.13126.

Beacom, E., Furey, S., Hollywood, L., Humphreys, P., 2021. Investigating food insecurity measurement globally to inform practice locally: a rapid evidence review. *Critical Reviews in Food Science and Nutrition*, 61, 20, 3319-3339. https://doi.org/10.1080/10408398.2020.1798347.

Belasco, W., 2007. *Appetite for Change: How the Counterculture took on the Food Industry and Won*. 2nd Edition, New York: Cornell University Press.

Berners-Lee, M., Kennelly, C., Watson, R., Hewitt, C.N., 2018. Current global food production is sufficient to meet human nutritional needs in 2050 provided there is radical societal adaptation. *Elementa: Science of the Anthropocene*, 6, 52. https://doi.org/10.1525/elementa.310.

Biermann, F., Kanie, N., Kim, R.E., 2017. Global governance by goal-setting: the novel approach of the UN Sustainable Development Goals. *Current Opinion in Environmental Sustainability*, 26-27: pp. 26-31.

Blas, J., Farchy, J., 2021. *The World for Sale: Money, Power and the Traders Who Barter the Earth's Resources*. London: Random House Business.

Caraher, M., 2019. High-cost cheap food. *The Blackwell Encyclopedia of Sociology* [Online], pp. 1-3. https://doi.org/10.1002/9781405165518.wbeos1494.

Caraher, M., Furey, S., 2018. *The Economics of Emergency Food Aid Provision*. London: Springer.

Caraher, M., Furey, S. 2017. *Is it appropriate to use surplus food to feed people in hunger? Short-term Band-Aid to more deep-rooted problems of poverty*, Food Research Collaboration, Centre for Food Policy, London.

Clapp, J., Isakson, S.R., 2018. Risky returns: the implications of financialization in the food system: debate: financialization in the food system. *Development and Change*, 49, 2: 437–460.

Clapp, J., Scott, C., 2018. The Global Environmental Politics of Food. *Global Environmental Politics*, 18, 2: 1–11.

Daly, A., Pollard, C.M., Kerr, D.A., Binns, C.W., Caraher, M., Phillips, M., 2018. Using cross-sectional data to identify and quantify the relative importance of factors associated with and leading to food insecurity. *Int. J. Environ. Res. Public Health*, 15, 12: 2620.

Daviron, B., Ponte, S., 2005. *The Coffee Paradox: Global Markets, Commodity Trade and the Elusive Promise of Development*. London: Zed Books.

De Schutter, O., 2014. *Final Report: The Transformative Potential of the Right to Food: Report of the Special Rapporteur on the Right to Food*. Washington: United Nations.

De Schutter, O., 2013. The right to food in times of crisis. *Just Fair Freedom from Hunger: Realising the Right to Food in the UK*. London: Just Fair, pp. 7–11.

Drèze, J., Sen, A., 1989. *Hunger and Public Action*. Oxford: Oxford University Press.

Fisher, A., 2017. *Big Hunger: The Unholy Alliance between Corporate America and Anti-Hunger Groups*. Cambridge, MA: MIT Press.

Food and Agriculture Organization of the United Nations (FAO) 2020. *The State of Food Security and Nutrition in the World 2020*. Rome: Food and Agriculture Organization.

Gibney, M.J., Forde, C.G. et al., 2017. Ultra-processed foods in human health: a critical appraisal. *The American Journal of Clinical Nutrition*, 106, 3: 717–724.

High Level Panel of Experts on Food Security and Nutrition (HLPE). 2021, *Food Security and Nutrition: Building a Global Narrative Towards 2030. A Report by the High-Level Panel of Experts on Food Security and Nutrition of the Committee on World Food Security*, Rome.

International Food Policy Research Institute (IFPRI) 2016. *Global Nutrition Report 2016: From Promise to Impact: Ending Malnutrition by 2030*. International Food Policy Research Institute, Washington DC.

International Panel of Experts on Sustainable Food Systems (IPES-Food) 2020. *COVID-19 and the Crisis in Food Systems: Symptoms, Causes, and Potential Solutions*. International Panel of Experts on Sustainable Food Systems, Brussels (www.ipesfood.org/pages/covid19).

Kenny, T., Sage, C., 2021. Surplus food redistribution and healthy, sustainable diets: Exploring the contradictions of charitable food provisioning. *The International Journal of Sociology of Agriculture and Food*, 27, 1: 71–86. https://doi.org/10.48416/ijsaf.v27i1.82.

Kobayashi, Y., Heinrich, T., Bryant, K.A., 2021. Public support for development aid during the COVID-19 pandemic. *World Development*, 138: 105248.

Leissle, K., 2018. *Cocoa*. Cambridge, UK: Polity Press.

Lorenz, S., 2012. Having no choice: Social exclusion in the affluent society. *Journal of Exclusion Studies*, 5, 1: 11–17.

Luiten, C.M., Steenhuis, I.H., Eyles, H., Ni Mhurchu, C., Waterlander, W.E., 2016. Ultra-processed foods have the worst nutrient profile, yet they are the most available packaged products in a sample of New Zealand supermarkets. *Public Health Nutrition*, 19, 3: 530–538.

Mason, P., Lang, T., 2017. *Sustainable Diets: How Ecological Nutrition Can Transform Consumption and the Food System*. London: Routledge.

Monteiro, C.A., Cannon, G., Levy, R.B. et al., 2019. Ultra-processed foods: What they are and how to identify them. *Public Health Nutrition*, 22, 5: 936–941.

Monteiro, C.A., Moubarac, J., Levy, R.B. et al., 2018. Household availability of ultra-processed foods and obesity in nineteen European countries. *Public Health Nutrition*, 21, 1: 18–26.

Moyo, D., 2010. *Dead Aid: Why Aid is Not Working and How There is a Better Way for Africa*. London: Penguin.

Navarro, V., 2020. The consequences of neoliberalism in the current pandemic. *International Journal of Health Services*, 50, 3: 271–275.

Neufeld, D., 2021. *UN Sustainable Development Goals: How Companies Stack Up*, 16 March edn, Visual Capitalist. https:// www .visualcapitalist .com/ sustainable -development-goals/.

Pan American Health Organization 2021. *Sugar-Sweetened Beverage Taxation in the Region of the Americas*. Pan American Health Organization, Washington DC.

Peña, M., Bacallao, J., 2000. *Obesity and Poverty: A New Public Health Challenge. Scientific Publication no 576*. Pan American Health Organization, Washington DC.

Perez, J., Kilian, B., Pratt, L., Ardila, J.C., Lamb, H., Byers, L., Sanders, D., 2017. Economic sustainability – price, cost, and value. In Folmer, B. (ed.) *The Craft and Science of Coffee*. London: Academic Press, pp. 133–160.

Prahalad, C.K., Hammond, A., 2002. Serving the world's poor, profitably. *Harvard Business Review*, 80, 9: 48–124.

Purcell, T.F., 2018. 'Hot chocolate': Financialized global value chains and cocoa production in Ecuador. *The Journal of Peasant Studies*, 45, 5–6: 904–926.

Radimer, K.L., Olson, C.M., Campbell, C., 1990. Development of indicators to assess hunger. *Journal of Nutrition*, 120: 1544–1548.

Ratcliffe, R., 2021. Concern grows for global coffee supply amid Vietnam lockdown. *The Guardian*, 1 September. https:// www .theguardian .com/ food/ 2021/ sep/ 01/ concern-grows-global-coffee-supply-vietnam-lockdown.

Richards, C., Kjærnes, U., Vik, J., 2016. Food security in welfare capitalism: Comparing social entitlements to food in Australia and Norway. *Journal of Rural Studies*, 43: 61–70.

Ryan, O., 2011. *Chocolate Nations: Living and Dying for Cocoa in West Africa*. London: Zed Books.

Sen, A., 1981. *Poverty and Famines: An Essay on Entitlement and Deprivation*. Oxford: Clarendon Press.

Sen, A., 1992. *Inequality Reexamined*. Oxford: Oxford University Press.

Sen, A., Drèze, J., 2012. *The Amartya Sen & Jean Drèze Omnibus*. New Delhi: Oxford University Press.

Silvasti, T., Kortetmäki, T., 2017. Nordic Welfare Universalism, Charity Food Aid and Environmental Ethics. In Matthies, A., Närhi, K. (eds) *The Ecosocial Transition of Societies: The Contribution of Social Work and Social Policy*. London: Routledge, pp. 219–233.

Stitt, S., 1996. An international perspective on food and cooking skills in education. *British Food Journal*, 98, 10: 27–34.

Tait, C., 2015. *Hungry for Change: The Final Report of the Fabian Commission on Food and Poverty*. London: Fabian Society.

Townsend, P.B., Whitehead, M., Davidson, N., 1992. *Inequalities in Health: The Black Report and the Health Divide*, 3rd edn. London: Penguin Books.

Williams, O., Fullagar, S., 2019. Lifestyle drift and the phenomenon of 'citizen shift 'in contemporary UK health policy. *Sociology of Health and Illness*, 41, 1: 20-35.

World Bank 2021. *Brief: Food Security and COVID-19* (Updated 17 August, 2021). The World Bank. https://www.worldbank.org/en/topic/agriculture/brief/food-security -and-covid-19.

6 Reconfiguring animals in food systems: an agenda for research[1]

Lewis Holloway

Introduction

Contemporary food systems have been responsible for significant transformations in the bodies and experiences of farmed nonhuman animals (henceforth farmed animals). As Derrida and Wills observed, the transformation of animals

> has occurred by means of farming and regimentalization at a demographic level unknown in the past ... the industrialisation of what can be called the production for consumption of animal meat ... the reduction of the animal not only to production and over-active reproduction (hormones, genetic crossbreeding, cloning and so on) of meat for consumption but also of all sorts of other end products. (Derrida and Wills, 2002: 394)

Similarly,

> the practices of maximising control over life and death, of 'making live' in Foucault's words, through eugenics, artificial insemination and selective breeding, pharmaceutical enhancement, inoculation, and the like are on display in the modern factory farm as perhaps nowhere else in biopolitical history. (Wolfe, 2012: 46)

At the most fundamental level, farmed animals have been reconfigured to 'fit' better into agricultural production systems, food processing and retail systems, and changing patterns of food consumption. Three key issues serve to illustrate this. First, the bodies of farmed animals have been largely reconfigured through changes in breeding and reproduction practices. The deployment of genetic knowledges and technologies has increasingly allowed interventions in the breeding of farmed animal populations which have focused on specific bodily characteristics and capacities including, for example, growth rates, milk yields and corporeal conformation. As just one example, Michael Watts describes changes in the growth rates, feed efficiency and body size of broiler chickens, writing that:

> Since 1940, the industry's feed conversion rate has declined precipitously from three pounds [1.36kg] of feed per pound [0.45kg] of liveweight to under two pounds [0.9kg]. Over the same period of the average broiler liveweight has increased from 2.89lb [1.31kg] to 4.63lb [2.1kg], and the maturation period ... has plummeted from over seventy days to less than fifty. (Watts, 2000: 297)

These animal bodies are seen as more productive and 'efficient' within an output-oriented agri-food system built around producing cheap food, and where they appear designed for disassembly and processing into the extensive range of food products demanded by retailers and consumers.

The second reconfiguration issue is that farmed animals have become increasingly entangled with continually developing on-farm technologies which are responsible for monitoring and managing their lives and bodies. Here, for example, increasing levels of automation have seen technologies such as automatic milking systems replace human labour-intensive milking practices with implications for how dairy cows are expected to behave and for their relationships with people (Holloway, 2007). Moreover, the deployment of monitoring technologies inserted on or into animal bodies produce increasing amounts of data which can be used to manage farmed animals, individually instead of at herd level, at the micro scale.

The third reconfiguration of farmed animals has involved changes in farming systems that have had significant implications for animal health and welfare. Changes in herd size are part of this story. For example, in the UK the Agriculture and Horticulture Development Board suggests that between 1996 and 2018, the mean number of cows in a dairy herd almost doubled, from 75 to 148 cows (with many much larger herds becoming established during that time too, see Holloway and Bear, 2011). In the US, the phenomenon of so-called CAFOs (Concentrated Animal Feeding Operations) or feedlots has resulted in the concentration of beef production in a relatively small number of very large operations (Gollehon et al., 2001; Imhoff, 2010). The USDA's Economic Research Service (2021) reports that CAFOs containing more than 1000 animals account for less than 5 percent of feedlots, but produce 80–85 percent of US beef cattle. Those feedlots with over 32,000 cattle produce around 40 percent of all beef cattle.

Herd size is not the whole story, however. The management of farmed animals within particular farm systems is also important. Endemic so-called 'production diseases', those diseases (such as lameness or mastitis), associated with or made more likely by the conditions in which farmed animals are kept and by the expectations placed on them to be productive in certain ways, are prevalent despite high levels of veterinary intervention (McEldowney et al., 2013). Trading patterns, and the circulation of animals over space and between farms, contribute to the persistence of infectious diseases such as BVD (Bovine Viral Diarrhoea) despite the existence of testing and vaccination regimes aiming to reduce or eradicate their presence. It might, indeed, be argued that such veterinary interventions, in attempting to react to the problems associated with problematic farming systems, contribute to the persistence of such health and welfare issues by normalising and attempting to remediate them, marginalising arguments that farming systems themselves, and the wider food systems that drive farming practices, could be altered so as to make production diseases less likely.

Developing the argument from these three issues, this chapter reviews several aspects of the reconfiguration of farmed animals in contemporary livestock agriculture, and develops an agenda for ongoing research into how such animals are transformed as they are caught up in the complex network of modern food systems. Focusing mainly on examples of animal agriculture and aquaculture in the Minority World, and in particular Western Europe and North America, the chapter looks at how the changing technologies and knowledge-practices of farming, and the changing nature and demands of food systems (from production to consumption), have been associated with changes in how farmed animals are bred, reared, understood and related to.

The remainder of this chapter is presented as follows. Section two focuses on the reconfiguring of farmed animal bodies and populations in contemporary farming systems. Section three explores the concurrent reconfiguration of farmed animal subjectivities and experiences as they are remade to fit into farming systems. Section four examines how the meaningfulness of farmed animals is restructured in contemporary food systems and also discusses changes in understandings of farmed animal agency. In each of these sections, contributions towards a developing research agenda are suggested. Finally, section five aims to draw these suggestions together and outline a research agenda for future research into the ongoing reconfiguration of farmed animals in contemporary food systems.

Reconfiguring Bodies and Populations

This section discusses the reconfiguring of farmed animals as individuals and populations within contemporary farming systems. It briefly outlines the emergence of selective breeding and explores its more recent manifestations which have increasingly made use of 'geneticised' techniques. The section outlines how these processes have focused on, and had implications for, farmed animals as both individual embodied creatures and as defined populations of animals at herd, breed, national or international scales. A key argument here is that the animals and the production systems are co-constituted. Although farmed animal bodies have been significantly transformed over time through breeding and management practices, their bodies have affordances (things they *can* do) and constraints (things which *limit* their reconfiguration) which affect what farming systems *can* evolve, while the systems which do evolve clearly have important effects on farmed animals. At the same time, then, as farmed animals are transformed over longer timescales to fit farming and food systems, they are affected individually and collectively by those systems in ongoing and immediate ways, both bodily (for example in terms of health or disease) and in terms of their subjective experience of being farmed. Because of the potentially detrimental effects on farmed animals, there are clearly ethical questions concerning what farming systems *should* be practiced, and these are returned to in subsequent sections.

Space precludes a detailed discussion of the emergence of selective breeding practices. However, it is necessary to begin by acknowledging the development of pedigree breeding in the 18th century, associated with the emergence of specific, so-called 'improved' breeds of livestock (as opposed to regional 'types'), many of which persist to the present day. Pedigree breeding practices have been associated with a wider transformation of agricultural systems, such as enclosure and the increasing incorporation of agriculture within capitalist modes of production, as well as the involvement of aristocratic landed interests along with 'progressive' farmers and stock breeders looking to enhance the financial, production and status value of their farmed animals. The history and effects of these practices has been explored in detail (see, for example, Ritvo, 1987; Derry, 2003). Selective, pedigree breeding, often using processes of close in-breeding (e.g. mating an animal with its own offspring), and the creation of breeds as identifiable kinds of farmed animal, were dependent on meticulous record keeping and the production of extensive databases regarding the animals concerned. In particular, parentage records – animals' pedigrees – were (and are) vital in recording the relationships between animals, being a mechanism for proving those relationships and thus establishing the quality of any individual animal on the basis of its parentage.

The construction of farmed animal breeds is significant in terms of the reconfiguration of animals' bodies because, in the absence of alternatives such as genetic proof of membership of a particular type, it was the *visual* appearance of an animal which informed prospective buyers, for example, that the animal concerned was indeed a member of a particular breed. As such, strictly policed 'breed standards' were written by the breed societies which were established to promote each breed. Breed standards tend to emphasise the appearance and aesthetic qualities of animals, emphasising colouration for example, often in great detail (Holloway and Morris, 2014). Animals which do not meet the standards may be ineligible to be recorded in the herd or flock books of the relevant breed society. Over time, there has thus been a set of tensions, played out differently with regard to different breeds, between a desire to retain the breed standard according to which breeds have been 'fixed' according to type, and a countervailing desire to 'improve' breeds to meet changing farming and market conditions, and/or changing aesthetic sensibilities. 'Improvement', in this sense, might mean continuing to seek reconfigurations of animal bodies by making them larger, more efficient, more productive or with different conformations. In some breeds, such as Belgian Blue or British Blue cattle, such reconfiguration has produced extremes of bodily conformation such as the 'double muscling' seen in these breeds (Stassart and Whatmore, 2003). Double muscling results from a genetic abnormality in cattle, which has been selectively bred in order to increase the animals' productivity, despite in many cases producing welfare issues such as problematic calving.

In this process of reconfiguring animal bodies, record keeping, the production of data, and certification as a way of instilling trust in the qualities of farmed animals, are crucial. The breeds are constituted in and by the data, and the data help reproduce the breed. This process has intensified over time as processes of performance recording, and more recently genetic assessment of animals' qualities, have grown in importance. Performance recording, for example of feed conversion efficiency, milk yields, growth rates, or 'killing out' percentages (the ratio of useful meat to bone etc. in a slaughtered animal) has increasingly supplemented pedigree records. This data feeds back into the reconfiguration of animals' bodies as breeding strategies aim to produce bodies with specific qualities. Importantly, the creation and use of this data is associated with changed understandings of farmed animals, so that they can be represented as populations with particular population-scale characteristics or norms, against which individuals can be compared (Holloway et al., 2009). These populations can be the herds or flocks on individual farms, but might also be breed or type populations, or national or even international populations, as breeding (through the circulation of live animals, embryos, eggs or sperm) is globalised. Considerations of farmed animals as populations can then lead to larger-scale interventions in breeding and management practices with implications for the configurations of animals, as what is sought is standardised and thus predictable and designed to conform to the needs of particular food processing and retailing segments and systems. Individual animals, measured against population norms, can be managed in different ways, including (for example) the culling of those which do not meet production standards.

In many breeds, performance data is now represented as aligned with animals' genetic qualities, presented in terms of the likelihood of them passing on certain genetic characteristics to their offspring which will be expressed in their phenotypes. Estimated Breeding Values (EBVs), based on performance recording, and genetic markers, derived from analysis of blood, semen or hair samples from animals are widely used in this context. Breeding animals can thus increasingly be selected according to a set of 'genetic' traits, allowing breeders to choose to emphasise, say, growth rate, calving ease or meat tenderness in making choices about which animals to breed with which. Indeed, for some commentators emphasising 'progressive' strategies, breeding based on the traditions of breeds, with an emphasis on animals' colour and so on, should become outmoded as these genetic techniques can better inform decision-making based on the performance and 'eating' qualities that actually matter (Holloway, 2005). Especially in pig and poultry breeding, for example, for most commercial farming there has been a move away from traditional breeds towards 'hybrids' created by large commercial companies based on their genetic qualities (Watts, 2000), and sold to farmers as trademarked types which will, assuming they are housed and fed correctly, perform in very predictable ways.

In much cattle and sheep breeding, by contrast, the breed as a concept and bodily manifestation retains a valency. Nevertheless, the establishment of new bodily configurations is happening in these species too, with the creation of new, branded 'composite' breeds (e.g. the Stabiliser cattle breed, or the so-called Easycare sheep, in the mid to late 20th century) claiming to combine the best qualities of several breeds into a new type of animal. As with poultry and pigs, the creation of such composites has tended to be associated with relatively recently formed breeding companies, taking breeding out of the hands of disparate groups of farmers with varying breeding objectives and skills, and concentrating it into the hands of companies who sell breeding animals on to individual farmers. In some cases, as in the further cases of food system companies who contract with farmers to rear animals to enter into their food processing (Holloway et al., 2015; Morgan et al., 2006), the companies' control extends to being able to influence how the farmers then manage and breed their animals, transforming relations of power in farmed animal breeding and influencing the ongoing reconfigurations of farmed animal bodies. In relation to all species, these processes are countered by organisations aiming to preserve traditional breeds for a variety of reasons (e.g. they have aesthetic and heritage value, and might be seen as retaining important genetic qualities for future farming scenarios). These organisations include the breed societies themselves as well as groups such as the Rare Breeds Survival Trust (in the UK) or the Livestock Conservancy (in the US) which retain a wider remit of protecting livestock genetic diversity in the face of a tendency for farming to focus on a narrower genetic pool.

To end this section, the above discussion leads to a set of questions as part of an agenda for research concerning farmed animals in changing food systems. First, it remains important to continue to trace the implications of the ongoing physical reconfigurations of animal bodies as farming systems and breeding techniques and practices change. As well as breeding, these interventions include the use of chemicals and pharmaceuticals such as hormones and antibiotics which both controversially facilitate certain kinds of food system practice, and have implications for the bodies and welfare of farmed animals. In breeding itself, techniques such as gene editing are becoming increasingly seen as offering the potential to rapidly 'improve' livestock populations, yet such techniques remain controversial in part because of their association with sustaining intensive forms of animal agriculture. Second, the changing relationships between understandings of individual farmed animals, and animals as populations, remains an important area of research as it influences how animals are conceptualised and treated. A third area of interest concerns breeds and breeding practices, and how the intensified application of genetic knowledge-practices is intertwined with the (re)constitution, or decline, of breeds. Relatedly, a fourth area for continued research is the changing power relations associated with these processes, which exist differentially across different farmed animal species and sectors, and vary geographically, but are connected to the increasing importance of companies and other organisations in breeding and managing farmed animals.

Reconfiguring Subjectivities

In this section the chapter builds on the discussion of the corporeal remaking of farmed animal bodies by exploring how farmed animal subjectivities and experiences are reconfigured as they are made to fit into farming systems. The section also examines how intersubjective relationships involving humans and farmed animals are affected by ongoing reconfigurations of animal bodies and subjectivities. Clearly, this multi-dimensional reconfiguration goes beyond the use of breeding strategies and technologies as farmed animals adapt to different farming systems. Here, subjectivity is not seen as an inherent characteristic of a (human or nonhuman) animal, but as something which is a relational effect of, in this case, specific farming systems and particular kinds of farming knowledges, practices, technologies and spaces (Holloway, 2007; Miele, 2016). The argument is that what it is to be a dairy cow, for example, can be different, depending on whether she is part of a more or less intensive farming system, what kinds of milking technology are used, what kinds of spaces she inhabits and so on. Two brief examples illustrate this.

First, at the same time as breeding for bodily characteristics such as size, colour or productivity, selective livestock breeding has also aimed at reconfiguring subjectivity. Breed society standards, for example, often refer to qualities of subjectivity which are expected to be apparent in breed members: references to 'breed character' for example suggest that individual animals express a shared breed personality. At the same time, some breeds in particular, especially those associated with more extensive, upland farming environments, are expected to exhibit sets of characteristics such as independence, self-sufficiency and resilience in the face of challenging environmental conditions. More widely, breeding strategies have attempted to breed more docile and pliable animals. Such animals might, first, present less danger to the people farming them, and second, might be more compliant with more intensified farming systems in which they experience crowding, noise, or close confinement. They might thus exhibit less stress in such systems, meaning that from the farmer's perspective they are likely to be more productive. Combining attempts to manipulate animal bodies with reconfiguring their subjectivity, discussion has even taken place regarding breeding chickens, and potentially other animals, to be blind, as a way of reducing the stress such animals experience in intensive farming conditions (Thompson, 2007). Taking this further, but for similar reasons, philosophical debates have considered the ethical implications of creating 'brainless' animals (Solon, 2012), which resonates with recent developments in the field of in vitro meat production where meat is 'grown' artificially rather than 'harvested' from the bodies of animals (see below). This effective removal of subjectivity is clearly a highly controversial suggestion, removing the integrity of the animal as an animal, but more widely these approaches to breeding for docility or resilience to the conditions of intensive farming come under sustained criticism for acting to facilitate and reproduce farming systems that many see as ethically problematic.

Second, certain technological changes have resulted in changing expectations being placed on farmed animals. What they are expected to do, associated with the constitution of a particular subjectivity, alters in relation to the introduction of new technology. For instance, the advent of automatic or robotic milking technologies on dairy farms means that cows are expected to choose to visit the milking robot to be milked, several times during each 24-hour period. This contrasts with 'conventional' parlour milking, in which the cows are milked together, as a herd, usually twice per day. Automatic milking represents the cow as an individual subject, able to choose when to be milked, and as having a freedom which conventionally milked cows lack. In terms of how the cow is subjectified in automated milking, however, this freedom is constrained by expectations that she *will* choose to be milked regularly, that she will be a productive herd member, and that she will not *resist* the system by either not choosing to be milked regularly enough, or by visiting the machine too regularly in the search for food (Bear and Holloway, 2019).

Beyond these elements of subjectivity, other aspects of farmed animal experience can be characterised in terms of their welfare. While understandings of animal welfare and the closely related concept of health have changed over time (see, for example, Buller and Roe, 2018), it is evident that welfare as the subjective experience of farmed animals is closely related to the specific nature of different farming systems and is part of the reconfiguration of animal bodies and subjectivities. Health and welfare are thus systematically part of farming systems, with specific welfare issues being constituted within those systems (McEldowney et al., 2013). For example, some health and welfare issues, such as lameness or mastitis, are specifically referred to as 'production conditions', and are associated with both the environments animals are kept in (for example, the use of concrete and slatted flooring for indoor animal production) and the physiological demands put on their bodies (for example, the significant metabolic demands put on dairy cows to produce high milk yields, or the effects on broiler chicken bodies of the very rapid growth rates they are genetically predisposed to achieve).

The reconfigurations of subjectivity briefly outlined here, and which are linked to changes in farming systems and farmed animal bodies, can also be associated with important reconfigurations in the intersubjective relations between humans and animals in farming. In this sense, the subjectivities of farmed animals and humans are co-produced in farming systems. Here, for example, important notions of what it is to be a 'good farmer' (Burton et al., 2021) have co-evolved with the changing bodies, subjectivities and experiences of farmed animals, and with growing demands from consumer groups, activist groups and private and public sector organisations for animal welfare to be considered in agriculture. Notions of what makes a good 'stockperson' (Butler and Holloway, 2016) or caregiver (Buller and Roe, 2018) have also changed in relation to some of the reconfigurations mentioned above. For example, Butler and Holloway (2016) show how what is expected of farmers and stockpeople in dairy farming has changed with the advent of automated milking systems which create large amounts of data about animal bodies and productivity: the people involved have to learn to know their animals in part through that data, and to make interventions in the lives of their animals on the basis of the data. More widely, new kinds of data stimulating different kinds of interventions are increasingly created by the various monitoring devices which are attached to animals (such as tags measuring activity levels), or literally placed within animals' bodies (such as boluses in cows' stomachs measuring rumen activity). Similarly, the increasing availability and use of 'genetic' information in livestock breeding reconfigures the relationships between breeders and their animals, at the same time as the animals' bodies are remade in genetically inflected breeding strategies. Breeders come to know their animals at least partly in terms of such data, supplanting or supplementing previous visual and haptic ways of knowing (Holloway and Morris, 2012). In this way, the increasing amounts of data available about farmed animals' bodies and behaviours become part of how animals' bodies, behaviours and subjectivities are reconfigured in contemporary agricultural systems.

As a further dimension of this, assessments of animal health and welfare have increasingly been driven by standardised auditing processes rather than by informal farmer judgements, often tied to accreditation and certification schemes which aim to reassure consumers that their food is being produced in acceptable ways. For example, dairy farmers are encouraged to conduct regular mobility scoring of their cows as a way of assessing the prevalence and severity of lameness, and to drive remedial measures which might include both changing the cows' environment and treating individuals for specific foot conditions. Auditing schemes create further layers of data, and themselves act to drive change in farming practices and animals' bodies and experiences and through their emphasis on the specific criteria they embody and measure. Such schemes represent a degree of institutionalisation in how animals are reconfigured, as external agencies (including veterinary organisations, accreditation organisations, and retailers) drive the adoption of sets of standards, and audit adherence to those standards as they are enacted through on-farm practice. Further evidence of such institutionalisation can be seen in industry-led schemes focusing on specific diseases. In England, for example, the BVDFree England programme aims to eradicate this viral cattle infection (which can affect animals' productivity and make them more susceptible to other diseases) through a programme of testing and vaccination. In this scheme, some animals are configured as 'Persistently Infected' (PI) cows which will pass on the infection to other animals and to their own calves. Farmers are expected to cull PIs so that other animals are protected from them. Herds of cattle are in this way reconfigured around the specific characteristics of a viral infection, with the aim, ultimately, of creating a national population of healthier animals (Shortall and Calo, 2021).

Finally, it is important to note the complexity and ambiguity of human–nonhuman intersubjective relationships in agriculture. For notwithstanding the emphasis on productivity, it is recognised that other kinds of relationships exist for some farmed animals which can be expressed, in alternative ways, through their breeding and care. Thus, while animals are evaluated in terms of their growth rates or milk yields, they can at the same time be regarded as companion animals (Holloway, 2001), and as individuals and groups with which farmers or care givers experience intense but problematic relationships of care (de La Bellacasa, 2017). For example, Convery et al. (2005) discuss the profound sense of loss and grief experienced by UK farmers whose animals were subject to compulsory slaughter as part of the measures taken in response to the outbreak of Foot and Mouth Disease in 2001. In cases like these, the attachment to certain sorts of animals points to processes of differentiation which distinguish between different kinds of farmed animals in farming systems, implying that there will be a differentiation of treatment and intersubjective relationship too. For example, breeding animals and pedigree animals kept in relatively small numbers are likely to be the subjects of 'closer' relationships than animals being rapidly reared for meat or being kept in very large numbers.

Such considerations open up a further set of questions informing a research agenda in this field. First, there is a need to continue exploring the production of nonhuman subjectivities as food systems, technologies and relationships change. As part of this, continuing to examine changing human–nonhuman animal relationships in agriculture remains important as these inform understandings of different human subjectivities, and the emergence and contestation of ethical relationships in farming. Second, there is a continuing need to focus on different dimensions of health and welfare issues in relation to farmed animals. How are persistent issues in this area addressed and how are they understood by different groups (including the nonfarming public as well as farmers, vets, policymakers and others)? This is a vitally important question alongside ongoing investigation of the implications of emergent health and welfare issues for animal bodies and subjectivities. Finally, emergent ethical issues surround the ongoing entanglement of animals with techniques and technologies, such as novel breeding processes, which reconfigure their experience and subjectivity as well as their bodies (Twine, 2010). These issues warrant research which examines the views of different interest groups, again including the nonfarming public, on the future of food systems and the often-problematic human–nonhuman animal relationships involved.

Reconfiguring the Agency and Meaning of Animals

This penultimate section of the chapter briefly addresses some of the ways that farmed animal agency, and the meaningfulness of animals in different situations, has been and is being reconfigured alongside the remaking of their bodies and subjectivities described earlier. First, this is because relationships between animals and different kinds of environmental issues are undergoing a form of renegotiation, partly as farmed animals have been constituted as environmental agents. That is, in some spaces they have been regarded as beneficial in attempts to conserve and manage certain ecosystems. The practice of 'conservation grazing' (WallisDeVries et al., 1998) for example has made use of often 'traditional' breeds of cattle and sheep, as their selective grazing allows the flourishing of particular vegetation species, and even their hoofprints might contribute to producing microenvironments assisting the conservation of invertebrate or bird species. Similarly, pigs have been used in woodland and scrub management. This might be seen as the configuring of farmed animals as providers of 'ecosystem services', expressed through their capacities as (for example) grazers and browsers. On the other hand, however, farmed animals, and perhaps more properly the farming of animals, have been figured as agents of environmental crisis. There are several dimensions to this (Sage, 2012). These include the increasing concern about the contributions to greenhouse gas emissions (GHG) made by cattle especially, emissions of other pollutants in manure, and thinking more systemically, concerns about significant transformations of environments such as rainforest into either grazing land or land used to produce crops grown to feed animals reared elsewhere. In this sense, animal bodies are figured as contributing to the climate crisis through their own bodily metabolisms and in terms of the systems which feed them. Concerns about animals' emissions of GHG or other pollutants influence other reconfiguration processes which directly affect animals bodies and experiences, for example through attempts to reduce their environmental impact through intervening in the interactions between animal bodies and environments (for instance by manipulating cows' physiological processes by altering their diets, or their rumen functioning) or through the genetic manipulation of animals to create, for instance, the Enviropig©, engineered to excrete less phosphorous (Forsberg et al., 2003).

A second form of agency attributed to farmed animals is their threats to health, not only their own wellbeing through various livestock diseases and biosecurity issues, but also to people through the transmission of zoonoses (i.e. diseases which can affect human and nonhuman animals). The potential of new diseases emerging from more intensive forms of contact between farmed animals and people has become a growing public policy concern. Animals thus become associated with risks to human health, and these concerns have been heightened as people have become more aware that the functioning of particular farming systems, and the specific practices involved, create pathogenic 'disease situations' (Hinchliffe et al., 2016) conducive to the spread of disease. For example, maintaining large populations of animals confined in indoor spaces means that disease transmission can be rapid, while the frequent long-distance movement of animals makes the spread of disease over larger geographical areas more likely. Responding to these concerns, a whole biosecurity infrastructure focusing on separating farmed animals from possible disease sources, and on tracking and recording animal movements, has arisen (Bingham et al., 2008; Hinchliffe et al., 2013; Hinchliffe et al., 2016). Consequently, the reconfiguring of animal bodies to fit into particular kinds of farming system serves as a feedback loop on those animals as they experience particular kinds of confinement and bodily intervention (such as the use of prophylactic medication) which itself may produce further anxieties such as those related to antimicrobial resistance (Morris et al., 2016). Prophylactic use of antibiotics, for example, has been used in some systems not only to try to protect animals against infection, but actually to promote rapid growth as farmers aim for more 'efficient' and speedy rearing. This raises concern not only about the evolution of the bacteria affecting farmed animals so that they are able to resist antimicrobials, but also that such resistance becomes more possible in those bacteria which might affect people.

Finally in this section, the meaning of farmed animals as food has undergone reconfiguration as food systems and consumption practices have changed: animal bodies' meaningfulness as meat in different food systems varies. Broadly, in systems associated with the mass consumption of animal bodies, there is a focus on production quantity, on qualities such as the efficiency and standardisation of production and on the relative cheapness of animal products. Contrasting with this, other systems are associated with an elite preoccupation with 'quality' products, defined in terms of the taste and texture of animal products and with sets of associated meanings linking those products to particular places, people and production processes (e.g. organic production) (Ilbery et al., 2005). In this latter case, particular kinds of animal become important, with some consumers seeking products from 'rare' or 'heritage' breeds, or meat associated with breeds embodying qualities of taste and texture such as Wagyu or Aberdeen Angus beef. Here again, the material and symbolic configuration of animals is linked to certification and protection regimes, as animal products are labelled with information guaranteeing the breed of animal or the way it was reared. Yet other groups of consumers are moving away from the consumption of animal products altogether, for a range of ethical, health and environmental reasons. This consumption trend may have implications for the future reconfiguration of farmed animals. For example, reduced consumption of animal products may mean that animals figure more in terms of the preservation of rural heritage, in much reduced numbers, rather than as units of production. At the same time the emergence of 'alternative' or substitutive modes of meat production, such as in vitro meat, radically changes understandings of what meat is as it becomes displaced from actual animal bodies (Sexton et al., 2019; see also Chapter 8 in this volume).

As in previous sections, the discussion above presents some further areas for inclusion in an emerging agenda for food systems research. These include a continued focus on changing relationships between farmed animals and environmental issues, on evolving biosecurity issues and 'disease situations' as they affect human and nonhuman animals and have recursive effects on farming practices and on the bodies and experiences of farmed animals, and on the implications of changing consumption patterns for food systems and farmed animals. The COVID-19 pandemic raises the profile of a further dimension of this. At the time of writing the causes of the pandemic are still being explored, however it is likely that the encroachment of farming practices onto previously uncultivated land, driven by situations where many small farmers are being excluded from their traditional lands, along with the use of 'wild' animals for food, presents opportunities for more encounters between people and 'new' viruses with the possibility that those viruses become able to infect, and become transmitted between, humans. The complexities and geographical and social variability of food systems and production–consumption relationships are likely to continue to mean that animals (both domesticated and 'wild') are configured very differently as they are caught up in different consumption practices and systems, with significant effects on what they mean in those systems, how they are treated, valued, and understood, and what effects they can have on human health.

Conclusions

This chapter has explored several dimensions of the ways that farmed animals have been reconfigured in contemporary food systems. In particular it has suggested that these processes of reconfiguration provide opportunities for future research that can scrutinise and interrogate the entanglement of animals with changing farming systems and practices and the wider political-ecologies of meat-oriented food systems (Emel and Neo, 2015). The chapter first discussed the remaking of individual, and populations, of animals through breeding and management practices. Second, it covered the remaking of farmed animal subjectivities and experiences, aspects of reconfiguration which are concurrent with the remaking of bodies but which also imply a need to pay attention to what farmed animals experience as a result of farming practices which focus on their bodies and their productivity, and what is expected of farmed animals in different farming systems. Third, the chapter explored some aspects of the reconfiguration of farmed animal agency, suggesting that the meaningfulness of animals is changed along with interventions in their bodies, subjectivities and experiences. In relation to each section, dimensions of a further research agenda have been suggested. Throughout, the emphasis has been on the relationships between farmed animals and farming and food systems: these are co-produced, so that an understanding of how farmed animals are reconfigured requires analysis of the practices and relationships encapsulated within specific systems.

Of course, this implies that a reconfiguration of animals is just one part of the systemic changes which need to be examined concurrently. If animals are regarded as actors and as sentient subjects, able to affect and be affected by how farming is done, then there is an ethical need to pay them particular attention in analyses of continuing and contested changes in farming and food systems. Such changes include ongoing rounds of enclosure (Watts, 2000), intensification and productivism, as well as divergent pathways which might emphasise, *inter alia*, processes of extensification, more sustainable, regenerative and agroecological modes of livestock farming, improvements in animal health and welfare, and even the reduction or ending of the consumption of animal products. While some may challenge the consumption of animal products and their bodies, as seen through the increasing adoption of vegan and vegetarian diets, for many more consumers there is at least a growing desire to know more about where their food comes from and to be able express their 'care' through their consumption choices. For most people outside farming there is limited knowledge or understanding of breeding techniques and how animal bodies are reconfigured, and they may know little about modern farming systems and practices. However, many are anxious about the conditions in which farmed animals are produced and kept, expressing this through a rejection of 'intensive' farming, and seeking welfare labelling and foods of known provenance, or through seeking reconnection with food producers (and thus by proxy with their animals and farms) through 'alternative' food networks of various sorts

(Kneafsey et al., 2008; Goodman et al., 2012). And yet there are also many consumers for whom this kind of re-engagement with, and expression of care for, sources of animal products is a luxury, or not remotely a concern.

Because of these differences in food system pathways (e.g. intensification or extensification) and in people's perspectives on farmed animals more generally, a research agenda in this field needs to pursue multiple lines of enquiry, focusing on different practices and visions for the future of food systems. If it assumes that some kind(s) of animal farming will persist, it needs to avoid simplistic assumptions about which farming practices are better and to engage with actual practices, experiences and human–nonhuman relationships which will be geographically specific and potentially very diverse. At the same time, it needs to acknowledge the multiple perspectives on the ethically problematic practice of farming animals, exploring the commonalities and differences evident in the views of different groups of farmers, different publics and others. This 'staying with the trouble' (Haraway, 2016) of livestock farming means addressing, rather than avoiding, difficult questions about the ongoing reconfigurations of animal bodies, subjectivities and agency.

Note

1. Some of the material in this chapter is drawn from work undertaken as part of the following funded research projects:
    *   Wellcome Trust 'Thinking forward through the past: linking science, social science and the humanities to inform the sustainable reduction of endemic disease in British livestock farming'. 209818/E/17/Z.
    *   Economic and Social Research Council. 'Robotic and information technologies in livestock agriculture: new relationships between humans, cows and machines'. RES-062-23-2086.
    *   Economic and Social Research Council. 'Genetics, genomics and genetic modification in agriculture: emerging knowledge-practices in making and managing farm livestock'. RES-062-23-0642.

References

Bear, C., Holloway, L., 2019. Beyond resistance: Geographies of divergent more-than-human conduct in robotic milking. *Geoforum*, 104: 212–21.

Bingham, N., Enticott, G., Hinchliffe, S., 2008. Biosecurity: Spaces, practices, and boundaries. *Environment and Planning A*, 40: 1528–33.

Buller, H., Roe, E., 2018. *Food and Animal Welfare*. Bloomsbury: London.

Burton, R. Forney, J., Stock, P., Sutherland, L., 2021. *The Good Farmer: Culture and identity in food and agriculture*. Earthscan: London.

Butler, D., Holloway, L., 2016. Technology and restructuring the social field of dairy farming: Hybrid capitals, 'stockmanship' and automatic milking systems. *Sociologia Ruralis*, 56: 513-30.

Convery, I., Bailey, C., Mort, M., Baxter, J., 2005. Death in the wrong place? Emotional geographies of the UK 2001 foot and mouth disease epidemic. *Journal of Rural Studies*, 21: 99-109.

de La Bellacasa, M., 2017. *Matters of Care: Speculative ethics in more than human worlds*. University of Minnesota Press: Minneapolis.

Derrida, J., Wills, D., 2002. The animal that therefore I am (more to follow). *Critical Inquiry*, 28: 369-418.

Derry, M., 2003. *Bred for Perfection: Shorthorn cattle, Collies and Arabian horses since 1800*. Johns Hopkins University Press: Baltimore, Maryland.

Emel, J., Neo, H., 2015. *Political Ecologies of Meat*. Routledge: Abingdon.

Forsberg, CW, Phillips, J., Golovan, S. et al., 2003. The Enviropig physiology, performance, and contribution to nutrient management advances in a regulated environment: The leading edge of change in the pork industry. *Journal of Animal Science*, 81: E68-E77.

Gollehon, N, Caswell, M., Ribaudo, M. et al., 2001. *Confined Animal Production and Manure Nutrients*. Department of Agriculture Economic Research Service: Washington DC.

Goodman, D., DuPuis, M., Goodman, M., 2012. *Alternative Food Networks: Knowledge, practice, and politics*. Routledge: Abingdon.

Haraway, D. 2016. *Staying with the Trouble: Making kin in the Chthulucene*. Duke University Press: Durham, NC.

Hinchliffe, S., Allen, J., Lavau, S. et al., 2013. Biosecurity and the topologies of infected life: From borderlines to borderlands. *Transactions of the Institute of British Geographers*, 38: 531-43.

Hinchliffe, S., Bingham, N., Allen, J., Carter, S., 2016. *Pathological Lives: Disease, space and biopolitics*. John Wiley: London.

Holloway, L., 2001. Pets and protein: Placing domestic livestock on hobby-farms in England and Wales. *Journal of Rural Studies*, 17: 293-307.

Holloway, L., 2005. Aesthetics, genetics, and evaluating animal bodies: locating and displacing cattle on show and in figures. *Environment and Planning D: Society & Space*, 23: 883-902.

Holloway, L., 2007. Subjecting cows to robots: Farming technologies and the making of animal subjects. *Environment and Planning D: Society & Space*, 25: 1041-60.

Holloway, L., Bear, C., 2011. DNA typing and super dairies: Changing practices and remaking cows. *Environment and Planning A*, 43: 1487-91.

Holloway, L., Morris, C., 2012. Contesting genetic knowledge-practices in livestock breeding: Biopower, biosocial collectivities, and heterogeneous resistances. *Environment and Planning D: Society & Space*, 30: 60-77.

Holloway, L., Morris, C., 2014. Viewing animal bodies: Truths, practical aesthetics and ethical considerability in UK livestock breeding. *Social & Cultural Geography*, 15: 1-22.

Holloway, L., Morris, C., Gibbs, D., Gilna, B., 2015. Making meat collectivities: entanglements of geneticisation, integration and contestation in livestock breeding. In Goodman, M., Sage, C. (eds), *Food Transgressions: Making Sense of Contemporary Food Politics*. Routledge: London.

Holloway, L., Morris, C., Gilna, B., Gibbs, D., 2009. Biopower, genetics and livestock breeding: (re)Constituting animal populations and heterogeneous biosocial collectivities. *Transactions of the Institute of British Geographers*, 34: 394-407.

Ilbery, B., Morris, C., Buller, H., Maye, D., Kneafsey, M., 2005. Product, process and place: An examination of food marketing and labelling schemes in Europe and North America. *European Urban and Regional Studies*, 12: 116-32.

Imhoff, D., 2010. *The CAFO Reader: The Tragedy of Industrial Animal Factories*. Watershed Media: Berkley, CA.

Kneafsey, M., Cox, R., Holloway, L. et al., 2008. *Reconnecting Consumers, Producers and Food: Exploring alternatives*. Bloomsbury Publishing: London.

McEldowney, J, Grant, W., Medley, G., 2013. *The Regulation of Animal Health and Welfare: science, law and policy*. Routledge: London.

Miele, M., 2016. The making of the brave sheep … or the laboratory as the unlikely space of attunement to animal emotions. *Geohumanities*, 2: 58-75.

Morgan, K, Marsden, T., Murdoch, J., 2006. *Worlds of Food: Place, Power and Provenance in the Food Chain*. Oxford University Press: Oxford.

Morris, C., Helliwell, R., Raman, S., 2016. Framing the agricultural use of antibiotics and antimicrobial resistance in UK national newspapers and the farming press. *Journal of Rural Studies*, 45: 43-53.

Ritvo, H. 1987. *The Animal Estate: The English and other creatures in the Victorian age*. Harvard University Press: Cambridge MA.

Sage, C., 2012. *Environment and Food*. Routledge: Abingdon.

Sexton, A., Garnett, T., Lorimer, J., 2019. Framing the future of food: The contested promises of alternative proteins. *Environment and Planning E: Nature and Space*, 2: 47-72.

Shortall, O., Calo, A., 2021. Novel industry–government governance mechanisms for the eradication of bovine viral diarrhoea in the UK and Ireland. *Journal of Rural Studies*, 81: 324-35.

Solon, O. 2012. Food projects proposes matrix-style vertical chicken farms. *Wired*, 15 February.

Stassart, P., Whatmore, S., 2003. Metabolising risk: Food scares and the un/re-making of Belgian beef. *Environment and Planning A: Economy and Space*, 35: 449-62.

Thompson, P., 2007. Welfare as an ethical issue: Are blind chickens the answer. In *Bioethics Symposium: Proactive approaches to controversial welfare and ethical concerns in poultry science*. https://naldc.nal.usda.gov/catalog/7016548.

Twine, R., 2010. *Animals as Biotechnology: Ethics, sustainability and critical animal studies* Earthscan: London.

USDA ERS 2021. https://www.ers.usda.gov/topics/animal-products/cattle-beef/sector -at-a-glance.

WallisDeVries, M., Bakker, J., van Wieren, S., 1998. *Grazing and Conservation Management*. Springer Science & Business Media: Berlin.

Watts, M. 2000. Afterword: Enclosure. In Philo, C. and Wilbert, C. (eds), *Animal Spaces, Beastly Places*. Routledge: London.

Wolfe, C. 2012. *Before the Law: Humans and other animals in a biopolitical frame*. University of Chicago Press: Chicago.

PART III

'Solutions?'

Introduction to Part III

If the chapters of Part II presented a bleak picture of a food system dominated by corporate concentration and where a narrative of productivism, with all of its attendant consequences for people (as workers and consumers), animals and climate prevailed, then readers will take solace from the writings that follow here. We are not yet in the 'sunny uplands' but we can now ask some important questions such as: can the incumbent corporate hegemony maintain its grip on the food system and how might it do so? And what prospect do subaltern voices have in executing a different vision for how we might feed ourselves?

In this Part there are five chapters offering very different insights into possible ways forward for the food system. They should not be regarded as mutually exclusive or as singular solutions but might well emerge, if not synergistically then as aspects of a diversifying food system with even entirely divergent trajectories marking various 'sub-systems' of food production and supply. In Chapter 7, David Rose and colleagues review technological developments in primary food production and prospects for what they call a 'Fourth Agricultural Revolution'. Helpfully, their historical backfill explains why this is the fourth and they counsel care in using the term 'revolution'. Still, digitalization does seem to promise rather a sharp change of direction as it underpins developments in artificial intelligence, robotics, remote sensing and so on. While smartphone devices and apps appear to be making some contribution to farmers in the Global South, the roll-out of precision farming in wealthier countries – involving drones, robotic milking parlours, advanced genetics, the Internet of Things – does suggest that Big Ag will remain firmly in control given the levels of financial investment heading into the sector. The chapter demonstrates a commendable secular agnosticism which helps us appreciate the potential contribution that new technologies might offer – especially if they were to be decoupled from the economic interests behind them. Their two cases of precision livestock technology and autonomous robotics provide a good basis by which to appreciate the potential benefits but also drawbacks of such innovations.

Beyond the fields, the mainstream food system is currently beset by breathless excitement surrounding the emergence of alternative proteins (AP) as a solution to the dilemma facing the 'ethical consumer'. Conscious that rearing animals to make patties for burgers comes with all sorts of trouble (Haraway, 2016), Silicon Valley start-ups saw an opportunity in an emerging market for plant-based food. Unsurprisingly, Big Meat were not slow to react and have also joined the field rebranding themselves in the process, leaders of a new Protein industry (Howard et al., 2021). In Chapter 8, Alex Sexton and Mike Goodman introduce us to the world of plant-based and cell-cultured AP and evaluate their current and potential impacts on the development of food systems within wealthier markets. Their analysis reveals the necessity of simultaneously possessing the capacity to understand the scientific-technical, legal-regulatory, and bio-ethical dimensions of such developments. Above all, however, the chapter explores the ways in which the proponents of AP are representing themselves as planetary saviours, capable of addressing the narratives of ecological crisis, anxiety, and urgency – and in which meat has become deeply entangled – by offering eaters the chance to take 'ethics off the table' while still enjoying the foods (burgers) to which they are accustomed. However, what are the implications of taking animals out of meat? What are the spatial and wider economic implications of 'death-free' eating and farming? This chapter offers some rich insights into such questions.

Chapter 9 sets out clearly and concisely a number of reasons why cities should be concerned with food systems. Urbanization means there are increasing numbers of mouths to feed in cities and food supply chains may be less resilient in a warming and more uncertain future. Issues of poverty and precarity are also confronting increasing numbers of people, and not simply in the poorest countries. Yet the last decade or so has seen the emergence of a number of international agreements and networks designed to encourage and support cities to engage with food. Jess Halliday, who is professionally engaged in such work, makes a powerful case to show not only what city governments can do about food, but what food can do for the city. Reviewing a range of policy initiatives as well as challenges, Chapter 9 provides a clear-eyed examination of the possibilities for greater municipal and civic engagement with the food system. Given the bridging functions that food can perform with other sectors (health, environmental quality, energy etc.) it provides cities with greater capacity for adaptive governance which would enhance resilience and contingency in order to improve the health and wellbeing of its citizens.

Extending and developing this approach, Chapter 10 first reminds us of the extractive, long-distance and linear nature of the prevailing food system that has generated such enormous costs for human and planetary health. However, introducing the principles and practices of a circular economy, Steffen Böhm and colleagues explain how these provide an integrated approach to addressing human, environmental and economic health via food systems transformation. Using the UK as a worked example, particularly the south-west where the writing team have conducted extensive engaged research practice, they set out and illustrate the ways in which three key principles can be realized. The synergistic benefits that are gained by operationalizing food systems at a regional scale are innumerable and demonstrates once more that there are very practical and successful alternatives to business as usual – providing we can convince governing institutions to engage with such initiatives.

The final chapter in this volume takes us into a realm which is all too frequently overlooked by food system studies: the domestic kitchen. An architect in professional practice, Kata Fodor, the author of this chapter, reveals for us some of the design secrets that have shaped our living spaces, and which have traditionally centred upon the nuclear family. As late-modern societies have experienced demographic and social change, including increasing numbers of single-person households, designers have been rethinking the space allocated to the kitchen and its many appliances. Moreover, digitalization is not only making an impact in farming and through global supply chains, but in the way we connect with proximate sources of food, whether raw ingredients or prepared meals. The sharing economy, which underpins the commercial success of Airbnb and Uber, seems to have resulted in more mixed fortunes in the food realm, and Chapter 11 takes us through some of its casualties. Nevertheless, online meal delivery services appear to be thriving; linking 'dark kitchens' on industrial estates with (mostly) urban customers either ill-equipped (kitchen space, utensils, skills) or too time pressed to prepare their own food. What does this mean for the food system? What does it mean for individuals as consumers of food? As discussed in Chapter 1, much will depend upon the food environment or, as Fodor terms it here, the foodscape. What are the infrastructural arrangements as well as the cognitive signals that might encourage us to assert greater control over what we choose to buy, prepare and eat? Do we, after all, need to rethink the traditional domestic kitchen but replace it with shared spaces that might encourage and facilitate more attention to what we put into our mouths? In this regard the design of hybrid food spaces that exist outside the home, including kitchens, pushes back against the individualization that the mainstream food system has so enthusiastically promoted.

As Fodor concludes, "Design at the end of the food system – in the realm of consumption – shapes the entire food system by the sheer collective power of the quantities involved". Design, then, is a great deal more than re-modelling space: it has a transformative power which can be used to rethink many of our existing practices. Indeed, perhaps it can also help dismantle the belief propagated by food companies and echoed by governments, that we are only ever consumers driven by economic rationality, whereas food system transformation will require us to become more collaborative food citizens.

References

Haraway, D., 2016. *Staying with the Trouble: Making Kin in the Chthulucene*. Durham, NC: Duke University Press.

Howard, P., Ajena, F., Yamaoka, M., Clarke, A., 2021. 'Protein' Industry Convergence and its Implications for Resilient and Equitable Food Systems. *Front. Sustain. Food Syst.* 5: 684181. https://doi.org/10.3389/fsufs.2021.684181.

7

The fourth agricultural revolution: technological developments in primary food production

David Christian Rose, Mondira Bhattacharya, Auvikki de Boon, Ram Kiran Dhulipala, Catherine Price and Juliette Schillings

Introduction

This chapter explores the past, present, and future of agricultural technology yet it is difficult to begin with an agreed definition of 'agri-tech', as a review of the literature will reveal. Some papers have attempted to define contemporary developments as the 'digital agricultural revolution' (Bertoglio et al., 2021), 'agriculture 4.0' (Barrett and Rose, 2020; Klerkx and Rose, 2020), 'precision agriculture' (see Miles, 2019), and other variants, such as 'precision livestock farming' (Berckmans, 2014). For many, agricultural technology includes developments such as artificial intelligence, robotics, remote sensing, and decision support systems, while for others lower tech 'tools' are also included. Some people speak of innovation, rather than technology, which can be defined as 'doing something differently' and thus is much broader than a tangible piece of equipment. A key lesson from the literature is, therefore, that policymakers, funders, and other actors who set the direction of agriculture, equate agricultural technology with 'high-tech' only at their peril – because it risks diverting attention away from existing technologies, which could be better implemented and for which evidence proves benefit (Klerkx and Rose, 2020).

For the purposes of this chapter, we do not make a tacit judgement of what agricultural technology specifically refers to. Rather, we attempt to provide an overview of the evolution of agricultural technology over time ('past', 'present' and 'future'), the spectrum of technologies from the high-tech to the low-tech and speculate what agriculture of the future might look like. We explore the possible benefits and drawbacks of the so-called fourth agricultural revolution, including who is most likely to win and lose from the increased use of sophisticated technology on-farm, and we also identify key questions to consider as we move towards this so-called 'revolution'.

Revolution? Or Evolution?

Agricultural change has been defined by long periods of stagnation and short periods of rapid change. Although demarcations of critical moments in agriculture vary, one school of thought is that there have been three previous agricultural revolutions: the first occurring when hunter-gatherer societies moved to settled agriculture; the second associated with new technologies developed before the Industrial Revolution in Britain; and the third coinciding with the post-Second World War 'Green Revolution' as new technologies (e.g. high-yielding seeds and agri-chemicals) were rolled out in in the developing world (Rose and Chilvers, 2018).

Research has shown, however, that this is a Western-centric and oversimplified view of agricultural change, focusing selectively on apparent headline moments, and ignoring the non-linear reality of technological development and uptake. As van der Veen (2010) argues, the term 'agricultural revolution' has often been used to describe the end point in which many different innovations have come together over a long period of time, adding up to a magnitude of change, worthy of a revolution. However, focusing on the moment of transformation ignores the slow, non-linear, incremental change that characterises technological change in agriculture. Development and uptake of technology can sometimes be quick (Lowenberg-DeBoer and Erickson, 2019), but this appears to be relatively rare. Two examples help to illustrate the non-linearity of change.

In 18th and early 19th century England, agricultural labourers earned a living by using a flail to manually harvest grains. In the first decades of the 19th century, however, threshing machines were invented and became increasingly popular with farmers who could save money on labour. A simplified chronological narrative may suggest that threshing machines were a better technology than the simple flail and thus were adopted relatively quickly and without argument. Yet, this would ignore the huge controversy created by the introduction of threshing machines, which were resisted by labourers. As people lost their jobs, a series of so-called 'Swing Riots' occurred across southern and eastern England with threshing machines smashed and burned. Though the impact of such resistance was relatively short-lived, there were examples of farmers returning to the old method of flailing, at least for a short time (MERL, 2021).

A more famous narrative of technological improvement in agriculture is the so-called 'third agricultural revolution' or the 'Green Revolution' as it is better known. Popular accounts of the Green Revolution tell a story of Western-led technological improvement across the Global South, particularly in Asia, where increased yields saved hundreds of millions of people from starvation. On the face of it, therefore, the Green Revolution appears to be an example of linear technology uptake, which led to positive benefits for all. Yet, scholars have critiqued this 'political myth of the averted famine' (Pielke Jr and Linnér, 2019), arguing that improved yields came largely as a result of improved weather and changing agricultural policies, as well as labour-saving mechanisation and plant breeding advancements. There are accounts of long-term innovation by farming communities across Asia and South America which led to improvements masked by the claim that Western technology saved the day (Kumar et al., 2017). Furthermore, there are many studies that explore the negative consequences of new technologies associated with the Green Revolution, from labour displacement, a loss of autonomy amongst rural communities, and a rise in social inequality (Shiva, 2016). Yet,

> [f]amine averted by the intervention of scientific genius is a much more straightforward narrative than a famine-free story of incremental, accumulating, multi-factor progress in local agricultural production due to a complex tapestry of societal and political actors. (Pielke Jr and Linnér 2019: 278–279)

Change is thus rarely caused by the introduction of a radical, 'high-tech' product, but rather by the accumulation of low-tech and non-tech innovations. Farmers still use old equipment; a BBC Farming Today tweet[1] to ask for examples of old machinery still in use today saw farmers respond with working tractors from the 1940s.

There can be no doubt, however, that agricultural technology has been transformative over the whole period of settled agriculture, but such transformation often takes time. 'Diffusion of innovations' does occur, if not perhaps in the linear fashion implied by those who use Rogers' (1962) framework. Precision agricultural technologies, such as GPS-guided tractors and variable rate seeding and chemical application, are now relatively widespread in developed countries, but this did not happen overnight (Griffin et al., 2017; Lowenberg-DeBoer and Erickson, 2019). In these countries and the developing world, farmers have started to use various technologies such as mobile phone apps and other decision support systems (FAO, 2019). But equally, new technologies have appeared by farmers 'tinkering'; retro-fitting new things to the old and shaping them to suit their farm (Klerkx and Rose, 2020). There are also examples of agricultural technologies that were never implemented at scale, such as the 'dungledozer' designed to spread manure, but these are readily forgotten from the annals of history.

Although this introduction to the history of technological change in agriculture is brief and simplifies the nuanced work of agricultural historians, its purpose is to show that 'evolution' is a better word to describe change in farming than 'revolution' (but we stick with 'revolution' for this chapter as this is currently the more commonly used phrase). Adoption of new technologies are often made possible by the convergence of a number of innovations in policy, society, and institutions, which have a much longer history. Sometimes technological change can be resisted, new technologies emerge through tinkering on the farm and not as a result of a scientific breakthrough attributed to a famous scientist or engineer, and old ideas return to the mainstream (e.g. traditional ideas of regenerative agriculture). Though the past can rarely be used to predict the future accurately, as the context is always different, it does suggest that the so-called 'fourth agricultural revolution' is unlikely to be rapid and that its benefits are unlikely to be spread evenly between actors and across different places in the world.

The Promise of a Fourth Agricultural Revolution

Digitalisation is occurring across the agricultural sector (Fielke et al., 2020) and contemporary developments are affecting smallholder farmers in developing countries, although inequality and the digital divide is still prevalent here, as in many rural areas of the Global North. The penetration of mobile phones, improving network connectivity, affordable smartphone devices, inexpensive mobile data, widespread adoption of mobile money platforms and social media, availability of satellite imagery, enhanced weather forecasting, and remote sensing, are some of the drivers that are leading to the use of digital innovations across the agri-food value chain in the Global South, with some examples provided by the World Bank (Schroeder et al., 2021) and the FAO (2019).

Moving beyond mere digitalisation of agriculture, we now may be in the midst of the so-called 'fourth agricultural revolution' (Rose and Chilvers, 2018). Though poorly defined, this has come to be associated with the use of particular technologies. These include, but are not limited to: gene editing, cultured meat, robotics, AI and machine learning, drones, blockchain, cameras and wearable tech to monitor animals, and the Internet of Things (IoT) (Klerkx and Rose, 2020). Robotic automated milking has been adopted to various degrees in different countries: on 30 percent of dairy farms in Iceland and Sweden; 20–25 percent in Denmark, the Netherlands, Norway, Belgium, and Switzerland; although with less than 10 percent adoption in Canada, the UK and the USA (Eastwood and Renwick, 2020).

In the context of precision farming, Miles (2019: 2) describes how emergent agricultural technologies are talked about in the popular press and marketing literature as 'changing agriculture for the better from degrees ranging from the cautiously optimistic to the epochal' (see also Duncan et al., 2021). This resonates with a study of how the fourth agricultural revolution is discussed in policy documents and media articles in the UK (Barrett and Rose, 2020). The language reminds us of how previous events of change were described, couched in an implicit or explicit lens of linearity of the 'technological sublime' (Matless, 2018).

Market research is predicting a significant increase in the value of the agri-tech market. Recent AgFunder investment reports found that investment in Farm Tech startups has grown 370 percent since 2013 and, in 2019, $19.8 billion was invested in agri-food tech across the world. Birner et al. (2021) show that the supply side of digital agriculture is continuing to grow rapidly. They argue that rapid growth is being powered by a 'dramatic' decline in the cost of digital infrastructure, such as high-speed internet and smartphones, as well as the drive to save input costs. The agri-tech market thus has the potential to create jobs and boost productivity across the economy and thousands of agricultural start-ups have already entered the digital revolution (Birner et al., 2021). It is certainly the case that some of the technologies associated with the fourth agricultural revolution offer potential solutions to sustainability challenges facing farmers. Table 7.1 summarises some of the potential benefits of this revolution with a selective list of sources for further information.

Agricultural technology is being projected as the solution to many different 'missions' (Klerkx and Begemann, 2020). A recent report from the World Bank called 'What's Cooking: Digital Transformation of the Agrifood System' (Schroeder et al., 2021) identifies new technologies as being key to address the Sustainable Development Goals, for example reducing poverty and famine (#1 'No poverty'; #2 'Zero Hunger'). De Clercq et al. (2018) argues that the world has to 'produce 70 percent more food by 2050, using less energy, fertilizer, and pesticide while lowering levels of greenhouse gas emissions and coping with climate change'. New technologies are seen as a way of achieving the

Table 7.1   Potential benefits of the fourth agricultural revolution

Theme heading	Theme description	Sources for further information
Opportunities for SMEs	Development of new technologies can create business opportunities	AgFunder (2019)
Contribution to economy	Agri-tech development can make a contribution to the wider economy	AgFunder (2019)
Monitoring and data collection	Facilitating fine-scale data collection from an individual plant or animal (e.g. wearable animal tech, sensors, decision support)	NFU (2020)
Higher yields and profitability	As a result of evidence-based decision-making, lower input costs, and the development of higher-yielding, more tolerant varieties (e.g. gene editing)	Hickey et al. (2019) Lowenberg-DeBoer and Erickson (2019)
Addresses some of the Sustainable Development Goals	Potential to address goals such as reducing poverty and hunger	Schroeder et al. (2021) Herrero et al. (2020)
Replaces dull, dangerous and dirty jobs. Improve lifestyles	Automation (e.g. AI/robotics) can replace manual jobs and free up time for the farmer	Rose et al. (2021b)
Addresses labour shortages	Automation could address labour shortages in parts of the world	Christiaensen et al. (2021)
Attracts new workers	Attract younger, high-skilled workers. Farming suffers from low formal skills, and an ageing workforce	Bock et al. (2020) RBC (2019)
Improved gender equality	Technology could change gender-based, false stereotypes of the industry	NFU (2020)
Improved eco-efficiency	Facilitating less chemical inputs, enabling land sparing, aiding agroecological system change (e.g. variable rate application, higher yielding varieties, using non-traditional land through vertical farming or cultured meat)	Dicks et al. (2019) De Clercq et al. (2018)

Theme heading	Theme description	Sources for further information
Contributes to net zero	Reducing animal emissions (methane capture), smaller robots plus electrification	NFU (2020) Rose et al. (2021b)
Connects with consumers	Social media, blockchain etc. may increase transparency and consumer trust in food	Phillips et al. (2019) Yiannas (2018)

sustainable intensification (creating more with less) of the food system (Dicks et al., 2019). Consequently, technologies such as drones, artificial intelligence and machine learning, and remote sensing offer the potential to drive better evidence-based decision-making by giving farmers an extra level of precision. If new technologies can collect data at the scale of individual animals or individual plants, rather than more generalised assessments of fields and herds, farmers can undertake more targeted interventions. These might include asking a robot to spray an individual plant, rather than a whole field, reducing inputs or adjust the nutrition of an individual animal to suit its needs and thereby offering financial, environmental, and even animal welfare benefits (Lowenberg-DeBoer and Erickson, 2019).

As well as this precision of monitoring, technologies have the potential to make resulting data more interpretable by farmers. As the World Bank (Schroeder et al., 2021) predict, the fact that we will move from a scenario where 190,000 data points are produced on-farm each day (2014 figure) to 4.1 million data points daily by 2050, means that new technologies are needed to allow simple decisions to be made. Such technologies may be able to replace dull, dangerous, and dirty jobs, which is particularly valuable if specific regions are suffering from a shortage of labour (Christiansen et al., 2020). Indeed, the increasing use of technology in agriculture may drive the recruitment of a younger, more skilled workforce who can design, operate, and repair machines, and occupy jobs in farming which have better defined career prospects (NFU, 2020). We know that many parts of the world, particularly in developed countries such as Japan, South Korea, NW Europe, USA, Canada, Australia and New Zealand, struggle to recruit their citizens to do jobs in agriculture because of the stigma of long hours, poor pay, and bad career prospects. Farming lifestyles could be improved if difficult, laborious jobs can be done by technology and there is some evidence that this is driving the uptake of robotic milking. The fourth agricultural revolution could change notions of what farming is and open up the sector to innovative new ideas from outside, as is already being seen with controlled environment agriculture and the development of cultured meat (Sexton, 2020). For example, it has been claimed that vertical farming boosts productivity and uses 95 percent less water, fertiliser, and nutritional supplements, whilst using no pesticides (De Clercq et al., 2018).

Social media is also allowing farmers to connect better with consumers and can be used for marketing (Phillips et al., 2019), and blockchain may increase data transparency (Yiannas, 2018). In a briefing paper on digital technology, the FAO (2019) use the example of a mobile phone application used by farmers in Kenya to reduce market distortions and plan better, which in some cases led to them receiving higher prices. Some innovators and companies are also exploring the use of the IoT and computer vision to solve the problem of manual grading and assaying, as well as food quality issues. Technologies, such as gene editing and genetic modification, have the potential to increase productivity further by creating higher-yielding varieties of crops or animals and reducing the susceptibility of crops to pests and diseases (Hickey et al., 2019). Also, drones may be used to identify crops in need of treatment before a human agronomist could with their naked eye. Electrification of farm vehicles could also play a major role in reducing the carbon emissions associated with agriculture. Furthermore, new technologies, such as small robots, offer the potential for farmers to adopt new production systems that are more environmentally friendly, including agroforestry and strip-cropping (since the robot can navigate in tight spaces) (Rose et al., 2021b).

The Ethics of the Fourth Agricultural Revolution

While the potential promises of technology are exciting, we should not forget to also consider their potential drawbacks. In recent years, an increasing number of researchers have warned that we need to be more cautious of the potential (unanticipated) negative consequences that technological development might bring, especially in relation to social aspects. They highlight that once new technologies are implemented, it becomes more difficult to counteract their negative consequences and, therefore, we need to carefully consider them throughout the entire innovation process and not address them as an afterthought (Eastwood et al., 2019; Klerkx and Rose, 2020; Stilgoe et al., 2013; Sveiby et al., 2009; Shepherd et al., 2018). When it comes to potential social consequences of new technologies, we need to be aware of the disruptive, normative, and political nature of technological innovation (de Boon et al., 2021). Regarding innovation as a change from an old to a new state, or a change in behaviour (Duru et al., 2015; McKenzie, 2013; Spielman et al., 2008), then innovation is clearly disruptive as it requires the destruction of the old. This disruption can emerge on a small scale, but it also has the potential to change entire societal structures (Blok, 2020; Loorbach et al., 2017; Voss and Bornemann, 2011).

However, the disruptive nature of technological innovation does not always have to be negative, and when used carefully, can help us to move away from unsustainable agricultural practices. Whether or not a certain disruption will be seen as positive or negative is a highly normative question. Potential changes brought by a new technology will be experienced and valued differently by different people. In addition, people will have different perceptions on the acceptability of potential (negative) consequences and the potential kinds of farming futures that the innovation will contribute towards (Köhler et al., 2019; Leach et al., 2007; Markard et al., 2012). For example, some people might prefer a technology driven farming sector where farmers do not have to work in the field, others might prefer the agricultural sector to be dominated by vertical farming or by agroforestry, while others might want the sector to become completely organic, and so on. Underlying all of this is the normative question of whether technological fixes to our problems is the solution, or if instead we need structural changes to the way we organise our society and treat the earth (Scott, 2011). This demonstrates the political nature of technological innovation, which becomes a contested space for different interests to compete in exercising influence over how the agricultural sector will develop, which views are taken into account and which ones are neglected. These processes ultimately shape how resources, life chances, and well-being are distributed in society (de Boon et al., 2021).

Thus, for the many promises offered by new agricultural technologies there is the potential for negative social, environmental, and ethical consequences. These are being increasingly investigated by social scientists, with much of this work brought together in reviews by Klerkx et al. (2019) and Fielke et al. (2020). New technologies are unlikely to be desirable for everyone (Fleming et al., 2018). Table 7.2 highlights some of the potential negative impacts of the fourth agricultural revolution with a selective list of sources for further information.

Whilst the collection of more data at a finer scale brings many potential benefits, there are concerns over who benefits from data collection and who owns it. In a survey of 1000 Australian farmers, Wiseman et al. (2019) found that only 9 percent had a good understanding of the terms and conditions of data collection by service providers and 67 percent would not feel comfortable if it was used to make profits for these providers. We have recently seen protests across India, partially driven by the perception that smallholder farmers were losing power over their farms, and there is widespread concern about the dilution of

Table 7.2 Potential drawbacks of the fourth agricultural revolution

Theme heading	Theme description	Sources for further information
Data ownership	Concerns over who owns and benefits from data collection	Wiseman et al. (2019) Lioutas et al. (2019)
Lack of interoperability	Technologies do not work together on the farm (e.g. made by different companies)	Kalatzis et al. (2019) Phillips et al. (2019)
More power to big companies/lack of benefits to individual farmers	Tech companies benefit most. Farmers locked into repairs and upgrades from the same manufacturer	Klerkx et al. (2019) Bronson (2019) Duncan et al. (2021)
Lack of innovative capacity	Smaller farms, with less staff, lower cash flow, fewer skills, and lower social capital find it harder to adapt	Rose and Chivers (2020) Vik et al. (2019)
Greater intensification of the food system	New technologies could facilitate more intensive monoculture	Miles (2019) Thomson et al. (2019)
Consumer backlash	Consumers might not like how food is being produced	Regan (2019) Specht et al. (2019)
Labour displacement	Loss of jobs for traditional agricultural workers who cannot re-train plus potential disruption to advisor roles	Rotz et al. (2019)
Increased energy use	Non-traditional systems (e.g. cultured meat, vertical farming) may have a high energy input	Mattick et al. (2015) Lynch and Pierrehumbert (2019)
Increased stress on farmers	New technologies can create an 'always on' culture and data can be difficult to deal with	Barrett and Rose (2020)
Loss of practical knowledge	More sophisticated technologies can reduce farmer autonomy and erode practical knowledge creating a 'cyborg farmer'	Brooks (2021) Carolan (2020) Higgins (2007) Miles (2019)

Theme heading	Theme description	Sources for further information
Health and safety	New technologies may not work within current regulations and may cause danger to workers or the public	Basu et al. (2020) Lowenberg-DeBoer et al. (2021) Sparrow and Howard (2020)
Cybersecurity	New technologies could be open to hacking and data theft	NCC (2020)

farmer expertise and autonomy. Brooks (2021) worries about the creation of so-called 'cyborg farmers' as they are configured to act with less autonomy in a world where 'algorithmic rationality' rules (Miles, 2019; Carolan, 2020). If we see the fourth agricultural revolution as a 'progressive transfer of autonomy to other human agents' (Higgins, 2007: 268), such as already powerful technology companies (and large ones rather than small and medium enterprises), the power to decide and to shape the means of production moves further away from the farmer. Practical knowledge may be diluted, and different stresses caused by new technology (Barrett and Rose, 2020). In parts of the world where corruption is rife, including in government, the use of technology to reduce the autonomy of smallholder farmers has an even greater potential to do harm.

Lack of data interoperability is a significant concern (Kalatzis et al., 2019). Different technologies used on-farm designed by different companies may not speak to one another, presenting a huge challenge to farmers trying to interpret the collected data. Furthermore, some farmers find it easier to adopt new technologies than others; for example, those with greater cashflows, more skilled staff, better rural infrastructure, and better social capital to network (Rose and Chivers, 2020). We have seen, for example with the development and implementation of automatic milking systems, that the existing societal structure of the industry has changed because smaller farms were not as capable to adapt to this innovation as larger farms. This resulted in the industry being left with fewer but larger farms (Tse et al., 2017; Vik et al., 2019). Benefits of the fourth agricultural revolution will, therefore, not be spread evenly across farming populations. Some of these adoption issues, such as poverty, low skills, and poor rural infrastructure, may be more pronounced in some parts of the world than others (Schroeder et al., 2021). Furthermore, there is the potential for digitalisation to benefit larger companies more than the thousands of SMEs that have recently entered the sector (Birner et al., 2021).

Whilst automation offers the potential to fill labour gaps and reduce dangerous jobs, there is a significant possibility of labour displacement of farm workers many of whom will find it difficult to re-train to suit a changed workplace (Rotz et al., 2019). It is important to note that many parts of the world are not suffering from a shortage of labour and whilst COVID-19 undoubtedly presents a short-term threat to safe working conditions on-farm, there is the potential for automation to exacerbate unemployment in parts of the world where traditional farm work is a major employer. Improving working conditions and pay may be an alternative to draw more workers towards farming rather than replacing them with technology. Moreover, health and safety concerns, as well as cybersecurity issues, have been raised by new technologies, such as autonomous robots. Although existing technologies cause many injuries and deaths to farm workers every year, new autonomous technologies also have the potential to injure or kill workers or members of the public accessing farmland (Sparrow and Howard, 2020). Determining the responsibility for injuries caused by autonomous machines is more challenging to navigate (Basu et al., 2020). Such technologies are also vulnerable to hacking and data theft (NCC, 2020).

As well as the possibility that new technologies will not deliver their promised benefits in practice, some unintended consequences of trying to make environmental gains may occur. Whilst cultured meat, for example, attempts to reduce the burden of traditional meat production, sparing land from being used by greenhouse gas-emitting livestock, research has suggested that alternative systems can have higher energy costs (Mattick et al., 2015; Lynch and Pierrehumbert 2019). We also do not know whether consumers will have concerns about new methods of producing food (Regan, 2019; Specht et al., 2019), for example cultured meat, or from controlled environment agriculture or livestock systems using wearable technologies (Schillings et al., 2021a).

Two cases of precision livestock technology and autonomous robotics help to show how a single piece of technology can offer both great potential to drive sustainability, helping people, production, and the planet (Rose et al., 2021a), but also simultaneously cause negative impacts, whether intended or unintended. Precision Livestock Farming (PLF) technologies are designed to help farmers monitor their animals and assist them in making effective management decisions which could result in improved productivity, better animal health and welfare, and reduction of costs (Berckmans, 2014). PLF technologies can monitor a variety of parameters in a real-time, automatic, and continuous way. These can, for example, detect diseases at an early stage and alert farmers through notifications on digital devices such as computers or smartphones, indicating which specific animal may require particular attention. However, there are potential drawbacks depending on how these technologies are used and how they may influence management decisions. Some of the potential benefits and challenges of using PLF technologies are described in Figure 7.1 (see also Schillings et al., 2021a; 2021b).

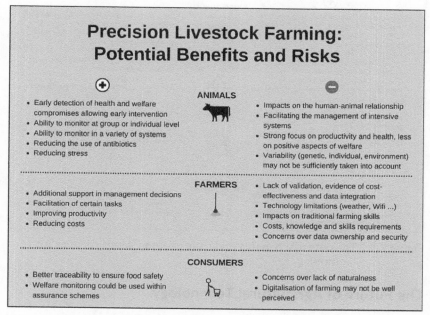

Figure 7.1 The potential benefits and risks of Precision Livestock Farming technologies

Likewise, autonomous robotics in farming offer great potential to address labour shortages, reduce chemical use, switch to agroecological systems, create new jobs, and reduce input costs (Rose et al., 2021b). However, there are concerns over their role in labour displacement in parts of the world where rural unemployment is high, as well as safety and cybersecurity threats, reliability, and cost issues, and that they could facilitate greater intensification (Sparrow and Howard, 2020). Figure 7.2 summarises these points.

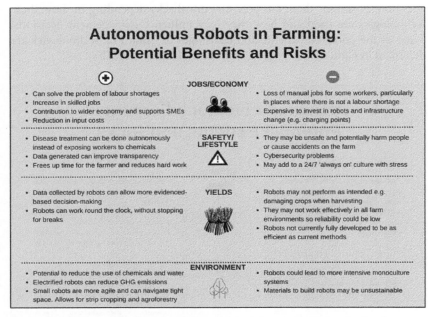

Figure 7.2   The potential benefits and risks of autonomous robotics in farming

The Future of Agricultural Technology

If we are on the cusp of a so-called fourth agricultural revolution, the future of agriculture may be very different from the past and present. Various reports, including 'Farmers of the Future' from the EU Commission (Bock et al., 2021) and 'Farmer 4.0' (RBC, 2019), project a digitalised future where farmers will need new skills and will perform non-traditional roles. However, there are different potential futures for agriculture including agroecology, the application of ecological concepts and principles in agriculture. Technologies include nutrient cycling, soil biological activity, organic matter accumulation, resource conservation and regeneration (soil and water), and natural control mechanisms including the biological control of weeds and insects along with disease suppression (Lang and Heasman, 2015). Agroecology is often presented as a 'bottom-up approach' providing an alternative set of principles and practices for organising the food system (Anderson et al., 2019; Lang and Heasman, 2015). Some people see high-tech futures as different from agroecological futures, but this often results from a misconception of how technologies can be used (Miles, 2019; Castell et al., 2021; Little, 2019).

To ensure that we can make use of the positive potential of technological innovation whilst simultaneously mitigating the potential negative consequences and being wary of its normative and political implications, it is essential that we do our best to anticipate potential consequences early on. Understanding governance of technologies means taking a step back and examining governance of the whole food system. Technologies add to the complex entanglement of challenges associated with the food system such as health, the environment, social values and trust, culture, jobs, and the wider economy (Lang, 2021). A clear example of this is the introduction of genetically modified maize in Mexico. For Mexicans, maize is culturally important as a crop and as food and is a fundamental component of both urban and rural people's diets (Carro-Ripalda et al., 2015; Fitting, 2014, 2006). The introduction of genetically modified maize was seen as a form of imposed globalisation with traditional practices of seed saving threatened (Carro-Ripalda et al., 2015). Just as with other areas of the world, corporations were benefiting from the introduction of GM maize as opposed to Mexican farmers and smallholders (Little, 2019).

If large corporations are seen as driving change without wider input, this can be problematic. They can dominate global and regional food systems, leading to the concentration of power (Howard, 2016; Lang and Heasman, 2015). For farmers, using agricultural technologies may mean they become tied to an organisation such as for servicing and repairs as has happened with John Deere (Dauvergne, 2020). Also, companies such as Bayer-Monsanto, BASF, and DowDuPont have long dominated the global market for seeds, fertilisers and agri-chemicals (Dauvergne, 2020; Howard, 2016; Lang and Heasman, 2015). Rather than challenging the underlying social, political and economic structures of the global food system, technologies may reinforce existing power structures.

For more responsible futures, therefore, all types of actors need to be involved in decision making processes, not least because building socio-technical networks is vital to the success of technology systems (Higgins, 2007). The main approach in the agricultural literature, and which is also endorsed by the European Union to help support these efforts, is Responsible Research and Innovation (RRI). It consists of four components that all address ways to improve our capacity to anticipate consequences and also highlight the importance of reacting to the new insights that we gain (Eastwood et al., 2019; Rose and Chilvers, 2018).

The first component is *anticipation*. Within this component the approach stresses the need to explore 'what if' questions, to systematically examine what we already know, consequences that may be likely, plausible, or possible, both in the short and in the long term and across all societal scales (Stilgoe et al., 2013). Examples of methods that can be used for these kinds of explorations include scenario studies (van de Poel et al., 2017) and foresighting (e.g. Fleming et al., 2018).

The second component, *reflexivity*, invites innovators to critically assess their own assumptions, perceptions, value system, actions, and the limits of knowledge, and to recognise that these might block or steer their imagination of potential consequences (Eastwood et al., 2019). Developing and using critical codes of conduct or standards could be helpful to support these reflections (Rose et al., 2021b). In addition, these conversations need to be opened up to the public so that conflicting views can be brought together and steps taken to reach compromise (Stilgoe et al., 2013).

Inclusion is the third component of the RRI approach. It relates to the inclusion of stakeholders throughout the innovation process. Potential methods that can be used for this purpose include workshops, user-centred design, and citizen panels (Eastwood et al., 2019). When including stakeholders into the innovation process it is important that the process is not dominated by the 'usual suspects' and that attention is given to power inequalities between the stakeholders. Including a wide range of stakeholders in the innovation process can help support anticipatory efforts as it broadens and diversifies the knowledge that can be considered in anticipatory exercises (Rose and Chilvers, 2018; Rose et al., 2021b).

The final dimension, *responsiveness*, highlights that none of the aforementioned components matter if we do not act on the insights that we gain through them. It stresses the importance to act upon newly gained insights, to adapt our innovations accordingly, and in some instances withdrawing the innovation altogether if it is not considered desirable by society. Potential methods to increase responsiveness include value-sensitive design and stage-gating (Eastwood et al., 2019; Stilgoe et al., 2013).

A recent perspective by Rose et al. (2021b) argued that a relatively small number of methods had been used to-date for the purpose of engaging publics on the issue of autonomous robotics in farming, mainly surveys or demonstration events. It is argued that more substantive methods of public engagement, such as citizen juries and deliberative workshops should be used, alongside innovative methods such as science-fiction movie nights, in order to stimulate the question of what future different people would like to see. One possibility to govern more responsible approaches is an observatory or coordinating body, and this has been proposed for gene editing (Burall, 2018).

An observatory or coordinating body enables different types of actors to ask questions and could stimulate conversations about an agreed set of standards, regulations, and codes of practice for the development and use of technology on-farm (see draft Australian code of practice for use of autonomous vehicles[2]). With gene editing, we should be asking what 'new beings, for whom, and out of whom' (Haraway, 2018: 58) are being produced? This question is important for agriculture, social and environmental justice, democracy, and the environment, because plants, animals, and seeds are becoming part of the bio-genetic economy, with companies profiting from life itself (Braidotti, 2019). Answering questions like this about technological futures in agriculture, means taking into account both science and the concerns associated with values and beliefs. However, deliberation activities only work if the background issues of who gets to ask a question, and which questions and concerns are excluded, are also addressed (Jasanoff and Hurlbut, 2018).

Conclusion

Though the fourth agricultural revolution and the technologies associated with it promise much, it is not the first time in history that farming has been on the cusp of change. We have shown how farmers have always innovated and that technological change does occur, but often in a non-linear way, punctuated by controversy, missteps, and the resurrection of old ideas. Technological change is disruptive and decisions over desirable trajectories are always normative. It would be unrealistic to think that the fourth agricultural revolution is going to see the rapid uptake of technologies without negative and unintended consequences. New technologies promise much to people, production, and the planet, and many of the innovations being heralded may well make a significant contribution to sustainability. But there will also be inevitable disruption. There will be winners and losers and the voices of the potential losers, those already with less power such as smallholder farmers and their families, are likely to be unheard unless decision-makers embrace methods of responsible innovation. Unchecked techno-optimism has the potential to sideline these important issues and put faith in high-tech silver bullets at the expense of low-tech or non-tech innovation, or socio-political change, that could make an equal or bigger contribution to achieving sustainability. The progress of the so-called revolution is most likely to be halted by the inadequate inclusion of citizens in determining desirable futures, leading to an unsatisfactory consideration of social, ethical, political, and legal issues. In setting futures, therefore, decision-makers should be mindful of the tinkerer, as well as the radical technologist.

The research community has a key role to play in ensuring that transitions towards new forms of agriculture are fair and just for all stakeholders and this will require a major trans-disciplinary effort. Several papers have identified key questions that need to be considered, including reviews by Klerkx et al. (2019) and Fielke et al. (2020), and a forward-thinking piece by de Boon et al. (2021), who specifically set questions for researchers, innovators, and society at large to examine collaboratively, aimed at exploring the normative, disruptive, and political dimensions of transitions alongside a list of possible methods to support these efforts. De Boon et al. (2021) argued that there are six partially overlapping stages of agricultural innovation processes at which various questions should be posed:

Stage 1: Problem and goal formulation – exploring perceptions on the underlying drivers of problems that need addressing and values that are strived for in the aimed for goals, as well as potential alternative problem and goal formulations.

Stage 2: Idea generation – investigating the values underpinning suggested ideas, for example specific technological solutions, and the consequences of different futures, closed-down alternative visions, trade-offs, and who these affect.

Stage 3: Concept/prototype development – articulating who the technological solution is for and benefits, the resources needed to develop it, and its consequences for farmers with differing capacities to adapt and innovate.

Stage 4: Concept/prototype testing – interrogating the criteria used to measure whether a tested technology is beneficial or not, and for whom, and whether they take into account the views of all stakeholders.

Stage 5: Implementation – exploring the trade-offs involved in implementation, whether the solution is beneficial for all, which farmers can adapt easier than others, and the consequences of implementation at scale for the structure of the farm industry.

Stage 6: Monitoring and evaluation – considering the criteria used for monitoring and evaluation, their underlying values, and whether lessons are learned to alter the technological solution or process.

Across all stages – exploring which stakeholders are involved, how they are involved, which types of knowledge are influential, and whether there are mechanisms in place to allow technology trajectories to be set by all actors equally (not just the most powerful).

Thus, there is considerable work to be done to explore the process and consequences of transitions towards a so-called fourth agricultural revolution and such research is likely to involve a range of participatory methodologies suggested by de Boon et al. (2021). Ultimately, we should be motivated to investigate not only the 'exciting' parts of the fourth agricultural revolution, but also the 'scary' aspects (Rose and Chivers, 2020), and this will require us to employ a range of critical social science approaches from across multiple disciplines (de Boon et al., 2021).

Notes

1. https://twitter.com/BBCFarmingToday/status/1390530582023655424.
2. https://www.harper-adams.ac.uk/news/203570/code-of-practice-for-autonomous -crop-equipment-planned.

References

Agfunder, 2019. AgFunder Agri-FoodTech Investing Report – 2019. https://agfunder .com/research/agfunder-agrifood-tech-investing-report-2019/.

Anderson, C. R., Maughan, C., Pimbert, M. P. 2019. Transformative agroecology learning in Europe: building consciousness, skills and collective capacity for food sovereignty. *Agriculture and Human Values* 36, 531–547. https://doi.org/10.1007/ s10460-018-9894-0.

Barrett, H., Rose, D. C., 2020. Perceptions of the fourth agricultural revolution: what's in, what's out, and what consequences are anticipated?, *Sociologia Ruralis*. https://doi .org/10.1111/soru.12324.

Basu, S., Omotubora, A., Beeson, M., Fox, C., 2020. Legal framework for small autonomous agricultural robots. *AI & Society* 35: 113–134.

Berckmans, D., 2014. Precision livestock farming technologies for welfare management in intensive livestock systems. *Revue scientifique et technique* 33, 1: 189-196.

Bertoglio, R., Corbo, C., Renga, F. M., Matteucci, M., 2021. The digital agricultural revolution: a bibliometric analysis literature review. https://arxiv.org/abs/2103.12488

Birner, R., Daum, T., Pray, C., 2021. Who drives the digital revolution in agriculture? A review of supply-side trends, players and challenges. *Applied Economics Perspectives and Policy*. https://doi.org/10.1002/aepp.13145.

Blok, V., 2020. What is Innovation? Laying the ground for a philosophy of innovation. *Techné: Research in Philosophy and Technology* 25, 1: 1-25.

Bock, A.K., Krzysztofowicz, M., Rudkin, J., Winthagen, V., 2020. Farmers of the future. EUR 30464 EN, Publications Office of the European Union, Luxembourg, ISBN 978-92-76-26332-6. https://doi.org/10.2760/680650, JRC122308.

Braidotti, R., 2019. *Posthuman Knowledge*. Cambridge: Polity Press.

Bronson, K., 2019. Looking through a responsible innovation lens at uneven engagements with digital farming. *NJAS – Wageningen Journal of Life Sciences* 90–91: 100294.

Brooks, S., 2021. Configuring the digital farmer: a nudge world in the making?. *Economy and Society*. https://doi.org/10.1080/03085147.2021.1876984.

Burall, S., 2018. Rethink public engagement for gene editing. *Nature* 555, 438–439.

Carolan, M., 2020. Automated agrifood futures: robotics, labor and the distributive politics of digital agriculture. *The Journal of Peasant Studies* 47: 184-207.

Carro-Ripalda, S., Astier, M., Artía, P., 2015. An analysis of the GM crop debate in Mexico. In Macnaghten, P., Carro-Ripalda, S. (eds) *Governing Agricultural Sustainability: Global Lessons from GM Crops*. Abingdon: Routledge, pp. 33–73.

Castell, S., Clemence, M., Kamvar, R., Reynolds, M., 2021. Living landscapes public dialogue on the future of land use. Conducted on behalf of the Royal Society. https://royalsociety.org/-/media/policy/Publications/2021/23-03-21-living-landscapes-full-report.pdf.

Christiaensen, L., Rutledge, Z., Taylor, E., 2021. Viewpoint: the future of work in agri-food. *Food Policy* 99. 101963.

Dauvergne, P., 2020. *AI in the Wild: Sustainability in the Age of Artificial Intelligence*. Cambridge, MA: The MIT Press.

de Boon, A., Sandström, C., Rose, D.C., 2021. Governing sustainable agricultural innovation: a comprehensive framework to support decision-making processes. *Journal of Rural Studies*. https://doi.org/10.1016/j.jrurstud.2021.07.019.

De Clercq, M., Vats, A., Biel, A., 2018. Agriculture 4.0: the future of farming technology, World Government Summit. https://www.oliverwyman.com/content/dam/oliver-wyman/v2/publications/2021/apr/agriculture-4-0-the-future-of-farming-technology.pdf

Dicks, L. V., Rose, D. C., Ang, F., Aston, S., Birch, N. E. et al., 2019. What agricultural practices are most likely to deliver 'sustainable intensification' in the UK?. *Food and Energy Security* 8, 1: e00148.

Duncan, E., Glaros, A., Ross, D. Z., Nost, E., 2021. New but for whom? Discourses of innovation in precision agriculture. *Agriculture and Human Values*. https://doi.org/10.1007/s10460-021-10244-8.

Duru, M., Therond, O., Martin, G., Martin-Clouaire, R. et al., 2015. How to implement biodiversity-based agriculture to enhance ecosystem services: a review. *Agronomy for Sustainable Development* 35, 4: 1259-1281.

Eastwood, C. R., Renwick, A., 2020. Innovation uncertainty impacts the adoption of smarter farming approaches. *Frontiers in Sustainable Food Systems*. https://doi.org/10.3389/fsufs.2020.00024.

Eastwood, C., Klerkx, L., Ayre, M., Dela Rue, B., 2019. Managing socio-ethical challenges in the development of smart farming: from a fragmented to a comprehensive approach for responsible research and innovation. *Journal of Agricultural and Environmental Ethics* 32: 741-768.

FAO, 2019. *Digital Technologies in Agriculture and Rural Areas*. Briefing Paper. Rome: FAO.

Fielke, S., Taylor, B., Jakku, E., 2020. Digitalisation of agricultural knowledge and advice networks: a state-of-the-art review. *Agricultural Systems* 180: 102763.

Fitting, E., 2006. The political uses of culture: maize production and the GM corn debates in Mexico. *Focaal—European Journal of Anthropology* 48: 17–34.

Fitting, E., 2014. Cultures of corn and anti-GMO activism in Mexico and Colombia. In Counihan, C., Siniscalchi, V. (eds) *Food Activism*. London: Bloomsbury Academic, pp. 175–192.

Fleming, A., Jakku, E., Lim-Camacho, L., Taylor, B., Thorburn, P., 2018. Is big data for big farming or for everyone? Perceptions in the Australian grains industry. *Agronomy for Sustainable Development* 38, 24.

Griffin, T. W., Miller, N., Bergtold, J. S. et al., 2017. Farm's sequence of adoption of information-intensive precision agricultural technology, *Applied Engineering in Agriculture* 33, 4: 521–527.

Haraway, D., 2018. *Modest_Witness @Second_Millennium. FemaleMan©_Meets_ OncoMouseTM*. 2nd edn. Abingdon: Routledge.

Herrero, M., Thornton, P. K., Mason-D'Croz, D. et al., 2020. Innovation can accelerate the transition towards a sustainable food system. *Nature Food* 1: 266–272.

Hickey, L.T., Hafeez, A.N., Robinson, H. et al., 2019. Breeding crops to feed 10 billion. *Nature Biotechnology* 37: 744–754.

Higgins, V. 2007. Performing users: the case of a computer-based dairy decision-support system. *Science, Technology, and Human Values* 32, 3: 263–286.

Howard, P., 2016. *Concentration and Power in the Food System*. London: Bloomsbury Academic.

Jasanoff, S., Hurlbut, B., 2018. A global observatory for gene editing. *Nature* 555: 435–437.

Kalatzis, N., Marianos, N., Chatzipapadopoulos, F., 2019. IoT and data interoperability in agriculture: a case study on the gaiasense™ smart farming solution. 2019 Global IoT Summit. 10.1109/GIOTS.2019.8766423

Klerkx, L., Begemann, S., 2020. Supporting food systems transformation: the what, why, who, where and how of mission-oriented agricultural innovation systems. *Agricultural Systems*, 1984: 102901.

Klerkx, L., Rose, D., 2020. Dealing with the game-changing technologies of agriculture 4.0: how do we manage diversity and responsibility in food system transition pathways?. *Global Food Security* 24: 100347.

Klerkx, L., Jakku, E., Labarthe, P., 2019. A review of social science on digital agriculture, smart farming and agriculture 4.0: new contributions and a future research agenda. *NJAS – Wageningen Journal of Life Sciences* 90–91: 1–16. https://doi.org/10.1016/j.njas.2019.100315.

Köhler, J., Geels, F. W., Kern, F. et al., 2019. An agenda for sustainability transitions research: state of the art and future directions. *Environmental Innovation and Societal Transitions*, 31: 1–32.

Kumar, R., Lorek, T., Olsson, T. C., Sackley, N. et al., 2017. Roundtable: new narratives of the green revolution. *Agricultural History* 91, 3: 397–422.

Lang, T., 2021. *Feeding Britain: Our Food Problems and How to Fix Them*. London: Penguin.

Lang, T. and Heasman, M., 2015. *Food Wars: The global battle for mouths, minds and markets*. 2nd edn. Abingdon: Routledge.

Leach, M., Bloom, G., Ely, A., Nightingale, P. et al., 2007. Understanding governance: pathways to sustainability, STEPS Working Paper 2, Brighton: STEPS Centre.

Lioutas, E. D., Charatsari, C., La Rocca, G., De Rosa, M., 2019. Key questions on the use of big data in farming: an activity theory approach. *NJAS – Wageningen Journal of Life Sciences* 90–91: 1–12. https://doi.org/10.1016/j.njas.2019.04.003.

Little, A., 2019. *The Fate of Food: What we'll eat in a bigger, hotter smarter world.* London: Oneworld.

Loorbach, D., Frantzeskaki, N., Avelino, F., 2017. Sustainability transition research: transforming science and practice for societal change. *Annual Review of Environment and Resources*, 42: 599–626.

Lowenberg-DeBoer, J., Erickson, B., 2019. Setting the record straight on precision agriculture adoption. *Agronomy Journal* 111, 4: 1552–1569.

Lowenberg-DeBoer, J., Behrendt, K., Ehlers, M-H. et al., 2021. Lessons to be learned in adoption of autonomous equipment for field crops. *Applied Economic Perspectives and Policy.* https://doi.org/10.1002/aepp.13177.

Lynch, J., Pierrehumbert, R., 2019. climate impacts of cultured meat and beef cattle. *Frontiers in Sustainable Food Systems.* https://doi.org/10.3389/fsufs.2019.00005.

Markard, J., Raven, R., Truffer, B., 2012. Sustainability transitions: an emerging field of research and its prospects. *Research Policy* 41: 955–967.

Matless, D., 2018. The Agriculture Gallery: displaying modern farming in the Science Museum. In Agar, J., Ward, J. (eds) *Histories of Technology, the Environment and Modern Britain.* London: UCL Press, pp. 101–122.

Mattick, C. S., Landies, A. E., Allenby, B. R., Genovese, N., 2015. Anticipatory life cycle analysis of in vitro biomass cultivation for cultured meat production in the United States. *Environmental Science & Technology* 49, 19: 11941–11949.

McKenzie, F., 2013. Farmer-driven innovation in New South Wales, Australia. *Australian Geographer* 44, 1: 81–95.

MERL (The Museum of English Rural Life), 2021. The evolution of rural protest. https://merl.reading.ac.uk/explore/online-exhibitions/evolution-rural-protest/.

Miles, C., 2019. The combine will tell the truth: on precision agriculture and algorithmic rationality. *Big Data & Society* 6, 1: 1–12.

National Farmers' Union (NFU), 2020. The future of food 2040. https://www.nfuonline .com/nfu-online/news/the-future-of-food-2040/.

NCC Group, 2020. Cyber security in UK agriculture. https://research.nccgroup.com/ wp-content/uploads/2020/07/agriculture-whitepaper-final-online.pdf.

Phillips, P. W., Relf-Eckstein, J-A., Jobe, G., Wixted, B., 2019. Configuring the new digital landscape in western Canadian agriculture. *NJAS – Wageningen Journal of Life Sciences* 90–91: 1–11. https://doi.org/10.1016/j.njas.2019.04.001.

Pielke Jr., R., Linnér, B-A., 2019. From green revolution to green evolution: a critique of the political myth of averted famine. *Minerva* 57: 265–291.

RBC, 2019. Farmer 4.0. How the coming skills revolution can transform agriculture. https://thoughtleadership.rbc.com/farmer-4-0-how-the-coming-skills-revolution -can-transform-agriculture/

Regan, A., 2019. Smart farming' in Ireland: a risk perception study with key governance actors. *Wageningen Journal of Life Sciences* 90–91: 1–10.

Rogers, E. M., 1962. *Diffusion of innovations.* New York: Free Press of Glencoe.

Rose, D. C., Chilvers, J., 2018. Agriculture 4.0: broadening responsible innovation in an era of smart farming. *Frontiers in Sustainable Food Systems* 2: 1–7.

Rose, D. C., Chivers, C-A., 2020. The fourth agricultural revolution is coming – but who will really benefit? https://theconversation.com/the-fourth-agricultural-revolution -is-coming-but-who-will-really-benefit-145810.

Rose, D. C., Wheeler, R., Winter, M., Lobley, M., Chivers, C-A., 2021a. Agriculture 4.0: making it work for people, production, and the planet. *Land Use Policy* 100: 104933.

Rose, D. C., Lyon, J., de Boon, A., Hanheide, M., Pearson, S., 2021b. Responsible development of autonomous robotics in farming. *Nature Food.* https://doi.org/10.1038/s43016-021-00287-9.

Rotz, S., Gravely, E., Mosby, I., Duncan, E. et al., 2019. Automated pastures and the digital divide: how agricultural technologies are shaping labour and rural communities. *Journal of Rural Studies* 68: 112–122.

Schillings, J., Bennett, R., Rose, D. C., 2021a. Animal welfare and other ethical implications of Precision Livestock Farming Technologies. *CABI Agriculture and Bioscience.* https://doi.org/10.1186/s43170-021-00037-8.

Schillings, J., Bennett, R., Rose, D. C., 2021b. Exploring the potential of Precision Livestock Farming technologies to help address farm animal welfare. *Frontiers in Animal Science.* https://doi.org/10.3389/fanim.2021.639678.

Schroeder, K., Lampietti J., Elabed, G., 2021. What's cooking: digital transformation of the agrifood system. Agriculture and Food Series. Washington, DC: World Bank. https://doi.org/10.1596/978-1-4648-1657-4.

Scott, D., 2011. The technological fix criticisms and the agricultural biotechnology debate. *Journal of Agricultural and Environmental Ethics* 24, 3: 207–226.

Sexton, A., 2020. Food as software: place, protein, and feeding the world Silicon Valley-style. *Economic Geography* 96, 5: 449–469.

Shepherd, M., Turner, J.A., Small, B., Wheeler, D., 2018. Priorities for science to overcome hurdles thwarting the full promise of the 'digital agriculture' revolution. *Journal of the Science of Food and Agriculture.* https://doi.org/10.1002/jsfa.9346.

Shiva, V., 2016. *The Violence of the Green Revolution: Third world agriculture, ecology, and politics.* Lexington: University Press of Kentucky.

Sparrow, R., Howard, M., 2020. Robots in agriculture: prospects, impacts, ethics and policy. *Precision Agriculture.* https://doi.org/10.1007/s11119-020-09757-9.

Specht, K., Zoll, F., Schümann, H., Bela, J. et al., 2019. How will we eat and produce in the cities of the future? From edible insects to vertical farming—a study on the perception and acceptability of new approaches. *Sustainability* 11, 16: 4315.

Spielman, D.J., Ekboir, J., Davis, K., Ochieng, C.M., 2008. An innovation systems perspective on strengthening agricultural education and training in sub-Saharan Africa. *Agricultural Systems* 98, 1: 1–9.

Stilgoe, J., Owen, R., Macnaghten, P., 2013. Developing a framework for responsible innovation. *Research Policy* 42: 1568–1580.

Sveiby, K.E., Gripenberg, P., Segercrantz, B., Eriksson, A., Aminoff, A., 2009. Unintended and undesirable consequences of innovation. In XX ISPIM conference, The Future of Innovation. Vienna.

Thomson, A., Ellis, E., Grau, H. et al., 2019. Sustainable intensification in land systems: trade-offs, scales, and contexts. *Current Opinion in Environmental Sustainability* 37: 37–43.

Tse, C., Barkema, H., DeVries, T.J., Rushen, J., Pajor, E., 2017. Effect of transitioning to automatic milking systems on producers' perceptions of farm management and cow health in the Canadian dairy industry. *Journal of Dairy Science* 100, 3: 2404–2414.

van de Poel, I., Asveld, L., Flipse, S., Klaassen, P. et al., 2017. Company strategies for Responsible Research and Innovation (RRI): a conceptual model. *Sustainability* 9, 11: 2045. https://doi.org/10.3390/su9112045.

van der Veen, M., 2010. Agricultural innovation: invention and adoption or change and adaptation?. *World Archaeology* 42, 1: 1–12.

Vik., J., Straete, E. P., Hansen, B. G., Naerland, T., 2019. The political robot – the structural consequences of automated milking systems (AMS) in Norway. NJAS – *Wageningen Journal of Life Sciences* 90–91: 100305.

Voss, J.P., Bornemann, B., 2011. The politics of reflexive governance: challenges for designing adaptive management and transition management. *Ecology and Society* 16, 2: art. 9.

Wiseman, L., Sanderson, J., Zhang, A., Jakku, E., 2019. Farmers and their data: an examination of farmers' reluctance to share their data through the lens of the laws impacting smart farming. NJAS – *Wageningen Journal of Life Sciences* 90–91: 100301.

Yiannas, F., 2018. A new era of food transparency powered by blockchain. *Innovations: Technology, Governance, Globalization* 12, 1–2: 46–56.

8

Of fake meat and an anxious Anthropocene: towards a cultural political economy of alternative proteins and their implications for future food systems

Alexandra E. Sexton and Michael K. Goodman

Introduction

In 2019, food technology company Beyond Meat, the makers of the plant based Beyond Burger, went public on the New York Stock Exchange (NYSE). The Los Angeles-based company was one of the earliest ventures to launch in the recent wave of alternative protein (AP) companies along with Eat Just and Impossible Foods in the US, as well as similarly high-profile ventures in Europe and Asia (Stephens et al., 2019). Beyond Meat is the first ever plant-based food company to list on the NYSE. The company's shares nearly tripled in value by the end of their first day of trading and at the time of writing the company is valued at over $1 billion (Murphy, 2019). Impossible Foods has had a similarly headline-grabbing time in recent years. Its pea-based products and proprietary ingredients that cause their burgers to bleed like conventional meat have led technology and market analysts to herald the company as 'revolutionaries' and 'the Tesla of food' (Hicks and Stein, 2016). The company raised $200 million in its 2020 funding round – bringing the company to a total of $1.5 billion raised since its founding in 2011 – and expanded its partnerships with Burger King, Walmart, Target, and other major food chains across the US (Poinski, 2020).

Like other biotechnologies before them, media coverage of APs has tended to skew to the celebratory (Painter et al., 2020), with the glitz of the latest investment cycle or prototype launch often overshadowing broader debate on what APs might mean for the future of food and farming, and what challenges remain for the sector. A great deal of this breathless coverage articulates the ways that the Impossible and Beyond Burgers are on the front lines of solving any and all crises related to the production and consumption of meat: from climate change, to the direct environmental destruction caused by livestock production, to health complications from the consumption of too much red and other animal-derived meats, yet all without sacrificing the taste and pleasure of meat eating (Sexton et al., 2019). As the Beyond Meat website states, their latest burger – the 'even-better Beyond burger' – is 'for your health, planet, [and] BBQ'. And it's not just AP companies who are pushing this win-all narrative. To the surprise of many in the AP sector, the biggest names in conventional meat processing and retail have jumped into AP development, launching their own product ranges and/or investing in AP start-ups. It is now commonplace to see senior executives from Tyson Foods, Cargill and other meat and dairy giants effuse about the world-saving benefits of 'expanding the future of protein' beyond solely animals, and rebranding themselves as 'protein leaders' (Tyson Foods, 2021).

Similar tropes have been echoed by the AP sector known as cellular agriculture. 'Cell-ag' involves the cultivation of animal-derived meat, but instead of through livestock husbandry and animal slaughter, animal cells are harvested from a host animal and grown in tissue culture, similar to that used in the growth and regeneration of human and other biological tissues. The most famous public performance of cell-ag was the unveiling of an in-vitro, cell-cultured burger in London in 2013. The burger reportedly cost $300,000 to create and involved investment from the likes of Sergey Brin, the progenitor of Google. A more recent unveiling marked another historic moment for the sector: the first public sale of cultured chicken nuggets was made in December 2020 at an exclusive members-only restaurant in Singapore. Created by San Francisco-based company Eat Just, the event followed the landmark approval of cultured meat by Singapore's food regulators – the first country in the world to approve a cultured meat product for public consumption. While there remain a number of technical and regulatory obstacles to achieving large-scale commercialisation and cost-effectiveness of cellular agriculture, this has not stopped those in and around the industry heralding its revolutionary potential in dealing with the ongoing and increasing crises of the Anthropocene, particularly those related to conventional livestock's impact on the environment. Like their plant-based counterparts, these are products that promise to be 'good for people, animals and the planet' (Clara Foods, cited in Sexton et al., 2019); a total fix that replaces the perceived inefficiencies of biology with the control and efficiency of technology. Cell-ag has similarly captured the imagination of animal rights and welfare types, yet unlike the substitutionist approach of plant-based alternative proteins, cell-ag proponents promise 'real', animal-derived meats and milks, but without the animal death, suffering, and zoonotic and ecological risks associated with industrialised meat production. Rather, a cell-ag 'post-animal bioeconomy' (Datar, 2015) is envisioned to either involve immortal cell lines (i.e. banks of cell lines that replicate without the need for animal inputs) and/or small 'donor' herds that provide a relatively limitless supply of cells from which to produce the likes of real hamburgers, pork, chicken, duck or shrimp, but this time in laboratory petri dishes and eventually in larger-scale bioreactors and fermentation tanks.

In this chapter, we consider the rise of plant-based and cell-cultured APs and critically assess their current and potential impacts on the development of food systems across the US, UK and Europe. In the latter half of this chapter, we focus specific attention on the rise of cell-ag given its potentially far-reaching ethical, material and spatial 'disruptions' to conventionally produced animal meat food systems. Our discussion and analysis are positioned within the broader landscape of recent research on APs. For example, studies have examined AP regulatory and legal considerations (Seehafer and Bartels, 2019), as well as technical challenges (Stephens et al., 2018; Post et al., 2020), and life-cycle analyses (LCAs) (Lynch and Pierrehumbert, 2019; Tuomisto, 2019). Consumer-focussed work on the acceptability of APs across demographic and cultural contexts has also comprised a large proportion of recent AP research (Bryant and Barnett, 2020), while narrative analyses (Morris et al., 2019; Sexton et al., 2019), bioethics and philosophy (Chauvet, 2018), and sociology of science approaches (Stephens, 2013) led early research interest in APs.

Across this past research, a core strand of social science work on APs has examined the contexts and processes through which this emergent industry has formed. For example, in their study of the cultured meat sector, Stephens et al. (2019) highlight the institutional and interpretative processes by which cultured meat has been made sense of by different publics and ultimately served to bring an industry and its future markets into being (see also Stephens and Ruivenkamp, 2016; Jönsson, 2016; Stephens, 2021). Others have looked across broader AP 'movements', mapping their material, cultural and spatial politics (Guthman and Biltekoff, 2020; House, 2019; Mylan et al., 2019; Clay et al., 2020), political economies (Yates-Doerr, 2015), economic geographies (Mouat and Prince, 2018; Sexton, 2020) and biopolitical outcomes (Sexton, 2018) that are materialising with and through recent AP development. This recent body of AP research builds on established interdisciplinary scholarship that has long been interested in animal-free practices and diets, from philosophical (Francione, 2012), to cultural (Cole and Morgan, 2011; Harper, 2012; Doyle, 2016), nutritional (Radnitz et al., 2015) and environmental perspectives (Lappé, 1971).

In building on this AP research landscape, we are particularly interested in exploring two themes. First, the market-making processes of this new industry: that is, how the possibilities of APs have been framed and contested by different interest groups (e.g. Jönsson, 2016); and second, the material, cultural and political economic implications these framings present to the future of food and farming. Our analysis draws on the broad conceptual lens of cultural political economy in general (e.g. Sayer, 2001; Jessop and Oosterlynck, 2008) and as applied to the study of food systems (e.g. Watts et al., 2018). In this, we explore the cultural politics of APs in their discursive construction as 'planetary saviours' in relation to their marketisation and materialisation as a burgeoning sector of the food economy, and as a potential reconfiguring force of the broader food system. In deploying this cultural political economy lens, we specifically analyse two 'moments' in the trajectory of APs that raise critical questions for the development of food systems. The first explores the promissory narratives and resistances they have encountered as they have been marketised and mainstreamed. Here we pay particular attention to the ways that the narratives of *crisis, anxiety* and *urgency*, as well as the *scale* of livestock-related problems in the Anthropocene, have (re)authorised the power of Big Food as central to solving these crises. Our second moment is more speculative and narrows our analysis to only cellular agriculture. Here we ask: what are the ethical and spatial implications of taking the animal 'out' of meat production via cell-culture technologies, and how will these implications be felt in different places and over different timeframes? We posit some of the ways that APs have the potential to reconfigure the ethical and spatial nature of food systems at the same time they have the potential to replicate and deepen the moralistic justifications of maintaining the current concentrated political economic structures of agri-food capitalism. We conclude with a series of questions designed to further develop research on APs in the context of the changing contours of the food system.

Promises and contestations: Making better 'Meat' for Anxious Times; or giving Big Food an Urgent Leg Up?

Food has the potential to nurture human health and support environmental sustainability. Instead, our food is **threatening** both.
Because food systems are a major driver of poor health and environmental degradation, global efforts are **urgently** needed to collectively transform diets and food production. Faced with the challenge of feeding about 10 billion people a healthy and sustainable diet by 2050, and with a rising number of environmental systems and processes being pushed beyond safe boundaries by food production, methods of food production need to be **urgently** reviewed. (Willett et al., 2019: 447, 450)

Food has continually provoked deep-rooted anxieties throughout human history (Belasco, 2006). Fears of not having enough food, not having the 'right' type, or exhortations to eat 'good' food and avoid the 'bad', all have been (re)produced throughout the ages, often shaping and being shaped by advancements in technological knowledge, and cultural and political economic trends (Jackson, 2015). Most recently, food has become a central concern in scientific and policy narratives about the so-called Anthropocene we are said to currently live in. Defined as the human-induced era of planetary ecological changes, the Anthropocene has come to represent an existential crisis that has in turn created a state of anxiety and urgency across societies, governments, and institutions.[1]

Some 'thing(s)' and 'something' *must* be done – and done *now* (urgency) – to confront the currently ongoing and potential future threats and catastrophic collapse (crises), or it will be too late (anxiety). In the context of food, related framings of crisis, anxiety and urgency are exemplified in the much-publicised EAT-Lancet report entitled *Food in the Anthropocene* where we are told that food systems are threatening human health and environmental sustainability. Yet, in an era *also* defined by a neo-liberalised 'disaster capitalism' (Klein, 2008), the narratives of crisis, urgency and anxiety that make-up the Anthropocenic condition are at the core of the paradoxical role agriculture and food are now seen to occupy in contemporary societies. On the one hand, food is a global-scale and multi-fronted threat to planetary survivability, resilience and prosperity, while on the other, it is an untapped opportunity for major health, sustainability and economic wins. As we will show below, the narratives of crisis, anxiety and urgency, coupled with the material development and timing of APs, have provided Big Food with the affective and market-friendly opportunities they need to remain key players in solving the problems they have had a very real and existential hand in creating.

In addition, within these debates, particular narratives about the *scale* of animal agriculture have featured as a central 'matter of concern' (Latour, 2004) in driving contemporary Anthropocene crises, including everything from climate change, soil degradation, chronic health illnesses and antimicrobial resistance (to name a few) (Godfray et al., 2018). The existing massive scale of livestock on the planet, the predicted increased demand for meat in industrialising economies coupled with projected global population increases over coming decades have collectively advanced a deepening sense of urgency for 'doing' animal agriculture differently, or indeed, doing away with it in many places (Neo and Emel, 2016).

It is against this backdrop of Anthropocene crises, its logics of anxiety and urgency, and the scale of both the challenge *and* opportunity of rethinking livestock production that recent AP activity has emerged. By no means the only food system solution put forward, APs have nevertheless gained widespread attention and support from powerful investors, mainstream media and most recently partnerships with incumbent Big Food corporates. Promissory narratives of what APs might achieve in response to Anthropocenic anxieties have formed a central part of their materialisation. In this, Sexton et al. (2019) outline a typology of five key promises: *healthfulness* (e.g. 'high protein' and 'disease-free' products); *global food security* (e.g. feeding the '9 billion by 2050' and the hungry '2 billion' today in Majority nations); *benefitting animals and the environment* (e.g. 'earth-friendly' and 'kinder' alternatives); *greater control in terms of food safety and functionality* (e.g. produced in 'safe, sterile, controlled conditions'); and *retaining the same eating experience as conventional animal foodstuffs* (e.g. 'the revolutionary plant burger that looks, cooks, and satisfies like beef'). These promissory narratives collectively work to 'make the ultimate promise of a better food system for all, and in turn a better food future for all' (ibid, 59).

Broad (2020) explores the promises of cell-cultured and plant-based meat products through the conceptual lens of metaphors. He notes two metaphors that dominate AP narratives: the metaphor that 'meat is made' which broadens the category of meat beyond solely animal bodies to also include cells and plants; and the 'metaphor of the market' which centres capitalist markets as the most effective forum for advancing AP innovation. Broad's conclusions on the implications of such metaphors for the possibilities of AP technologies echo the concerns raised by Guthman and Biltekoff (2020), who argue that AP promises have functioned as an obfuscation of what is (or not) being disrupted in the name of Anthropocenic crises. A primary critique across both studies concerns how techno-optimist promises can black-box the technologies in question and 'make it difficult, if not impossible, for the public to meaningfully assess the promises and their potential consequences, much less hold their proponents accountable to anything but pecuniary concerns' (Guthman and Biltekoff, 2020: 16). Consequently, commentators have argued that the ability to imagine or create alternative ways of *doing* AP innovation has been narrowed and de-legitimised (Sexton, 2020) and the concerns and values of different publics are at risk of being overlooked (Broad, 2020). Others note that critical voices from outside the industry are largely missing in mainstream coverage of, and decision-making in, AP development (Painter et al., 2020).

Despite the overwhelming positive framing the AP industry has received in mainstream coverage, its promise of multiple wins for people, planet and profits has met with significant resistances from different interest groups. Perhaps unsurprisingly, a primary group of counterclaims has emerged from incumbents involved in conventional livestock production. Powerful lobby groups and farmer organisations have questioned the technical viability, legality and 'realness' of AP products (Sexton et al., 2019). Characterisations of APs as 'Frankenfood' and ultra-processed products have drummed up fears of further separating us from where our food comes from and advancing the corporate capture of food systems (Blythman, 2018). A number of high-profile lawsuits have been filed in the US by livestock industry incumbents contesting the labelling of AP products as 'meat', prompting counter-suits from the AP industry that in many cases are still ongoing (Stephens et al., 2019). In addition, the framing of APs as a direct and complete replacement of global livestock production has been pushed by a number of key individuals and publications from the AP industry. For example, Pat Brown, CEO of plant-based meat company Impossible Foods, has repeatedly stated in public interviews that he wants to make livestock farming obsolete through his products (Greenfield, 2021). A recent report by RethinkX (2019) that was widely cited amongst the AP industry made headlines for its dramatic prediction that 90 percent of jobs in US beef and dairy production and their associated industries will be lost by 2035. Farming communities were further angered when in 2018 prominent AP institutions and individuals pushed for the sector to adopt 'clean meat' as a new name for their cell-cultured and plant-based products. This framing was seen by many in conventional food and farming circles as explicitly and antagonistically positioning conventional meat as the 'dirty' option (Stephens et al., 2019).

Yet, and importantly for this chapter, at the same time as resistance has risen from some parts of the Big Food landscape, a particular group of agri-food industry players has ended up leading the charge on a more celebratory, incumbent engagement with the AP sector. Multinational livestock processing companies such as Tyson Foods and PHW Group, along with major food retailers and fast-food chains (e.g. Tesco, McDonald's) have been notable for their lack of resistance to APs. On the contrary, they have actively invested in and started their own development of APs and done so much sooner than the AP industry anticipated. In 2020, California-based Memphis Meats secured the biggest investment for a cultured meat company to date (at the time of writing), raising $161 million in their Series B funding round which included Cargill and Tyson Foods amongst its backers. In early 2021, Netherlands-based Mosa Meat announced it had closed an $85 million Series B funding round with key investors including global animal nutrition firm Nutreco and the CEO of online food delivery company JustEatTakeaway.com. This round follows their Series A funding in 2018 which was led by M Ventures and European meat processing giant Bell Food Group. Major names in supermarket retail (e.g. Tesco, Walmart) and global fast-food chains (e.g. KFC, McDonald's, Burger King) have made landmark partnerships with Beyond Meat, Impossible Foods and other recent plant-based AP companies over recent years. Multiple high-street food retailers have launched their own plant-based product lines (e.g. M&S's 'Plant Kitchen' range) and in 2018 Tesco hired a Director of Plant-based Innovation. In a further public commitment to AP futures, Tyson Foods made headlines in 2018 for announcing it was rebranding from a 'meat company' to a 'protein company'.

For us, it is these narratives of crises, anxiety and urgency – as well as the more implied concerns over the scale of the livestock sector – that have specifically worked to authorise Big Food (and specifically Big Meat) as critical and, indeed, unavoidable actors in solving the Anthropocenic problems associated with meat production and consumption. Agri-food giants have sought to rapidly and unequivocally position themselves as a core set of players able to solve the food-related Anthropocene crisis, to do so urgently given the problems humanity faces, and to deal with the state of societal anxiety surrounding, in particular, climate change. They have, in effect, made themselves indispensable – and thus critical nodes of power that shape the AP sector and its trajectories – through two principle means. First, they have deployed the 'too big to ignore' arguments used by other multinationals (e.g. Unilever; see Doyle et al., 2020) that suggest that only *they* have the technological, investment and knowledge capital to innovate, scale-up and bring APs to market. For example, Tyson Foods CEO stated in a 2018 Bloomberg interview about APs that '[Tyson is] so big that the industry can't change if we don't lead' (Little, 2018). Second, given the amount Big Food has already invested in APs in terms of capital – albeit small for the overall agri-food sector, yet large compared to investment capital in the AP space – many have developed a tangible rationale for their authorisation as important and powerful actors to shape AP innovation and marketisation. As a recent Bloomberg article detailing Big Food investment in APs puts it:

> Tyson isn't the only player in the conventional meat industry making unconventional investments. Cargill Inc. bought into Memphis Meats, too. Perdue Farms Inc. is investing in humane processing equipment, slow-growth chicken breeds, and niche organic brands. Even Hormel Foods Corp., maker of Spam, is developing animal-free products. If Tyson doesn't stay ahead of the game, it runs the very real risk of falling behind. "We want to actively disrupt ourselves", says Hayes [CEO of Tyson Foods). "We don't want to be Kodak". (Little, 2018)

Thus, to (re)authorise themselves as sustainable food actors and legitimate 'honest brokers' in the Anthropocene, Big Food has developed its own unique set of promissory narratives in relation to APs: namely, their *outsized role* in food systems, their *expertise*, their *economic and political capital*, and their already *existing investments in APs* collectively work to position themselves as best-placed to solve the urgent crises and anxieties of the Anthropocene. In true disaster capitalist fashion, the self-proclaimed 'fixers' are those who played no small part in driving food systems to their current social and environmental states. A key outcome, then, of the AP sector's appeals to urgency, anxiety and crisis, coupled with the market-friendly opportunities it represents, has simultaneously allowed Big Food to position itself as *the* legitimate and necessary actor in bringing about a better, fairer and more sustainable protein future for all.

Taking the Animal Out of Meat: Speculations on the Ethical, Material, and Spatial Implications of Cellular Agriculture

> Our goal is to take ethical considerations off the table, and to make the best choices from the perspective of sustainability, climate change, global health, and animal welfare. (Bruce Friedrich, Executive Director of GFI, cited in Illing, 2016)

This cultural-political economic analysis of APs highlights the ways in which Anthropocenic crises, anxieties and urgencies have authorised novel and incumbent corporates across the food sector to 'disrupt' the food system, and that a key part of this so-called disruption is in fact the preservation of business-as-usual in agri-food capitalism. We now turn to a more speculative discussion of the potential impacts of APs on the future of food systems. Building directly on Morris et al. (2021) research priorities on the de-meatification of food systems, we assess the possible implications for how cellular agriculture might reconfigure core aspects of the food system. More specifically, we ask: what are the potential *ethical, material* and *spatial* implications of removing animal death from the production and consumption of meat? We are, of course, very wary about attempts to predict the future in general and specifically in relation to the future of food. Rather, in the spirit of this volume's desire to develop a food systems research agenda, we present a series of prompting questions and discussion points designed to not just illuminate critical areas worthy of future research, but also develop some sense of the potential pathways (animal) food systems might travel with the further mainstream marketisation of cellular agriculture. As a reminder we focus here mainly on the Minority world and the potential and specific impacts of cellular agriculture.

As mentioned briefly above, there are currently two predominant imaginaries for a *post-animal bioeconomy* (Datar, 2015) facilitated by the technologies of cultured meat. The first imagines, in effect, the complete removal of the animal from the food system: cell lines are initially extracted from, for example, cows, chickens or pigs, to then become 'immortally' replicated through infinite cellular regeneration from which the resulting meat is then produced ad infinitum and at scale (Stephens et al., 2018). Animals are theoretically no longer needed in this process. Such an approach represents the most absolute version of a post-animal bioeconomy. The second process involves so-called donor herds whereby cells are continually extracted from the various animals, to then be produced into meat also ad infinitum and at scale. In this process, the animal is not completely side-lined but rather a considerably reduced number of much smaller herds globally can be kept alive as a kind of cell stock. Thus, while animals are still a fundamental part of this process of cellular agriculture, there is no direct animal slaughter involved in the production of meat. Both of these approaches offer up a form of 'no direct death' cellular agriculture that have important implications for the ethical, material and spatial futures of food systems[2].

The discussion below is not exhaustive in its coverage of these potential implications, but rather is intended to both highlight existing themes and prompt new questions that build on recent reviews of AP impacts (e.g. Hamdan et al., 2018; Chauvet, 2018; Stephens et al., 2018; Newton and Blaustein-Rejto, 2021). While the different implications we explore overlap to a large extent – for example, any material and spatial changes to food systems from cellular agriculture will, by their very existence or characteristics, have ethical implications – we have separated them below for clarity and focus.

The Potential Ethical Implications of Cellular Agriculture: Eating and Producing without Death to Save the Planet

The possible ethical implications of the production of meat through cellular agriculture are in some ways the most obvious: we get to eat meat that promises to be free of direct death, exploitation and cruelty. By taking animals off the table in this way, proponents of APs see these technologies as a way to take ethics off the table per the quote opening this section. By this logic, consumers will effectively have no reason to consider the ethics of their choices around meat any longer. Along with the end of animal death, so too could there be the 'death' of ethical consumerism or other variants of consumers choosing the 'right' or 'good' form of meat (Johnston, 2008). All consumption of cultured meat becomes ethically good in this way: it does away with the moral quandaries about eating something produced through death and with a high ecological footprint while, at the same time, providing meat that promises to be good to eat in terms of a familiar and pleasurable experience.

It is important to highlight here that there are still significant question marks over cultured meat being able to deliver its win-all promises once production is scaled up. The process is expected to require relatively high energy consumption (Lynch and Pierrehumbert, 2019) and it remains to be seen how other promises relating to antibiotic use, nutritional quality and other ecological impacts will fare against the pressures of becoming technically and economically scalable. Since 2019 a number of cellular agriculture companies have announced plans to start building pilot plants in the US, Europe and Israel (VegEconomist, 2021). Time will tell what trade-offs are potentially made during this next stage of the industry's evolution. There remains considerable optimism within the cellular agriculture sector, at least publicly, that their processes will deliver a choice of meat at scale that is good for our bodies and our bank accounts, good for animals and the planet, and also good for the agricultural corporates they have partnered with.

A set of core questions for further exploration include the following: how and in what ways will cellular agriculture shift and change our ethical – along with other multi-varied, contextual and contingent – relationships to meat, livestock animals and nature in the broadest possible terms? In particular, does cellular agriculture prompt us to develop novel relations and ethics of care to 'companion species' (Haraway, 2003) as donor herds or perhaps remnant animal herds designed to stay on the landscape for tourists and/or grassland management (van der Weele and Driessen, 2013)? Does eating cultured meat become an ethical eating practice designed to allow us to care for other, geographically 'far away' humans impacted by climate change, agricultural pollution and/or food insecurity? Critically this last question spotlights the problematic ethical framings of the cellular agriculture industry that often draw on a kind of neo-Malthusian 'hunger-scape' in which overpopulation and insufficient agricultural production, and specifically of protein supply, at the global scale are foregrounded as the primary challenges of current and future food systems (Sexton et al., 2019).

A second core set of questions revolves around the ontological status of what is meant by 'meat' given the technological and biological affordances of cellular agriculture. Will meat produced through cellular agriculture – which at the molecular level is expected to be the same biological product as conventionally-derived animal meat – be judged to have the same ontological status as 'real' meat derived from animal production and slaughter? It appears as if the definition of what 'meat' is and can be is slowly dissolving with the introduction of cellular agriculture, plant-based 'meat' and the possibilities available from insects (House, 2018). There have already been legal and social battles over how we define 'meat' and 'milk' (Stephens et al., 2019). How will these continue to play out in coming years if the AP industry continues to grow in economic and cultural power, and what are the implications for both the cell-cultured and plant-derived meat markets? Another important question surrounds the ways that 'real' meat is infused with masculinity and gendered politics (e.g. Adams, 1990; Roe, 2018): if cellular agriculture produces animal-derived meat but through its lab-based process, what implications does this have for how it is defined in gendered terms for consumers and the possible easier ride to acceptance by male eaters? Could it be more acceptable to male consumers and eschew the more plant-based epitaphs of 'soy boy' or the ways that vegan diets are often coded as 'female' and/or as a threat to hyper-masculine tropes of physical strength and virility?

More than likely what we will see, at least in the short term, is a bifurcation in markets for cell-cultured, plant-based and animal-derived meats as they all come to exist simultaneously in food systems. Ethical eating choices and responsibilised consumers will thus remain front and centre as these respective markets develop and evolve in relation to each other. Commentators have raised the very real possibility for cellular agriculture products to simply *add* to existing meat systems rather than *replace* their conventional animal-derived counterparts, at least in the short to medium term (cf. Newton and Blaustein-Rejto, 2021). This is potentially one of the biggest ethical and material concerns about AP development, especially given the current culture of urgency that calls for radical change to have any hope of avoiding worse-case scenarios of planetary breakdown. A near-future scenario where plant-based and cellular alternatives have simply added to the overall pie of industrial food production and consumption will have done very little to disrupt the ongoing power of Big Food – despite claims of 'self-disruption' from the likes of Tyson – and the economic, social and environmental injustices that prop up their business models.

Much of the industry and media boosterism surrounding cellular agriculture frames it as a replacement for animal-derived meat, whereby demand for cultured meat goes up and, correspondingly, demand for slaughtered livestock meat goes down (Dutkiewicz and Rosenberg, 2020). Yet if the history of ethical consumerism and previous 'saviour-like' products are anything to go by, we will most likely see an expanding demand for meat alternatives in addition to existing animal meat demands, plus the capture of new vegetarian and vegan consumers who may have previously avoided fast food and other restaurants because of a lack of choice. Some of this additionalism[3] of meat alternatives is already evidenced in a recent statement by the CEO of Burger King's parent company who stated that they were '…not seeing guests swap the original Whopper for the Impossible Whopper. We're seeing that it's attracting new guests' (Newkey-Burden, 2020). The head of communications at Veganuary sees it this way: 'Fast-food restaurants don't have a particular vested interest in serving up dead animals. …. They just want to serve products they can make a profit on. So, if we can help them make a profit on products that don't involve dead animals that can only be a good thing' (Newkey-Burden, 2020). Yet, if the desire to reduce the number of livestock for ethical and ecological reasons is to be realised, then additionalism poses a significant threat to this end goal and should be much more fully investigated for its ethical and ecological quandaries in the face of climate change, the power of Big Food and the often-stated purpose of cellular agriculture to transition us away from the farming and death of 'real' animals.

With cellular agriculture and its promises and potentialities, it is hard to not offer up some science fiction-esque questions in light of this possible bifurcation of meat production and consumption systems. Is there a possible future whereby the masses consume an affordable, scaled-up, readily available cell-cultured meat and the well-to-do eat 'real', slaughtered animal meat? Does animal death become a form of reputational capital only afforded by the richest amongst us or, at a global scale, the richest on the planet? In this scenario, poor consumers eat 'clean' meat with a clean conscious – if they think about it at all – and the rich continue to eat animal-derived meat with little conscious concern – if they think about it at all. There is, of course, the opposite possibility whereby the wealthy are those who can afford cultured meat – as appears to be happening now given the current high prices – and they are the ones eating 'good', cultured meat and accruing the ethical capital of solving climate change through their shopping trips and family meals. Eating cultured meat may thus become a form of virtue signalling for the wealthy as responsibilised consumers who can afford to eat cultured meat to save animals, people and the planet. Either way, the ethical, racial, class and gendered dilemmas embedded in the rise of cellular agriculture is worthy of much further consideration.[4]

The Potential Material and Spatial Implications for Cellular Agriculture: Assessing the Future Economic Geographies of Death-free Eating and Farming

The mainstreaming and growth of cellular agriculture holds many potential material and spatial implications for food supply chains, agri-food networks and socioeconomic change. We only have space to introduce and discuss a few and have chosen those most applicable to cultured meat and those we feel bring some of the timeliest issues currently faced by this emergent sector to the fore.

First, like the development of any good novel capitalist market, cellular agriculture will work to produce new forms of commodification of biological resources, technological processes, production methods and, of course, goods to be sold on markets to consumers. From animal cell lines and serum ingredients, donor herds and new breeds of animals, to fermentation processes and intellectual property surrounding the whole of the cultured meat enterprise, commodification will drive economic development and vice versa as markets develop. Several critical questions are important to ask in this context: will these forms of commodification and the intellectual property surrounding cultured meat reinforce the economic concentration evident in current Big Food-owned supply chains? Will it allow new and different players – such as Big Pharma – to capture (more) parts of the food system? Or will cultured meat be diversified and devolved to more/other innovators who can then develop their own power in food systems and disrupt existing supply chains to a certain extent?

On more specific details: with infinitely replicable cell lines and/or donor herds, who will own these and control them, and where in the world will they exist? Some in the cellular agriculture sector see a possible future in a kind of devolved and diversified system of small donor herds that supports innovation and economic development across a variety of types of animals, types of landscapes and types of 'meat'. In this imagined future, what scope is there for cultured meat to revitalise smaller, craft-led, agroecological livestock farming? What are the barriers to entry, and how might this differ across Minority and Majority World contexts? Again, a bifurcated meat supply chain seems more likely at least in the short to medium term, with donor herds in existence and potted around various landscapes while more traditional animal livestock systems that harvest meat after slaughter still remain viable and likely. Indeed, 'real' meat might become more valuable and support the continuing – or even expanded – existence of these farming systems in smaller, rural communities that depend on their economic viability. This of course depends greatly on the ability of cellular agriculture to prove itself technically and economically beyond the scale of the lab, as well as barriers to entry being addressed in terms of knowledge and technological accessibility, consumer acceptance and regulatory approval being achieved beyond Singapore.

Second, the expansion of cellular agriculture into something we eat everyday has the potential to impact on environments, landscapes and livelihoods in important ways. There are, for example, the large-scale ecological implications of transitioning to cellular agriculture which reduces the overall number of livestock in agri-food systems. Will this be sufficient to support the reduction of carbon emissions to reach net-zero as promised by national governments through the Paris Accord? How will the energy required to make cultured meat mitigate these reductions? In addition to the possible ecological impacts of widespread cellular agriculture, the potential reduction in numbers of livestock on the land holds important possible implications for livelihoods and landscapes. For example, with the reduction of livestock, what happens to farmers, farming jobs and rural communities? Do they disappear to a large extent or concentrate into smaller and fewer locales? Does fewer livestock mean *more* people on the landscape because there is effectively more room, or *fewer* people if the land is given over to re-wilding and conservation services? Will these reimagined landscapes create more and different jobs in food and farming (e.g. as cell scientists or biochemical engineers) or reimagine rural livelihoods away from agriculture towards conservation and eco-tourism?

On this latter point, a key vision of the cellular agriculture movement is the expansion of re-wilding and the development of landscapes full of past native species. Former farmers may become more akin to rural land managers, designing landscapes to further suck up carbon emissions and contribute to net-zero targets. Livestock-related land and water pollution might also begin to disappear with reductions in livestock numbers leading to reductions in manure run-off and contaminants in the production of animal feed. There is, of course, the counter argument that we cannot have sustainable agricultural systems without some livestock replenishing nutrients in the soil, in addition to concerns over the cultural relevance of the rural idyll, lifestyles and cultures that might be altered as livestock leave the land through cellular agriculture. A recent study of UK attitudes to landscapes found that sheep, cows and trees were voted the top three most popular landscapes, highlighting the deep cultural significance (albeit often heavily romanticised) of seeing livestock animals in our landscapes (Rust et al., 2021). It is these concerns that raise one of the most fundamental questions in the shadow of the widespread shift to cultured meat: who and what is the countryside for, who decides this, and how might these fundamentally political and geographical questions play out in often marginal, powerless and economically depressed rural areas?

These points all collectively speak to a bigger issue concerning the process by which *transitions* towards cellular agriculture may play out over shorter, medium and longer terms in different places and at different scales. As we have mentioned, it is predicted that cellular agriculture and plant-based products will exist alongside conventional animals for some time, rather than instigate a complete and immediate substitution effect despite some relatively dramatic predictions to that effect (e.g. RethinkX, 2019). This has implications for the extent to which APs can deliver on their environmental and health promises in the short and medium term if they are simply increasing *overall* production and consumption of food. For example, will the growing demand for food crops like wheat, pea and soya – the most popular bases for plant-based meat substitutes and potential ingredients for cultured meat growth serum – further entrench intensive production systems around the world and exacerbate local-ised food insecurity, particularly in poorer nations dependent on agricultural exports?

Longer term forecasts predict that the short term additionalism that APs will likely create is simply an initial and necessary step in a broader shift that will eventually see conventional livestock products reduce in number, particularly as AP competition and changes in climate, regulations and rep-utational pressures render livestock the next 'stranded assets' (Scott, 2019). There is little, however, in AP narratives that challenges the continued culture of over-consumption that is at the heart of its innovation model and its short-term forecasts of scaling from lab to initial production. The dominant promise of APs is not about *eating less but better* meats and milks, but about continuing to eat the *same if not more* of these foods without the ecological and ethical guilt that comes with conventional animal agriculture. How, and indeed if, this latest expression of green consumerism bucks the trend and delivers on its promises over the coming years requires continued critical assessment.

These points emphasise the need to critically examine AP implications across different timescales to understand where and by whom their effects and ben-efits will be felt. For example, we have seen that much effort has been spent by the AP industry itself and incumbent agri-food corporates on centring Big Food as key facilitators of AP development in the short to medium term. This centring has largely been justified by the latter's economic and material means being deemed the most effective at scaling up the production and promised benefits of APs *quickly* in response to the era of planetary urgency. In other words, partnerships with Big Food have become a *necessary* short-term step that can buy us and the planet time for more radical, systemic reform later on; this is very reminiscent of the 'put out the fire first so there is still a house to rebuild later' argument. While these justifications often belie a sense of 'there is no other way' and 'we don't have time to do it differently', it is important to recognise that transition pathways such as this are made up of choices – choices of who gets to decide, who gets to lead and who is missing from the table; of what social contracts, ethical values and innovation models are priori-tised; and of where and how technological development and its mainstreaming takes place. The *choice* by AP proponents to partner with incumbent agri-food corporates in the short term has important and very material effects over different timescales. For example, is it reasonable to expect that accessibility to AP technologies for smaller producers will increase in the medium to longer term if Big Food takes the reins in the short term? If Big Food with its big budgets takes on the high risk and expense of early R & D, how might we expect the intellectual property landscape of APs to develop over the coming decades? Whose interests will be served and what lock-ins will be created by choosing to take AP production out of the lab and into initial production through partnerships with Big Food (and Big Pharma)?

In sum, *how* the AP industry scales up and instigates a transition away from conventional livestock production will determine who will benefit, and when and where these impacts will be felt. Thinking across timeframes as well as places and scales is, we argue, a fundamental part of these discussions. Yet far from needing to re-invent the wheel in this endeavour, there is a wealth of research that has explored pathways and challenges for 'just transitions' within food and farming (e.g. Blattner, 2020), and in other industrial sectors (e.g. see Newell and Mulvaney, 2013 on energy transitions). There is much scope for the AP industry itself and researchers more broadly to draw on these frameworks to think through a more holistic vision that ensures notions of justice and sovereignty are embedded in larger-scale transitions away from conventional animal agriculture towards APs (Broad, 2019), and that lessons are learnt from previous encounters between AFNs and the mainstream.

Conclusions: Taking APs Forward in Food Systems Research

While the food technologies we discuss in this chapter are ostensibly new, the promises they claim, the ethical dilemmas they raise, and the critical questions they prompt are largely familiar to researchers of (alternative) food systems and food-related innovation and technological change: namely, what constitutes a 'better' future for food and farming? Who gets to decide how this better future is imagined and put into place? Who or what is overlooked, and what role should technology, markets, food movements and corporations play in transitions to just and sustainable food systems? Our aim here has been to begin thinking through some of these themes in relation to APs and to signpost future directions for food systems researchers to produce further in-depth critical work on the continuing development of APs and their current and potential impacts on food systems.

We focussed first on the role Big Food has and continues to play in shaping the politics of possibility of APs, and how this is having very real implications on what APs are, what they might deliver, when, and for whom. We showed how the contemporary moment of planetary urgency, anxiety and crisis – and their scaled politics – coupled with the market-friendly model of the AP sector, has created yet another opportunity for Big Food to centre itself in the 'reinvention' of the food system. While we have shared our concerns based on historic precedence of this 'too big to fail' and/or 'too big to ignore' flavour of green capitalism, more critical work is needed to assess whether these specific actors and the reinvented futures they are proposing are best placed to bring about the radical social, ecological and political economic change that is needed in the construction of sustainable food systems.

Second, we argued that it is important to continually reflect on the various implications of APs across place, scale and over different timeframes as the AP industry continues to scale up. There has been a tendency in the AP sector to eschew critical debate on the technological (i.e. high-tech) and ideological (market-based) approach that has largely underpinned AP development to date. Appeals to urgency, anxiety and crisis have in part been used to close down such reflections on the basis that there isn't time to *not do something*, or that the old critiques of market-based approaches are at best unrealistic and at worst obstructive to bringing about the urgent change we need. Rather, what would happen if we positioned APs – and their framings of urgency, anxiety and crisis – as central to asking the most important question of all in these turbulent and alarming times. What, in the broadest possible sense, are food systems *for* and *how* and *by whom* should they be controlled? Clearly critical research on the place-based, scalar and temporal promises and material changes embedded in APs must continue and be further extended as these foods increasingly enter the mainstream of current and future food systems.

We are of course generalising across an entire and currently emergent sector that does not always itself identify as a singular movement or industry and is made up of diverse people, geographies, motivations, products and technologies. There are some directly involved in AP development who are concerned about the points we have raised in this chapter, and those who are working to think differently about how best to 'do' AP innovation that does not lead to yet more (or indeed the same) Goliaths controlling the global food system. A crucially under-developed area for facilitating these types of conversations is the lack of meaningful engagement between those working in AP development, conventional farming and alternative food communities. To date AP discourse has been dominated by increasingly incendiary and binary arguments – in both academia and popular culture – of what food is and what it should be in the face of contemporary crises, with little understanding or, in some cases, purposeful mischaracterisation of what is contested and shared across AP and more conventional farming divides. There is much potential and a critical need to bring the rich knowledge base of different farming and food systems communities across different geographies, as well as responsible innovation and food sovereignty/justice movements, into conversation with AP development as a key part of opening this emergent sector to alternative possibilities and outcomes.

Notes

1. See Sklair (2020) for more on the controversial definitions of the Anthropocene.
2. At the time of writing, foetal bovine serum (FBS) is still used as a key component in cell-ag growth medium. FBS is a by-product of the dairy and meat industries, harvested from the blood of cow foetuses separated from pregnant cattle during slaughter. Several companies are currently working on the development of a serum-free medium for truly 'no-death' meats (McCormick 2021).
3. In some ways, this is an interesting novelty to the agro-food system innovation processes of 'substitutionism' and 'appropriationism' articulated by Goodman et al. (1987) where we are beginning to see a kind of 'additionalism' to current food systems through the development of novel markets for APs.
4. These questions should be asked in addition to those related to the ethical and moral concerns about racialised and gendered labour and ecological exploitation throughout the industrial food system – and its alternatives.

References

Adams, C.J., 1990. *The Sexual Politics of Meat: A Vegetarian Critical Theory*. New York, NY: Continuum.

Belasco W., 2006. *Meals to Come: A History of the Future of Food*. Berkeley, CA: University of California Press.

Blattner, C., 2020. Just transition for agriculture? A critical step in tackling climate change. *Journal of Agriculture, Food Systems, and Community Development, 9*, 3: 53–58.

Blythman J., 2018. The Quorn revolution: The rise of ultra-processed fake meat. *The Guardian*. https:// www .theguardian .com/ lifeandstyle/ 2018/ feb/ 12/ quorn -revolution-rise-ultra-processed-fake-meat (accessed: 26 July 2021).

Broad, G.M., 2019. Plant-based and cell-based animal product alternatives: An assessment and agenda for food tech justice. *Geoforum*, 107: 223–226. https://doi.org/doi: 10.1016/j.geoforum.2019.06.014.

Broad, G.M., 2020. Making meat, better: The metaphors of plant-based and cell-based meat innovation. *Environmental Communication*, 14, 7: 919–932.

Bryant, C., Barnett, J., 2020. Consumer acceptance of cultured meat: An updated review (2018–2020). *Applied Sciences*, 10, 15, 5201.

Chauvet, D.J., 2018. Should cultured meat be refused in the name of animal dignity?. *Ethical Theory and Moral Practice*, 21, 2: 387–411.

Clay, N., Sexton, A.E., Garnett, T., Lorimer, J., 2020. Palatable disruption: The politics of plant milk. *Agriculture and Human Values*, 37, 4: 945–962.

Cole, M., Morgan, K., 2011. Vegaphobia: Derogatory discourses of veganism and the reproduction of speciesism in UK national newspapers. *The British Journal of Sociology*, 62, 1: 134–153.

Datar, I., 2015. Food of the future: The post-animal bioeconomy. Keynote given at SXSWECO. October 6. https://www.youtube.com/watch?v=Aj2LQ5W_MgU.

Doyle, J., 2016. Celebrity vegans and the lifestyling of ethical consumption. *Environmental Communication*, 10, 6: 777–790.

Doyle, J., Farrell, N., Goodman, M.K., 2020 The cultural politics of climate branding: Project Sunlight, the biopolitics of climate care and the socialisation of the everyday sustainable consumption practices of citizens-consumers. *Climatic Change*, 163: 117–133.

Dutkiewicz, J., Rosenberg, G., 2020. Burgers won't save the planet – but fast food might. *Wired*. https://www.wired.com/story/opinion-burgers-wont-save-the-planet-but-fast-food-might/ (accessed: 6 July 2022).

Francione, G.L., 2012. Animal welfare, happy meat, and veganism as the moral baseline. In Kaplan, D. (ed.) *The Philosophy of Food*. Berkeley: University of California Press, pp. 169–189.

Godfray, H.C.J., Aveyard, P., Garnett, T. et al., 2018. Meat consumption, health, and the environment. *Science*, 361, 6399.

Goodman, D., Sorj, B., Wilkinson, J. 1987. *From Farming to Biotechnology*. Oxford: Blackwell.

Greenfield P., 2021. 'Let's get rid of friggin' cows' says creator of plant-based 'bleeding burger'. https://www.theguardian.com/environment/2021/jan/08/lets-get-rid-of-friggin-cows-why-one-food-ceo-says-its-game-over-for-meat-aoe (accessed 26 July 2021).

Guthman, J., Biltekoff, C., 2020. Magical disruption? Alternative protein and the promise of de-materialization. *Environment and Planning E: Nature and Space*, 2514848620963125.

Hamdan, M.N., Post, M.J., Ramli, M.A., Mustafa, A., 2018. Cultured meat in Islamic perspective. *Journal of Religion and Health*, 57, 6: 2193–2206.

Haraway, D., 2003. *The Companion Species Manifesto: Dogs, People and Significant Others*. Chicago: Prickly Paradigm Press.

Harper, A.B., 2012. Going beyond the normative white 'post-racial' vegan epistemology. In: Forson P., Counihan, C. (eds) *Taking Food Public: Redefining Foodways in a Changing World*. New York, NY: Routledge, pp. 155–174.

Hicks, K., Stein, J., 2016. Why this 'bloody' veggie burger may become the Tesla of food. *Vox*. https://www.vox.com/2016/7/7/12106708/impossible-foods-ezra-klein-show (accessed: 2 August 2021).

House, J., 2018. Insects as food in the Netherlands: Production networks and the geographies of edibility. *Geoforum*, 94: 82–93.

House, J., 2019. Insects are not 'the new sushi': Theories of practice and the acceptance of novel foods. *Social and Cultural Geography*, 20, 9: 1285–1306.

Illing, S., 2016. Ethical arguments won't end factory farming. Technology might. *Vox*. https://www.vox.com/conversations/2016/10/11/13225532/bruce-friedrich-good -food-institute-meat-factory-farming-vegetarianism (accessed: 26 July 2021).

Jackson, P., 2015. *Anxious Appetites: Food and Consumer Culture* (Vol. 2). London: Bloomsbury Publishing.

Jessop, B., Oosterlynck, S., 2008. Cultural political economy: On making the cultural turn without falling into soft economic sociology. *Geoforum*, 39: 1155–1169.

Johnston, J., 2008. The citizen-consumer hybrid: Ideological tensions and the case of Whole Foods Market. *Theory and Society*, 37, 3: 229–270.

Jönsson, E., 2016. Benevolent technotopias and hitherto unimaginable meats: Tracing the promises of in vitro meat. *Social Studies of Science*, 46, 5: 725–748.

Klein, N., 2008. *The Shock Doctrine: The Rise of Disaster Capitalism*. London: Penguin.

Lappé, F.M., 1971. *Diet for a Small Planet*. New York, NY: Ballantine Books.

Latour, B., 2004. Why has critique run out of steam? From matters of fact to matters of concern. *Critical Inquiry*, 30: 225–248.

Little, A., 2018. Tyson isn't chicken. Virtually all of the company's revenue comes from animal slaughter and processing. Now its new CEO is pouring money into animal-free alternatives. Bloomberg. https://www.bloomberg.com/news/features/2018-08-15/tyson-s-quest-to-be-your-one-stop-protein-shop (accessed: 2 August 2021).

Lynch, J., Pierrehumbert, R., 2019. Climate impacts of cultured meat and beef cattle. *Frontiers in Sustainable Food Systems*, 3, 5.

McCormick, E., 2021. Eat Just is racing to put 'no-kill meat' on your plate. Is it too good to be true? *The Guardian*. https://www.theguardian.com/food/2021/jun/16/eat-just -no-kill-meat-chicken-josh-tetrick (accessed: 6 July 2022).

Morris, C., Mylan, J., Beech, E., 2019. Substitution and food system de-animalisation: The case of non-dairy milk. *The International Journal of Sociology of Agriculture and Food*, 25, 1.

Morris, C., Kaljonen, M., Aavik, K., Balázs, B. et al., 2021. Priorities for social science and humanities research on the challenges of moving beyond animal-based food systems. *Humanities and Social Sciences Communications*, 8, 1: 1–12.

Mouat, M.J., Prince, R., 2018. Cultured meat and cowless milk: On making markets for animal-free food. *Journal of Cultural Economy*, 11, 4: 315–329.

Murphy, M., 2019. Beyond Meat soars 163% in biggest-popping U.S. IPO since 2000. https://www.marketwatch.com/story/beyond-meat-soars-163-in-biggest-popping -us-ipo-since-2000-2019-05-02 (accessed: 6 July 2022).

Mylan, J., Morris, C., Beech, E., Geels, F.W., 2019. Rage against the regime: Niche-regime interactions in the societal embedding of plant-based milk. *Environmental Innovation and Societal Transitions*, 31: 233–247.

Neo, H., Emel, J., 2016. *Geographies of Meat: Politics, Economy and Culture*. Abingdon: Routledge.

Newell, P., Mulvaney, D., 2013. The political economy of the 'just transition'. *The Geographical Journal*, 179, 2: 132–140.

Newkey-Burden, C., 2020. More fast-food chains are offering plant-based food – but should vegans be celebrating? *The Guardian*. https://www.theguardian.com/lifeandstyle/shortcuts/2020/jan/07/more-fast-food-chains-are-offering-plant-based -food-but-should-vegans-be-celebrating (accessed: 26 July 2021).

Newton, P., Blaustein-Rejto, D., 2021. Social and economic opportunities and challenges of plant-based and cultured meat for rural producers in the US. *Frontiers in Sustainable Food Systems*, 5, 10.

Painter, J., Brennen, J.S., Kristiansen, S., 2020. The coverage of cultured meat in the US and UK traditional media, 2013–2019: Drivers, sources, and competing narratives. *Climatic Change*, *162*, 4: 2379–2396.

Poinski, M., 2020. Impossible Foods closes $200M funding round. *Food Dive*. https://www.fooddive.com/news/impossible-foods-closes-200m-funding-round/583529/ (accessed: 6 July 2022).

Post, M.J., Levenberg, S., Kaplan, D.L., Genovese, N. et al., 2020. Scientific, sustainability and regulatory challenges of cultured meat. *Nature Food*, *1*, 7: 403–415.

Radnitz, C., Beezhold, B., DiMatteo, J., 2015. Investigation of lifestyle choices of individuals following a vegan diet for health and ethical reasons. *Appetite*, *90*: 31–36.

RethinkX, 2019. Rethinking food and agriculture 2020–2030: The second domestication of plants and animals, the disruption of the cow, and the collapse of industrial livestock farming. https://www.rethinkx.com/food-and-agriculture (accessed 28 July 2021).

Roe, E.J., 2018. Sun's out, buns out: Exploring the alfresco ritual of meat, fire, man's work, and sustainability. In: *Global Food Security*. https://www.foodsecurity.ac.uk/blog/suns-out-buns-out-exploring-the-alfresco-ritual-of-meat-fire-mans-work-and-sustainability/ (accessed: 25 January 2021).

Rust, N.A., Rehackova, L., Naab, F., Abrams, A. et al., 2021. What does the UK public want farmland to look like?. *Land Use Policy*, *106*, 105445.

Sayer, A., 2001. For a critical cultural political economy. *Antipode*, *33*, 687–708.

Scott, M., 2019. Could climate change make cows the next stranded asset? *Forbes*. https://www.forbes.com/sites/mikescott/2019/09/04/could-climate-change-make-cows-the-next-stranded-asset/ (accessed: 26 July 2021).

Seehafer, A., Bartels, M., 2019. Meat 2.0: The regulatory environment of plant-based and cultured meat. *Eur. Food and Feed L. Rev.*, *14*, 323.

Sexton, A.E., 2018. Eating for the post-Anthropocene: Alternative proteins and the biopolitics of edibility. *Transactions of the Institute of British Geographers*, *43*, 4: 586–600.

Sexton, A.E., 2020. Food as software: Place, protein, and feeding the world Silicon Valley-style. *Economic Geography*, *96*, 5: 449–469.

Sexton, A.E., Garnett, T., Lorimer, J., 2019. Framing the future of food: The contested promises of alternative proteins. *Environment and Planning E: Nature and Space*, *2*, 1: 47–72.

Sklair, L. (ed.), 2020. *The Anthropocene in Global Media: Neutralizing the Risk*. London: Routledge

Stephens, N., 2013. Growing meat in laboratories: The promise, ontology, and ethical boundary-work of using muscle cells to make food. *Configurations*, *21*, 2: 159–181.

Stephens, N., 2021. Join our team, change the world: Edibility, producibility and food futures in cultured meat company recruitment videos. *Food, Culture and Society*, *25*, 1: 32–48.

Stephens, N., Ruivenkamp, M., 2016. Promise and ontological ambiguity in the in vitro meat imagescape: From laboratory myotubes to the cultured burger. *Science as Culture*, *25*, 3: 327–355.

Stephens, N., Di Silvio, L., Dunsford, I., Ellis, M., Glencross, A., Sexton, A. 2018. Bringing cultured meat to market: Technical, socio-political, and regulatory challenges in cellular agriculture. *Trends in Food Science & Technology*, *78*: 155–166.

Stephens, N., Sexton, A.E., Driessen, C., 2019. Making sense of making meat: Key moments in the first 20 years of tissue engineering muscle to make food. *Frontiers in Sustainable Food Systems*, *3*, 45.

Tuomisto, H L., 2019. The eco-friendly burger: Could cultured meat improve the environmental sustainability of meat products?. *EMBO reports*, *20*, 1, e47395.

Tyson Foods, 2021. Leading the future of plant protein. The Food Blog. https://thefeed .blog/2021/01/08/leading-the-future-of-plant-based-protein/ (accessed: 6 July 2022).

van der Weele, C., Driessen, C., 2013. Emerging profiles for cultured meat: Ethics through and as design. *Animals*, *3*, 3: 647–662.

VegEconomist, 2021. MeaTech to open Belgium factory to 3D print 'real meat cuts' like steak and chicken breast. *VegEconomist*. https://vegconomist.com/companies-and -portraits/meatech-to-open-belgium-factory-to-3d-print-real-meat-cuts-like-steak -chicken-breast/ (accessed: 26 July 2021).

Watts, D., Little, J., Ilbery, B., 2018. 'I am pleased to shop somewhere that is fighting the supermarkets a little bit'. A cultural political economy of alternative food networks. *Geoforum*, 91: 21–29. https://doi.org/10.1016/j.geoforum.2018.02.013.

Willett, W., Rockström, J., Loken, B., Springmann, M. et al., 2019. Food in the Anthropocene: The EAT–Lancet Commission on healthy diets from sustainable food systems. *The Lancet*, *393*, 10170: 447–492.

Yates-Doerr, E., 2015. Does meat come from animals? A multispecies approach to classification and belonging in highland Guatemala. *American Ethnologist*, 42, 2: 309–323. https://doi.org/10.1111/amet.12132.

9 Urban food systems: the case for municipal action

Jess Halliday

Introduction

For much of the past two to three thousand years, food provisioning has been a preoccupation for the governments and residents of cities. Human settlements were generally sited on or near a fertile basin suitable for growing food, yet as populations swelled and trade relations expanded foodstuffs have made up an increasing proportion of imported products. The development of new modes of transportation, especially of railway networks during the 19th and early 20th centuries, as well as the development of food preservation technologies were critical to the extension and industrialisation of food supply chains serving cities, particularly those in countries of the global North (Lang, 2003). During the second half of the 20th century a globalised food system emerged in which agri-commodities are produced either in low- and middle-income countries (LMIC) utilising cheap labour and under-valued resources, or in high-income countries using advanced technologies, and then moved in large volumes over great distances through global supply chains. One of the features of this globalised food system has been the nutrition transition in LMIC characterised by increasing consumption of processed foods including animal proteins, a process that has been accompanied by rising levels of non-communicable disease (Popkin et al., 2012).

The prevailing mode of governance of the globalised food system is neo-liberal and market-based, with a relatively small number of powerful corporations extracting value and setting conditions for other supply chain players (Lang, 2003; see Clapp, Chapter 2 in this volume). With the exception of regulatory baselines on food safety and quality, national governments have tended to conflate food and agricultural policy. Consequently, food has largely been regarded as a rural issue, with an over-riding assumption that if production is sufficient, food will find its way into cities (Crush and Riley, 2018) to be distributed through the major retailers. In this respect city authorities are relieved of responsibility for availability and access to food for their citizens. While other human necessities such as shelter, water, and sanitation, have informed urban planning decisions, food has tended to be overlooked (Pothukuchi and Kauffman, 1999).

The assumption that cities' food needs will be met by the market has been challenged over the last two decades. An increasing number of cities have begun asserting responsibility for their food system through the development and implementation of policies and programmes, and the installation of food governance mechanisms. This shift in perspective, driven by a realisation that food supply chains are vulnerable, are often socially and environmentally harmful, and do not deliver the best outcomes for consumers (see section two below), has been a gradual process. Much of the early thinking was from cities in high-income, industrialised countries such as the United States, Canada, the UK, and mainland Europe (Bassarab et al., 2019; Ilieva, 2016), although a handful of cities in lower-middle income countries are also counted among the pioneers, such as Belo Horizonte in Brazil (Rocha and Lessa, 2009). Since 2015 the movement has picked up pace with a stream of new cities – including some in Latin America, Africa and (to a lesser extent) Asia – taking up the challenge (MUFPP, n.d.).

This chapter explores the drivers of cities' re-awakened concern for their food system, and examines the potential they have to shape it, bearing in mind the different degrees of political autonomy of local governments under different national legal institutional frameworks. Before embarking on this exploration, however, it is necessary to define some key concepts in this emerging field of policy and practice.

First, the term 'urban food system' refers to the food system of which a city is part, that is configured to serve urban consumers. In keeping with the food systems approach, this includes all activities and interactions between actors at all stages of the value chain, as well as societal and nature-based contextual factors and all socio-economic and environmental impacts and outcomes, on all value chain actors, in all places (FAO, 2018). The conventional, globalised food system can be considered as inherently urban (Clendenning et al., 2016), since it delivers convenient, processed, and packaged foods that are ubiquitous in cities of the global North, whose component ingredients originate from far afield. Even minimally or unprocessed foodstuffs, such as fruit, vegetables and raw meat, are frequently delivered to urban areas via long supply chains.

Second, the term 'city region food system' has emerged as a territorial conceptualisation that encompasses a larger urban centre – or conglomeration of smaller urban centres – and the surrounding and interspersed peri-urban and rural hinterland (Rodríguez-Pose, 2008). As such, a city region food system is "the complex network of actors, processes and relationships that are involved in food production, processing, marketing and consumption in a given city region", with rural–urban linkages at the centre (FAO, 2016a: 2). The city region food system approach does not advocate serving cities exclusively through regional or local food supply chains, but rather valorising local food capabilities and assets to enable diverse supply chains of varying lengths. A key lesson from situations of food supply chain disruption (due to, for example, political unrest, industrial action, climate shocks and stresses, or infection control measures during pandemics such as COVID-19) is that diversity in food sources and supply chains increases resilience. If one source or supply chain is compromised, others can step up to ensure food availability (Blay-Palmer et al., 2021; Smith et al., 2015).

A third useful conceptualisation in work on urban food systems is the 'food environment'. The food environment is the physical interface between the food system and the day-to-day food experiences of residents (FAO, 2016b). Herforth and Ahmed (2015) identified a number of core dimensions of the food environment: availability, affordability, convenience, and desirability. Turner et al. (2018) built on these works by attributing these four dimensions to the 'personal' domain of the food environment – that is, those that are experienced at the individual level. Alongside this, they identified a parallel 'external' domain that is driven by dynamics within the wider food system: availability, prices, vendor and product properties, and marketing and regulation. Combined, these two domains influence acquisition and consumption on the part of urban residents, and in turn health and nutrition outcomes.

The remainder of this chapter is structured as follows. Section two outlines six reasons why cities should be – and in many cases are – increasingly concerned with their food systems. Section three then explains what cities can do to reshape their food system (depending on local powers and responsibilities), with policy actions ranging from single-issue initiatives through to fully integrated strategies implemented by all relevant municipal departments. This highlights the potential of food policy action to help address other entrenched urban issues such as poverty and social exclusion. Section four sets out the challenges that cities may encounter in securing and retaining political will for the food agenda, securing funds, and implementing actions. It provides examples of how some cities have overcome or circumvented these challenges. Section five discusses various governance models that local governments may put in place or participate in, with particular attention to multi-stakeholder platforms such as food policy councils, and structural and operational considerations. Finally, section six identifies areas where more research is needed to support food action by cities, to extend and magnify the impact of their efforts, and to shore up resilience of urban and city region food systems to multiple hazards of the early 21st century.

Why Cities Should be Concerned with Food Systems

There are multiple compelling reasons why modern cities should be concerned with, and assert responsibility for, their food systems. First, activities geared towards providing food for urban populations make major contributions to the drivers of environmental change. With the world in the throes of climate emergency, urgent action is required by 2030 to keep global warming to a maximum of 1.5°C, regarded as a tipping point for environmental break-down (IPCC, 2018). Yet the food system that serves cities is responsible for 34 percent of all anthropogenic greenhouse gas emissions (Crippa et al., 2021), and cattle ranching and soy and palm oil production alone are responsible for 40 percent of tropical forest loss (FAO and UNEP, 2020). Agriculture is the reason why 86 percent of the 28,000 species at risk of extinction are under threat, and agricultural intensification causes serious soil degradation, impairing future yield potential (Kopittke et al., 2019).

Second – and perversely, given cities' contribution to climate change – the food supply chains serving cities are highly vulnerable to disruption, be it due to extreme weather events, political events, or disease infection control measures (Blay-Palmer et al., 2021; Smith et al., 2015). Not only does this severely compromise food and nutrition security, but food shortages and subsequent price spikes for basic staples can incite civil unrest, as seen in several countries during the Arab Spring events of 2011 (Soffiantini, 2020; Morgan and Sonnino, 2010). Supply chain disruption can contribute to a significant increase in food loss and waste, exacerbating an already serious issue in many lower and lower-middle income country contexts with poor or archaic infrastructure (Rolle, 2020).

Third, rapid urbanisation means there are increasing numbers of mouths to feed in cities, yet the ability to do so is impaired by ageing farming populations and urban sprawl encroaching on peri-urban productive land. It is projected that 68 percent of the world's population will live in urban areas by 2050 (up from 55 percent in 2018), with the most rapid urbanisation in low and lower-middle income countries (UNDESA, 2019a). Along with overall population growth to 9.7 billion over the next three decades (UNDESA, 2019b), rural–urban migration is a major driver of this unprecedented demographic shift. With rural farm livelihoods ever more precarious as a result of inequitable food value chains and vulnerability to climate impacts, young people are moving from the countryside to cities in search of stable, better-paid work, leaving behind a depleted, ageing, farm workforce to provide for larger, denser cities (FAO, 2017). Moreover, land use tensions arise as cities sprawl outwards to accommodate the population influx, encroaching on farmland and further reducing productive capacity from within the agricultural region (Bren d'Amour et al., 2016).

Fourth, inequitable access to affordable, healthy, safe food in cities leads to food insecurity and all forms of malnutrition, with social and economic implications. Some neighbourhoods have abundant shops, stalls and restaurants offering healthy food, while others are so-called 'food deserts' that lack retail outlets selling food, especially fresh fruit and vegetables. The term 'food swamps' has been applied to neighbourhoods where there is a concentration of outlets selling ultra-processed foods with high fat and sugar content and little nutritional value (Cooksey-Stowers et al., 2017; Bridle-Fitzpatrick, 2015). The urban poor have little to no elasticity in household budgets to accommodate food price increases, leaving them more likely to be tipped into food insecurity in times of crisis and scarcity (FAO et al., 2020). The consequences of food insecurity – the failure of children to thrive, micronutrient deficiencies causing chronic disease, and diets that underpin obesity – prevent individuals from fulfilling their life potential and realising their contribution, either directly or through the burden it places on family members who care for those who are unable to work (Bloom et al., 2011).

A fifth reason why cities have begun to pay more attention to food systems is that local policy makers have a closer view of the tangible consequences for their citizens of the inherent problems with the globalised food system (often due to advocacy and awareness raising by civil society). Some commentators attribute the development of municipal food policies in some cities as an attempt to bridge the policy void created by their national governments' persistent commitment to the neo-liberal approach to food governance (Caraher et al., 2013; Derkzen and Morgan, 2012). This policy void does not apply in all country contexts; Knuth (2011) reported that at least 106 countries have embedded the right to food in their national constitutions or other legal instruments. However, such measures are no guarantee of implementation at either national or local level.

A sixth reason for cities to express greater interest in food systems is the emergence of international and transnational agreements and networks over the past decade that provide explicit encouragement and support to the vanguard of cities introducing initiatives around food. For example, on the international front, the United Nations' 2030 Agenda for Sustainable Development sets out 17 Sustainable Development Goals (SDG) and 169 targets in pursuing, for example, the elimination of poverty and hunger (SDG 1 and 2), the achievement of greater equality (SDG 4, 5, 10) and the sustainable management of natural resources (SDG 12, 15). In practice the SDGs and targets are closely interlinked, although SDG 11 is explicit in recognising the need to 'Make cities and human settlements inclusive, safe, resilient and sustainable'. Likewise, the UN Habitat New Urban Agenda, adopted in Quito in October 2016, highlights the need to 'strengthen food system planning', with commitments from signatories including the integration of food security and nutrition in urban planning, as well as promoting sustainable production and consumption. Both the SDGs and the NUA are signed by national governments of United Nations Member States. As such, they may stimulate more national attention to urban food system issues or provide a mandate for cities to take action in the absence of a national lead.

Transnationally, the Milan Urban Food Policy Pact (MUFPP) was signed by 100 cities in all parts of the world when it was launched in 2015 – and that number has grown to 210 by early 2021 (MUFPP, n.d.). The MUFPP functions as a voluntary framework providing strategic options to signatory cities aiming to achieve more sustainable food systems. The MUFPP has garnered significant media attention and serves as a platform for city-to-city exchange, often across international boundaries and contexts, undoubtedly serving as a stimulus for more cities to act. Other existing networks of local governments have begun to pay more attention to food through their own workstreams and partner with expert food organisations to offer technical guidance to their members. For example, C40 formed a partnership with the EAT Initiative to form the C40 Food System Network; and ICLEI Local Governments for Sustainability joined forces with RUAF to establish the ICLEI-RUAF CITYFOOD Network.

What Can City Governments Do?

At the outset of their food policy journey, local government actors are often unaware of what they can do to actively influence food provisioning arrangements, to reduce their negative impacts throughout the food system, and to shape the food environment.

In fact, in many countries local governments already exercise food-related responsibilities or activities under discrete local government departments.

For instance, environmental health often includes food safety through the inspection and certification of food service outlets; public health can include information campaigns on healthy eating; social welfare teams may issue referrals for emergency food services such as food banks; urban planning includes zoning for agricultural activities, and designation of building uses, such as types of food outlet, within particular urban areas; local economic development teams can provide incentives and support for certain kinds of business start-ups, including food enterprises of all kinds. Because these food responsibilities and activities are only part of a wider remit of the respective department, and in some cases are secondary to their main activities, they are often not acknowledged as contributing to food system planning.

Moreover, without any concerted coordination between the food responsibilities of different departments, there is a danger of policy incoherence – that is, when one department inadvertently counteracts the activities of another because their priority considerations are different, resulting in zero sum gains for the food system. Equally siloed working carries a risk that vital food-related services will fall through the cracks and no department will deliver them (Morgan, 2014; Caraher et al., 2013; Pothukuchi and Kaufman, 1999; Haughton, 1987).

Thus, the question of 'what can the city do about food' brings to the surface all these food-related activities. However, as Mah and Thang (2013) have acknowledged in the context of the Toronto Food Strategy (Toronto Public Health, 2010), this is only part of the question. All of these food activities are lodged within different departments because they contribute to that department's core role, often contributing to managing entrenched problems such as child obesity, health inequalities, unemployment, or poor livelihoods. Therefore, it is helpful to turn the question around and also ask what food can do for the city, so as to recognise the multi-faceted benefits of concerted, sustainable, and healthy food arrangements across multiple agendas (IPES-Food, 2017; Mah and Thang, 2013).

Urban food policy is defined as "concerted action on the part of city government to address food-related challenges" (IPES-Food, 2017: 9), with policies envisaged as occupying a spectrum. At one end of the spectrum are single issue policies, with targeted actions towards achieving specific primary goals (although they may also have secondary benefits for other policy agendas). Policies are implemented through programmes or, where a programme is not attached to an explicit policy, the involvement of local government suggests it is implicitly in line with policy. Box 9.1 provides a selection of single-issue policies.

At the other end of the spectrum are integrated, cross-departmental strategies that seek to actively break down silos between food responsibilities of government departments and leverage synergies where possible (Wiskerke and Viljoen, 2012). For example, the Vancouver Food Strategy, adopted in 2013, is intended "to integrate individual food policies into a more coordinated food systems approach, and align food system goals within broader City plans and processes" (City of Vancouver, 2013: 4). In Milan, Italy, the 2015 food strategy is implemented through the work of various boards of management, municipal companies, and other urban stakeholders. Institutional coordination is led by civil servants in the Mayor's office, and a Board of Interdepartmental Coordination has been established (Comune di Milano, 2015).

Box 9.1   Examples of Single-Issue Urban Food Policies and Instruments

- **Malmö, Sweden** introduced its *Policy for Sustainable Development and Food* in 2010 with the aim of reducing the climate change contribution of food in public canteens. The main instrument is public procurement (Moragues-Faus and Morgan, 2015).
- **La Paz, Bolivia** has a policy of enabling citizens to grow food on public land on a temporary basis, out of a combined desire to make use of public spaces, promote food security at the household level, and enhance biodiversity. The policy was introduced through a legal instrument (LM 321/2018) (La Paz, 2018)
- **Baltimore, USA**, introduced the Grocery Store Incentive Area Personal Property Tax Credit in 2012, a fiscal instrument to incentivise grocery store owners to set up in underserved areas of the city. The policy is part of the Healthy Food Environment Strategy (City of Baltimore, 2018)
- **Newcastle, UK** sought to limit the number of hot food takeaway outlets serving unhealthy food near to schools and playgrounds using a planning instrument – the Hot Food Takeaway Supplementary Planning Document (Newcastle, 2016)
- **Fort Portal, Uganda**, integrated the addition of new street lighting and water points into municipal council plans, and gazetted dedicated space for street vendors who comply with the rules of their own association. The aim was to facilitate the sale of safe, nutritious street food in the city; the outlawing of street food vending by the outdated 1935 Public Health Act had led to the emergence of an unmonitored informal sector (Halliday and Gomes, 2020).

Often, cities start with a single policy as an entry point, in a department where the imperative has been acknowledged and there is a will to act, using available instruments. From this entry point, they may then be able to move along the spectrum, drawing in other departments and working towards an integrated strategy. For example, in Nairobi, Kenya, the 2015 Nairobi Urban Agriculture Promotion and Regulation Act was the City County government's first foray into food-related policy (IPES-Food, 2017), after which a Food Systems Strategy was developed (as of 2021 it is still in draft form) (NCC, 2021).

An integrated strategy can also have an initial entry point – that is, a policy imperative that allows food to be put on the agenda – while at the same time acting on other objectives that are not currently seen as priorities by the administration. For example, in London, UK, public health issues (particularly obesity) drew then-Mayor Ken Livingstone to support the city's first food strategy in 2006 (updated in 2018), but the strategy itself retained broad policy objectives on food access, affordability, education and production (Reynolds, 2009). From 2011, the focus under Livingstone's successor, Boris Johnson, shifted to the local economy, but the document was capacious enough to accommodate the new prerogative (Halliday, 2015). The 2018 London Food Strategy (GLA, 2018), while coordinated by officers in the Regeneration and Economic Development team, seeks to address not only local economic development and job creation but also food insecurity, social welfare, public health, green infrastructure; biodiversity, carbon emissions and air quality, and food waste.

What are the Challenges and How Can They be Circumvented?

The previous section showed that there is huge potential for cities to take action to improve food system sustainability, and the positive examples cited showed that many are acting on that potential. However, the road is beset with challenges that, while not always insurmountable, must be handled deliberatively and if possible pre-emptively.

First, securing political will is notably difficult when food itself is not high on the agenda and there is no obvious department that has explicit overall responsibility for the food system. As mentioned above, it can help to select the most amenable 'entry point', and to frame arguments in terms of contributions to high-agenda problems. Often it is a matter of building networks over a long period of time, as in the case of the 2015 Nairobi Urban Agriculture

Promotion and Regulation Act, which was developed after more than a decade of sustained networking by civil society actors (IPES-Food, 2017). Another tactic is to draw in a champion who is prepared to introduce and make the case for food policy within the corridors of power (Giambartolomei et al., 2021). For instance, in the case of the Fort Portal, Uganda, local organisations have sought to engage a national politician to introduce the need to revise or repeal the outdated 1935 Public Health Act that outlaws street food vending (Halliday and Gomes, 2020).

Second, even once political will is established, there is no guarantee that it will endure, particularly through electoral change. Even well-established and institutionalised food policies and programmes can find themselves at risk with the introduction of a new leader. For instance, the Toronto Food Policy Council has found itself under threat due to cuts in provincial public health budgets since the election of populist Ontario premier Doug Ford in 2018 (TFPC, 2019), and before that saw some of its programmes curtailed under the Mayoral term of Ford's brother from 2010 to 2013 (Mah and Thang, 2013).

Some cities have sought to establish a measure of protection against electoral change. For instance, the Healthy Weight Programme in Amsterdam is a 30-year programme to address child obesity, but this 'marathon' is broken down into smaller periods with reporting more-or-less in line with electoral cycles. The expectation is that it will be much harder for an incoming leader to cancel a programme that has recently reported positive results (IPES-Food, 2017). Another tactic is to ensure that governance is shared between local government and civil society and/or the private sector, as it is also harder to cancel a programme that has multiple, non-governmental participants. Even if the government pulls out, activities may still continue under the auspices of other organisations. For example, in Antananarivo, Madagascar, the Food Policy Council focuses on projects with joint-governance. In the words of Deputy Mayor Oliver Andrianarisoa:

> We do not locate the policy in the City Council as, if the Mayor leaves, the projects are lost. Rather, we lead and facilitate as the major stakeholder and focus on the projects. We identify stakeholders with high potential and we partner with them, and we fit them like pieces of the puzzle towards a sustainable food system. (Andrianarisoa et al., 2019: 30)

Third, it can be hard to secure sufficient budgets to action food work. Often projects are initiated with only a small, time-limited pot of money, meaning there is a need to re-apply for funding if they are to continue. Funds from outside organisations may also come with conditions attached that necessitate some trade-off between values and actions. Both these issues have been experienced by the city-region entity, the Golden Horseshoe Food and Farming Alliance in Canada, of which one member municipality wished its annual contribution to be spent on projects of its own choosing (IPES-Food, 2017). One way to ensure availability of a minimum amount of funds is for food work to be written into a budget year-on-year. Another is to request actions be implemented by departments using existing budgets. This latter approach has been taken in Amsterdam, where the Healthy Weight Programme was deliberately attributed no budget in its initial phase to encourage government departments to find ways to contribute – and funding to do so – without requiring additional resources (IPES-Food, 2017).

In times of economic crisis, sustainability actions are sometimes regarded as non-essential. This means they are first in line for cuts or cancellation. Food policies and programmes that have an entry point and/or institutional home that is deemed more crucial – such as economic development – are in a stronger position than those linked to departments that are less high up on the political agenda. For example, the AGRUPAR participatory urban agriculture programme in Quito, Ecuador, has seen more investment since the inclusion of the food economy in the city's Resilience Strategy, despite the city facing economic constraints (Resilient Cities, n.d.). It can also be helpful to keep some flexibility in terms of framing food policies so that benefits can be highlighted in line with the issue *du jour*. That does not mean that the other issues are side-lined but rather the most relevant benefits are talked-up at a given moment. For instance, in 2011 the London Food Programme developed a Food Strategy Action Plan that was focused to a great extent on sustainability, but in August 2011 the Greater London Authority agenda changed overnight following rioting, one cause of which was marginalised and disaffected young people. As such the new Action Plan was not published and the work of the London Food Board pivoted towards youth opportunities (Halliday and Barling, 2018).

Fourth, the best intentions notwithstanding, sometimes intended food policies or plans cannot be implemented because the necessary powers lie outside of local government responsibilities, or local government is constrained by policies at the regional or national level to which it must adhere. One example relates to public procurement of local food for canteens. Although local government buyers may wish to support the local or regional economy, EU procurement law requires that all economic operators should have equal access to procurement procedure without unjustified obstacles to competition (Directive 2014/24/EU). As such, public procurement teams wishing to procure more sustainable food avoid the term 'local' since it would exclude some operators, using instead terms like 'fresh', 'seasonal', and 'organic', which are often *de facto* local (Foodlinks, 2013). In rare cases, local governments successfully challenge constraints on their powers. This was the case in Detroit, USA, where the city planning department had to negotiate an exception to the state-level Michigan Right to Farm Act to introduce an ordinance on urban agriculture (IPES-Food, 2017).

Governance Models

Local governments that are prepared to take responsibility for their food system must put in place an internal structure or arrangements to coordinate food issues between departments. In some cities this involves giving responsibility for coordination to an officer (or more than one) within a particular department or office. For instance, in Baltimore, USA, the Food Policy Director leads the Baltimore Food Policy Initiative, which involves cooperation between several departments, from within the Department of Planning. Elsewhere, such as Ede in the Netherlands, a 'food interest group' was established comprising members of various government departments, each of which has food responsibilities as a part of their job description (Halliday et al., 2019). Very rarely a local government establishes an entire department or agency under which all food-related work is centralised, as was the case in Belo Horizonte with the creation in 1993 of the Municipal Secretariat for Food Supply (SMAB, now known as the SMASAN) which, subsequently, lost its status as a stand-alone agency and became a sub-division of the Department of Social Policies (IPES-Food, 2017).

Whatever internal structures are established, however, local governments do not seek to govern the urban food system in a top-down manner. In keeping with the de-centralised shift towards 'governance', they initiate or participate in a multi-stakeholder governance platform, alongside a host of other actors who are involved in the food system such as: civil society organisations, community groups, private businesses of all sizes and types, trade associations, unions, research institutes and academics, consultants, media, and others. This is crucial, since although city governments may be new to food system work, often there are already active networks of non-governmental stakeholders and others – including those with a role in supply chains – that are lobbying for change, running programmes, and raising awareness of the need for food systems transformation at the grassroots level.

Such multi-stakeholder platforms go by a variety of names, including food policy councils, food networks, food boards, food coalitions, food partnerships, and food labs. Whatever the chosen nomenclature, they are united by a desire for sustainable, healthy, and just food systems transformation, and the need to ensure the interests of food chain participants are taken into account (RUAF, 2019).

In North America, where the first examples arose in the 1980s and where they have proliferated since the 2000s, multi-stakeholder platforms are commonly known as 'food policy councils' (FPC). According to the Johns Hopkins Centre for a Liveable Future, at the end of 2017 there were 341 FPC active, in development, or in transition in the USA and Canada (Bassarab et al., 2019). In the UK, the term 'food partnership' has been favoured by Sustainable Food Places, a civil society-led network of over 50 local and regional government areas with a multi-stakeholder food platform (SFP, 2021).

Although the concept of multi-stakeholder food platforms originated in developed countries of the global North, it is gaining traction in other countries. For instance, in 2020 the city of Lusaka in Zambia formally launched its food policy council (Lwizi, 2020). The Milan Urban Food Policy Pact also contributes to multi-stakeholder collaboration, since its recommendations include enhancing participation at the city level (MUFPP, n.d.).

While the general form of multi-stakeholder platform is replicated from place to place (often with cities learning from each other), the structure and function varies, depending on a number of factors. These include the degree of political buy-in, the policy entry point to working on food, the origins of the initiative (whether it was started by local government or at the behest of civil society), and the level of social capital – that is, the shared understandings, trust, values, and norms that underscore relationships within society. Common variables are the institutional home of the platform, its membership composition, and its precise role and mandate.

Institutional home. Where there is a local government food programme the multi-stakeholder platform may be hosted by local government. In these scenarios, non-governmental stakeholders are invited to participate by the government, which retains a strong steering hand. The benefit of this arrangement is that the platform has legitimacy that can open doors, and often a clear route to decision-making circles. The downsides, however, are that the agenda of the food group may be constrained by that of the local government administration; moreover, being closely associated with a particular administration can make the food group vulnerable to being disbanded following electoral change, as a newly elected Mayor may sweep away the flagship projects of the previous incumbent (Halliday and Barling, 2018).

In other situations, the institutional home is outside of local government, with representatives participating outside their usual workplace yet still in a formal capacity. It may be hosted by a civil society organisation that provides secretariat services and some administrative support, as in the case of the Golden Horseshoe Food and Farming Partnership, which is housed by the Toronto and Region Conservation Authority (IPES-Food, 2017). In other instances, the food platform is entirely independent, existing in a neutral civil society space where it would ideally be incorporated and able to apply for funding. This independence gives members more freedom to set their own agenda, and means they are not so vulnerable to electoral change (although government support may be withdrawn, it is easier to re-organise as an advocacy group). The downside is that the channels into local government tend to be weaker and depend heavily on the position and seniority of local government representatives. For instance, members at departmental director level or cabinet members of the Mayor who have food as part of their portfolio are far and away more helpful than junior-ranking civil servants who must seek support from their seniors at every turn.

Membership. It is a pre-requisite that local government be involved in the multi-stakeholder platform in some way, as without it the platform would be an advocacy group with no connection to the seat of policy making (Schiff, 2008). Civil society participation is also extremely valuable as a source of ideas, energy, specialist know-how, and capacity for action that can complement that of local government (Derkzen and Morgan, 2012). When it comes to businesses, however, some seek representation from across the food system, while others specifically seek small businesses and or social enterprises whose values are considered more convergent, eschewing multi-nationals that are seen as the power-holders with different definitions of sustainability.

Some platforms specifically seek involvement of engaged citizens, such as the Toronto Food Policy Council (Blay-Palmer, 2009). The Lusaka Food Policy Council, mentioned above, is notable for its concerted inclusion of informal marketers, whose needs and interests are often overlooked by policy makers as they operate outside the system (Lwizi, 2020). Such efforts towards inclusiveness are helpful as they give a voice to those who will be most affected by future policy actions (RUAF, 2019).

Role and mandate. The role of multi-stakeholder platforms can vary considerably, including a combination of any of the following: gathering knowledge and information; identify emerging issues that require attention; making policy recommendations or drafting policies; brokering connections with stakeholders who are able to implement actions; leading implementation through members' own organisations; monitoring and reporting on implementation of policies and programmes; advocacy and lobbying role; and holding local government to account.

The question of mandate is closely connected to institutional home and degree of buy-in of city leaders. The London Food Board, for example, provides information and advice to the Mayor's food advisor, and although neither they nor the Mayor are bound to act upon it, the fact that there is a channel makes it more likely that recommendations find their way into policy (Halliday and Barling, 2018).

An Eye to the Future: Research Needs for Stronger Food Cities

By way of conclusion, the final section of this chapter identifies some areas where more research is required to bolster and consolidate municipal authorities' efforts, giving them the best chance of enduring over the long term, magnifying their contribution to food systems transformation, and strengthening the resilience of urban and city region food systems.

First, institutionalisation within legal frameworks and budgets is often regarded as the 'holy grail' of food policy work, establishing it as a core, non-negotiable part of the local government. Both SMASAN in Belo Horizonte, Brazil and the Toronto Food Policy Council in Canada effectively achieved institutionalisation. As a result, they are two of the longest standing urban food policy initiatives in the world; however as noted above, neither has proven completely invulnerable to restructuring or budget withdrawal. In an age where populist leaders are prepared to uproot established social programmes from one day to the next, there is a need for more research on protecting food policy from drastic political change that could set the agenda back decades.

Second, supportive multi-level governance frameworks reduce the risk that cities' food initiatives will be constrained or even over-written by inclement regional or national policies, intentionally or not (Marsden et al., 2006). They can also actively nurture action that starts at the city level, promoting scale-up or proliferation to new areas and accelerating sustainable food systems transformation. There is some evidence of cities prompting regional or national level policy change through lobbying, as in the case of Detroit discussed above, and in Philadelphia, USA, which lobbied for regional tax incentives to promote the sale of fresh foods on local markets (Sonnino, 2014). In a few places the success of pioneering local initiatives have attracted attention at the national level and subsequently scaled up, such as in Belo Horizonte, Brazil, where elements of SMASAN's work served as a model for the federal *Fome Zero* (Zero Hunger) programme introduced in 2003, and which in-turn gave support to SMASAN through grant allocations (IPES-Food, 2017). Such examples are rare, however, and in the case of Brazil came about at a particular moment of political alignment between levels. There is a need for more creative thinking about how national governments could be brought around from a market-led approach to the food system to one where they actively support their cities' food system transformation efforts, and which actors or sectors are best positioned to convince them (e.g. international organisations, the private sector, or the citizens of those cities themselves).

Third, hard data to demonstrate the efficacy of a policy can make the difference between city leaders deciding to continue an initiative or to terminate it, particularly when there is a change of government (as in the case of Amsterdam's Healthy Weight Programme noted above). However, proving that a particular policy has made a material impact on alleviating entrenched problems is not straightforward because there are often confounding factors. The benefits of an action may be masked by the counteractive effects of other local or national policies or programmes; conversely, an underperforming initiative might be given false credit for gains made by other, more effective policies or programmes (IUFN, 2015). Some useful tools have been recently developed to help cities establish methodologically-sound monitoring of actions and their contribution to the desired direction of travel; the MUFPP indicator framework and accompanying handbook are useful tools to help cities do this (Carey and Cook, 2021). How these tools are used in practice, and whether they yield useful data to prove efficacy and motivate continued action, must be studied over the coming years.

Finally, urban food governance structures and processes are critical to effective, coordinated efforts to transform the urban food system, but establishing them is not a one-time task. Rather, continuous review and adaptation – or 'reflexive governance' (Voss and Kemp, 2006) – is required, both to take past experiences into account and to be best able to address upcoming tasks and challenges. In addition, in light of the increase in sudden, dramatic hazards impacting urban food systems, such as climate events and pandemic control measures, there is pressing need for adaptive governance capacity in urban food systems (Hatfield-Dodds et al., 2007) – that is, governance structures and processes with built in contingency that allow for food arrangements to pivot at a moment's notice. Close study of the adaptive capacity of cities in dealing with the food system impacts of COVID-19 measures and major climate events is required urgently, to establish factors that facilitate adaptation or hinder it. The lessons learned will be beneficial to all city governments striving to build more resilient food systems that can weather the many (literal or figurative) storms of the coming decades – whether they are establishing governance structures and processes for the first time or reviewing existing ones.

References

Andrianarisoa, O., Zuleta Ferrari, C., Currie, P., Coetzee, I., 2019. Antananarivo Food Policy Council: Policy as Practice. *Urban Agriculture Magazine*, [online] (36), pp. 29–30. https://ruaf.org/document/urban-agriculture-magazine-no-36-food-policy-councils/ [Accessed 31 March 2021].

Bassarab, K., Santo, R. and Palmer, A., 2019. *Food Policy Councils Report 2018*. [online] Baltimore: Johns Hopkins Center for a Livable Future. https:// assets .jhsph .edu/ clf/mod_clfResource/doc/FPC%20Report%202018-FINAL-4-1-19.pdf [Accessed 9 March 2021].

Blay-Palmer, A., 2009. The Canadian Pioneer: The Genesis of Urban Food Policy in Toronto. *International Planning Studies*, 14, 4: 401–416.

Blay-Palmer, A., Santini, G., Halliday, J. et al., 2021. City Region Food Systems: Building Resilience to COVID-19 and Other Shocks. *Sustainability*, 13, 3: 1325.

Bloom, D., Cafiero, E, Jané-Llopis, E. et al., 2011. *The Global Economic Burden of Noncommunicable Diseases*. Geneva: World Economic Forum. http:// www3 .weforum.org/docs/WEF_Harvard_HE_GlobalEconomicBurdenNonCommunicab leDiseases_2011.pdf [Accessed 31 March 2021].

Bren d'Amour, C., Reitsma, F., Baiocchi, G. et al., 2016. Future Urban Land Expansion and Implications for Global Croplands. *Proceedings of the National Academy of Sciences*, 114, 34: 8939–8944.

Bridle-Fitzpatrick, S., 2015. Food Deserts or Food Swamps?: A Mixed-Methods Study of Local Food Environments in a Mexican City. *Social Science & Medicine*, 142: 202–213.

Caraher, M., Carey, R., McConell, K., Lawrence, M., 2013. Food Policy Development in the Australian State of Victoria: A Case Study of the Food Alliance. *International Planning Studies*, 18, 1: 78–95.

Carey, J., Cook, B., 2021. *The Milan Urban Food Policy Pact Monitoring Framework, a Practical Handbook for Implementation*. Rome: FAO, MUFPP, RUAF. www.fao .org/documents/card/en/c/cb4181en [Accessed 13 July 2021].

City of Baltimore, 2018. *Heathy Food Environment Strategy*, Department of Planning, City of Baltimore. https:// planning .baltimorecity .gov/ baltimore -food -policy -initiative/healthy-food-retail [Accessed 28 March 2021].

City of Vancouver, 2013. *What Feeds Us: Vancouver Food Strategy*. City of Vancouver. https:// vancouver .ca/ files/ cov/ vancouver -food -strategy -final .PDF [Accessed 28 March 2021].

Clendenning, J., Dressler, W., Richards, C., 2016. Food Justice or Food Sovereignty? Understanding the Rise of Urban Food Movements in the USA. *Agriculture and Human Values*, 33, 1: 165-177.

Comune di Milano, 2015. *The Food System in Milan: Five Priorities for a Sustainable Development*. Comune di Milano. https://www.foodpolicymilano.org/wp-content/uploads/2015/04/Milan_food_system_EN1.pdf [Accessed 28 March 2021].

Cooksey-Stowers, K., Schwartz, M., Brownell, K., 2017. Food Swamps Predict Obesity Rates Better Than Food Deserts in the United States. *International Journal of Environmental Research and Public Health*, 14, 11: 1366.

Crippa, M., Solazzo, E., Guizzardi, D., Monforti-Ferrario, F. et al., 2021. Food Systems are Responsible for a Third of Global Anthropogenic GHG Emissions. *Nature Food*, 2, 3: 198-209.

Crush. J., Riley, L., 2018. Rural Bias and Urban Food Security. In Battersby, J., Watson, V. (eds), *Urban Food Systems Governance and Poverty in African Cities*. Abingdon: Routledge, pp. 42-55.

Derkzen, P., Morgan, K., 2012. Food and The City: The Challenge of Urban Food Governance. In Viljoen, A., Wiskerke, J. (eds), *Sustainable Food Planning: Evolving Theory and Practice*. Wageningen: Wageningen Academic Publishers, pp. 61-67.

FAO, 2016a. *Food for the Cities Programme: Building Sustainable and Resilient City Region Food Systems*. City Region Food System Programme. Rome: Food and Agriculture Organisation of the United Nations, RUAF Foundation, City Region Food System Alliance. http://www.fao.org/3/i5502e/i5502e.pdf [Accessed 31 March 2021].

FAO, 2016b. *Influencing Food Environments for Healthy Diets*. Rome: Food and Agriculture Organisation of the United Nations. http://www.fao.org/3/a-i6484e.pdf [Accessed 31 March 2021].

FAO, 2017. *The State of Food and Agriculture: Leveraging Food Systems for Inclusive Rural Transformation*. Rome: Food and Agriculture Organisation of the United Nations. http://www.fao.org/3/a-I7658e.pdf [Accessed 31 March 2021].

FAO, 2018. *Sustainable Food Systems: Concept and Framework*. Rome: Food and Agriculture Organisation of the United Nations. http://www.fao.org/3/ca2079en/CA2079EN.pdf [Accessed 31 March 2021].

FAO, IFAD, UNICEF, WFP and WHO. 2020. The State of Food Security and Nutrition in the World 2020. Transforming Food Systems for Affordable Healthy Diets. Rome, Food and Agriculture Organisation of the United Nations. http://www.fao.org/3/ca9692en/online/ca9692en.html [Accessed 31 March 2021].

FAO and UNEP, 2020. The State of the World's Forests 2020. Forests, Biodiversity and People. Rome: Food and Agriculture Organisation of the United Nations. https://doi.org/10.4060/ca8642en [Accessed 31 March 2021].

Foodlinks, 2013. *Revaluing Public Sector Food Procurement in Europe: An Action Plan for Sustainability*. https://base.socioeco.org/docs/foodlinks_report_low.pdf [Accessed 28 March 2021].

Giambartolomei, G., Forno, F., Sage, C. 2021. How Food Policies Emerge: The Pivotal Role of Policy Entrepreneurs as Brokers and Bridges of People and Ideas. *Food Policy*, 103: https://doi.org/10.1016/j.foodpol.2021.102038.

GLA, 2018. *The London Food Strategy: Healthy and Sustainable Food for London*. London: Greater London Authority. https://www.london.gov.uk/sites/default/files/final_london_food_strategy.pdf [Accessed 28 March 2021).

Halliday, J., 2015. *A New Institutionalist Analysis of Local Level Food Policy in England between 2012 and 2014*. PhD thesis. Centre for Food Policy, City University London.

Halliday, J., Barling, D., 2018. The Role and Engagement of City Mayors in Local Food Policy Groups in England: Comparing the Cases of London and Bristol. In Barling, D., Fanzo, J. (eds), *Advances in Food Security and Sustainability*, Volume 3, Cambridge: Elsevier Academic Press, pp. 177–209.

Halliday, J., Platenkamp, L., Nicolarea, Y., 2019. *A Menu of Actions to Shape Urban Food Environments for Improved Nutrition*. Geneva: GAIN, Milan Urban Food Policy Pact, RUAF. https://www.gainhealth.org/sites/default/files/publications/documents/gain-mufpp-ruaf-a-menu-of-actions-to-shape-urban-food-environments-for-improved-nutrition-2019.pdf [Accessed 31 March 2021].

Halliday, J., Gomes, M., 2020. *A Food Systems Assessment of the Sustainable Diets for All programme in Uganda and Zambia*. The Hague: Hivos and IIED. https://sustainablediets4all.org/document/a-food-systems-assessment-of-the-sustainable-diets-for-all-programme-in-uganda-and-zambia/ [Accessed 31 March 2021].

Hatfield-Dodds, S., Nelson, R., Cook, D., 2007. *Adaptive Governance: An Introduction, and Implications for Public Policy*. Paper presented at the 51st Annual conference of the Australian Agricultural and Resource Economics Society, Queenstown NZ, 13–16 February 2007. Available at: Adaptive Governance: An Introduction and Implications for Public Policy. https://ageconsearch.umn.edu/record/10440/?ln=en [Accessed 31 March 2021].

Haughton, B., 1987. Developing Local Food Policies: One City's Experiences. *Journal of Public Health Policy*, 8, 2: 180.

Herforth, A., Ahmed, S., 2015. The Food Environment, its Effects on Dietary Consumption, and Potential for Measurement Within Agriculture–Nutrition Interventions. *Food Security*, 7, 3: 505–520.

Ilieva, R., 2016. *Urban Food Planning: Seeds of Transition in the Global North*. London: Routledge.

IPCC, 2018. Global Warming of 1.5°C. An IPCC Special Report on the impacts of global warming of 1.5°C above pre-industrial levels and related global greenhouse gas emission pathways, in the context of strengthening the global response to the threat of climate change, sustainable development, and efforts to eradicate poverty. Geneva: World Meteorological Organization. https://www.ipcc.ch/sr15 [Accessed 31 March 2021].

IPES-Food, 2017. *What makes urban food policy happen? Insights from five case studies*. Leuven: International Panel of Experts on Sustainable Food Systems. http://www.ipes-food.org/_img/upload/files/Cities_full.pdf [Accessed 31 March 2021].

IUFN, 2015. *Mesurer l'impact de l'approche territoriale de l'alimentation? Etude sur l'impact des Systemes alimentaires territorialises, L'alimentation durable dans les projets de territoires. Rapport operationnel novembre 2015*. Nantes: International Urban Food Network. https://www.pat-cvl.fr/wp-content/uploads/2021/03/VF-Rapport-operationnel-IUFN-MEDDE-1.pdf [Accessed 30 March 2021].

Knuth, L., 2011. Constitutional and Legal Protection of the Right to Food around the World. Rome: Food and Agriculture Organization of the United Nations. http://www.fao.org/3/ap554e/ap554e.pdf [Accessed 31 March 2021].

Kopittke, P., Menzies, N., Wang, P., McKenna, B., Lombi, E., 2019. Soil and the Intensification of Agriculture for Global Food Security. *Environment International*, 132: 105078.

La Paz, 2018. *Ley Municipal Autonomica No. 321*. Gobierno Autonomo Municipal de La Paz. http://wsservicios.lapaz.bo/normativa_externa/ConsultaExternaDocumento.aspx?archivo=2018/LM_7602_2018_00321.pdf [Accessed 28 March 2021].

Lang, T., 2003. Food Industrialisation and Food Power: Implications for Food Governance. *Development Policy Review*, 21, 5-6: 555-568.

Lwizi, G., 2020. Lusaka Food Policy Council Formed. *Zambian Business Times*. https://zambianbusinesstimes .com/ lusaka -food -policy -council -formed [Accessed 28 March 2021].

Mah, C. and Thang, H., 2013. Cultivating Food Connections: The Toronto Food Strategy and Municipal Deliberation on Food. *International Planning Studies*, 18, 1: 96-110.

Marsden, T., Murdoch, J., Morgan, K., 2006. *Worlds of Food: Place, Power, and Provenance in the Food Chain*. Oxford: Oxford University Press.

Moragues-Faus, A., Morgan, K., 2015. Reframing The Foodscape: The Emergent World of Urban Food Policy. *Environment and Planning A: Economy and Space*, 47, 7: 1558-1573.

Morgan, K., 2014. Nourishing the City: The Rise of the Urban Food Question in the Global North. *Urban Studies*, 52, 8: 1379-1394.

Morgan, K., Sonnino, R., 2010. The Urban Foodscape: World Cities and the New Food Equation. *Cambridge Journal of Regions, Economy and Society*, 3, 2: 209-224.

MUFPP, n.d. *Milan Urban Food Policy Pact*. Milan Urban Food Policy Pact. https://www.milanurbanfoodpolicypact.org [Accessed 9 March 2021].

NCC, 2021. *Nairobi City County Food System Strategy: Fourth Draft*. Nairobi.go.ke. https:// nairobi.go .ke/ download/ nairobi -city -county-food-system -strategy -fourth -draft [Accessed 24 June 2021].

Newcastle, 2016. *Hot Food Takeaway Supplementary Planning Document*. Newcastle City Council. https://www .newcastle .gov .uk/ sites/ default/ files/ 2019 -01/ hot_food _takeaway_spd_-_october_2016_-_final_0.pdf [Accessed 28 March 2021].

Popkin, B., Adair, L., Ng, S., 2012. Global Nutrition Transition and the Pandemic of Obesity in Developing Countries. *Nutrition Reviews*, 70, 1: 3-21.

Pothukuchi, K., Kaufman, J., 1999. Placing the Food System on the Urban Agenda: The Role of Municipal Institutions in Food Systems Planning. *Agriculture and Human Values*, 16: 213-224.

Resilient Cities, n.d. *The Transformative Impact of Quito's Resilient Food Security Program, Resilient Cities Network*. Resilient Cities Network. https:// re silientcit iesnetwork.org/urban_resiliences/quito-food-program [Accessed 28th March 2021]

Reynolds, B., 2009. Feeding a World City: The London Food Strategy. *International Planning Studies*, 14, 4: 417-424.

Rocha, C., Lessa, I., 2009. Urban Governance for Food Security: The Alternative Food System in Belo Horizonte, Brazil. *International Planning Studies*, 14, 4: 389-400.

Rodríguez-Pose, A., 2008. The Rise of the "City-Region" Concept and its Development Policy Implications. *European Planning Studies*, 16, 8: 1025-1046.

Rolle, R., 2020. *Mitigating Risks to Food Systems During COVID-19: Reducing Food Loss and Waste*. Rome: Food and Agriculture Organisation of the United Nations. http://www.fao.org/3/ca9056en/ca9056en.pdf [Accessed 27 March 2020].

RUAF, 2019. *Food Policy Councils, Urban Agriculture Magazine*, #36. https://www.ruaf .org/ua-magazine-no-36-food-policy-councils [Accessed 31 March 2021].

Schiff, R., 2008. The Role of Food Policy Councils in Developing Sustainable Food Systems. *Journal of Hunger & Environmental Nutrition*, 3, 2-3: 206-228.

Smith, K., Lawrence, G., MacMahon, A., Muller, J., Brady, M., 2015. The Resilience of Long and Short Food Chains: A Case Study of Flooding in Queensland, Australia. *Agriculture and Human Values*, 33, 1: 45-60.

Soffiantini, G., 2020. Food Insecurity and Political Instability During the Arab Spring, *Global Food Security*, 26, 100400.

Sonnino, R., 2014. The New Geography of Food Security: Exploring the Potential of Urban Food Strategies. *The Geographical Journal*, 182, 2: 190–200.

Sustainable Food Places (SFP), 2021. Members, Sustainable Food Places. https://www.sustainablefoodplaces.org/members/ [Accessed 28 March 2021].

TFPC, 2019. *Policy Council Unanimously Passes Motion Asking the Ontario Government to Reverse Cuts to Public Health*, 23 May 2019, Toronto Food Policy Council. https:// tfpc .to/ toronto -food -policy -council -unanimously -passes -motion -asking -the -ontario-government-to-reverse-cuts-to-public-health [Accessed 30 March 2021].

Toronto Public Health, 2010. *Cultivating Food Connections: Toward a Healthy and Sustainable Food System for Toronto*. Toronto Public Health. https://www.toronto .ca/ legdocs/ mmis/ 2010/ hl/ bgrd/ backgroundfile -30483 .pdf [Accessed 28 March 2021].

Turner, C., Aggarwal, A., Walls, H., Herforth, A. et al., 2018. Concepts and Critical Perspectives for Food Environment Research: A Global Framework with Implications for Action in Low- and Middle-Income Countries. *Global Food Security*, 18: 93–101.

UNDESA, 2019a. *World Urbanization Prospects: The 2018 Revision*. United Nations, Department of Economic and Social Affairs, Population Division (ST/ ESA/SER.A/420). New York: United Nations. https:// population .un .org/ wup/ Publications/Files/WUP2018-Report.pdf [Accessed 31 March 2021].

UNDESA, 2019b. World Population Prospects 2019: Highlights. United Nations, Department of Economic and Social Affairs, Population Division (2019). ST/ ESA/SER.A/423. New York: United Nations. https:// population .un .org/ wpp/ Publications/Files/WPP2019_Highlights.pdf [Accessed 31 March 2021].

Voss, J-P., Kemp, R., 2006. Sustainability and Reflexive Governance: Introduction. In Voss, J.P., Bauknecht, D., Kemp, R. (eds), *Reflexive Governance for Sustainable Development*. Cheltenham, UK and Northampton, MA, USA: Edward Elgar Publishing, pp. 3–30.

Wiskerke, J., Viljoen, A., 2012. Sustainable Urban Food Provisioning: Challenges for Scientists, Policymakers Planners and Designers. In Viljoen, A., Wiskerke, J. (eds), *Sustainable Food Planning: Evolving Theory and Practice*. Wageningen: Wageningen Academic Publishers, pp. 67–78.

10 Circular food systems: a blueprint for regenerative innovations in a regional UK context

Steffen Böhm, Rebecca Sandover, Stefano Pascucci, Laura Colombo, Sophie Jackson and Matt Lobley

Introduction

The global food system is under pressure to supply affordable, nutritious and appetising products. To maximise production and affordability, the food system has become extractive, linear and excessively reliant on imports and long supply chains (D'Odorico et al., 2018; Rockström et al., 2020). Some island communities in the Caribbean, for example, rely on more than 80 percent of food imports to feed themselves (Thomas, Moore & Edwards, 2018). Even a big, rich and fertile country, such as the United Kingdom, imports more than half of its food requirements (Lang, 2020). This has resulted in harmful environmental, human and economic health impacts (Godfray et al., 2010), including increased greenhouse gas emissions; biodiversity loss; high levels of food waste; poor diets; preventable diseases; poorly paid jobs; low productivity and so on. The average UK diet, for example, does not meet nutritional recommendations and has a higher carbon footprint than many other high-income countries (Steenson & Buttriss, 2021). Moreover, the UK imports increasing and unsustainable amounts of foods from climate vulnerable countries, threatening future food security.

The most promising solutions to these challenges will emerge from a shift to more diverse, regional food systems that adopt low-carbon and regenerative agriculture principles, engaging consumers to increasingly consume local, sustainable produce. Based on the principles of closing loops, designing effective and resilient food systems, and enhancing diversity, multi-stakeholder cooperation, place-based food culture, participation and empowerment, as well as value retention, we contend that regional circular food systems can create multiple, interconnected health benefits.

This chapter will introduce a blueprint for a regional circular food system from a UK perspective, which we believe is best achieved through a dynamic process of cooperation amongst multiple stakeholders (policymakers, businesses, citizens, NGOs) at the regional level, thereby addressing multiple environmental, social and economic challenges within a specific geography. We define circularity as the practice of identifying and optimising feedback processes within systems to enable them to regenerate; reduce their dependency on external inputs; and maximise the optimisation value to system actors and to the system as a whole (Fassio & Tecco, 2019; Alhawari et al., 2021; Sreeharsha & Mohan, 2021; Kowalski & Makara, 2021). Circular Economy principles and practices are extended here to take an integrated approach to addressing human, environmental and economic health via food systems transformation.

To instigate transformational change, we will outline three institutional innovations that are of relevance in the UK context, namely community-supported agriculture schemes, food hubs and public food procurement partnerships. Discussing existing cases of these institutional innovations, we will show how we can move beyond feted 'field-to-fork' approaches, providing a more integrated approach that aims to transform regional food systems. However, a word of caution. Our emphasis on 'regional' does not imply a protectionist or isolationist agenda that dovetails with the UK's recent exit from the European Union. On the contrary, a predominantly regional focus of food system intervention does not preclude global cooperation and sharing between regions for mutual co-benefit and global human, environmental and economic health gain (Sibbing, Candel & Termeer, 2021).

Indeed, our circular approach to food systems closely aligns with a number of Sustainable Development Goals (SDGs) and other governmental and inter-governmental policy agendas. Most notably, regional circular food systems would help to radically reduce greenhouse gas emissions, helping the world tackle global climate change and also address other environmental challenges, such as biodiversity loss, soil health and water quality and security (Rockström et al., 2020; Schreefel et al., 2020). Our approach aims to improve food security by providing better access to safe, sustainable and nutritious food, particularly for the most vulnerable members of society, while reducing childhood and adult obesity and other diet-related health conditions. It also aims to radically improve economic wellbeing amongst small-scale food producers and workers, which are amongst the lowest paid in many economies (Böhm, Spierenburg & Lang, 2020).

Currently, many local initiatives exist to address the problems of the food system. Yet, they largely operate individually, with little opportunity for coordination between them. What is needed is to link and coordinate local food initiatives to promote a 'politics of possibility' and 'new economic imaginary' (Gibson-Graham, 2006) within networks of place-based action for food systems change across regions. An integrated regional circular food system enables creative, locally embedded movements to become exemplars of new economic activity that brings to the fore human and environmental health.

The Current Food System: Extractive and Linear

The evidence on the impacts of conventional and linearly designed food systems points to the need to re-think the design of food provisioning processes, considering simultaneously human, environmental and economic aspects (Moreau et al., 2017). Linearly-designed food systems have provided unprecedented agricultural productivity growth, advanced an abundance of technologies and infrastructure dedicated to food production and distribution, and in so doing, generated wealth and generous returns on investments for several food system actors (Pascucci, 2020). However, despite its promise, this approach to food provisioning, from production to market and distribution mechanisms, seems to be unable to feed the world (FAO et al., 2015), ensuring environmental and social benefits for all. Linear food provisioning approaches are characterised by economic factors, often organised in large-scale and highly industrialised processes defined by centralisation, dependence on external inputs (e.g. fossil fuels), competition, domination of nature, specialisation, and exploitation (Pascucci & Duncan, 2017; Rockström et al., 2017).

All these factors have contributed to the emergence of highly extractive food provisioning systems, with growing evidence indicating their lack of resilience and sustainability. Today, agricultural expansion is the leading driver of deforestation, accounting directly for the loss of 420 million hectares of forest since 1990 (FAO & UNEP, 2020). Additionally, agriculture directly contributes up to 8.5 percent of global greenhouse gas emissions with an additional 14.5 percent of greenhouse gas emissions derived from land use change (IPCC, 2019). This indicates the emergence of diffused food provisioning systems that are highly extractive, creating specific pressures on finite resources such as water, soil and biodiversity. These pressures are systemic and affect food systems at different scales and levels, creating a protracted and deepening socio-ecological crisis. Inherently linked to the linear and extractive design model of conventional food provisioning systems, from production through distribution to consumption, such systems are typically organised in value chains in which natural resources are extracted, made into products (food, feed or fibre), consumed and disposed of, generating waste, detrimental emissions, and pollution. This wasteful, exploitative and resource-intensive approach creates short-term economic benefits but often at the cost of human and environmental health.

The UK is a good case on which to focus as, for longer than any other highly developed country, it has been characterised by a linear and extractive food system, resulting in high rates of dependency on food imports. For example, for fresh fruit and vegetable supplies, the UK imports 84 percent and 47.3 percent respectively (Food Foundation, 2020). In consequence, multiple harmful human, environmental and economic health impacts and risks are rising in the shape of, for example: obesity (28 percent of all people in England); poor diets (only 26 percent of UK adults adhere to the five-a-day guidance of fruit and vegetables intake); incidence of chronic non-communicable diseases; and increasing evidence of microbial and pest resistance (due to overuse of antibiotics and other artificial inputs in intensive agricultural systems). Environmental impacts include excessive greenhouse gas emissions, biodiversity loss (e.g. breeding birds on farmland have declined by 45 percent from 1970 to 2018), waste pollution, and degradation of soils, freshwater and other ecosystems. The economic costs of these impacts are immense (e.g. UK soil degradation was calculated in 2010 to cost £1.2 billion a year). Meanwhile, those employed in the food system often experience poor working conditions, with jobs tending to be low-paid and precarious.

In the last few decades, there have been attempts to tackle these issues by encouraging more sustainable practices in all dimensions of food provisioning, as well as increasing the measuring and monitoring of negative impacts of activities using tools such as life cycle assessment (LCA), carbon footprint, and other eco-efficiency approaches (Verfaillie & Bidwell, 2000; Braungart et al., 2007). These concepts are all, in one way or another, concerned with using less resources and producing less emissions, and thus aspire to greater efficiency and environmental sustainability. Eco-efficiency approaches attempt to minimise the speed, toxicity and volume of material flows, but fail to challenge, let alone reimagine, the linear and extractive approach of food provisioning systems. From an economic point of view, eco-efficiency can result in a short-term cost reduction as a result of using fewer materials. However, in the long(er) term, eco-efficiency implies continued economic growth at the expense of the environment and human health. Thus, a key limitation of eco-efficiency approaches to sustainability is that harmful wastes and negative impacts remain an outcome of the production process.

Moving away from this extractive and linear model requires more than just adaptation but rather a systemic approach, in which food provisioning is re-imagined and re-designed to celebrate regenerative and restorative processes. If 'Business-as-usual is no longer an option' (IAASTD, 2009), where do we start? How do we design our way out of a system that has a destructive impact on human, social and environmental health? In an attempt to address the limitations of linearly designed food systems, we draw inspiration from the concept of regenerative food provisioning systems.

Designing Regenerative, Circular Food Systems: Three Principles

In regenerative food provisioning systems, the aim is to counter the 'taken, used and disposed of' tradition of conventional food production and, instead, design approaches where natural resources can be used and safely returned back to ecosystems (Pascucci and Duncan, 2017). More specifically, regenerative food provisioning systems are intentionally re-designed around a set of three key principles: (i) closing loops and designing for effective and resilient systems; (ii) celebrating diversity through sharing, participation and cooperation; and (iii) place-based value retention and creation. The premise of this approach is that localised food provisioning systems are best suited for aligning human, economic and environmental health outcomes. This is because closer proximity allows for designing circular and regenerative systems that take account of local topography and ecosystems, local cultures and infrastructures.

Figure 10.1 schematically depicts our regional circular food system approach where the inner circle symbolises the food chain (producing, processing, distributing, accessing, consuming and waste recycling), while the outer circle categorises the human, environmental and economic health dimensions of food systems. The model depicts the design of a circular system that optimises the food chain not only for the economic benefit of food producers, distributors and consumers but also includes the human and environmental health dimensions as key parts. In short, it is not enough to produce food efficiently and in ever greater quantity so that consumers have an ever-wider choice, paying lower prices. This is linear thinking championed by an extractive regime. Instead, a whole systems approach needs to be taken, which functions according to the three principles outlined below.

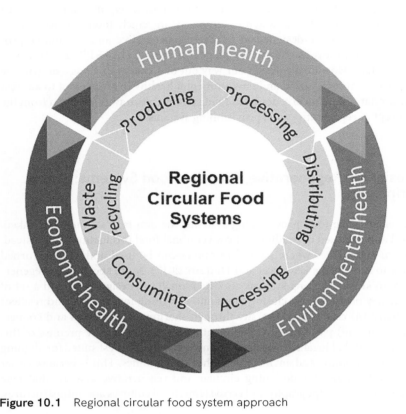

Figure 10.1   Regional circular food system approach

Closing Loops and Designing for Effective and Resilient Systems

Following this principle, food production, distribution, and consumption processes should be designed around the use of renewable energy and materials, taking into account the properties of ecosystems. The aim is to design processes capable of returning biological nutrients safely back into natural cycles (D'Amato et al., 2019; Borrello et al., 2020). As such, a truly regenerative food system is able to produce and distribute food avoiding the use of fossil fuels, and in general to use renewable energy and resources. Following this principle, food provisioning systems need to be designed eco-effectively; that is, in such a way that the use of hazardous and toxic materials is eliminated (Borrello et al., 2020). In this way, any food product would contribute to design metabolisms, promoting a positive synergistic relationship between ecological and social systems, economic growth and human health (Pascucci & Duncan, 2017). Closing loops and regenerating also means addressing the re-utilisation of materials. Inspired by industrial ecology, in a regenerative economy food products are designed to be used and consumed such that their biological and technical (non-biological) components (i.e. packaging) are not mixed (Borrello et al., 2020). Avoiding the mix of biological and technical materials means designing food products, and managing materials during the process, in ways that facilitate easy separation and re-use. Issues related to how residual outputs (i.e. packaging, or wastewater) will be used by another actor/partici-pant in the cycle after usage/consumption are incorporated in the design of the product (Tukker, 2015; Borrello et al., 2020). In this way, within a circular food approach, it is not only products that are being designed, but also 'streams' of nutrients. In practice, this means that the design of a food product will include the use of biodegradable or compostable packaging, or any packaging which can be upcycled as a technical nutrient in a given metabolism (e.g. paper, glass, plastics). Key to the design process is avoiding the use of materials that mix biological and non-biological nutrients. This results in a waste product that cannot easily be returned to the system, leading some to label such materials as 'monstrous hybrids' (Braungart & McDonough, 2002). A typical example of a monstrous hybrid would be packaging where cellulose and aluminium are mixed together in a way that they cannot be disassembled nor easily re-used (e.g. drinks cartons).

In linearly designed food provisioning systems, there is an inherent trade-off between resource efficiency and resilience (Borrello et al., 2020). While resil-ience calls for an interconnection and diversification of food systems, such that perturbations can be absorbed by and deal with the different compo-nents (actors) of the system, efficiency is oriented to streamline production processes and celebrate standardisation in isolation. Diversified systems are more likely to be resilient and adaptive but are not always efficient in the short run (Ulanowicz et al., 2009). Vice versa: highly specialised systems may gain efficiency in terms of resource use in the short run, but because they rely on resource-intense and standardised processes and depend on external inputs, they may lose adaptability to change, thus being highly inefficient in the long-run (Ulanowicz et al., 2009). A food provisioning system designed around sharing resources aims at reconciling efficiency and resilience through adaptive optimisation processes. For example, at farm level, efforts to optimise the adoption of technology might include more careful use of fertilisers and water (precision farming); crop rotations; reduced tillage (or use of 'no-till' techniques); even the adoption of permaculture or other agro-ecological practices (Pascucci & Duncan, 2017). Optimising along the supply chain also aims at prolonging the life-span of key materials, for example, re-using and up-cycling packaging (Borrello et al., 2020). At distribution level, it also deals with eliminating food waste, for example by improving the use of big data and

IT-based platforms to better organise operations and inventories in the retailing space (e.g. optimising the storage capacities of retailers). At consumption level, reducing food waste entails engaging in changing food habits, fighting obesity, starvation and the desertification of food landscapes.

Celebrating Diversity through Sharing, Participation and Cooperation

The re-balancing of efficiency and resilience is also reinforced by the principle of celebrating diversity. This is a system-wide approach inviting actors involved in the food provisioning system to think about local communities, justice and power imbalances, as well as to collaborate in designing decision-making mechanisms to govern the food system. As Clapp demonstrates in Chapter 2 of this volume, the food system is highly concentrated and dominated by a handful of global corporations which arguably makes the system less resilient. The call to celebrate diversity, then, is to encourage people to think about how to foster collaborative interactions and democratise food systems, to make them more inclusive and ultimately more resilient. This entails a decolonisation process that allows local communities to take charge of their own food provisioning, in line with their local traditions and cultures, providing economic opportunities. A system designed for most people to shop in large supermarkets, which are owned by international shareholders in distant cities and countries, is not a diverse system that provides opportunities for the many. Instead, it encourages a culture of dependency on long supply chains, which, during crisis, are vulnerable. To overcome dependency, food systems need to be designed for sharing, participation and cooperation, giving voice and material stakes to local communities (Bharucha et al., 2020).

Circular food system initiatives are intrinsically collaborative (Pascucci, 2020). Often constituted as the outcome of a process of multi-stakeholder interactions, they rely on cooperation to survive and thrive. Community-supported agriculture schemes, for example, create stable networks of mutual support among citizens and with farmers (e.g. sharing skills, knowledge and resources). For example, food hubs allow producers and consumers to come together and empower each other, generating new routes to market and improving local food accessibility. Public food procurement partnerships are grounded on the relationship between public authorities and local farmers, creating opportunities for deeper institutional change. Not only do these interactions and collaborations enhance local-regional food production, distribution and trade, but they also create non-material goods (such as 'relational goods'), which are produced and consumed within the local community. The importance of relational goods for strengthening social capital and wellbeing is widely acknowledged by researchers and practitioners (Donati, 2019). Increasing social capital is essential for overcoming human and economic health crises, such as food related illnesses and economic exclusion and lack of opportunity.

The UK has a diverse food movement, comprising a wealth of actors and organisations working as advocates for food systems change in a range of ways. These include contributions to consultation processes such as the recent National Food Strategy, or to the House of Lords Select Committee on Food, Poverty, Health and the Environment. Clearly, the knowledge produced by civil society food organisations is informing current policy debates on food and sustainability, whilst also contributing to academic knowledge production. Academics have a long history of researching social movements but in recent years more participatory approaches are being deployed where academics research alongside partners in social movements, civil society organisations and informal community groups (Gillan & Pickerill, 2012; Sandover, 2020). Indeed, this is an approach pursued by the authors of this chapter who have been engaged in collaborative work with research partners and with whom we have been able to gain particular insights on concerns relating to sustainability within the food system, while at the same time sharing our expertise with partners to help drive change on the ground. This collaborative approach enables knowledge production processes that support community empowerment through food practices. Examples include the recent Food for Change Programme that operated in Cornwall to support people back into employment, volunteering or training. Food for Change ran community-based food skills training via cooking and growing workshops, alongside one-to-one mentoring, to support participants who lacked food skills, experienced food insecurity, poor health and experienced loneliness. Similar programmes that empower communities through food are being supported by civil society organisations across the UK (Blake, 2019).

Place-based Value Retention and Creation

Academics, entrepreneurs and policymakers often assume that larger scale equates with greater impact. In the management literature, scaling is usually referred to as 'scaling-up' and considered a synonym for organisational growth and success (Ruggiero, Martiskainen & Onkila, 2018; Macqueen et al., 2020). Business strategies are thus often dominated by the search for economies-of-scale and the desirability of organisational growth is rarely in question. The assumption that global is the optimal scale is also reflected in current international trade negotiations by the UK government, in which food and agricultural products feature prominently.

However, initiatives that embrace integrated, circular approaches to food systems (e.g. community-supported agriculture schemes, food hubs and public food procurement partnerships) challenge these assumptions. Largely operating at a local-regional level, whilst engaging in multinational cooperation and solidarity, these initiatives are connected by a web of complex relations and the willingness to address the global challenges that threaten our future. In the context of alternative food networks, the question of scale is a question of purpose. What is scaling for? Circular food systems require changing the goal: from endless growth to thriving in balance (Raworth, 2017). Consequently, this requires changing the way scale and scaling are considered: a global scale is not necessarily optimal; nor is scaling up always a route to impact.

Research on diverse economies and alternative food networks shows that innovations scale through different routes, including impacting policies (scaling-up); impacting culture (scaling-deep); and impacting greater numbers (scaling-out). Different scaling routes involve different strategies, such as advocacy and campaigning (scaling-up); replication and diffusion (scaling-out); and storytelling, transformative learning and community of practice (scaling-deep) (Moore, Riddell & Vocisano, 2015). Transforming food systems requires action at different levels, including at local and regional scales. This is where circular food initiatives are often situated and where they thrive. Operating at a local-regional scale means increasing the opportunities for different stakeholders to participate in the food system. In a virtuous circle, participation strengthens trust that, in turn, reinforces cooperation (Jarosz, 2000). Short supply chains enable the development of local food cultures, improving the sense of belonging and wellbeing; and food sovereignty allows both producers and consumers to have more influence and control over food production, distribution and trade.

Whilst operating at a local-regional scale, circular food initiatives rely on each other to increase their impact (scaling-with) (Colombo, 2020). For example, they gather in local networks and constitute food hubs, support each other through creating solidarity economy districts and join international networks such as La Via Campesina. Building networks and partnerships is a vital strategy that allows diverse enterprises to retain economic, social and environmental value locally; and exercise their influence globally. Circular food systems is a term aligned with other descriptors used for local or place-based food systems, such as Local-Regional or City-Region Food Systems and Civic Food Networks (Renting et al., 2012; see also Halliday, Chapter 9 in this volume). It denotes action towards addressing contemporary food issues including complex issues of power, social justice and community resilience, amongst others. A key focus is on local value retention and creation. While a system that is monopolised by a handful of powerful actors transfers value out of local places into the hands of distant executives and shareholders, a place-based approach secures local value retention and creation. A community-supported agricultural farm business, for example, supports local jobs, enhances local social capital and produces food within a local ecosystem environment. 'Value' should here not be seen as simply economic value, but as an integrated value system that aims to optimise human, environmental and economic health dimensions.

A place-based approach to envisioning and delivering a circular food system fits with wider food policy scholarship and the work of key civil society organisations, which contends that place-based food policies are effective in addressing complex food issues (Sonnino et al., 2016; Moragues-Faus & Morgan, 2015). Place-based food initiatives are being deployed at a range of scales across the UK, from city to county-wide projects, as exemplified by the networks convened by The Sustainable Food Places Network, Food Power Alliances and Feeding Britain projects. Place-based approaches take into account context-specific environments and can take a more integrated approach that works across policy sectors and silos. In the UK, a plethora of Local Food Initiatives have arisen in response to England's food policy vacuum (although there is hope that this will change via the work of the National Food Strategy). The ongoing work of the Sustainable Food Places network, with its 57 UK-wide members, undertaking place-based food policy and pro-gramme change, demonstrates the momentum of activity behind place-based approaches to food systems transformation.

Institutional Innovations for Regional Circular Food Systems

To transform regional food systems, new, innovative institutional models are required, which are able to synergise previously disparate activities. In the UK, for example, there have been many local, small-scale attempts to bring about positive change in the food system. The 'Making Local Food Work' cam-paign, for example, 'aimed to reconnect people and land through local food by increasing access to fresh, healthy, local food with clear, traceable origins' (Sustain, 2021). This resulted in many positive projects, such as the establish-ment of food hubs, food co-ops and buying groups, the mapping of local and regional food systems, and the improvement of hospital food (Hinrichs & Charles, 2012; Kirwan & Maye, 2013). These were meaningful projects that created change in local communities, helping to rebuild local food cultures and economies (Santo & Moragues-Faus, 2019). Yet, they were rarely supported by institutional actors, such as local authorities and other large so-called 'anchor organisations' (Mount, 2012). Change efforts were hence rarely sustained, keeping dominant food regime structures in place. The dominance by UK supermarkets is unbroken (Murray & Caraher, 2019), supply chains are getting longer, and UK high-streets are marked by an ever-greater proliferation of fast-food outlets, serving unhealthy food with low or no nutritional value (Hubbard, 2017). Meanwhile, the human, environmental and economic health indicators associated with the UK food system are becoming worse, heightened by the COVID pandemic, with obesity rates increasing exponentially over the past two years. The UK government has taken some action by introducing the Soft Drinks Industry Levy (HM Treasury, 2018) or so-called 'sugar tax' in 2018. Focused on reducing consumption of sugary soft drinks, it has reportedly made a difference to sugar consumption, particularly amongst children: that is, it is working (Jones, Wu & Buse, 2021). Aware of the multiple factors involved in the UK food crisis, the government also commissioned a National Food Strategy (2021). Despite these positive first steps, the UK food system does not yet appear to be on course for a more sustainable future.

We suggest that new institutional approaches are needed to create sustained, transformative change in the UK food system. While large institutions, such as local authorities as well as central government, play an important role in driving change, it is important to not only think about change as a top-down process. As our discussion of scale and placed-based approaches indicated above, cooperation amongst small-scale, more localised actors can also generate sustained, transformative change that is able to create multiple value benefits for local communities, ecosystems and economies. We will now outline three institutional innovations as examples of how transformative change might appear within regional circular food systems.

Public Food Procurement Partnerships

In the UK, the public sector spends about £2.4bn per year procuring food and catering services (DEFRA, 2014). Given the significant spending power and number of people the different public institutions feed, the decisions made by public sector purchasers influence every aspect of the food system as well as a myriad of externalities. As the UK government's 'A Plan for Public Procurement' (DEFRA, 2014) notes, effective public procurement can deliver a range of benefits including: supporting a thriving local economy; rewarding food producers for operating to high animal welfare standards; building training opportunities into contracts to ensure a well-skilled food and farming sector; tackling health issues by enabling people to eat well across the public sector; tackle food poverty, which has been rising exponentially during the

COVID-19 pandemic; helping school children value their food by knowing where their food comes from, and how to cook healthy meals. By choosing to purchase food that is locally and sustainably produced, as well as highly nutritious, the public sector is uniquely placed to drive transformational change that will put a sustainable environment, healthy people and healthy local economies at the heart of the UK food system.

Yet, in practice, the enormous potential for public sector procurement to drive change has barely been tapped. Instead, cost-reduction remains an overriding objective for purchasing managers (Marshall et al., 2020) due to the lack of compelling evidence to prove the value in procuring sustainable food as well as the lack of enablers to make that procurement possible and feasible (i.e. policy, technology, logistics and supply). Due to their significant spending power, large 'anchor' institutions (e.g. local authorities, schools, universities, hospitals, prisons, etc.) are ideally placed to transform the agri-food system by demanding higher standards of suppliers. The Preston model (Whyman, 2021) suggests that anchor organisations can produce positive knock-on effects beyond the immediate supplier-procurer relationship, positively influencing local and regional economies. Yet, across the UK, thousands of small, regional suppliers of nutritious, sustainably produced food find themselves excluded from procurement chains in favour of larger national or multinational operators (Stahlbrand, 2018). We view this disconnect as a profound market failure, because smaller-scale and regional suppliers have the potential to support public sector organisations in driving positive environmental, health and economic outcomes.

We contend that the food chain (see inner circle of Figure 10.1) can be made more resilient by linking public sector buyers with a network of producers, delivering multiple human, environmental and socio-economic health benefits (outer circle of Figure 10.1). Our perspective is both informed and supported by non-academic partners with direct experience of the challenge of sustainable food procurement and its potential for transformative multiple health benefits. A recent report highlights that this regional approach does not have to be more expensive – while at the same time it can support local, seasonally produced food, which is often healthier for the consumer, has lower food miles, and chimes with the government's own 'net zero' and future farming ambitions (House of Commons, 2021). This confirms that regional public procurement 'has the potential to produce major reductions in food carbon footprints' (Devon Climate Emergency Response Group, 2020). Giving local producers access to public sector procurement would create local jobs and increase economic resilience of rural communities. Those employed in the food system often experience poor working conditions, with jobs tending to

234 A RESEARCH AGENDA FOR FOOD SYSTEMS

be low-paid and precarious (Lewis et al., 2015). Cutting out intermediaries and forging direct and equitable business relationships with major procurers would improve livelihoods for local producers.

Food Hubs

Food hubs, which aggregate food typically from local and smaller producers distributing it to a local customer base, have emerged in the UK as an innovative alternative to the current linear agri-food model dominated by large scale producers, processors, distributors and retailers. Frequently grounded on the principles of open innovation, food hubs are characterised by collaborative working and a focus on effectiveness-orientated agro-ecological principles (Psarikidou et al., 2019; Guzman & Reynolds, 2019). Whilst food hubs aim towards relocalising the food economy by supporting local food distribution, they can have a variety of meanings within academic literature, community organisations and social enterprises. Guzman and Reynolds' report found that:

> In practice, we have found food hubs, both here and in the US, to be very varied in composition and purpose. Some are focused solely on building an alternative local and/or more sustainable food supply chain, while others also aim to deliver wider social, economic and environmental benefits. (Guzman & Reynolds, 2019: 4)

Place-based food organisations such as Food Exeter, Bristol Food Network, Food Durham and others, see local food hubs as potentially fulfilling two roles: (1) a collaborative approach to creating new routes to market that enable small-scale local food producers to access new consumers; and (2) providing a physical space for community food practises that empower communities via affordable access to local fresh produce and which doubles up as a learning space for sharing food skills and consuming food for example a. community café (Lewis, 2015; Food Exeter, 2019; Blake, 2019). Guzman and Reynolds (2019) found that food hubs adopted a range of operational approaches that depended on their assets and capacities, such as whether they had access to a physical space from which to run a hub. Alternatively, telephone or increasingly virtual formats were deployed to link local food producers and consumers. Innovation in local food distribution is being trialled in the UK by a number of organisations at a range of scales including The South West Food Hub, Supply Devon, Tamar Valley Food Hubs, with the aim of supporting small-scale producers to access new customer bases, including local authority procurers.[1]

At the heart of a food hub approach is the idea that food is not only a question of provisioning but also entails other important social dimensions. Local and regional food hubs can provide jobs and economic security for local producers (Berti & Mulligan, 2016) as well as foster local food security and justice, which have been highlighted as challenges particularly during the COVID pandemic (Bellamy et al., 2021). Whereas food hubs focus on distributing food in an inclusive and just way, the community-supported agriculture model takes one step further by letting consumers participate directly in food production.

Community-Supported Agriculture (CSA)

The CSA model has been around for many decades, allowing citizens and consumers to directly get involved with food producers (Hvitsand, 2016). CSA is an umbrella term for a range of so-called 'prosumer' models, enabling close collaboration between food producers and consumers. There are three main CSA types: (a) shareholder CSAs which are formed and coordinated by members and hire a farmer; (b) subscription CSAs, which are owned and coordinated by the farmer and invite consumers to participate; and (c) cooperative CSAs that operate as non-profit social enterprises for the benefit of their members (Harmon, 2014). CSAs are generally believed to have increased in popularity, alongside box schemes and other local food initiatives, particularly during the COVID pandemic (Wheeler et al., 2020), allowing people direct access to local farms and their produce. CSAs create new social and geographically rich connections amongst producers and communities, which provide vital economic and social benefits (Brinkley, 2017). In some countries, such as France, there has been a deep-seated culture of supporting small-scale, local producers, and hence CSAs, referred to as AMAP (association pour le maintien d'une agriculture paysanne; association for the support of peasant agriculture), and which have grown exponentially over the past twenty years, now involving more than 50,000 families (Peterson, Taylor & Baudouin, 2015).

CSAs can operate in different ways, ranging from more commercially focused businesses to models that favour cooperative approaches. Yet, they all entail long-term partnerships and risk-sharing between food producers and their consumers, which mostly live in close proximity to each other (Henderson & Van En, 2007). Consumers normally pay the producer a monthly subscription or some other form of medium to long-term commitment is established, providing the producer with some economic security. Producers get to know their customers and often organise social events (e.g. farm walks) that help foster a close-knit community. Depending on the agreement, members of the community might provide labour, particularly at harvest or other crucial times in the agricultural calendar. Often, entire families are involved, providing opportunities for children to learn about where food comes from and how it is grown. People also get vital access to the countryside and green spaces, which have reportedly improved mental health and wellbeing (Bharucha et al., 2020).

While CSAs can clearly experience 'growing pains' (Brinkley, Manser & Pesci, 2021), it is generally agreed that they can deliver human health, socio-economic and environmental benefits for participants, both on the producer and consumer side. Due to the close-knit communities that are created by CSAs, they can foster social connections amongst citizens as well as between producers and consumers like few other local food models (Espelt, 2020). As modern, hyper-competitive societies often struggle with social alienation and individualism (McDonald, Wearing & Ponting, 2007), CSAs can provide vital opportunities for rebuilding social fabrics and solidarity amongst communities (Diekmann, Gray & Thai, 2020). Economically too, CSAs can provide a lifeline for small-scale, local food producers who are often disadvantaged by a food system dominated by national and international companies (Shideler et al., 2018). From an environmental perspective, CSAs often use agroecological, organic and other more sustainable farming techniques that have a much smaller ecological footprint than traditional food production methods (Espelt, 2020).

Conclusions

Given the challenges faced by the global food system – producing manifold negative human, economic and environmental health outcomes – this chapter has argued that a shift to more diverse, regional food systems, which follow low-carbon, participatory and regenerative principles, would create multi-layered benefits. Based on a review of existing evidence, we have provided a blueprint for what we have termed a 'regional circular food system model' that operates according to three main principles: (i) closing loops and designing for effective and resilient systems; (ii) celebrating diversity through sharing, participation and cooperation; and (iii) place-based value retention and creation. We believe that the regional level is best suited for designing food systems along these principles, simultaneously delivering human, socio-economic and environmental health benefits. This is because a nested, circular food system creates multiple feedback loops that allow social, economic and ecological values to cycle within a region, compared to value being lost through long supply chains that are often wasteful and operate for the benefit of financiers rather than communities and places.

In this chapter we have outlined three specific institutional innovations that provide practical entry points to our model, namely community-supported agriculture schemes, food hubs and public food procurement partnerships. While in the UK and many other countries such local food schemes have existed for a long time, we have argued that there is now a need to create a new economic imaginary by linking local, small-scale initiatives to larger institutions. We need a step change in the quest for the transformation of local food systems. Our model of an integrated regional circular food system enables creative, locally embedded movements to become exemplars of new economic activity that brings to the fore human and environmental health.

Note

1. The South West Food Hub: https://www.thesouthwestfoodhub.co.uk/; Supply Devon: https://www.applegate.co.uk/supply/devon; Tamar Valley Food Hubs: https://www.tamarvalleyfoodhubs.org.uk/.

References

Alhawari, O., Awan, U., Bhutta, M., Ülkü, M., 2021. Insights from circular economy literature: A review of extant definitions and unravelling paths to future research. *Sustainability*, 13, 2: 859.

Bellamy, A. S., Furness, E., Nicol, P., Pitt, H., Taherzadeh, A., 2021. Shaping more resilient and just food systems: Lessons from the COVID-19 Pandemic. *Ambio*, 50, 4: 782–793.

Berti, G., Mulligan, C., 2016. Competitiveness of small farms and innovative food supply chains: The role of food hubs in creating sustainable regional and local food systems. *Sustainability*, 8,7: 616.

Bharucha, Z. P., Weinstein, N., Watson, D., Böhm, S., 2020. Participation in local food projects is associated with better psychological well-being: evidence from the East of England. *Journal of Public Health*, 42, 2: e187–e197.

Blake, M., 2019. More than Just Food: Food insecurity and resilient place making through community self-organising. *Sustainability*, 11, 2942.

Böhm, S., Spierenburg, M., Lang, T., 2020. Fruits of our labour: Work and organisation in the global food system. *Organization*, 27, 2: 195–212.

Borrello, M., Pascucci, S., Cembalo, L., 2020. Three propositions to unify circular economy research: A review. *Sustainability*, 12, 10: 4069.

Braungart, M., McDonough, W., 2002. *Cradle to Cradle; Remaking the Way We Make Things*. New York: North Point Press.

Braungart, M., McDonough, W., Bollinger, A., 2007. Cradle-to-cradle design: creating healthy emissions – a strategy for eco-effective product and system design. *Journal of Cleaner Production*, 15, 13–14: 1337–1348.

Brinkley, C., 2017. Visualizing the social and geographical embeddedness of local food systems. *Journal of Rural Studies*, 54: 314–325.

Brinkley, C., Manser, G. M., Pesci, S., 2021. Growing pains in local food systems: A longitudinal social network analysis on local food marketing in Baltimore County, Maryland and Chester County, Pennsylvania. *Agriculture and Human Values*, 1–17.

Colombo, C., 2020. Scaling without growth? The scaling approaches of social agricultural cooperatives in Italy, PhD thesis, University of Exeter.

D'Amato, D., Korhonen, J., Toppinen, A., 2019. Circular, green, and bio economy: How do companies in land-use intensive sectors align with sustainability concepts? *Ecological Economics*, 158: 116–133.

DEFRA, 2014. A plan for public procurement: food and catering. https://www.gov.uk/government/publications/a-plan-for-public-procurement-food-and-catering.

Devon Climate Emergency Response Group, 2020. The Devon carbon plan. https://www.devonclimateemergency.org.uk/devon-carbon-plan/.

Diekmann, L. O., Gray, L. C., Thai, C. 2020. More than food: The social benefits of localized urban food systems. *Frontiers in Sustainable Food Systems*, 4, 169.

D'Odorico, P., Davis, K. F., Rosa, L. et al., 2018. The global food–energy–water nexus. *Reviews of Geophysics*, 56, 3: 456–531.

Donati, P., 2019. Discovering the relational goods: Their nature, genesis and effects. *International Review of Sociology*, 29, 2: 238–259. https://doi.org/10.1080/03906701.2019.1619952.

Espelt, R., 2020. Agroecology prosumption: The role of CSA networks. *Journal of Rural Studies*, 79: 269–275.

FAO and UNEP, 2020. The state of the world's forests 2020. Forests, biodiversity and people. Rome: FAO. https://doi.org/10.4060/ca8642en.

FAO, IFAD, WFP., 2015. The state of food insecurity in the world: Meeting the 2015 international hunger targets: Taking stock of uneven progress. Rome: Food and Agriculture Organization of the United Nations.

Fassio, F., Tecco, N., 2019. Circular economy for food: A systemic interpretation of 40 case histories in the food system in their relationships with SDGs. *Systems*, 7, 3: 43.

Food Exeter, 2019. Exploring Community Food Hubs in Exeter. https://foodexeter.org.uk/wp-content/uploads/Exploring-Community-Food-Hubs.Food-Exeter.pdf.

Food Foundation, 2020. Monitoring imports of fruit and veg into the UK. https://foodfoundation.org.uk/covid_19/monitoring-imports-of-fruit-and-veg-into-the-uk.

Gibson-Graham, J. K., 2006. A Postcapitalist Politics (NED-New edition). University of Minnesota Press. http://www.jstor.org/stable/10.5749/j.ctttt07.

Gillan, K., Pickerill, J., 2012. The difficult and hopeful ethics of research on, and with, social movements. *Soc. Mov. Stud*, 11: 133–143.

Godfray, H. C. J., Crute, I. R., Haddad, L. et al., 2010. The future of the global food system. *Phil Trans R Soc Lond B Biol Sci*, 365, 1554: 2769–77.

Guzman, P., Reynolds, C., 2019. Food Hubs in the UK: Where are we and what next?. Food Research Collaboration Food Discussion Paper. https://foodresearch.org.uk/publications/food-hubs/.

Harmon, A., 2014. Community supported agriculture: A conceptual model of health implications. *Austin Journal of Nutrition and Food Sciences*, 2, 4.

Henderson, E., Van En, R., 2007. *Sharing the harvest: a citizen's guide to Community Supported Agriculture*. White River Junction, VT: Chelsea Green Publishing.

Hinrichs, C., Charles, L., 2012. Local food systems and networks in the US and the UK: Community development considerations for rural areas. In Shucksmith, M., Brown,

D., Shortall, S. et al. (eds) *Rural Transformations and Rural Policies in the US and UK*. Abingdon: Routledge, pp. 176-196.

HM Treasury, 2018. Soft drinks industry levy comes into effect. https://www.gov.uk/government/news/soft-drinks-industry-levy-comes-into-effect.

House of Commons, 2021. Public sector procurement of food. HC469, 21 April 2021. https://committees.parliament.uk/publications/5509/documents/54917/default/.

Hubbard, P., 2017. *The Battle for the High Street*. London: Palgrave Macmillan.

Hvitsand, C., 2016. Community supported agriculture (CSA) as a transformational act: Distinct values and multiple motivations among farmers and consumers. *Agroecology and Sustainable Food Systems*, 40, 4: 333-351.

International Assessment of Agricultural Knowledge, Science and Technology for Development (IAASTD). 2009. Synthesis Report: A synthesis of the global and sub-global IAASTD reports. Washington, D.C.: Island Press.

IPCC, 2019. Climate change and land: An IPCC special report on climate change, desertification, land degradation, sustainable land management, food security, and greenhouse gas fluxes in terrestrial ecosystems. https://www.ipcc.ch/srccl/.

Jarosz, L., 2000. Understanding agri-food networks as social relations. *Agriculture and Human Values*, 17, 3: 279-283.

Jones A, Wu J., Buse K., 2021. UK's sugar tax hits the sweet spot *BMJ*, 372, n463. https://doi.org/10.1136/bmj.n463.

Kirwan, J., Maye, D., 2013. Food security framings within the UK and the integration of local food systems. *Journal of Rural Studies*, 29: 91-100.

Kowalski, Z., Makara, A., 2021. The circular economy model used in the Polish agro-food consortium: A case study. *Journal of Cleaner Production*, 284, 124751.

Lang, T., 2020. *Feeding Britain: Our Food Problems and How to Fix Them*. Harmondsworth: Penguin.

Lewis, H., Dwyer, P., Hodkinson, S., 2015. Hyper-precarious lives: Migrants, work and forced labour in the Global North. *Progress Human Geography*, 39, 5: 580-600.

Lewis, T., 2015. Access to markets for Bristol food producers. Report for Bristol Food Producers. https://bristolfoodproducers.uk/wp-content/uploads/2015/03/Shared-Distribution-Report.Final-Nov15_with-Appendices.compressed.pdf.

Macqueen, D., Bolin, A., Greijmans, M., Grouwels, S., Humphries, S., 2020. Innovations towards prosperity emerging in locally controlled forest business models and prospects for scaling up. *World Development*, 125, 104382.

Marshall, R. et al., 2020. Procuring food for the future. https://feedbackglobal.org/wp-content/uploads/2020/11/FF-Procurement-Report-Final-November-2020.pdf.

McDonald, M., Wearing, S., Ponting, J., 2007. Narcissism and neo-liberalism: Work, leisure, and alienation in an era of consumption. *Loisir et Société/Society and Leisure*, 30, 2: 489-510.

Moore, M. L., Riddell, D., Vocisano, D., 2015. Scaling out, scaling up, scaling deep: Strategies of non-profits in advancing systemic social innovation. *Journal of Corporate Citizenship*, 58: 67-84. https://www.jstor.org/stable/jcorpciti.58.67.

Moragues-Faus, A., Morgan, K., 2015. Reframing the foodscape: The emergent world of urban food policy. *Environment & Planning A*, 47: 1558-1573.

Moreau, V., Sahakian, M., Van Griethuysen, P., Vuille, F., 2017. Coming full circle: Why social and institutional dimensions matter for the circular economy. *Journal of Industrial Ecology*, 21, 3: 497-506.

Mount, P., 2012. Growing local food: Scale and local food systems governance. *Agriculture and Human Values*, 29, 1: 107-121.

Murray, S., Caraher, M., 2019. Food retail and distribution: A focus on supermarkets. In Lawrence, M., Friel, S. (eds), *Healthy and Sustainable Food Systems*. Abingdon: Routledge, pp. 93-102.

National Food Strategy, 2021. National Food Strategy. An independent review for government. The plan. https://www.nationalfoodstrategy.org/.

Pascucci, S., 2020. Circular food economies. In Duncan, J., Carolan, M., Wiskerke, H. (eds) *Routledge Handbook of Sustainable and Regenerative Food Systems*. Abingdon: Routledge, pp. 318-335.

Pascucci, S., Duncan, J., 2017. From pirate islands to communities of hope. In Duncan, J., Bailey, M. (eds) *Sustainable Food Futures: Multidisciplinary Solutions*. New York: Routledge.

Peterson, H., Taylor, M., Baudouin, Q., 2015. Preferences of locavores favoring community supported agriculture in the United States and France. *Ecological Economics*, 119: 64-73.

Psarikidou, K., Kaloudis, H. et al., 2019. Local food hubs in deprived areas: De-stigmatising food poverty? *Local Environment*, 24, 6: 525-538.

Raworth, K., 2017. *Doughnut Economics: Seven Ways to Think Like a 21st-Century Economist*. White River Junction, VT: Chelsea Green Publishing.

Renting, H., Shermer, M., Rossi, A., 2012. Building food democracy: Exploring civic food networks and newly emerging forms of food citizenship. *Int. Jrnl. of Soc. of Agr. & Food*, 19, 3: 289-307.

Rockström, J., Edenhofer, O., Gärtner, J., DeClerck, F., 2020. Planet-proofing the global food system. *Nature Food*, 1, 1: 3-5.

Rockström, J., Williams, J., Daily, G. et al., 2017. Sustainable intensification of agriculture for human prosperity and global sustainability. *Ambio*, 46, 1: 4-17.

Ruggiero, S., Martiskainen, M., Onkila, T., 2018. Understanding the scaling-up of community energy niches through strategic niche management theory: Insights from Finland. *Journal of Cleaner Production*, 170: 581-590.

Sandover, R., 2020. Participatory food cities: Scholar activism and the co-production of food knowledge. *Sustainability*, 12: 3548

Santo, R., Moragues-Faus, A., 2019. Towards a trans-local food governance: Exploring the transformative capacity of food policy assemblages in the US and UK. *Geoforum*, 98: 75-87.

Schreefel, L., Schulte, R., de Boer, I. et al., 2020. Regenerative agriculture: The soil is the base. *Global Food Security*, 26: 100404.

Shideler, D., Bauman, A., Thilmany, D., Jablonski, B., 2018. Putting local food dollars to work: The economic benefits of local food dollars to workers, farms and communities. *Choices*, 33, 3: 1-8.

Sibbing, L., Candel, J., Termeer, K., 2021. The potential of trans-local policy networks for contributing to sustainable food systems: The Dutch city deal: food on the urban agenda. *Urban Agriculture & Regional Food Systems*, 6, 1: e20006.

Sonnino, R., Marsden, T., Moragues-Faus, A., 2016. Relationalities and convergences in food security narratives: Towards a place-based approach. *Trans. Inst. Br. Geogr.*, 41: 477-489.

Sreeharsha, R., Mohan, S., 2021. Symbiotic integration of bioprocesses to design a self-sustainable life supporting ecosystem in a circular economy framework. *Bioresource Technology*, 124712.

Stahlbrand, L., 2018. Can values-based food chains advance local and sustainable food systems? Evidence from case studies of university procurement in Canada and the UK. *International Journal of Sociology of Agriculture and Food*, 24, 1: 77-95.

Steenson, S., Buttriss, J., 2021. Healthier and more sustainable diets: What changes are needed in high-income countries?. *Nutrition Bulletin*, 46, 3: 279-309.

Sustain, 2021. Archive: Making local food work. https://www.sustainweb.org/.

Thomas, A., Moore, A., Edwards, M., 2018. Feeding island dreams: Exploring the relationship between food security and agritourism in the Caribbean. *Island Studies Journal*, 13, 2: 145-162.

Tukker, A., 2015. Product services for a resource-efficient and circular economy: A review. *Journal of Cleaner Production*, 97: 76-91.

Ulanowicz, R. E., Goerner, S. J., Lietaer, B., Gomez, R. (2009). Quantifying sustainability: Resilience, efficiency and the return of information theory. *Ecological Complexity*, 6, 1: 27-36.

Verfaillie, H., Bidwell, R., 2000. Measuring eco-efficiency: A guide to reporting company performance. Geneva, World Business Council on Sustainable Development.

Wheeler, A., Dykstra, P., Black, J., Soares, N., 2020. COVID-19: UK Veg Box report. Food Foundation.

Whyman, P. B., 2021. The economics of the Preston Model. In Manley, J., Whyman, P. (eds) *The Preston Model and Community Wealth Building*. Abingdon: Routledge, pp. 128-149.

11 Design at the end of the food system: hybrid foodscapes in the realm of consumption

Kata Fodor

Introduction: The Kitchen – a Provocation

One remarkable 2021 television and YouTube advertisement for an online meal delivery brand, Foodora,[1] depicts a mundane situation: a young blonde couple (carrying their child) are shown around a sleek urban apartment by a real-estate agent. As they walk into the kitchen, the agent routinely says – '… and this is the kitchen'. The scene here cuts to the couple, who in reaction, now appear completely puzzled. After a moment of silent bafflement, the woman asks back 'Kitchen?!' – clearly having no idea what this specific room is supposed to be for, or even what that word 'kitchen' might mean. The skit ends there, and we see the familiar logo of the meal delivery brand pop up. The message, of course, is as simple as it is provocative: online meal delivery service has made life so convenient for its users, that it renders the idea and functionality of a kitchen as a basic component of one's home, as simply obsolete. Inevitably, this advertisement hits a nerve for a range of different audiences. First, it ridicules traditionalist ideas about the home and domestic life, challenging the old adage that the kitchen is the heart of the home. Second, it mocks the ignorance of millennials and their hopeless reliance on smartphone apps. And, third, the native, white, middle-class, heteronormative family life, large city apartment and sleek kitchen, which are all shown in the ad, are not necessarily an existing combination of real-life circumstances, let alone options, for a large segment of the meal delivery app's actual users, thereby perhaps provoking yet another kind of subtle frustration with the fictional scene. In effect, the advertisement becomes memorable while operating independently of whichever specific interpretation of its subtext is assumed.

The idea, or prediction, of 'the kitchen' becoming obsolete is nothing new, however, and online meal delivery is merely the latest culprit hailed to bring about the 'death of the kitchen' (Q-Series, UBS Evidence Lab, 2018).

243

Previously, utopian socialists and material feminists of past centuries had long argued for moving the kitchen – and the domestic labour associated with it – out of the private and into the larger community's realm (Hayden, 1979; Hayden, 1982). Moreover, removing this basic food function from the home, by rendering it superfluous, has always been one frontier of lucrative residential real-estate ventures in dense urban areas (McKinley, 2012; Boffey, 2017; Sullivan, 2021). In these cases, the focus is typically more on relieving an already tight private unit – a room, bedsit, studio apartment or micro apartment, and so on – of the spatial, infrastructural and cost burdens a kitchen would entail. The function is then either delegated to the surrounding city, and the available food outlets it offers (Fodor, 2021), or is concentrated into shared or centralised service facilities. In contrast, as Hayden thoroughly outlines in *The Grand Domestic Revolution* (1982), the material feminists were more concerned about how exactly the question would be resolved and the labour distributed and organised anew. In short, there are multiple contrasting angles to approach the same question about the future of the kitchen: reorganising social dynamics and gender roles; exploring and exploiting new technological and market opportunities whether for cost and resource optimisation in housing or, alternatively, for sustainability initiatives, community building and mutual aid. However, looking beyond the array of ideologies associated with these varied approaches, three major factors can be identified that make renewed speculation about the future of the kitchen more relevant today than ever before: digitalisation, increasing environmental vulnerability, and social change. While a more detailed elaboration on each of these factors is to follow later, the ultimate purpose of this chapter is to challenge our typically rigid presumptions about the familiar physical forms, models and spatial typologies that constitute our foodscapes. By revisiting the above question, the chapter aims to emphasise the importance and timeliness of actively re-imagining the spatial structures and infrastructures of food – from housing to hospitality – in service of accommodating desirable changes in urban food consumption. Moreover, if we assume that redesigning the food environment can help facilitate sustainable urban food systems, then it is worth further elaborating, what exactly desirable foodscapes mean in practice, or more specifically, what they mean in urban, spatial and design practice. This chapter will consider these questions and reflect on the ways these affect the food system itself.

The Shift to Feeding Heterogeneous Urban Societies in the 21st Century

To consider the possible demise of the kitchen it is important to first summarise what the model actually is, in terms of design. The conventional western model of this room largely follows the 'Frankfurt kitchen' design by Margarete Schütte-Lihotzky, dating back to 1926–27. Her ingenious plan organised and optimised the kitchen in a way that was fully focused on the internal dynamics of that space, as tailor-made to the typical household of a German family from a hundred years ago. In terms of its food provisioning, that meant a 5-6-member nuclear family, where one person was a fulltime housewife, another a 'breadwinner', while the rest (children and possibly a grandparent) could provide occasional helping hands, as well as company for sharing meals, also subtly assuring the transfer of food customs, know-how and tradition over time. In short, the model of this kitchen is inseparable from that of the nuclear family itself (Fodor, 2018). The then contemporary principles of 'scientific management' were so carefully applied to the design of this space, it made the kitchen optimal for exactly that social arrangement. What could epitomise this better, than the idea of the 'kitchen work triangle', that is the 'appropriate' spatial relationship between stove top, sink and larder/refrigerator, as the key nodes in the everyday processes undertaken by *the* housewife (Baraona Pohl, Puigjaner and Nájera, 2012). Inevitably, what follows is that deviating from the traditional model of the nuclear family compromises the very design functionality and aptness of its kitchen. Thus, the question that follows is how we can rethink that design itself to better accommodate the shifted task of feeding our far more demographically heterogeneous urban societies.

Social and Demographic Change

Returning to the three key factors affecting the role of the kitchen – digitalisation, increasing environmental vulnerability, and social change – we can begin to see that each of these developments encourages a shift of focus from the previously described family logic of this domestic space into the larger infrastructural, service and social connections of the urban environment. Most obviously, the model of the nuclear family itself has become far less dominant: the average household size has been steadily decreasing in most metropolitan regions of the affluent Western world, to the point where single/one-person households now in some urban areas even outnumber them (Klinenberg, 2013; Københavns Kommune, 2013; Housing In London, 2015; Tervo and Hirvonen, 2020).

Simultaneously, gender roles have changed significantly, with far more women participating in the paid labour force (hence fewer full-time housewives), while men's share of household chores has also increased somewhat (Dotti Sani, 2014). But whether we observe the modern family household or the increasing segment of its alternatives, their housekeeping and food provisioning practices correspondingly have become far more diverse and complex and negotiated in more globalised and heterogeneous urban societies. The mere prevalence of one-person households (of any gender and, with longer life-spans, also more elderly people) in itself calls for revisiting the ideas of feminist collective house-keeping traditions since, in a way, the same issues that used to have a strong emphasis on gender have thus become far more universal practical *human* concerns. What were once considered women's issues, are to some degree becoming every person's practical challenges, when living alone.

Technological Development and Digitalisation

The unprecedented technological development since the onset of the Frankfurt kitchen model has not only brought about improved home appliances easing food preparation and storage inside the kitchen, but by changing the trans-port, preservation, and preparation of food, it also reshaped our food retail environments and our global food systems at large. The food items reaching our kitchens today – whether they are ready meals, consumer packaged goods or raw groceries – have far more complex supply chains in terms of both pro-cessing and organisation, as well as geography, seasonality and logistics. But we are yet to recognise the full extent to which digitalisation transforms the role of our home kitchens, and the exact new purposes they will serve within the larger changed context. In particular, the ways in which this technological boom increasingly ties together the private domestic space of our homes, with the often hidden, automated, black box architectures and remote operations of dark kitchens, courier services, (semi)automated warehouses, and even data centres, whether in adjacent urban settings or in far-distant globally connected remote locations. The Internet of Things (IoT), 'smart' appliances, and on-demand online grocery and meal delivery services are just a few of the latest technologies that have already demonstrated a capacity to create entirely novel spatial logics around food practices. Their power in reorganising how our spaces correspond to the various stages along the food provisioning – food purchasing decision continuum; with consequences for the conduct of finan-cial transactions; the organisation and performance of related logistical tasks; as well as determining relationships with the people involved in producing and supplying much of our food, groceries and meals demonstrates this unprece-dented capability (Fodor, 2021).

Arguably, ever since the venture-capital-funded giant 'sharing economy' enterprises, Airbnb and Uber, transformed their respective industries, there has been an excited anticipation – especially among investors and entrepreneurs – that some kind of equivalent must soon come to sweep the world of food consumption too. Would it take the form of people sharing their kitchens with strangers? Of home cooks preparing and selling food to their neighbours on demand? For years, plenty of experimental enterprises (such as Josephine, Eatwith or Restaurant Day)[2] have kept betting on versions of these P2P (peer-to-peer) ideas, yet none have so far come close to anything resembling commercial success, ability to scale, or even to maintain a stable flow of interest from their users. Presumably, the failure of such enterprises – beyond their ability to secure venture capital investment – is connected to how rigidly bound food is to the specific spatial pre-conditions and relations around it. That is to say, a new digital platform around food can hardly change its ecosystem without the insertion of new material, spatial or infrastructural elements. A case in point is the relative success of online meal delivery services, which not only provide access to aggregated platforms of all available take-away options at once, but directly take on and 'optimise' the burden of delivery tasks through new logistical arrangements that tie together home eaters via fleets of flexible gig economy couriers with dark kitchen operations. Similarly, the latest on-demand grocery businesses[3] offering groceries often within ten minutes of ordering, operate from strategically located mini urban storage units able to provision a selection of locally popular items at unprecedented speed and convenience to their customers in dense urban areas. While such platforms are often branded as immaterial digital technologies, it is the heavily material and costly logistical setups (of spaces, transport vehicles, and workers) coordinated by them that actually create the new irresistible conveniences. Overall, the various frontiers of the sharing economy applied to urban food consumption include the niches of instantaneous communication channels (such as for surplus food redistribution, e.g., Olio, Karma, TooGoodToGo, ResQ[4]), outsourcing the logistical efforts of getting both groceries and cooked meals (as detailed before), and SaaS (software-as-a-service) coming to the kitchen in the form of smart gadgets (appliance-as-a-service) and new fremium and subscription/rental models applied to home appliances (such as 'pay-per-use' solutions by Homie[5]). The common thread is the much-discussed move away from simple *ownership* toward *services* and *access*. While the positive potential of that idea persists, since the predominant optimism from the early onset of the age of 'collaborative consumption', this same shift has revealed itself as far more complex (Martin, 2016) and riddled with pitfalls, yet to be resolved (Morrison, 2021; Song, 2021).

Growing Environmental Vulnerability

The third factor pressing for re-thinking the design of our kitchens and broader food environments, is our growing environmental vulnerability. One desirable aspect of a promised 'age of access' was going to be its potential to reduce our environmental footprint: the idea of optimising our resource use by making use of things underutilised. In other words, owning less individually but having more *intensity of use* together. ICTs (information and communications technologies) would mediate that sharing with hitherto unimaginable ease and convenience, creating trust and accountability between neighbours and strangers. Moreover, our ever-changing needs in life (for variety) were to be flexibly satisfied without the endless pursuit of consumerist material possessions or involve compromises on quality. While these idealistic aspirations (Martin, 2016) of the sharing economy remain relevant today, their gloss has perhaps been tarnished by a deeper appreciation of the problems that can arise (Schor, 2014) from commercially driven, unregulated operations that result in exploitation of unprotected workers, 'enforced' participation, and the further 'commodification of everything'. Indeed, the comfortable lifestyles that have become available to an unprecedented large number of Western citizens in urban areas, are hardly imaginable in an ever-hotter, resource-constrained future, let alone extendable to more people, considering the devastating environmental consequences this comfort has traditionally entailed. Undoubtedly, the way Schor (2014: 2) describes the activities of the sharing economy as 'recirculation of goods, increased utilization of durable assets, exchange of services and sharing of productive assets' could not be more relevant for this challenge of making more effective use of 'doing more with less'.

Specifically in relation to urban food consumption, then, the design brief would need to embrace critical principles. In order to ensure that diets collectively resulted in significantly less environmental damage – in terms of atmospheric emissions, other waste streams and pollutants, as well as biodiversity loss and so on – food consumption practices will require close scrutiny. In other words, minimising or eliminating those practices regarded as harmful – while maximising the utility and joy of those that remain – will be vital (Sage et al., 2021). Moreover, we would find ways to make the most of what is still available and relatively sustainable: renewable energy and resources, durable, reusable or compostable material goods, and an assumed general shift toward more sustainably balanced diets. Lastly, we would need to engage in restorative practices for ecosystem (soil, water, air) and societal health, cultural preservation (technical know-how, education, community engagement) and innovation for building more resilience to the inevitable series of shocks yet to come. While such an idealistic agenda may sound far too simplistic from an academic or policy perspective, it is an essential tool from a design perspective. It helps us envision new realities, which rather than resolve all relevant questions separately, instead provide synthesis in practice – ideally, at an optimal intersection of multiple contending considerations. Such an approach can be particularly instrumental when attempting to apply learnings as complex as the multi-criteria analysis of sustainable diets argued for by Lang (2021).

Designing Foodscapes

Further related to the multi-criteria analysis of sustainable diets, several established and experimental modes of analysis hold relevant learnings to design the study of specific food environments. First, the 'food system approach' has the capacity to consider complexity far beyond life cycle analysis (LCA) approaches. While, as a consequence, it presents the inevitable challenge of setting system boundaries, it can help identify opportunities for improvement, as it draws attention to how actors and their activities interact, the natural resources used, as well as on impacts and outcomes (Westhoek et al., 2014). Furthermore, combining material flow analysis (MFA) with 'social practice theory' is a novel experimental approach that can be applied on multiple spatial, organisational, and temporal scales, as it focuses on the notion of activity, as well as the stocks, flows and processes of energy and materials that are involved in fulfilling a specific human need (Leray, Sahakian, and Erkman, 2016). Similarly, reverse LCA approaches also focus on needs rather than products as their starting point, in order to find alternative innovative systems of products and services that can then fulfil that need (Wangel, 2018). However, how do these matters apply more directly to the related questions of design?

While the term *foodscape* has no single definitive meaning, its increasing use across academia, policy and practice suggests that this elusive word captures something vague yet relevant that other more technical terms (such as 'food environment') do not encompass. According to the review study by Vonthron, Perrin and Soulard (2020), in the use of the term beyond tangible spatial characteristics, there are significant sociocultural, behavioural and systemic approaches increasingly taken into consideration when analysing people's subjective and personalised food realities. In spatial terms, it is both dynamic and multi-scalar: from the micro to the global, that is, from packaging and presentation, through display furniture, enclosed space (store, room), urban setting, to regional and global supply chains. As MacKendrick (2014: 16) explains 'the foodscape is never fixed; its boundaries shift depending on how the food environment expands and contracts'. It follows, that foodscapes are also dynamic over time (such as changing with the opening hours of food outlets or one's mobility options). Moreover, they encompass the non-material environment, for example, digital media, which coincidentally also becomes increasingly personalised,[6] the sociocultural environment (specific traditions, norms, social signalling, mental models, and aspirations), as well as the policy environment and economic circumstances. How the physically available components of the food environment are practically accessible to people, is thus an incredibly complex enmeshment of all these factors. Yet, the concept of foodscapes appears to adequately capture this in-flux, hybrid, and multi-scalar configuration, that is necessarily rendered through an individual's personal momentary circumstances. It thus follows, that there might be as many different foodscapes as there are people, and even those innumerable foodscapes are in constant change over time. This complexity entailed in 'foodscapes' is highly challenging for design to address, yet it helps us avoid the dangers of solving the wrong technical questions that could easily result from oversimplification and generalisation. Thus, if the aim remains – as this chapter set out – to facilitate sustainable diets, then one main challenge is that the re-design of foodscapes must happen on a large scale, even though our foodscapes significantly differ from one another's to begin with.

Three of the most evident ways this challenge might be addressed are as follows. First, through direct spatial means of redistribution: provision of public space; institutions and infrastructure; as well as affordable mobility and housing. Such interventions could help secure better access and lower barriers to more sustainable diets and food practices including, for example, improved availability and access to adequate food retail options, cooking facilities, the necessary space to sit down for meals, to store food safely or to sort waste. Second, through the practice of design (as visions, imaginaries and prototypes), we can shape people's subjectivities. For it is not only that the living environments we construct shape our subjectivities (including our political subjectivity) as David Harvey's work argues (2008), but that the reverse is true as well. As *The Buell Hypothesis* (Martin, Meisterlin, and Kenoff, 2011) suggests – drawing parallels with Harvey on the relationship between the 'American dream' and suburban housing – they argue that the way to change the city is by changing the 'dream': that is, by re-imagining the narratives guiding it. Finally, acknowledging that the foodscapes of people vary from one person to the next, as well as hour by hour, effective solutions will inevitably need to address the sheer diversity of personalised needs. One size fits all approaches (e.g., six square metre fitted Frankfurt kitchens installed into each new apartment unit is a typical legal requirement in contemporary housing developments) are unlikely to be efficiently utilised in heterogeneous urban societies, as compared to the provision of a range of varied accessible options (e.g., the way car sharing services provide a fleet of different cars to best accommodate their users' ever-changing needs).

Hybridity appears to be one of the key attributes of contemporary urban foodscapes. They are hybrid in the sense that they exist as the enmeshment of physical and virtual realities, as well as a consequence of socio-economic circumstances and mental models; the specific constellation of which varies individually and temporally. But our foodscapes are also hybrid in another sense: they cross spatial and organisational domains (Fodor, 2021). The way our domestic environments increasingly accommodate retail functions via digital services, such as online grocery shopping, is a perfect example of this. Moreover, our foodscapes can be hybrid in yet another important sense, by enabling a degree of fluidity in various access and control conditions, an issue that deserves some elaboration here. First, however, it is necessary to distinguish food spaces in terms of their organisational design that creates three distinct categories: individual (e.g., one's own kitchen at home); shared (e.g., a kitchen used by several tenants in a house-share); or top-down institutionally choreographed (such as canteens, restaurants, or supermarkets). From the individual through the shared to the institutional, each type possesses unique advantages (as well as disadvantages) over the others. Aspirational hybridity across these categories, then, would need to encompass collaborative and/or cooperative organisational and design solutions, that are neither purely individual, nor solely collective-communal, but instead exploit the upsides of both while minimising their drawbacks.

A small kitchen in a one-person household is the most iconic example of an atomised, individual food space. It provides autonomy, independence, comfort, and safety from the germs of strangers, but comes with the potential burdens of increased social isolation (often described as depressing), greater resource intensity, expensiveness (or often unaffordability) and full ownership of the related maintenance, costs and responsibilities. On the other end of the spectrum, institutional food spaces, such as a school canteen are convenient to use, affordable and highly resource efficient (through economies of scale). Typically, they rely on professionalised services and, due to their necessary compliance with strict regulatory measures on hygiene, the maintenance responsibilities are clearly accepted and taken care of. At the same time, a lack of personal attributes, the need to ensure adaptation to the needs of other users and the possible social frictions that may arise, alongside potential exposure to biosecurity hazards (airborne pathogens), still remain potential drawbacks here.

Shared use, in-between these two extremes, is often inconvenient for it requires a certain degree of adaptation to others, while occasional social frictions are inevitable. It is however more affordable and resource efficient than individual use, and even the maintenance responsibilities get distributed. The key distinction to make here between *shared* and *collaborative/cooperative* in this understanding is, that 'shared' stands for an asset that is used by multiple parties, but is not formally different from its 'individual' counterpart, only in how its use is organised. In contrast, the 'institutional' is not only different in its highly choreographed use, but is altogether a formally different spatial asset purposely designed for accommodating and mediating between multiple parties. A hybrid condition would therefore facilitate, and mediate between, multiple users but without having to imply rigid top-down choreographed organisational arrangements. It inherits elements of each category, while simultaneously being qualitatively different from all three. Thinking through the relative qualities across the spectrum from institutional to individual food spaces is represented in Figure 11.1.

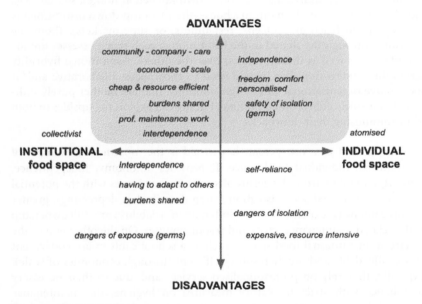

ADVANTAGES

community - company - care
economies of scale
cheap & resource efficient
burdens shared
prof. maintenance work

collectivist   interdependence

independence
freedom comfort
personalised
safety of isolation
(germs)

atomised

**INSTITUTIONAL
food space**

Interdependence
having to adapt to others
burdens shared

**INDIVIDUAL
food space**

self-reliance

dangers of isolation

dangers of exposure (germs)

expensive, resource intensive

DISADVANTAGES

Source: The author.

Figure 11.1 Qualities of institutional versus individual food spaces

Such hybrid types of collaborative-cooperative urban food spaces, when over-laid upon an existing landscape of typical non-hybrids (that is, both atomised and institutional food spaces), could meaningfully enrich and diversify the existing foodscapes of large urban populations. Such spaces could ideally provide local community access to an infrastructure of durable goods and services better able to harness renewable energy sources for their operation, while also assuring safe and resilient use. Indeed, such infrastructure might be regarded as a modern extension of the traditional public drinking water fountains once proudly installed by cities. Hybrid spaces could potentially also learn more explicitly from 'fremium' models, whereby some fundamental elements and functionality of a product or service is provided free of charge, while other 'premium' features come with a certain subscription rate or at a price. This principle is in fact nothing new and is already used implicitly in many university and workplace canteens, as well as in some small (outdoor) restaurants. Free access to such spaces typically encompasses (in the case of canteens): one's licence to enter, be sheltered and sit at a table; to pick up a clean plate and cutlery (even to be used for consuming items that were not necessarily purchased on site); to take tap water for drinking; and even, in some cases, to have free access to microwave ovens and worktop surfaces by which to reheat meals and take care of minor meal preparation and serving tasks. Beyond these, users can also typically purchase a range of groceries, snacks, and cooked meals in these canteens. Given these developments, it is appropriate to ask whether it is not overly ambitious to imagine an extension of such arrangements to providing space for simple cooking?[7] Even for that to be performed in groups who might share the meals collectively cooked? And by taking part in such maintenance responsibilities earning community and even individual benefits as a consequence?

Hybrid food spaces in the heart of the community have a potentially enormous range of benefits that would contribute to a more sustainable and inclusive food system. They might provide for the safe storage and provision of sustainable, healthy, and culturally appropriate foods that might otherwise be difficult for local residents to access. Community kitchens make available cooking facilities that can be rented by small-batch artisan producers or used by refugees and their support groups to offer spaces for celebrating their culturally important cuisines. Collective procurement enables them to bulk buy durable reusable and/or fully compostable utensils, reducing the need for disposable and single-use packaging. Providing a welcoming space for preparing and eating food together enhances a strong sense of mutualism and conviviality at the heart of the community (see Sage, Chapter 3 in this volume). Finally, effective management of waste streams – sorting, recycling, reutilising, composting, and cleaning – achieves a higher level of resource efficiency and embeds good practices amongst individuals. However, even beyond these desirable separate functions, hybrid spaces have the potential to become urban platforms for social learning, enhanced governance and greater community resilience: indeed, they could facilitate the creation and strengthening of urban food citizenship.

Conclusions

The chapter has sought to address the challenges facing contemporary food environments and has made a case for tackling the design of our increasingly hybrid foodscapes. This task will entail prototyping future visions that incorporate the latest critical learnings from green design and green architecture, social innovation projects, as well as progressive technological developments. These different disciplinary challenges will need to be addressed in equal measure while also demonstrating a deep understanding of the food system as it continues to evolve. As this chapter has outlined, changing demographic characteristics, growing environmental vulnerabilities, and sweeping technological changes together make it more urgent than ever to rethink the prevailing arrangements and conditions (physical forms, interfaces, and materialities) that constitute the contemporary food nexus.

One aspect of this conundrum, the chapter has argued, lies in the domestic kitchen. Given its place and design in the home, one of the most relevant questions is, perhaps, how we can reframe and extend the benefits and possibilities presented by the latest technologies at hand? At present, we have several commercially driven examples of IoT and smart gadgets entering our private and domestic food spaces. This is most prevalent as expensive kitchen equipment enters upmarket individual households (e.g., 'smart' refrigerators), and the ways in which giant technology corporations increasingly find their way to support these spaces and appliances (such as Amazon and Google, companies heavily investing in this new frontier); besides the home food delivery enterprises discussed earlier. Ultimately, however, the question for us in considering the future is this: how might these technological capabilities be put into the service of enhancing collaboration and support of individual households without further reinforcing corporate control of the food system? That is to say, how can appropriate technologies help address changing social conditions (austerity, precarity) and environmental burdens (through reduced resource use) in such a way as to progress the ethos and promise of the sharing economy?

Design at the end of the food system – in the realm of consumption – shapes the entire food system by the sheer collective power of the quantities involved, irrespective of whether it intends to. Recognising this power and the ways it can be redirected through deliberative, intelligent design provides us with a strong sense of optimism in forging an alternative path forward. However, such work requires considerable multi-disciplinary expertise, utilising theory and practice, learning by doing, trying and failing, and by prototyping new possibilities in iterative ways. To conclude this chapter, then, we identify three of the many critical questions that require further research in the field of designing more sustainable food consumption practices.

First, we need a deeper qualitative understanding of the food provisioning practices of people living in non-familial urban housing setups. That is to say, gaining a better understanding of how the very condition of living outside nuclear family units, but which vary enormously across age, gender, socio-economic and cultural divides, affects food provisioning practices and solutions in this heterogeneous group. Are there any common denominators between them, and if so, what are they? Conversely, what are the dominant factors that determine possible differences? Second, we will require more research and experimentation on the very practice of 'sharing' itself, that is, the ways in which 'sharing' and 'collaboration' can be more effectively accommodated by purposeful design decisions. Finally, cross-disciplinary expertise calls for more focus group engagements where multiple stakeholders get to discuss together and identify the challenges of the idealistic design brief described in this chapter. Such engagements could help locate where exactly the biggest practical obstacles lie, as well as help to find more ways to facilitate future prototyping opportunities. Such focused and collaborative encounters in themselves could help in bringing about a more integrated understanding of the many challenges confronting us as a consequence of the contemporary food system – and the ways we can effect change by a redesign at its end.

Notes

1. This 2021 ad spot was produced for the Finnish market of Foodora – a German-founded brand, currently operating across the Nordics. https://www.youtube.com/watch?v=9yqus4oRIV4.
2. See more about how they failed or pivoted away at https://thespoon.tech/josephine-a-sharing-economy-marketplace-for-home-cooking-shuts-down/, https://www.eatwith.com/, https://www.facebook.com/RestaurantDayFinland/.
3. As of 2021, examples include companies such as Gorillas, Zapp, Getir or Weezy https://gorillas.io, https://tryzapp.com, https://getir.com/, https://weezy.co.uk.

4. See more at https://olioex.com, https://www.karma.life, https://toogoodtogo.org, https://www.resq-club.com.
5. See more at https://www.homiepayperuse.com/en.
6. As we move away from fixed radio and tv channels toward algorithmic on-demand content, advertisements and information bubbles.
7. For recent/ongoing examples of such experimental collaborative urban food space projects see https://www.katafodor.com.

References

Baraona Pohl, E., Puigjaner, A., Reyes Nájera, C., 2012. Blurring the Kitchen Work Triangle. *Volume*, 33: 118-122.

Boffey, D., 2017. "No Cooking in the Kitchen": Disbelief at Amsterdam Rental Flat Rules. *The Guardian*, 10 August 2017. https://www.theguardian.com/world/2017/aug/10/no-cooking-in-kitchen-disbelief-amsterdam-rental-flat-rules.

Dotti Sani, G., 2014. Men's Employment Hours and Time on Domestic Chores in European Countries. *Journal of Family Issues*, 35, 8: 1023-1047. https://doi.org/10.1177/0192513X14522245.

Hayden, D., 1982. *The Grand Domestic Revolution: A History of Feminist Designs for American Homes, Neighbourhoods and Cities*. Cambridge, MA: The MIT Press.

Hayden, D., 1979. Charlotte Perkins Gilman and the Kitchenless House. *Radical History Review*, 21, 23: 225-247. https://doi.org/10.1215/01636545-1979-21-225.

Housing In London, 2015. The Evidence Base for the Mayor's Housing Strategy, 2015. Greater London Authority. https://www.london.gov.uk/sites/default/files/housing_in_london_2015.pdf.

Fodor, K., 2021. The Hybridization of Food Spaces: Changing Spatial Logics in Urban Food Systems and Prospects for Sustainable Diets. *International Journal of Sociology of Agriculture and Food*, 27, 1: 102-118. https://doi.org/10.48416/ijsaf.v27i1.83.

Fodor, K., 2018. Lessons from Launching an Alternative Architectural Practice. *Architectural Design* 88, 3: 62-67. https://doi.org/10.1002/ad.2302.

Harvey, D., 2008. The Right to the City. *New Left Review*, 53: 18.

Klinenberg, E., 2013. *Going Solo: The Extraordinary Rise and Surprising Appeal of Living Alone*. Harmondsworth: Penguin Books.

Københavns Kommune, 2013. Housing Barometer 2013: Copenhagen! Housing. www.kk.dk/boligbarometer.

Lang, T., 2021. The Sustainable Diet Question: Reasserting Societal Dynamics into the Debate about a Good Diet. *International Journal of Sociology of Agriculture and Food*, 27, 1: 12-34. https://doi.org/10.48416/ijsaf.v27i1.88.

Leray, L., Sahakian, M., Erkman, S., 2016. Understanding Household Food Metabolism: Relating Micro-Level Material Flow Analysis to Consumption Practices. *Journal of Cleaner Production*, 125: 44-55. https://doi.org/10.1016/j.jclepro.2016.03.055.

MacKendrick, N., 2014. Foodscape. *Contexts*, 13, 3: 16-18. https://doi.org/10.1177/1536504214545754.

Martin, C., 2016. The Sharing Economy: A Pathway to Sustainability or a Nightmarish Form of Neoliberal Capitalism? *Ecological Economics*, 121: 149-159. https://doi.org/10.1016/j.ecolecon.2015.11.027.

Martin, R., Meisterlin, L., Kenoff, A. (eds) 2011. *The Buell Hypothesis: Rehousing the American Dream*. The Temple Hoyne Buell Center for the Study of American Architecture, Columbia University Graduate School of Architecture, Planning, and Preservation https:// www .arch .columbia .edu/ books/ catalo/ 112 -the -buell -hypothesis.

McKinley, J., 2012. Must Haves For the Micro-Pad. *The New York Times*, 12 July 2012. https://www.nytimes.com/2012/07/12/garden/furnishing-a-tiny-apartment.html.

Morrison, S., 2021. Peloton's Mandatory Treadmill Memberships Show How You Never Fully Own Your Connected Devices. Vox Recode. 23 June 2021. https://www .vox .com/ recode/ 2021/ 6/ 23/ 22545534/ peloton -tread -membership -now -required -recall.

Q-Series, UBS Evidence Lab., 2018. Is the Kitchen Dead? Zurich, Switzerland: UBS.

Sage, C., Quieti, M-G., Fonte, M. 2021. Sustainable Food Systems <--> Sustainable Diets. *The International Journal of Sociology of Agriculture and Food*, 27, 1: 1–11. https://doi.org/10.48416/ijsaf.v27i1.449.

Schor, J., 2014. Debating the Sharing Economy. https:// www .icscarsharing .it/ wp -content/uploads/2019/02/2014-Schor-Debating-the-Sharing-Economy.pdf.

Song, V., 2021. In 2030, You Won't Own Any Gadgets. Gizmodo. 7 June 2021. https:// gizmodo .com/ in -2030 -you -wont -own -any -gadgets -1847176540 ?utm _source = pocket_mylist.

Sullivan, H., 2021. Rest Room: Tiny Vancouver 'Micro Studio' Combines Bedroom and Toilet. *The Guardian*, 6 July 2021. https://www.theguardian.com/world/2021/jul/06/rest-room-tiny-vancouver-micro-studio-combines-bedroom-and-toilet.

Tervo, A., Hirvonen, J., 2020. Solo Dwellers and Domestic Spatial Needs in the Helsinki Metropolitan Area, Finland. *Housing Studies*, 35, 7: 1194–1213. https:// doi.org/ 10 .1080/02673037.2019.1652251.

Vonthron, S., Perrin, C., Soulard, C-T., 2020. Foodscape: A Scoping Review and a Research Agenda for Food Security-Related Studies. *PLoS ONE*, 15, 5. https://doi .org/10.1371/journal.pone.0233218.

Wangel, A., 2018. Back to Basics – the School Lunch. *The International Journal of Life Cycle Assessment*, 23, 3: 683–689. https://doi.org/10.1007/s11367-016-1110-0.

Westhoek, H., Ingram, J., van Berkum, S., Herrick, J., Hajer, M., 2014. A Food System Approach for the Identification of Opportunities to Increase Resource Use Efficiency. In Proceedings of the 9th International Conference on Life Cycle Assessment in the Agri-Food Sector (LCA Food 2014), San Francisco, CA, USA, 8–10 October 2014; pp. 1505–1511.

Index

Printed and bound by CPI Group (UK) Ltd, Croydon, CR0 4YY

16/04/2025

14658485-0004